Lab Manual to Accompany

A+ Guide to Managing and Maintaining Your PC

SEVENTH EDITION

Jean Andrews, Ph.D.

Todd Verge

COURSE TECHNOLOGY
CENGAGE Learning™

Australia • Canada • Mexico • Singapore • Spain • United Kingdom • United States

COURSE TECHNOLOGY
CENGAGE Learning™

Lab Manual to Accompany
A+ Guide to Managing and Maintaining Your PC,
Seventh Edition
Jean Andrews/Todd Verge

Vice President, Career and Professional Editorial:
  Dave Garza

Executive Editor: Stephen Helba

Acquisitions Editor: Nick Lombardi

Managing Editor: Marah Bellegarde

Senior Product Manager: Michelle Ruelos Cannistraci

Developmental Editor: Jill Batistick

Editorial Assistant: Sarah Pickering

Vice President, Career and Professional Marketing:
  Jennifer McAvey

Marketing Director: Deborah S. Yarnell

Senior Marketing Manager: Erin Coffin

Marketing Coordinator: Shanna Gibbs

Production Director: Carolyn Miller

Production Manager: Andrew Crouth

Content Project Manager: Jessica McNavich

Art Director: Jack Pendleton

Cover photo or illustration: Shutterstock

Manufacturing Coordinator: Julio Esperas

Copyeditor: Katherine A. Orrino

Proofreader: Christine Clark

Compositor: Integra

Library of Congress Control Number: 2009940008

ISBN-13: 978-1-435-48740-6

ISBN-10: 1-435-48740-0

Course Technology
25 Channel Center Street
Boston, MA 02210
USA

Some of the product names and company names used in this book have been used for identification purposes only and may be trademarks or registered trademarks of their respective manufacturers and sellers.

Microsoft and the Office logo are either registered trademarks or trademarks of Microsoft Corporation in the United States and/or other countries. Course Technology, a part of Cengage Learning, is an independent entity from the Microsoft Corporation, and not affiliated with Microsoft in any manner.

Any fictional data related to persons or companies or URLs used throughout this book is intended for instructional purposes only. At the time this book was printed, any such data was fictional and not belonging to any real persons or companies.

Course Technology and the Course Technology logo are registered trademarks used under license.

Course Technology, a part of Cengage Learning, reserves the right to revise this publication and make changes from time to time in its content without notice.

The programs in this book are for instructional purposes only. They have been tested with care, but are not guaranteed for any particular intent beyond educational purposes. The author and the publisher do not offer any warranties or representations, nor do they accept any liabilities with respect to the programs.

Cengage Learning is a leading provider of customized learning solutions with office locations around the globe, including Singapore, the United Kingdom, Australia, Mexico, Brazil, and Japan. Locate your local office at: **international.cengage.com/region**

Cengage Learning products are represented in Canada by Nelson Education, Ltd.

For your lifelong learning solutions, visit **course.cengage.com**

Visit our corporate website at **cengage.com**.

Printed in the United States of America
4 5 6 7 12 11

Table of Contents

Preface

This lab manual is designed to be the best tool on the market to enable you to get the hands-on practical experience you need to learn to troubleshoot and repair personal computers and operating systems. It contains more than 100 labs, each of which targets a practical problem you're likely to face in the real world when troubleshooting PCs. Every attempt has been made to write labs that allow you to use generic hardware devices. A specific hardware configuration isn't necessary to complete the labs. In learning to install, support, and troubleshoot operating systems, you learn to support Windows Vista and Windows XP Professional and to use the command prompt. Each chapter contains labs designed to provide the structure novices need, as well as labs that challenge experienced and inquisitive students.

This book helps prepare you for the new A+ 2009 Certification exams offered through the Computer Technology Industry Association (CompTIA): A+ Essentials (220–701) and A+ Practical Application (220-702). Because the popularity of this certification credential is quickly growing among employers, becoming certified increases your ability to gain employment, improve your salary, and enhance your career. To find more information about A+ Upgrade Certification and its sponsoring organization, CompTIA, go to the CompTIA Web site at *www.comptia.org*.

Whether your goal is to become an A+ certified technician or a PC support technician, the *Lab Manual for A+ Guide to Managing and Maintaining Your PC, Seventh Edition, Comprehensive*, along with Jean Andrews's textbooks, will take you there!

FEATURES

To ensure a successful experience for both instructors and students, this book includes the following pedagogical features:

- **Objectives**—Every lab opens with learning objectives that set the stage for students to absorb the lab's lessons.
- **Materials Required**—This feature outlines all the materials students need to complete the lab successfully.
- **Lab Preparation**—This feature alerts instructors and lab assistants to items to check or set up before the lab begins.
- **Activity Background**—A brief discussion at the beginning of each lab provides important background information.
- **Estimated Completion Time**—To help students plan their work, each lab includes an estimate of the total amount of time required to complete it.
- **Activity**—Detailed, numbered steps walk students through the lab. These steps are divided into manageable sections, with explanatory material between each section.
- **Figures**—Where appropriate, photographs of hardware or screenshots of software are provided to increase student mastery of the lab topic.
- **Review Questions**—Questions at the end of each lab help students test their understanding of the lab material.
- **Web Site**—For updates to this book and information about other A+ and PC Repair products, go to *http://www.cengage.com/coursetechnology/*

ACKNOWLEDGMENTS

Jean and Todd would first like to thank Jill Batistick for her hard work and attention to detail throughout the editorial process. They would also like to extend their sincere appreciation to Michelle Ruelos Cannistraci, Nicole Ashton, Jessica McNavich, and all the Course Technology/Cengage staff for their instrumental roles in developing this lab manual. Many thanks to all the instructors who offered great suggestions for new labs and encouraged us to make other changes to the previous editions. Keep those suggestions coming!

Todd gives special thanks to his wife, Janine, and daughters Katie and Ella for their love and support. Finally, he would like to again thank Jean Andrews for her generosity in giving him this opportunity and all the doors it has opened.

Many thanks to the peer reviewers:

Keith Conn, Cleveland Institute of Electronics, Cleveland, OH

Scott Johnson, Crete High School, Crete, NE

Brandon Lehmann, Terra Community College, Fremont, OH

Vincent March, Palomar College, San Marcos, CA

Terry Sadorus, Lewis-Clark State College, Lewiston, ID

Jim Siscoe, Moore Norman Technology Center, Norman, OK

CLASSROOM SETUP

Lab activities have been designed to explore many different hardware setup and troubleshooting problems while attempting to keep the requirements for specific hardware to a minimum. Most labs can be done alone, although a few ask you to work with a partner. If you prefer to work alone, simply do all the steps yourself. Most lab activities have been designed to work in either Windows Vista or Windows XP Professional. In some cases, a particular operating system will be required.

Typical labs take 30 to 45 minutes; a few might take a little longer. For several of the labs, your classroom should be networked and provide access to the Internet. When access to Windows setup files is required, these files can be provided on the Windows installation CD/DVD, a network drive made available to the PC, or some other type of removable storage media.

These are the minimum hardware requirements for Windows Vista:

- 800MHz or better Pentium-compatible computer (1GHz preferred)
- 512MB of RAM (1GB preferred)
- 20GB hard drive (40GB preferred)
- An NTFS partition that can be the partition where Windows Vista is installed
- A user account with administrative privileges

These are the minimum hardware requirements for Windows XP Professional:

- 233MHz or better Pentium-compatible computer (300MHz preferred)
- 64MB of RAM (128MB preferred)
- 1.5GB hard drive (2GB preferred)
- An NTFS partition that can be the partition where Windows XP is installed
- A user account with administrative privileges

When the OS isn't of concern, the minimum hardware requirements are as follows:

- 233MHz or better Pentium-compatible computer
- 64MB of RAM
- 1.5GB hard drive
- A PC toolkit with an antistatic ground bracelet (ESD strap)

A few labs focus on special hardware. For example, one lab requires the use of a USB flash drive, one lab requires a wireless card and router, and another lab uses a PC camera. Another lab requires the use of a multimeter, and some labs require software that can be freely downloaded from the Internet.

LAB SETUP INSTRUCTIONS

CONFIGURATION TYPE AND OPERATING SYSTEMS

Each lab begins with a list of required materials. Before beginning a lab activity, each student workgroup or individual should verify access to these materials. Then make sure the correct operating system is installed and in good health. Note that in some cases, installing an operating system isn't necessary. When needed, the Windows setup files can be made available on the Windows CD/DVD, a network drive, or some type of removable media storage. In some labs, device drivers are needed. Students can work more efficiently if these drivers are available before beginning the lab.

PROTECT DATA

In several labs, data on the hard drive might get lost or corrupted. For this reason, it's important that valuable data stored on the hard drive is backed up to another medium.

ACCESS TO THE INTERNET

Several labs require access to the Internet. If necessary, you can use one computer to search the Internet and download software or documentation and another computer for performing the lab procedures. If the lab doesn't have Internet access, you can download the required software or documentation before the lab and bring the files to lab on some sort of storage medium.

THE TECHNICIAN'S WORK AREA

When opening a computer case, it's important to have the right tools and to be properly grounded to ensure that you don't cause more damage than you repair. Take a look at the items that should be part of any technician's work area:

- Grounding mat or bench (with grounding wire properly grounded)
- Grounding wrist strap (attached to the grounding mat)
- Non-carpet flooring
- A clean work area (no clutter)
- A set of screwdrivers
- 1/4-inch Torx bit screwdriver
- 1/8-inch Torx bit screwdriver

◢ Needlenose pliers
◢ A PLCC (plastic leadless chip carrier)
◢ Pen light (flashlight)
◢ Several new antistatic bags (for transporting and storing hardware)

At minimum, you must have at least two key items. The first is a grounding strap. If a grounding mat isn't available, you can attach the grounding strap to the computer's chassis and, in most cases, provide sufficient grounding for handling hardware components inside the computer case. The second key item is, of course, a screwdriver. You won't be able to open most cases without some type of screwdriver.

PROTECT YOURSELF, YOUR HARDWARE, AND YOUR SOFTWARE

When you work on a computer, harming both the computer and yourself is possible. The most common accident when attempting to fix a computer problem is erasing software or data. Experimenting without knowing what you're doing can cause damage. To prevent these sorts of accidents as well as physically dangerous ones, take a few safety precautions. The following sections describe potential sources of damage to computers and explain how to protect against them.

POWER TO THE COMPUTER

To protect yourself and the equipment when working inside a computer, turn off the power, unplug the computer, and always use an antistatic grounding strap. Consider the monitor and the power supply to be "black boxes." Never remove the cover or put your hands inside this equipment unless you know the hazards of charged capacitors. Both the power supply and the monitor can hold a dangerous level of electricity even after they're turned off and disconnected from a power source.

STATIC ELECTRICITY OR ESD

Electrostatic discharge (ESD), commonly known as static electricity, is an electrical charge at rest. A static charge can build up on the surface of a nongrounded conductor and on nonconductive surfaces, such as clothing or plastic. When two objects with dissimilar electrical charges touch, static electricity passes between them until the dissimilar charges are made equal. To see how this works, turn off the lights in a room, scuff your feet on the carpet, and touch another person. Occasionally you see and feel the charge in your fingers. If you can feel the charge, you discharged at least 3000 volts of static electricity. If you hear the discharge, you released at least 6000 volts. If you see the discharge, you released at least 8000 volts of ESD. A charge of less than 3000 volts can damage most electronic components. You can touch a chip on an expansion card or system board and damage the chip with ESD and never feel, hear, or see the discharge.

ESD can cause two types of damage in an electronic component: catastrophic failures and upset failures. A catastrophic failure destroys the component beyond use. An upset failure damages the component so that it doesn't perform well, even though it might still function to some degree. Upset failures are the most difficult to detect because they aren't easily observed.

PROTECT AGAINST ESD

To protect the computer against ESD, always ground yourself before touching electronic components, including the hard drive, system board, expansion cards, processors, and memory modules, by using one or more of the following static control devices or methods:

- *Grounding strap or antistatic strap:* A grounding strap is a bracelet you wear around your wrist. The other end is attached to a grounded conductor, such as the computer case or a ground mat, or it can be plugged into a wall outlet. (Only the ground prong makes a connection!)
- *Grounding mats:* Grounding mats can come equipped with a cord to plug into a wall outlet to provide a grounded surface on which to work. Remember, if you lift the component off the mat, it's no longer grounded and is susceptible to ESD.
- *Static shielding bags:* New components come shipped in static shielding bags. Save the bags to store other devices that aren't currently installed in a PC.

The best way to protect against ESD is to use a grounding strap with a grounding mat. You should consider a grounding strap essential equipment when working on a computer. However, if you're in a situation where you must work without one, touch the computer case before you touch a component. When passing a chip to another person, ground yourself. Leave components inside their protective bags until you're ready to use them. Work on hard floors, not carpet, or use antistatic spray on carpets.

There's an exception to the ground-yourself rule. Inside a monitor case, the electricity stored in capacitors poses a substantial danger. When working inside a monitor, you *don't* want to be grounded, as you would provide a conduit for the voltage to discharge through your body. In this situation, be careful *not* to ground yourself.

When handling system boards and expansion cards, don't touch the chips on the boards. Don't stack boards on top of each other, which could accidentally dislodge a chip. Hold cards by the edges, but don't touch the edge connections on the card.

After you unpack a new device or software that has been wrapped in cellophane, remove the cellophane from the work area quickly. Don't allow anyone who's not properly grounded to touch components. Don't store expansion cards within one foot of a CRT monitor because the monitor can discharge as much as 29,000 volts of ESD from the screen.

Hold an expansion card by the edges. Don't touch any of the soldered components on a card. If you need to put an electronic device down, place it on a grounding mat or a static shielding bag. Keep components away from your hair and clothing.

PROTECT HARD DRIVES AND DISKS

Always turn off a computer before moving it. Doing so protects the hard drive, which is always spinning when the computer is turned on (unless the drive has a sleep mode). Never jar a computer while the hard disk is running. Avoid placing a PC on the floor, where users could accidentally kick it.

Follow the usual precautions to protect CDs and floppy disks. Protect the bottom of CDs from scratches and keep them away from heat and direct sunlight. Keep floppies away from magnetic fields, heat, and extreme cold. Don't open the floppy shuttle window or touch the surface of the disk inside the housing. Treat disks with care, and they'll usually last for years.

Introducing Hardware

Labs included in this chapter:

- **Lab 1.1:** Gather and Record System Information
- **Lab 1.2:** Identify Computer Parts
- **Lab 1.3:** Use Software to Examine a Computer, Part 1
- **Lab 1.4:** Use Software to Examine a Computer, Part 2
- **Lab 1.5:** Compare Costs of Systems
- **Lab 1.6:** Plan an Ideal System

LAB 1.1 GATHER AND RECORD SYSTEM INFORMATION

OBJECTIVES

The goal of this lab is to use a system's physical characteristics and operating system to determine how the system is configured. After completing this lab, you will be able to:

⊿ Gather system information by observing a system

⊿ Use available Windows tools to access specific system information

MATERIALS REQUIRED

This lab requires the following:

⊿ Windows Vista/XP operating system

⊿ Individuals or a workgroup of 2 to 4 students

LAB PREPARATION

Before the lab begins, the instructor or lab assistant needs to do the following:

⊿ Verify that Windows starts with no errors.

ACTIVITY BACKGROUND

When working with a computer system, it's a good idea to know what components are installed on the system. This lab helps you identify some of these components as you gather information by observing the system and by using system tools.

ESTIMATED COMPLETION TIME: 15 Minutes

 Activity

Observe the physical characteristics of your system and answer the following questions:

1. Does the outside of the case have any identification on it indicating manufacturer, model, or component information? If so, list this information:

   _____

2. How many CD or DVD drives does your system have?

   _____

3. Describe the shape or type of the connection your mouse uses:

   _____

4. How many USB ports are in the back of your system? How many are in the front?

   _____

5. How many internal hard drives does your system have? Explain how you got your answer:

   _____

Most versions of Windows allow users to customize the display of information to suit their tastes. Windows XP and Vista can mimic the way previous versions of Windows presented menus and settings for users who are more comfortable with these presentations. Complete the following steps to restore Windows defaults to your system:

1. Boot your system and log on, if necessary. Click **Start,** and then click **Control Panel** to open the Control Panel window.

2. If Classic view has been enabled, select **Control Panel Home** in Vista or click **Switch to Category View** in XP. Figure 1-1 shows the Control Panel in Category view for Vista.

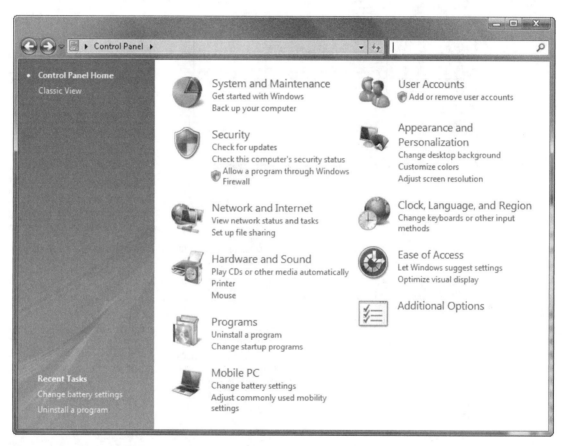

Figure 1-1 Windows Vista Control Panel in Category view
Courtesy: Course Technology/Cengage Learning

3. With Category view enabled, click the **Appearance and Personalization (Appearance and Themes** in XP) category. The Appearance and Personalization window opens.

4. In the Appearance and Personalization window, click **Folder Options** in the Control Panel icons list to open the Folder Options dialog box.

5. On the General tab of the Folder Options dialog box, click the **Restore Defaults** button (see Figure 1-2), and then click **Apply.**

6. Click the **View** tab in the Folder Options dialog box (see Figure 1-3). Click the **Restore Defaults** button, and then click **OK** to apply the settings and close the dialog box.

7. In the Appearance and Personalization window, click the **Taskbar and Start Menu** icon. The Taskbar and Start Menu Properties dialog box opens.

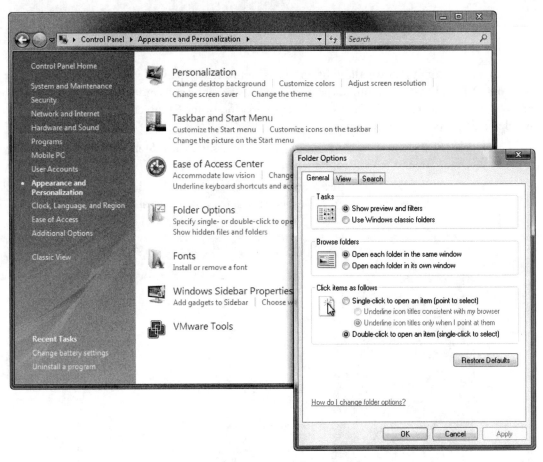

Figure 1-2 Use the Folder Options dialog box to restore Windows defaults to a folder
Courtesy: Course Technology/Cengage Learning

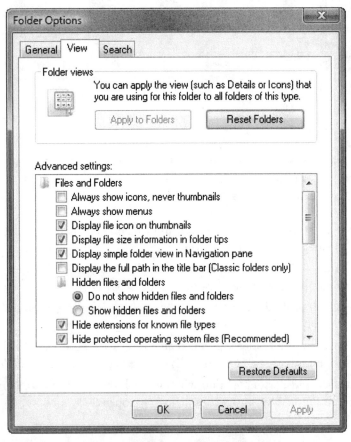

Figure 1-3 The View tab of the Folder Options dialog box
Courtesy: Course Technology/Cengage Learning

8. On the Taskbar tab, verify that all check boxes in the Taskbar appearance section are selected, except for Auto-hide the taskbar and Show Quick Launch, as shown in Figure 1-4. Click **Apply** if any changes were made.

Figure 1-4 Use the Taskbar and Start Menu Properties dialog box to control how the taskbar appears and functions
Courtesy: Course Technology/Cengage Learning

9. Click the **Start Menu** tab in the Taskbar and Start Menu Properties dialog box. Verify that the Start menu option button is selected, as shown in Figure 1-5. Click **OK** to apply the settings and close the dialog box. Close the Appearance and Personalization window.

From the Start menu, open the Control Panel and click the **System and Maintenance (Performance and Maintenance** in XP) category. The System and Maintenance window opens. In the System and Maintenance window, click the **System** icon to open the System Properties dialog box. Record the following information:

1. Which OS is installed and what is the version number?

_____

2. Have any service packs been installed?

_____

3. To whom is the system registered?

_____

4. What kind of CPU (type and speed) is installed in your system?

_____

Figure 1-5   The Start Menu tab of the Taskbar and Start Menu Properties dialog box
Courtesy: Course Technology/Cengage Learning

5. How much RAM is installed in your system?

6. Vista provides a rating called a Windows Experience Index to help you rate and improve your system's performance. Click **Windows Experience Index** to gather further details. What is your computer's base score?

7. Close the System Properties dialog box and the Performance and Maintenance window.

At this point, click **Start,** click **Computer** (**My Computer** in XP), and locate the following information:

1. How many hard disk drives are listed, and which drive letters are assigned to them?

2. How many devices with removable storage are listed, and which drive letters are assigned to them?

3. How many network drives are listed, and what are their names?

4. Move the mouse pointer over the icons to determine information about the drives. What is the total amount of free hard drive space on your system?

REVIEW QUESTIONS

1. List two categories available in Control Panel that were not mentioned in the lab:

   _____

   _____

2. Based on the Windows Experience Index, what component of your computer would you upgrade first? Why?

   _____

   _____

3. What differences, if any, are there between a list of components derived from a physical inspection versus a list of components derived from My Computer and System Properties?

   _____

   _____

LAB 1.2 IDENTIFY COMPUTER PARTS

OBJECTIVES

The goal of this lab is to examine your computer to identify the parts inside and outside the case. After completing this lab, you will be able to:

◢ Identify computer components outside the case

◢ Identify computer components inside the case

MATERIALS REQUIRED

This lab requires the following:

◢ A computer that can be disassembled

◢ A Phillips-head screwdriver

◢ An antistatic ground bracelet (wrist strap)

◢ Workgroup of 2 to 4 students

◢ A display of four or more computer parts to be identified by students

LAB PREPARATION

Before the lab begins, the instructor or lab assistant needs to do the following:

◢ Provide a computer that can have the cover removed for each student workgroup.

◢ Gather up four or more computer parts for display in each student workgroup or area of the lab.

ACTIVITY BACKGROUND

When working with a computer system, you must be able to identify the hardware components, both inside and outside the case. Components are not always labeled adequately, especially those inside the case. This lab helps you learn to recognize these components.

Activity

Observe the physical characteristics of your system and answer the following questions:

1. What size monitor do you have? Measure from the upper-left corner to the lower-right corner (the diagonal) on the monitor screen. Is the measurement what you expected for the size of the monitor?

   _____

2. How many keys are on your keyboard?

   _____

3. What other external components does your PC have (speakers, printer, and so forth)? Describe each component with as much detail as you can.

   _____

   _____

   _____

4. Look at the back of your PC and list all cables and cords connected to ports and other connections. Fill in the following chart:

Describe the port or connector to which the cable or cord is connected	Purpose of the cable or cord
1.	
2.	
3.	
4.	
5.	
6.	

5. What other ports on the PC are not being used? List them:

   _____

   _____

   _____

   _____

Next, you'll open the PC case (see Figure 1-6) and examine the components inside. As you work, make sure you do not touch anything inside the case unless you're wearing an antistatic ground strap that's clipped to the case so that any electrical difference between you and the case is dissipated.

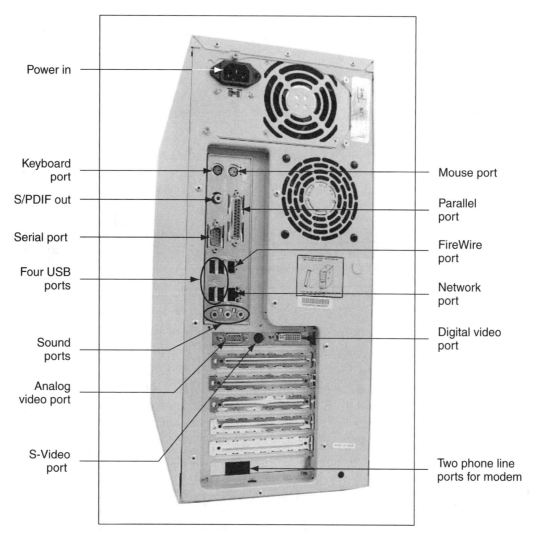

Power in

Keyboard port

S/PDIF out

Serial port

Four USB ports

Sound ports

Analog video port

S-Video port

Mouse port

Parallel port

FireWire port

Network port

Digital video port

Two phone line ports for modem

Figure 1-6 Common ports and connectors found on the back of a PC
Courtesy: Course Technology/Cengage Learning

To remove the cover from a PC with screws, follow these steps:

1. Power down the PC and unplug it. Next, unplug the monitor, printer, and any other device that has its own external power supply. Do not disconnect any cables or cords (other than the power supply cord) connected to the back of the PC case.

2. Case manufacturers use slightly different methods to open the case. Many newer cases require that you remove the faceplate on the front of the case first. Other cases require removing a side panel first, and very old cases require removing the entire sides and top as a single unit first. Study your case for the correct approach.

> **Notes** In the steps that follow, you will find general guidelines for disassembling a PC. If any of these steps do not seem to apply to your system, you'll need to consult the user manual or download a PDF of the manual from the manufacturer's Web site for more detailed instructions.

3. For a desktop or tower case, locate and remove the screws on the back of the case. Be careful not to unscrew any screws besides the ones attaching the cover. The other screws are probably holding the power supply in place.

4. After you remove the cover screws, slide the cover back to remove it from the case, as shown in Figure 1-7.

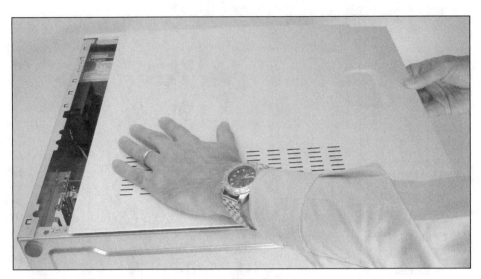

Figure 1-7 Slide a side panel to the rear and then lift it off the case
Courtesy: Course Technology/Cengage Learning

5. To remove the cover from a tower PC with no visible case screws, power down the PC and unplug it from its power outlet. Next, unplug the monitor and any other device with an external power source from the power outlet.

6. On some cases, you must pop the front panel off the case before removing the side panels. Look for a lever on the bottom of the panel and hinges at the top. Squeeze the lever to release the front panel and lift it off the case (see Figure 1-8). Then remove any screws holding the side panel in place, as shown in Figure 1-9, and slide the side panel to the front and then off the case.

> **Notes** Some case panels don't use screws at all; these side panels usually have buttons or tabs to release the cover.

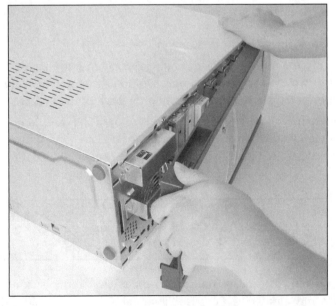

Figure 1-8 Some cases require removing the front panel before removing the side panels of a computer case
Courtesy: Course Technology/Cengage Learning

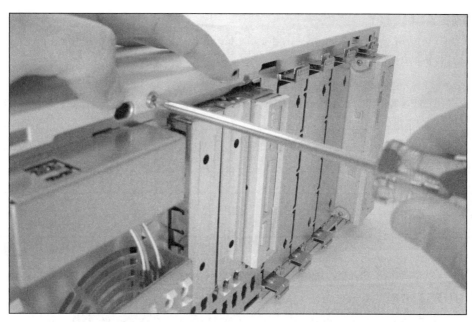

Figure 1-9 Screws hold the side panel in place
Courtesy: Course Technology/Cengage Learning

With the cover removed, you're ready to look for some components. As you complete the following, you may wish to refer to the drawings and photos in Chapters 4 through 8 of *A+ Guide to Hardware* or consult the Internet for additional information on the specific components in your system.

1. Put on your antistatic ground strap and connect the clip to the side of the computer case.

2. Identify and describe the following major components. List any other components you find inside the case. Fill in the following chart:

Component	Description—Include the manufacturer and model name (if listed) as well as its distinguishing characteristics
Power supply	
Motherboard	
Hard drive(s)	
CD/DVD-ROM drive(s)	
CPU	
RAM	
Cooling fan (not inside the power supply)	
Video card (if not onboard)	
Network card (if not onboard)	
Sound card (if not onboard)	

CHALLENGE ACTIVITY

If your instructor has prepared a display of four or more assorted computer parts, fill in the following chart:

Identify the part	Describe how you determined your answer
1.	
2.	
3.	
4.	
5.	
6.	

REVIEW QUESTIONS

1. Describe how you decided which expansion card was the video card:

   _____

2. Describe how you identified the type of CPU you have:

   _____

3. Does your system have much room for adding new components? What types of expansion bus slots are available for adding new cards?

   _____

4. Is there space for upgrading the RAM? If there isn't, what could you do to still upgrade?

   _____

5. Where (specifically) would you go on the Internet to download a PDF of the motherboard or system manual? What information would be required?

   _____

   _____

LAB 1.3 USE SOFTWARE TO EXAMINE A COMPUTER, PART 1

OBJECTIVES

The goal of this lab is to use Sandra Lite to examine your system. After completing this lab, you will be able to:

◢ Download a file from the Internet

◢ Install Sandra Lite

◢ Use Sandra Lite to examine your system

MATERIALS REQUIRED

This lab requires the following:

◢ Windows Vista/XP operating system

◢ Internet access

◢ If necessary, software such as WinZip to uncompress a downloaded file

LAB PREPARATION

Before the lab begins, the instructor or lab assistant needs to do the following:

◢ Verify that Internet access is available.

◢ For labs that don't have Internet access, download these files to a file server, flash drive, CD-R, or other media available to students in the lab:

  • Sandra Lite executable file downloaded from *www.sisoftware.net*.

  • If Windows cannot uncompress the file, an uncompress utility, such as WinZip, can be downloaded from *www.winzip.com*.

ACTIVITY BACKGROUND

Good PC support people are always good investigators. In previous labs, you learned how to gather information about your computer through the operating system and by a physical inspection. In this lab, you will download a diagnostic program from the Internet. These programs can be used to learn about your system, establish a benchmark of its speed and other characteristics, and even diagnose some common problems. If you have a classroom printer available, you'll print a report from the downloaded software about the hardware and software on your computer.

ESTIMATED COMPLETION TIME: 45 Minutes

 Activity

> **Notes** If the SiSoftware Web site is unavailable, you can use a search engine to locate the program.

1. Open your browser and go to **www.sisoftware.net**.
2. Click the link called **Download & Buy**. You will be downloading a free evaluation copy of Sandra Lite.
3. Follow one of the links pointing to a location for downloading Sandra Lite (Evaluation).
4. Follow the instructions on the site you selected to begin the download process.
5. When the File Download dialog box opens, save the file to your PC desktop. You can then disconnect from the Internet. What is the name of the downloaded file?

Next, follow these steps to install Sandra on your PC:

1. If the file has a .zip file extension, double-click it to uncompress the Sandra zip file and extract the setup file.

2. Run the setup program by double-clicking the executable file, which has an .exe file extension. (It might be the downloaded file or the extracted file.) If an Open File - Security Warning dialog box appears, click **Run**. In the installation wizard, use English as the language selection, accept the end user license agreement (EULA), and accept the default settings throughout. Click **Finish** to complete the installation. The Sandra installation creates a new item in your All Programs menu and adds an icon to your desktop.

   Note: The installation may require you to install or update DirectX.

3. When you finish the installation, Sandra will start. If a Customize Rank Engines box appears, close it. Read the Tip of the Day, click the **Module Options** tab, uncheck the **Show Tips and News on Start-up** check box, and then click **OK** to close. You should see a screen similar to the one in Figure 1-10.

Figure 1-10   SiSoftware Sandra main window
Courtesy: Course Technology/Cengage Learning

You can run each utility by double-clicking its icon, or you can create a composite report of the results of each selection. To learn more, complete the following:

1. Double-click the **Hardware** icon and then double-click **Computer Overview**. The Computer Overview utility starts and gathers information about your system before displaying it in a format similar to Device Manager, with devices listed by type. According to this utility, what kind of video adapter is your system using?

2. Click the red X at the bottom of the Computer Overview – SiSoftware Sandra window or press **Esc** to close the Computer Overview utility.

3. Next, click the **Software** tab and double-click the **Operating System** icon to start that utility. Scroll down and note the information types that are listed. According to this utility, which version of Windows are you using?

4. What is the path to the Temporary folder on your system?

5. What is your Windows installation product key?

_____

6. Click the red X at the bottom of the Operating System – SiSoftware Sandra window or press **Esc** to close the Operating System utility.

7. Next, double-click the **Physical Disks** icon (in the Hardware section). The utility begins to gather information about your drives. Do not move the mouse or touch the keyboard while this procedure is in progress. How much total space does your main hard drive contain? What interface type does it use and what is its cache size?

_____

_____

8. Click the red X at the bottom of the Physical Disks – SiSoftware Sandra window or press **Esc** to close the Physical Disks utility.

9. Find and double-click the **Memory Usage** icon to start that utility. What is the name and location of the page file?

_____

10. Close the Memory Usage utility.

You can also use Sandra Lite to create a composite report of your system. To learn more, follow these steps:

1. From the SiSoftware Sandra interface, click the **Tools** tab and click the **Create Report** icon.

2. Click **Next** (right-pointing arrow) to begin the creation.

3. In the Step 1 of 9 window, select **Make choices and generate report**, if necessary, in the drop-down list, and click **Next** to continue.

4. In the Hardware section (Step 2 of 9), click the **Clear All** (red X over a box) button. Click to select **Mainboard** and click **Next** to continue.

5. In the Benchmarks section (Step 3 of 9), click the **Clear All** button. Click **Memory Bandwidth** and click **Next** to continue.

6. In the Software section (Step 4 of 9), click the **Clear All** button, and then click **Next** to continue.

7. In the Support section (Step 5 of 9), click the **Clear All** button, and click **Next** to continue.

8. In the Comments on report section (Step 6 of 9), add any comments, if you like, and then click **Next** to continue.

9. In the Delivery section (Step 7 of 9), click the **Print or Fax** option in the drop-down list, and then click **Next** to continue.

10. In the Print or Fax dialog box, select your printer and click **OK** (green check mark). When Sandra has finished printing your report, you can click the **Exit** button (red X) to close the wizard and then collect your report from the printer.

11. Continue to explore each utility in Sandra, and then close it. You'll use Sandra again in later chapters, so don't uninstall it.

In this lab, you downloaded Sandra from the SiSoftware Web site, but many popular utilities are available from multiple sources on the Internet. To see for yourself, follow these steps:

1. Attempt to find Sandra at _www.zdnet.com_.

2. Is the program available through this avenue as well? Print the Web page or pages to support your answer.

_____

REVIEW QUESTIONS

1. From your printed report, what type of memory module(s) are installed in your system?

   _____

2. From your printed report, what is the maximum front side bus (FSB) speed of your mainboard?

   _____

3. Use the Analysis and Advice feature in the Tools section to generate a report. In your opinion, what is the most important advice contained in this report? Why?

   _____

   _____

   _____

4. How might Sandra be used when upgrading your computer?

   _____

   _____

LAB 1.4 USE SOFTWARE TO EXAMINE A COMPUTER, PART 2

OBJECTIVES

The goal of this lab is to use Belarc Advisor to examine your system. After completing this lab, you will be able to:

◢ Download a file from the Internet

◢ Install Belarc Advisor

◢ Use Belarc Advisor to examine your system

MATERIALS REQUIRED

This lab requires the following:

◢ Windows Vista/XP operating system

◢ Internet access

LAB PREPARATION

Before the lab begins, the instructor or lab assistant needs to do the following:

◢ Verify that Internet access is available.

◢ For labs that don't have Internet access, download Belarc Advisor (Advisor.exe) from *www.belarc.com* and make the file available to students in the lab.

ACTIVITY BACKGROUND

Good PC support people know that there's always more than one way to do something. In Lab 1.3, you learned to use Sandra to investigate your system. In this lab, you use another shareware utility, Belarc Advisor, to examine your system. Follow these directions to find and download this utility that you can use to diagnose PC problems. Then you print a report from the downloaded software about the hardware and software on your computer.

If your lab doesn't have Internet access, ask your instructor for the location of files downloaded previously for you to use. Write the path to those files here:

ESTIMATED COMPLETION TIME: 30 Minutes

 Activity

1. Open your browser and go to **www.belarc.com**.
2. Click the **FREE DOWNLOAD** link.
3. Follow one of the links pointing to a location that offers Belarc Advisor for download.
4. Follow the instructions on the site you selected to begin the download process.
5. When the File Download dialog box opens, save the file to your PC desktop. You can then disconnect from the Internet. At the time that this book was written, the downloaded filename was Advisor.exe, but sometimes Web sites and filenames change. What is the name of your downloaded file?

Notes If the Belarc Web site is unavailable, you can use a search engine to locate the shareware.

Next, follow these steps to install Belarc Advisor on your PC:

1. Run the setup program by double-clicking the downloaded executable file, **Advisor.exe** (or the name of your downloaded file). If an Open File - Security Warning dialog box appears, click **Run**. In the installation wizard, accept the EULA and click **Install**. If the installation prompts you to check for new definitions, click **No**. The Belarc Advisor installation automatically takes a snapshot of your computer, and then creates an item in your Start menu and adds an icon to your desktop.
2. When you finish the installation, Belarc Advisor uses your default Web browser to show the results of the snapshot. If you're using Internet Explorer, you should see a screen similar to the one in Figure 1-11.

Answer the following questions to learn what Belarc Advisor is telling you about your system:

1. What is the name of the manufacturer and model of the motherboard installed on your system?

---

2. What is the version of Windows you're using?

---

3. What is the product key for Windows?

---

4. What is the speed and model of the processor for the system?

---

5. Are there any security updates that need to be applied?

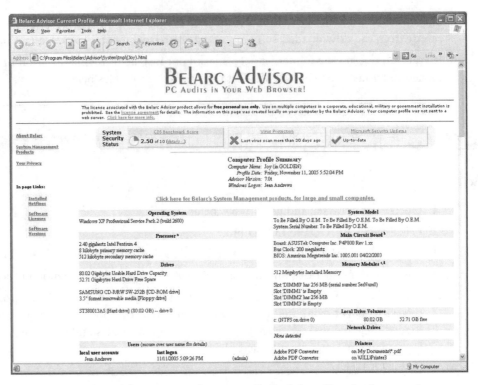

Figure 1-11 Belarc Advisor uses your browser to display information about your system
Courtesy: Course Technology/Cengage Learning

6. How much total space does the hard drive contain? How much free space does the hard drive contain? What type of file system does the hard drive use?

_____

_____

7. To print the Belarc results, click **File**, **Print** from your browser's menu. In the Print dialog box, click **Print**. Take a few minutes to explore the report that Belarc Advisor generated. List three other items of information not mentioned already in this lab that you think might be useful when troubleshooting a computer:

_____

_____

_____

8. Exit from your browser when you are finished.

You'll use Belarc Advisor again in later chapters, so don't uninstall it.

In this lab, you downloaded Belarc Advisor from the Belarc Web site, but many popular utilities are available from multiple sources on the Internet. To see for yourself, follow these steps:

1. Attempt to find Belarc Advisor at _www.zdnet.com_.

2. Is the program available through this avenue as well? Print the Web page or pages to support your answer.

_____

REVIEW QUESTIONS

1. What URL can you use to find a link to download Belarc Advisor?

   _____

2. What tool do you use to get a printed report from Belarc Advisor?

   _____

3. What type of software is Belarc Advisor?

   _____

4. Compare Belarc Advisor to Sandra that you downloaded and used in Lab 1.3. Which utility do you think is the most useful, and why? Which is easier to use?

   _____

   _____

LAB 1.5 COMPARE COSTS OF SYSTEMS

OBJECTIVES

The objective of this lab is to compare a preassembled system with the components that could be assembled to build a comparable system. After completing this lab, you will be able to:

◢ Identify the key components of a preassembled system

◢ Locate prices for components needed to assemble a comparable system

◢ Compare the cost of a preassembled system and a self-assembled system

MATERIALS REQUIRED

This lab requires the following:

◢ Internet access and/or access to a printed computer publication, such as *Computer Shopper*

LAB PREPARATION

Before the lab begins, the instructor or lab assistant needs to do the following:

◢ Verify that Internet access is available.

ACTIVITY BACKGROUND

In this lab, you compare the cost of a brand-name system with the cost of a system having similar specifications but assembled from separate components. Brand-name manufacturers typically build their systems from parts that only they market; these parts are called "proprietary" parts. Therefore, it's unlikely that you'll be able to find exact matches for brand-name components. However, you can find comparable components. For example, if a Gateway computer has a 500 GB hard drive installed, find another 500 GB hard drive for your list of parts. The idea is to find a close match for each major component so that you can compare the total cost of a brand-name system and a similar system built from parts. Use the Internet and available computer-related publications as your sources for information.

ESTIMATED COMPLETION TIME: 45 Minutes

 Activity

1. Find an advertisement for a complete, preassembled system similar to the one in Figure 1-12. Some manufacturers you might want to check out are Gateway (*www.gateway.com*), Dell (*www.dell.com*), and HP (*www.hp.com*).

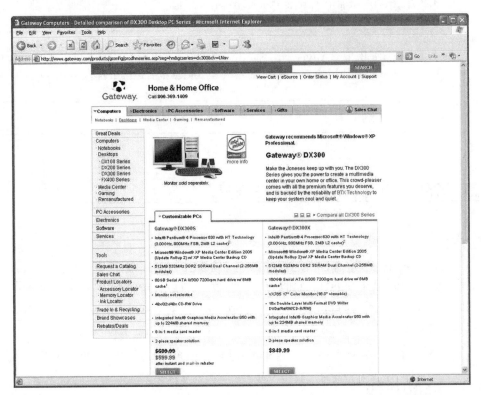

Figure 1-12   Complete, preassembled system
Courtesy: Course Technology/Cengage Learning

2. Study the advertisement and list the following specifications:

    ◢ Processor/MHz _____

    ◢ RAM: _____

    ◢ OS: _____

    ◢ HDD capacity: _____

    ◢ Monitor: _____

    ◢ Video card: _____

    ◢ Sound/speakers: _____

    ◢ Other drives: _____

    ◢ Bonus items: _____

    ◢ Bundled software: _____

    ◢ Total price: _____

3. Find advertisements similar to those in Figure 1-13. Notice that the items are grouped by component type.

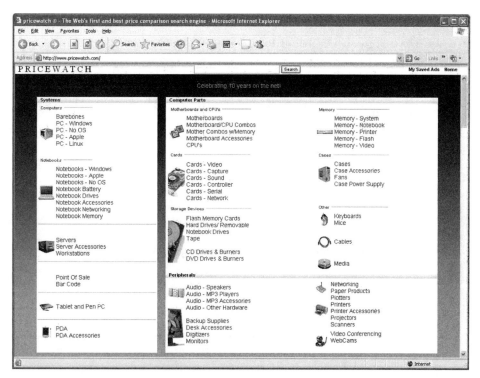

Figure 1-13 Components for sale
Courtesy: Course Technology/Cengage Learning

4. Using the following chart, list and describe the comparable components, their prices, and the source of your information. You might want to check several sources to find the best price. Remember, most mail-order or online purchases have shipping costs. If you can determine an exact shipping price for each component, include this information as part of the component's price. If you can't find the exact shipping price, include a 10 percent fee as part of the price for each shipped component. You might have to include tax, depending on the taxing laws that apply. Sometimes the shipping cost is offset by not having to pay sales tax on an item. Also, because you're early in the course, you might not know enough details about matching components inside the computer case, such as matching a processor to a motherboard. How to find correct matches is covered later in the book, but for now, a close match is all that's necessary.

Component	Description	Source	Price
Processor/MHz			
Motherboard			
RAM			
Case and power supply			
HDD type and capacity			
CD/DVD-ROM drive			
Other drives			
Monitor			
Sound/speakers			
Bonus items (such as video card)			
Operating system			
Bundled software			
TOTAL SYSTEM PRICE			

REVIEW QUESTIONS

1. Which approach to acquiring a system seems to be less expensive?

   _____

2. What is the single most expensive component of a system built from separate components?

   _____

3. What was the estimated cost of shipping (if any) for the component-built system?

   _____

   _____

4. What are some potential pitfalls of building your own PC? Rewards?

   _____

   _____

> **Notes** As you continue with this course, you'll be better able to answer this last question based on your own experiences.

LAB 1.6 PLAN AN IDEAL SYSTEM

OBJECTIVES

The objective of this lab is to plan and price your own ideal system within a budget. After completing this lab, you will be able to:

- Describe what you want your system to be able to do
- Pick components that best meet your goal
- Stay within a budget

MATERIALS REQUIRED

This lab requires the following:

- Internet access and/or access to a computer publication, such as *Computer Shopper*

LAB PREPARATION

Before the lab begins, the instructor or lab assistant needs to do the following:

- Provide Internet access in the lab or announce that students need to bring computer publications, such as *Computer Shopper*, to the lab.

ACTIVITY BACKGROUND

In the future, you might be in a position to build a system to your specifications from separate components. Within a budget of $800, what system would you put together? In this lab, you determine the answer based on your current knowledge and experience. Expect that your opinions will likely change as you continue in this course.

ESTIMATED COMPLETION TIME: 30 Minutes

Activity

1. On a separate piece of paper, make a chart similar to the one used in Lab 1.5. Use it to list the components you would like to include in your system, the cost of each component, and the source for each component. To begin, list everything you want without considering price.

2. After you have determined the total price of all the components you want to include in your ideal system, add up the prices and see whether you are within your $800 budget.

3. If you are under budget, consider including additional components or better versions of components. If you're over budget, determine what components you need to exclude or whether you need to use less expensive versions of some components. Either way, record what components you choose. Also, note how you altered your ideal system to meet your budget.

CHALLENGE ACTIVITY (ADDITIONAL 30 MINUTES)

Not all systems have the same requirements. A server might require lots of RAM and storage space, while a gaming machine would benefit from a more powerful video card. Design a custom $1500 system as either an optimal gaming machine or a media center. Create a one-page advertisement listing both the benefits and the technical specifications of your system.

REVIEW QUESTIONS

1. What is the goal of your original system? In other words, how do you plan to use your system? Explain your choices for components.

_____

_____

_____

2. How would you change your choices if you were to use this computer in a corporate office as a business workstation?

_____

_____

_____

3. What changes would you make if you had an extra $200 in the budget?

_____

_____

4. How might you change your design if your budget was only $600?

_____

_____

Tip   Keep your responses to this lab for later reference. As you learn more about PCs in this course, you can look back at these responses and see where you might change your mind based on new information you have learned.

CHAPTER 2

Introducing Operating Systems

Labs included in this chapter:

- Lab 2.1: Examine Files and Directories
- Lab 2.2: Convert Binary and Hexadecimal Numbers
- Lab 2.3: Investigate Operating Systems—Mac OS
- Lab 2.4: Investigate Operating Systems—Linux
- Lab 2.5: Compare Operating Systems
- Lab 2.6: Use Windows Keyboard Shortcuts

LAB 2.1 EXAMINE FILES AND DIRECTORIES

OBJECTIVES

The goal of this lab is to use different methods to examine files and directories. After completing this lab, you will be able to:

◢ Use the command line to view information about files and directories

◢ Use Computer (My Computer in XP) to view information about files and directories

◢ Display information about files and directories in other ways

MATERIALS REQUIRED

This lab requires the following:

◢ Windows Vista/XP operating system

LAB PREPARATION

Before the lab begins, the instructor or lab assistant needs to do the following:

◢ Verify that Windows starts with no errors.

ACTIVITY BACKGROUND

You can access information about a PC's file structure in several ways. At the Windows desktop, you can use Windows Explorer or My Computer to view the files and directories. From the command line, you can use the DIR command to list the same information. In the following lab, you practice using the DIR command and My Computer.

ESTIMATED COMPLETION TIME: 30 Minutes

 Activity

Follow these steps to access file information via the command line:

1. To open a command prompt window, click **Start**, type **cmd** in the Start Search box, and press **Enter**. (In XP, click **Start**, click **Run**, type **cmd**, and press **Enter**.)

2. When the command prompt window opens, type **help** and press **Enter** to view a list of commands that are available. You can get additional information about a command by typing help and the name of the command.

3. Type **help dir** and press **Enter**. Information and parameters (also called "switches" or "options") for the DIR command are displayed. How many different parameters does the command have?

_____

4. In a command prompt window, the prompt indicates the current directory. Type **dir** and press **Enter**. A detailed list of files and directories in the current directory is displayed. If there are many files and directories, only the last several are visible on the screen.

5. Use Help to examine the /p and /w switches for the dir command, and then try these variations and explain how the information is displayed:

dir /p _____

dir /w _____

6. Examine the results of the DIR command. The results vary with different versions of Windows, but each listing should include the following information:

  ◢ The date and time the file was created

  ◢ The directory markers (directories do not include an extension; instead, they are indicated by a <DIR> marker tag)

  ◢ The file size in bytes

  ◢ The name of a file or directory (most files have an extension)

  ◢ A summary, including the number of files and directories in that directory, the number of bytes those files use, and the number of bytes of free space on the drive

To print this file information, you can copy the contents of the command prompt window to Windows Clipboard, open the Notepad program, paste the file information into Notepad, and then use the Notepad Print command. To try that technique now, follow these steps:

1. On the far left of the command prompt window's title bar, click the **Command Prompt** icon. A drop-down list appears.

2. On the drop-down list, point to **Edit**, and then click **Mark**. A blinking cursor then appears at the top of the command prompt window.

3. Click and drag the cursor over the information you would like to copy to the Clipboard; the information should then be highlighted. You might need to scroll the window to capture all the necessary information.

4. After you have highlighted all the information you want to copy, click the **Command Prompt** icon on the title bar.

5. On the drop-down list, point to **Edit**, and then click **Copy**. The highlighted contents are copied to the Clipboard.

6. To open Notepad, click **Start**, point to **Programs** (**All Programs** in XP), point to **Accessories**, and click **Notepad**.

7. Click **Edit**, and then click **Paste** from the Notepad menu.

8. Click **File**, and then click **Print** from the Notepad menu. Use the print options to print your document.

9. Close the command prompt window and Notepad without saving the file.

In addition to the command prompt window, you can use Windows Explorer to examine files and directories. Windows Explorer can display information in a variety of ways. Before you view files and directories with this tool, you need to change some settings to control how information is displayed. To change settings in Windows Vista, follow these steps:

1. Click **Start**, and then click **Control Panel**.

2. Click **Appearance and Personalization**, and then click **Folder Options** from the menu. The Folder Options dialog box opens.

3. In the Folder Options dialog box, click the **View** tab, click to select the **Show hidden files and folders** button, and uncheck the **Hide extensions for known file types** check box.

4. Click **Apply**, and then click **OK** to close the Folder Options dialog box.

To change settings in Windows XP, follow these steps:

1. To open the My Computer window, click **Start**, and then click **My Computer**.

2. Click **Tools**, and then click **Folder Options** from the menu. The Folder Options dialog box opens.

3. In the Folder Options dialog box, click the **View** tab (if necessary), click to select the **Show hidden files and folders** button, and click to clear the **Hide extensions for known file types** check box.

4. Click **Apply**, and then click **OK** to close the Folder Options dialog box.

Now that you have changed the way information is displayed, you're ready to use Windows Explorer through Computer (My Computer in XP) to access specific information about your system's files and directories. Complete the following:

1. Click **Start**, and then click **Computer** (**My Computer** in XP). Maximize the Computer window, and click the icon representing drive C; you'll see details about the drive displayed in the bottom or left pane.

2. How much free space is available on drive C? What is the total size of the drive?

_____

3. Based on total size and free space, how much space is used on drive C?

_____

4. Double-click the drive C icon. What information about each folder is displayed in this window?

_____

_____

5. Windows uses different icons for different file types. Describe three different icons and the files they represent:

_____

_____

_____

6. From the Computer menu, click **View**, and then click **Details**. Notice that this command displays the same information as the DIR command.

7. Close all open windows.

REVIEW QUESTIONS

1. What command displays a list of files and directories at the command line?

_____

2. Does Windows display all system files by default?

_____

3. How can you change the way Windows displays file extensions?

_____

_____

4. In Computer, what type of graphic displays information about a drive?

_____

5. How does Windows graphically distinguish between different file types?

_____

LAB 2.2 CONVERT BINARY AND HEXADECIMAL NUMBERS

OBJECTIVES

The goal of this lab is to practice converting numbers between decimal, binary, and hexadecimal forms. After completing this lab, you will be able to:

▲ Convert decimal numbers (base 10) to hexadecimal and binary form

▲ Convert hexadecimal numbers (base 16) to binary and decimal form

▲ Convert binary numbers (base 2) to decimal and hexadecimal form

MATERIALS REQUIRED

This lab requires the following:

▲ A pencil and paper and/or Windows Calculator

▲ Access to the online content "The Hexadecimal Number System and Memory Addressing," downloaded from *www.cengage.com/coursetechnology/*

▲ Windows Vista/XP operating system

LAB PREPARATION

Before the lab begins, the instructor or lab assistant needs to do the following:

▲ Announce to students that, before they come to lab, they should read the online content "The Hexadecimal Number System and Memory Addressing." They might like to bring this content to class in printed form.

ACTIVITY BACKGROUND

Sometimes you need to know what resources, such as memory addresses, are being reserved for a device. This information is often displayed on a computer using the binary or hexadecimal (hex) numbering system. Often, you'll want to convert these numbers into more familiar decimal numbers to get a better picture of which resources are reserved for a device.

ESTIMATED COMPLETION TIME: 60 Minutes

 Activity

1. Convert the following decimal numbers to binary numbers using a calculator or by following the instructions in the online content "The Hexadecimal Number System and Memory Addressing." (To access Windows Calculator, click **Start**, point to **All Programs**, point to **Accessories**, and then click **Calculator**. If necessary, click **View**,

and then click **Scientific** from the Calculator menu to perform the conversions in these steps.)

⊿ 14 = _____

⊿ 77 = _____

⊿ 128 = _____

⊿ 223 = _____

⊿ 255 = _____

2. Convert the following decimal numbers to hexadecimal notation:

⊿ 13 = _____

⊿ 240 = _____

⊿ 255 = _____

⊿ 58880 = _____

⊿ 65535 = _____

3. Convert the following binary numbers to hexadecimal notation:

⊿ 100 = _____

⊿ 1011 = _____

⊿ 111101 = _____

⊿ 11111000 = _____

⊿ 10110011 = _____

⊿ 00000001 = _____

4. Hexadecimal numbers are often preceded with "0x." Convert the following hex numbers to binary numbers:

⊿ 0x0016 = _____

⊿ 0x00F8 = _____

⊿ 0x00B2B = _____

⊿ 0x005A = _____

⊿ 0x1234 = _____

5. Convert the following hex numbers to decimal:

⊿ 0x0013 = _____

⊿ 0x00AB = _____

⊿ 0x01CE = _____

⊿ 0x812A = _____

6. Convert the following binary numbers to decimal:

⊿ 1011 = _____

⊿ 11011 = _____

⊿ 10101010 = _____

⊿ 111110100 = _____

⊿ 10111011101 = _____

⊿ 11111000001111 = _____

A network card, also called a network adapter or NIC, is assigned an address that identifies the card on the network. The address is called the Media Access Control (MAC) or physical address. The address assigned to the network card is expressed in a series of paired hexadecimal numbers separated by dashes. In the following steps, you find out the network address for your network card and then convert the address to a binary number:

1. Open the command prompt window (see Lab 2.1), type **ipconfig /all**, and press **Enter**.

2. Write down the following information for your system:

   ◢ Network adapter address in hexadecimal form: _____

   ◢ Network adapter address in binary pairs: _____

3. Referring to Figure 2-1, convert the numbers in the network adapter's memory range and determine how many bytes, expressed in a decimal number, are in its memory address range.

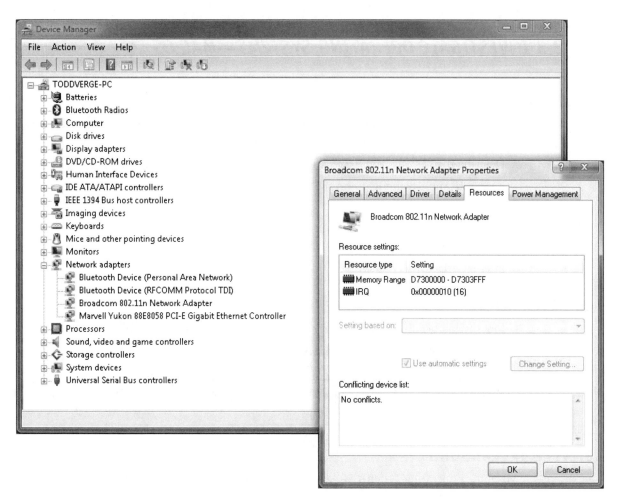

Figure 2-1 Memory range and input/output range expressed as hex numbers
Courtesy: Course Technology/Cengage Learning

CRITICAL THINKING (ADDITIONAL 15 MINUTES)

A typical video card uses a color depth of 8 bits to define the screen color in safe mode. Eight bits can form 256 different numbers from 00000000 to 11111111 in binary (0 to 255 in decimal) so 256 different colors are possible. How many colors are available with a 16-bit color depth? What about a 24-bit or 32-bit depth?

REVIEW QUESTIONS

1. How long, in bits, is a typical MAC address?

_____

2. Computers often express numbers in _____ format, which is a base 16 numbering system.

3. Most people are more comfortable working with a(n) _____, or base 10, numbering system.

4. In the hexadecimal system, what decimal value does the letter A represent?

_____

5. Hexadecimal numbers are often preceded by _____ so that a value containing only numerals is not mistaken for a decimal number.

LAB 2.3 INVESTIGATE OPERATING SYSTEMS—MAC OS

OBJECTIVES

The goal of this lab is to familiarize you with Macintosh operating systems and the hardware they support. After completing this lab, you will be able to:

◢ Describe the various Apple operating systems, hardware, and applications

◢ Research Apple technology on the Apple Web site (*www.apple.com*)

MATERIALS REQUIRED

This lab requires the following:

◢ Internet access

LAB PREPARATION

Before the lab begins, the instructor or lab assistant needs to do the following:

◢ Verify that Internet access is available.

> **Notes** If a Macintosh system is available, instructors might want to give a brief demonstration for students.

ACTIVITY BACKGROUND

Macintosh operating systems are designed to be used only on Macintosh (Mac) computers (see Figure 2-2). Many developers (including Apple, the company that created the Macintosh computer) have created Macintosh applications. The Apple Web site (*www.apple.com*) is the best source of information about Macintosh products. In this lab, you investigate Macintosh operating systems, hardware, and applications.

ESTIMATED COMPLETION TIME: 30 Minutes

 Activity

1. Open your browser and go to **www.apple.com**. Explore the site, and when you're done, return to the main page. Use the links on the site to answer the questions in this lab.

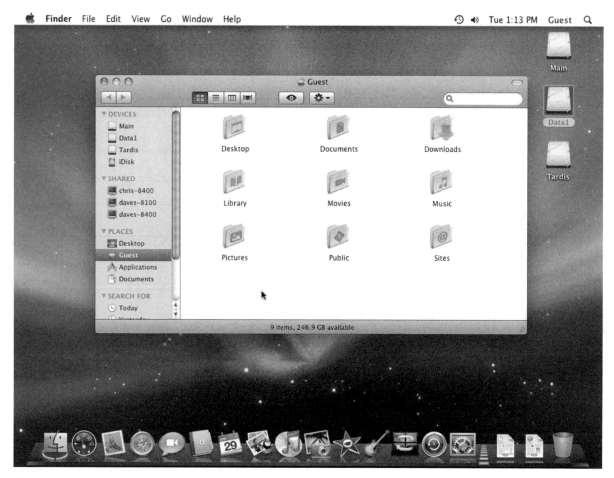

Figure 2-2 A typical OS X desktop
Courtesy: Course Technology/Cengage Learning

2. What is the latest version of the Mac operating system available for a new iMac?

_____

3. What is the cost of upgrading your operating system to the latest version of OS X?

_____

4. Compare the iMac, Mac mini, and Mac Pro systems available for sale on the Apple Web site. What are the speeds or frequencies of the processors in each computer?

_____

5. How much does the fastest 24-inch iMac cost?

_____

6. What software comes bundled with an iMac?

_____

7. What is a MacBook?

_____

8. How much does the most expensive MacBook Pro cost?

_____

9. What features are included with the least expensive MacBook?

10. Describe the features of an Apple Mighty Mouse:

11. What is the function of an AirPort Extreme Base Station?

12. What is the difference between the AirPort Extreme and the AirPort Express?

13. What is the purpose of QuickTime software?

14. Describe what the iWork software does:

15. Describe the purposes of iLife software:

REVIEW QUESTIONS

1. What is one advantage of using an Apple computer instead of a PC?

2. What is one disadvantage of using an Apple computer instead of a PC?

3. Why do you think it's easier for Apple to provide compatibility between hardware and the operating system than it is for Microsoft or Linux?

4. Why can't OS X run on a typical PC?

LAB 2.4 INVESTIGATE OPERATING SYSTEMS—LINUX

OBJECTIVES

The goal of this lab is to find information about Linux. After completing this lab, you will be able to:

- Research Linux on the Linux Web site (*www.linux.org*)
- Compare Linux with other operating systems
- Use the Linux tutorial on the Linux Web site

MATERIALS REQUIRED

This lab requires the following:

- Internet access
- A blank CD
- A CD burner and compatible burning software

LAB PREPARATION

Before the lab begins, the instructor or lab assistant needs to do the following:

- Verify that Internet access is available.

ACTIVITY BACKGROUND

UNIX is a popular OS used to control networks and support applications on the Internet (see Figure 2-3). Linux is a scaled-down version of UNIX that is provided, in basic form, free of charge and includes open access to the programming code of the OS. Linux can be used as both a server platform and a desktop platform, but its greatest popularity has come in the server market. In this lab, you search the *www.linux.org* site for general information on Linux and survey the Linux tutorial.

ESTIMATED COMPLETION TIME: 45 Minutes

 Activity

1. Open your browser and go to **www.linux.org**. Spend a few minutes exploring the site on your own, and then return to the main page.

2. Click the **General Info** link (on the navigation bar). Using the information on the "What is Linux" page, answer the following:

   - What is the current, full-featured version of the Linux kernel?

     _____

   - Who is credited with inventing the Linux kernel?

     _____

   - How is Linux licensed? Read the GNU General Public License. Give a brief description of the terms and conditions of this license:

     _____

     _____

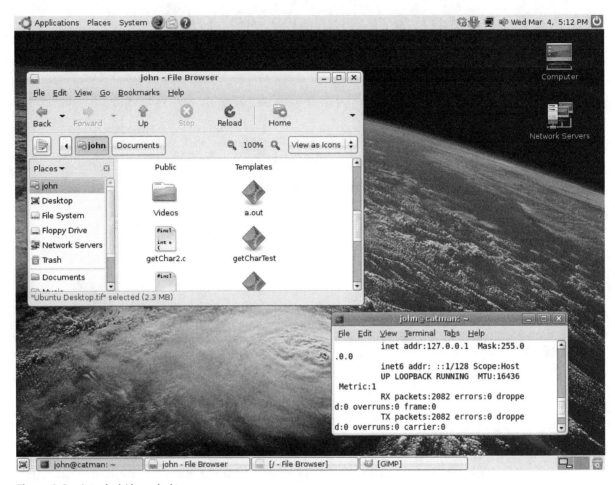

Figure 2-3 A typical Linux desktop
Courtesy: Course Technology/Cengage Learning

◢ How much does Linux cost?

For an operating system to be useful, applications must be written for it. Suppose a small business is interested in using Linux on its desktop computers. Will this business be able to run common business-type applications on its Linux desktops? To find out, click the **Applications** link (on the navigation bar). The types of applications are listed by category. Search this page and its links to answer the following questions:

1. Will the business be able to send faxes from a Linux machine?

2. List two Web browsers suitable for Linux.

3. How many antivirus software packages are available for Linux? List at least two.

4. After searching under Office and Word Processor, list at least three word-processing applications available for Linux.

5. How many accounting applications are available for Linux? List at least two and the URLs where you found them.

_____

_____

Now you can continue exploring the Linux Web site. Follow these steps to compare Linux to other operating systems:

1. Click the **Documentation** link on the navigation bar.

2. Read about the Linux Documentation Project.

3. Use the information on the Linux Web site to answer the following questions:

   ◢ What is the Linux Documentation Project?

   _____

   _____

   ◢ Who is responsible for writing documentation for the Linux operating system?

   _____

Next, follow these steps to explore the Web site's Linux tutorial:

1. Return to the home page, scroll down to display the heading **Linux 101,** and then click **more** at the bottom of that section.

2. Scroll down, and then click **Getting Started with Linux – Beginner's Course.** Browse through this tutorial and answer the questions in this lab.

3. What might you consider when deciding which version (distribution) of Linux to install?

   _____

   _____

4. Can you install Linux on a computer that has another operating system already installed (print the Web page supporting your answer)?

   _____

5. If you don't have a high-speed Internet connection or a CD-burner, what is another way you can get a copy of Linux for your home PC?

   _____

Continue exploring the Web site by completing the following:

1. Click the **Distributions** link. A link to the source code for Linux kernels is available on this page. Notice the Distribution search area. When searching for a distribution of Linux, if you don't narrow your search, you might get an overwhelming number of returns. The subsequent steps of this lab limit your search.

2. Click **English** in the Language drop-down list.

3. Click **Mainstream/General Public** in the Category drop-down list.

4. Click **Intel compatible** in the Platform list, and then click **Go.** How many distributions do you see listed?

   _____

5. Browse through the list, looking for openSUSE, Debian, and Fedora Linux. Which distribution appears to be easiest to use? What is its intended purpose?

_____

6. Can Linux be used on other systems that don't run Intel-compatible processors? Print the Web page supporting your answer:

_____

REVIEW QUESTIONS

1. What are some of the "costs" associated with installing a "free" operating system such as Linux?

_____

2. Why might a company not want to use Linux on its desktop computers?

_____

_____

3. What is one advantage of using Linux rather than a Windows operating system on a desktop?

_____

4. Based on what you learned from the Linux Web site, how do you think companies that provide Linux make the most profit?

_____

CRITICAL THINKING (ADDITIONAL 45 MINUTES)

Many distributions of Linux will run directly off a bootable CD called a Live CD. Go to *www.ubuntu.com* and download the latest version of the Ubuntu distribution of Linux. Burn the .ISO image you downloaded to a CD and use it to boot your computer. Take some time to explore the interface and then answer the following questions:

1. What does the button in the upper-left corner of the screen allow you to do?

_____

2. Does Ubuntu use the Gnome or KDE graphical interface by default?

_____

3. Name an Internet browser that is included with the operating system.

_____

LAB 2.5 COMPARE OPERATING SYSTEMS

OBJECTIVES

The goal of this lab is to help you learn about the history of PC operating systems and appreciate why many of today's operating systems share similar features. After completing this lab, you will be able to:

◢ Better understand the relationship among operating systems

MATERIALS REQUIRED

This lab requires the following:

◢ Internet access

LAB PREPARATION

Before the lab begins, the instructor or lab assistant needs to do the following:

◢ Verify that Internet access is available.

ACTIVITY BACKGROUND

Modern operating systems, such as Windows, Linux, and Mac OS, have many similar features because they share a common history. Figure 2-4 shows some highlights of this history. The arrows indicate a direct or indirect influence from an earlier operating system.

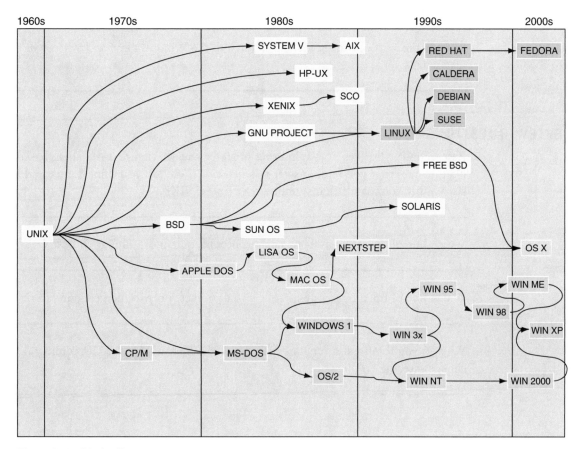

Figure 2-4 OS timeline
Courtesy: Course Technology/Cengage Learning

ESTIMATED COMPLETION TIME: 30 Minutes

 Activity

Use your favorite search engine, such as *www.google.com*, to answer the following questions:

1. Search for the "history of operating systems." List the URLs of three sites that you think do a good job of explaining this history.

2. What are two similarities and two differences between the original Mac OS and Windows?

_____

3. How is OS/2 loosely connected to Windows NT?

_____

4. What is the relationship of QDOS to CP/M and MS-DOS?

_____

5. Modify the timeline by adding any other past operating systems, such as BeOS or VMS, that you think are important.

CHALLENGE ACTIVITY (ADDITIONAL 15 MINUTES)

1. Extend the timeline into the future by adding any new operating systems with their expected release dates.

2. What is the next operating system planned in the Windows line and when will it be released?

_____

REVIEW QUESTIONS

1. Research OS timelines on the Internet (or refer back to Figure 2-4). Then, based on the OS timelines that you find, answer this question: Why do you think Linux and UNIX share more commands than Windows XP and UNIX?

_____

2. Which line of operating systems has recently become more similar to UNIX?

_____

3. Which line of operating systems split into two lines, only to merge again later?

_____

4. Why do you think most versions of Linux and Windows use the CD command to change directories?

_____

LAB 2.6 USE WINDOWS KEYBOARD SHORTCUTS

OBJECTIVES

The goal of this lab is to introduce you to some keyboard shortcuts. After completing this lab, you will be able to use the keyboard to:

◢ Display the Start menu

◢ Switch between open applications

◢ Launch utilities with the Windows logo key

MATERIALS REQUIRED

This lab requires the following:

◢ Windows XP operating system

◢ A keyboard with the Windows logo key

LAB PREPARATION

Before the lab begins, the instructor or lab assistant needs to do the following:

◢ Verify that Windows starts with no errors.

ACTIVITY BACKGROUND

You can use certain keys or key combinations (called keyboard shortcuts) to perform repetitive tasks more efficiently. These shortcuts are also useful when the mouse isn't working. In this lab, you learn to use some common keyboard shortcuts. You can find a full list of keyboard shortcuts by searching for "keyboard shortcuts" in the Windows Help and Support Center.

ESTIMATED COMPLETION TIME: 30 Minutes

 Activity

The F1 key is the universal keyboard shortcut for launching Help. To learn more, follow these steps:

1. Open Paint and then minimize it.

2. Open Notepad and then minimize it.

3. Click the desktop, and then press **F1**. Windows Help and Support opens.

4. Close Windows Help and Support, and restore Paint.

5. Press **F1**. Because Paint is now the active window, Windows Help and Support opens with information on Paint. Close this window.

6. Restore Notepad, and then press **F1**. Windows Help and Support opens with information about Notepad.

You can activate many shortcuts by pressing the Windows logo key in combination with other keys. An enhanced keyboard has two Windows logo keys, usually located between the Ctrl and Alt keys on either side of the spacebar. Try the combinations listed in Table 2-1, and record the result of each key combination in the Result column. (Close each window you open before proceeding to the next key combination.)

Key or Key Combination	Result
Windows logo	
Windows logo+E	
Windows logo+F	
Windows logo+R	
Windows logo+Break	
Windows logo+M	

Table 2-1 Key combinations using the Windows logo key

Suppose for some reason that your mouse isn't working and you have to print a text file. You would have to use the keyboard to find, select, open, and print the document. To learn more, follow these steps:

1. Boot the computer, wait for the Windows desktop to appear, and then unplug the mouse.

2. Press **Tab** a few times until one of the desktop icons is highlighted.

3. Use the arrow keys to highlight **Recycle Bin**.

4. Press **Enter**. The Recycle Bin opens.

5. Press **Tab** a few times and observe all the choices being highlighted. You can use a combination of Tab, arrow keys, and Enter to select almost anything in an open window.

6. Use this method to find, select, and open the Notepad program (from **Start, Programs, Accessories, Notepad**) and type "Have a Nice Day."

7. Notice in the Notepad window that one letter of each menu item becomes underlined after you press **Alt**. You can select menu options by holding down the Alt key while you press this underlined letter. For example, to open the File menu in Notepad, hold down the **Alt** key and press **F**. After the menu is open, you can use the arrow keys to move over the menu and select an option by pressing **Enter**, or you can type the underlined letter of a menu option. With the **Alt** key pressed down, press **F**. The File menu opens.

8. Press **P** to select Print. The Print dialog box opens.

9. Verify that the correct printer is selected. (To select a different printer, use the arrow keys.)

10. To send the print job to the printer, press **Tab** until the Print button is active, and then press **Enter** (or you can press **Alt+P**).

11. Practice editing text, using the following shortcuts for cutting, copying, and pasting:

    ◢ To delete one or more characters, move your cursor to the beginning of the text you want to delete, hold down the **Shift** key, and use the arrow keys to highlight the text. (If you were using a mouse, you could hold down the left mouse button and drag the mouse until the entire block was highlighted.)

    ◢ With the text highlighted, hold down the **Ctrl** key, press **X**, and then release both keys. This action cuts the highlighted text from its original location and moves it to the Clipboard. You can then paste it in another location.

    ◢ To copy a highlighted block of characters to the Clipboard (without removing it from its original location), hold down the **Ctrl** key, press **C**, and then release both keys. A copy of the highlighted block of characters is placed in the Clipboard. You can then paste it in another location.

    ◢ To paste text from the Clipboard to a new location, move the cursor to the desired location, press and hold the **Ctrl** key, press **V**, and then release both keys.

CRITICAL THINKING (ADDITIONAL 15 MINUTES)

Using the keyboard skills you have learned in this lab, perform the following steps without using the mouse and answer the respective questions:

1. Open Device Manager and view resources for the mouse. What status does Device Manager report about the mouse?

---

2. Open the calculator and select the scientific view. How would you express the decimal number 17 in hexadecimal?

---

3. Open Windows Explorer and select the hard drive. How much space is available on the hard drive?

_____

REVIEW QUESTIONS

1. What key is universally used to launch Help?

_____

2. How many Windows logo keys are usually included on an enhanced keyboard?

_____

3. What shortcut combination can you use to paste a block of text?

_____

4. What key combination can you use to switch between open applications? (*Hint*: Check Windows Help and Support.)

_____

5. Is it possible to open the Start menu by pressing only one key?

_____

Working with People in a Technical World

Labs included in this chapter:

- **Lab 3.1:** Understand IT Codes of Ethics
- **Lab 3.2:** Provide Customer Service
- **Lab 3.3:** Practice Help Desk Skills
- **Lab 3.4:** Practice Good Communication Skills
- **Lab 3.5:** Understand the Help Desk Procedures for a Company

LAB 3.1 UNDERSTAND IT CODES OF ETHICS

OBJECTIVES

The goal of this lab is to help you become familiar with the concept of a Code of Ethics for IT professionals. After completing this lab, you will be able to:

▲ Examine a Code of Ethics for IT professionals

▲ Consider different values when making an ethical decision

MATERIALS REQUIRED

This lab requires the following:

▲ A workgroup of 2 to 4 students

▲ Access to the Internet

LAB PREPARATION

Before the lab begins, the instructor or lab assistant needs to do the following:

▲ Read through the IEEE Code of Ethics and be prepared to discuss it with each group.

ACTIVITY BACKGROUND

Most companies and professional organizations have a *Code, of Ethics* or *Code of Conduct* that they expect their employees to uphold. It typically outlines the rights and responsibilities of employees as well as their customers. Certain practices such as respecting confidentially or avoiding conflicts of interest are common to most codes, while other behaviors are industry specific. In addition, many businesses publish a *Statement of Values* that outlines the values or qualities that guide their actions. In this lab, you will examine a Code of Ethics developed by the Institute of Electrical and Electronics Engineers (IEEE) and consider the values it represents.

ESTIMATED COMPLETION TIME: 60 Minutes

 Activity

1. Begin by going to **www.ieee.org** and searching for the IEEE Code of Ethics. Print a copy of this code.

   ▲ Discuss this code among your group. What do you, as a group, consider to be the most important guideline in the list?

   _____

   _____

   _____

   ▲ Find at least one other technological organization or company that posts a Code of Ethics. Name the organization and respective URL below:

   _____

   _____

◢ Describe any significant similarities or differences between the IEEE code and the code from your one additional organization:

_____

_____

_____

2. Ethical decisions are often constructed around a set of priorities called *values*. These values include fairness, equality, and honesty.

◢ In your group, brainstorm for as many unique values as you can in 10 minutes. You may wish to research "ethical values" on the Internet for inspiration. When you're finished, discuss them with your group and try to agree on what you consider to be the seven most important values. Remember that there are no right or wrong answers; you're just trying to determine what's most important to the members in your group.

◢ List the values below:

1. _____

2. _____

3. _____

4. _____

5. _____

6. _____

7. _____

◢ What values from your brainstormed list are also represented by the IEEE Code of Ethics?

_____

_____

_____

_____

3. Case study: You are working in the IT department of a large company. Your employer has asked you to monitor the e-mail and Internet activity of select individuals in the company and report back at the end of the week.

◢ Does your employer have the right to monitor this information? Does it have a responsibility to do so?

_____

_____

_____

◢ Does your employer have a responsibility to inform its employees that their e-mail and Internet activity are being monitored?

_____

_____

◢ What should you do if you discover an illegal activity during your investigation? What if your employer doesn't agree with your decision?

_____

_____

_____

◢ What would you do if you discovered that your employer was engaged in illegal activity like using pirated software?

_____

_____

_____

◢ If your best friend is found to be using the Internet for job hunting, would you mention it in your report?

_____

_____

_____

REVIEW QUESTIONS

1. Did your groups have any trouble agreeing on the seven most important values?

_____

2. Do you think having a company Code of Ethics makes ethical decisions any easier? Why?

_____

_____

3. Do you think most people share a fundamental set of values?

_____

_____

4. What can you do in cases where your personal values conflict with the values of your employer?

_____

_____

LAB 3.2 PROVIDE CUSTOMER SERVICE

OBJECTIVES

The goal of this lab is to help you appreciate some of the issues involved in providing excellent customer service. After completing this lab, you will be able to:

▲ Evaluate the service needs of your customers

▲ Plan for good customer service

▲ Respond to customer complaints

MATERIALS REQUIRED

This lab requires the following:

▲ A workgroup of 2 to 4 students

LAB PREPARATION

Before the lab begins, the instructor or lab assistant needs to do the following:

▲ Read through the customer service scenarios and be prepared to discuss them with each group.

ACTIVITY BACKGROUND

A PC technician needs to be not only technically competent, but also skilled at providing excellent customer service. Acting in a helpful, dependable, and, above all, professional manner is a must, whether the technician deals directly with customers or works with other employees as part of a team.

To complete this lab, work through the following customer service scenarios. When you are done, compare your answers with the rest of your group and see whether you can arrive at a consensus. Keep in mind that there might not be a single right answer to each question.

ESTIMATED COMPLETION TIME: 60 Minutes

Activity

1. A customer returns to your store complaining that the upgraded computer he just picked up doesn't boot. You remember testing the computer yourself before the pickup, and everything was fine.

   ▲ What can you do to remedy the situation?

   _____

   _____

   ▲ How can you avoid this kind of problem in the future?

   _____

   _____

2. You're working in a call center that provides support to customers who are trying to install your product at home. While working with an inexperienced customer over the telephone, you realize that she's having trouble following your directions.

  ◢ What are some ways you can help customers even when they can't see you in a face-to-face environment?

  _____

  _____

  _____

  _____

  _____

  ◢ How can you communicate clearly with your customers while avoiding the impression that you're talking down to them?

  _____

  _____

  _____

3. You arrive on a service call, and the overly confident office supervisor shows you the malfunctioning computer. She begins to explain what she thinks is the problem, but you can tell from the computer's operation that it's something else. You suspect that the office supervisor might have caused the malfunction.

  ◢ How can you troubleshoot the problem without offending your customer?

  _____

  _____

  _____

  ◢ Would it be a mistake to accuse the customer of causing the problem? Why?

  _____

  _____

4. An irate customer calls to complain that he's not satisfied with service he has received from your company and tells you he plans to take his future business elsewhere.

  ◢ Should you apologize even if you don't think your company acted improperly?

  _____

  _____

  ◢ How can you give the customer the impression that you and your company are listening to his complaints?

  _____

  _____

REVIEW QUESTIONS

1. Did the other members of your group come up with any viewpoints you hadn't considered?

   _____

2. Did you have any trouble coming to a consensus about how to deal with each situation?

   _____

3. Why is an understanding of good customer service important for a technician who doesn't work directly with the public?

   _____

   _____

4. How could you go about improving your listening skills with customers?

   _____

   _____

   _____

LAB 3.3: PRACTICE HELP DESK SKILLS

OBJECTIVES

The goal of this lab is to help you learn how to work with a customer using a chat session. After completing this lab, you will be able to:

◢ Use help desk skills in a chat session and on the phone to solve customer problems

MATERIALS REQUIRED

This lab requires the following:

◢ Two or more Windows Vista/XP computers connected by the Internet or a network for each student workgroup

◢ Access to instant messaging software such as MSN Messenger

◢ Phone (or cell phone) for each student

LAB PREPARATION

Before the lab begins, the instructor or lab assistant needs to do the following:

◢ Make available two networked Windows Vista/XP computers for each student workgroup of two or more students.

◢ Verify that messaging software is able to communicate

◢ Tell students to bring their cell phones to the lab, or provide telephones in the lab.

ACTIVITY BACKGROUND

In the past, help desk support was solely by telephone, but more and more companies are offering technical support for their hardware and software products by way of chat sessions between the company help desk and the customer. Help desk personnel need to know how to ask questions, connect with the customer in a friendly and personal tone, and solve the customer's problem using telephone or chat. These chat sessions are typically started by clicking a link on the company's Web site. For example, in Figure 3-1, you can see where to click to start a live chat session with Linksys support.

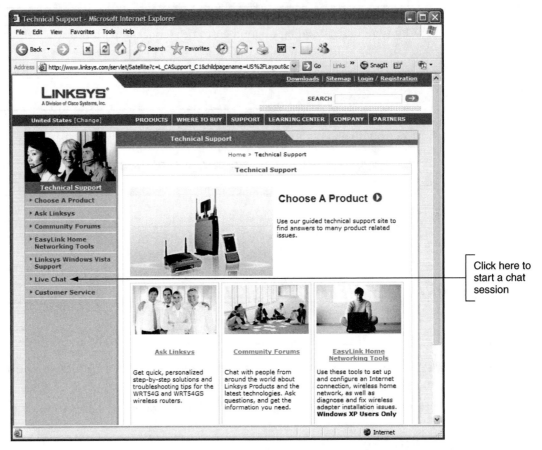

Figure 3-1   Chat sessions for technical support are often available by way of manufacturer Web sites
Courtesy: Course Technology/Cengage Learning

ESTIMATED COMPLETION TIME: 60 Minutes

 Activity

Imagine that Jesse is having problems securing his wireless network. The multifunctional router that serves as his wireless access point was giving problems, so he pressed the Reset button on the router to give it a fresh start. The router began working, but he then discovered he had reset the router back to factory default settings, undoing all his wireless security settings. When Jesse tried to reconfigure the router, he could not find the router documentation, which included the username and password to the router firmware utility. After giving up his search for the documentation, he now decides to contact Linksys for help.

TROUBLESHOOTING

Jesse goes to the Linksys Web site and clicks the SUPPORT link, which opens the page shown in Figure 3-1. He clicks the Live Chat link, and on the next page, enters his name, phone number, e-mail address, and product name. After he submits this information, a chat window opens similar to the one in Figure 3-2. Ryan is working the help desk at Linksys and responds.

Figure 3-2 Chat window with technical support
Courtesy: Course Technology/Cengage Learning

Working with a partner in your workgroup, use network and chat software such as MSN Messenger or AIM to do the following:

1. Select one person in your workgroup to play the role of Jesse, the customer. Select another person to play the role of Ryan, the help desk technician.

2. Jesse initiates a chat session with Ryan. What is the first thing Ryan says to Jesse in the chat session?

3. In the chat session between Jesse and Ryan, Ryan does the following:

   Ryan asks Jesse for the serial number of the router. This number is embedded on the bottom of the router.

   Ryan knows the default username and password for this router to be a blank entry for the username and "admin" for the password. Ryan wants Jesse to know it would have been better for him to have reset the router by unplugging it and plugging it back in, rather than using the Reset button. Ryan also suggests to Jesse that for security reasons, he needs to enter a new username and password for the router.

4. Print the chat session. If your chat software does not have the print option, then copy and paste the chat session text into a document and print the document. As a courtesy to their customers, many companies e-mail to the customer a transcription of the chat session with technical support.

5. Critique the chat session with others in your workgroup. Make suggestions that might help Ryan to be more effective, friendly, and helpful. Use telephones to simulate a help desk conversation.

Use the same troubleshooting scenario, but this time reverse roles between Jesse and Ryan. Do the following:

1. Jesse calls Ryan, and Ryan answers, "Hello, this is Ryan Jackson with the Linksys help desk. May I please have your name, the product you need help with, your phone number, and e-mail address?"

2. After the information is collected, Ryan allows Jesse to describe the problem and steps him through the solution.

3. When the problem is solved, Ryan ends the call politely and positively.

4. Make suggestions that might help Ryan to be more effective, friendly, and helpful.

In the next help desk session, Joy contacts technical support for her company, complaining of too many pop-up ads on her desktop. Do the following:

1. Select someone to play the role of Joy and another person to play the role of Sam, the help desk technician.

2. Using chat software, Joy starts a chat session with Sam, and Sam solves the problem. Assume that Joy is a novice user who needs a little extra help with keystrokes.

3. Sam decides to have Joy turn on the IE 6 pop-up blocker, use previously installed antivirus software to scan for viruses, and download, install, and run Windows Defender software from the Microsoft Web site.

4. Print the chat session and discuss it with the workgroup. Do you have any suggestions for Sam to improve his help desk skills?

5. Using telephones, reverse roles for Joy and Sam and solve the same problem. Do you have any suggestions for Sam to improve his help desk skills?

REVIEW QUESTIONS

1. After doing your best, but finding you still cannot solve a customer's problem, what is the appropriate next step?

_____

_____

2. Your cell phone rings while working with a customer. You look at the incoming number and realize it's your sister calling. How do you handle the call?

_____

_____

3. Why is it not a good idea to tell a customer about the time you were able to solve the computer problem of a very important person?

_____

_____

4. A customer is angry and tells you he will never buy another product from your company again. How do you respond?

_____

_____

LAB 3.4: PRACTICE GOOD COMMUNICATION SKILLS

OBJECTIVES

The goal of this lab is to help you learn how to be a better communicator. After completing this lab, you will be able to:

◢ Be a better listener

◢ Work with a customer who is angry

◢ Act with integrity to customers

MATERIALS REQUIRED

This lab requires the following:

◢ Student workgroups of 2 or more students

LAB PREPARATION

No lab preparation is necessary.

ACTIVITY BACKGROUND

PC support technicians are expected to be good communicators. Many times, technical people find this to be a difficult skill, so practice and training are very important. In this lab, you discover some ways to be an active listener and better communicator.

ESTIMATED COMPLETION TIME: 60 Minutes

 Activity

Work with a partner to learn to be a better listener. Do the following:

1. Sit with paper and pencil before another student who will play the role of a customer. As the customer describes a certain computer problem he or she is having, take notes as necessary.

2. Describe the problem back to the customer. Were you able to describe the problem accurately without missing any details? Have the customer rate you from one to ten, ten being the highest rating for good listening skills.

3. Now switch roles as you, the customer, describe a problem to the support technician. Then have the technician repeat the problem and its details. Rate the technician for good listening skills on a scale of one to ten.

4. Now describe an increasingly more difficult problem with more details. Rate the technician on a scale of one to ten for good listening skills.

5. Switch roles and listen to a detailed, difficult problem described. Then repeat the problem and have the customer rate your listening skills.

Being a good communicator requires being able to deal with angry and difficult people. Make suggestions as to the best way to handle these situations:

1. An angry customer calls to tell you that she has left you numerous phone messages that you have not answered. She is not aware that you receive about 25 voice messages a day and are trying hard to keep up with the workload. What do you say?

_____

_____

2. What can you say when an angry customer begins to use abusive language?

   _____

   _____

3. You have tried for over two hours, but you cannot fix the customer's boot problem. You think the motherboard has failed, but you are not sure. Before you make your conclusions, you want to try a POST diagnostic card. The customer demands that you fix the problem immediately before she leaves the office at 4:45 PM—about 10 minutes from now. What do you say to her?

   _____

   _____

4. Discuss in your workgroup the ethical thing to do in each situation below. Write down the group consensus to each problem:

   1. You work on commission in a computer retail store, and after working with a very difficult customer for over an hour, he leaves without buying a thing. As he walks out the door, you notice he dropped a twenty-dollar bill near where you were talking. What do you do?

      _____

      _____

   2. A customer is yelling at a coworker in a retail store. You see your coworker does not know how to handle the situation. What do you do?

      _____

      _____

   3. You are working in a corporate office as a technical support person trying to fix a scanner problem at an employee's workstation. You notice the employee has left payroll database information displayed on the screen. You know this employee is not authorized to view this information. What do you do?

      _____

      _____

   4. Your supervisor has asked you to install a game on his computer. The game is on a CD-R and is obviously a pirated copy. What do you do?

      _____

      _____

   5. You work for a retail store that sells a particular brand of computers. A customer asks your opinion of another brand of computer. What do you do?

      _____

      _____

6. You are asked to make a house call to fix a computer problem. When you arrive at the appointed time, a teenage girl answers the door and tells you her mother is not at home, but will return in a half hour. What do you do?

_____

_____

Have a little fun with this one! Working in a group of three, one member of the team plays the role of tech support. A second team member writes down a brief description of a difficult customer and passes the description to a third team member. (The tech support person cannot see this description.) The third team member plays out the described customer role. Use the following scenarios:

1. A customer calls to say his notebook will not start. The LCD panel was broken when the customer dropped the notebook, but he does not willingly disclose the fact that the notebook was dropped.

2. A customer complains that his CD drive does not work. The CD is in the drive upside down, and it is clear that the customer does not want the tech to ask him about such a simple issue.

REVIEW QUESTIONS

1. When working at a retail store that also fixes computers, what five items of information you should request when a customer first brings a computer to your counter?

_____

_____

2. List three things you should not do while at a customer's site:

_____

_____

3. When is it acceptable to ask a customer to refrain from venting?

_____

_____

4. When is it appropriate to answer a cell phone call while working with a customer?

_____

_____

5. When is it appropriate to install pirated software on a computer?

_____

_____

LAB 3.5 UNDERSTAND THE HELP DESK PROCEDURES FOR A COMPANY

OBJECTIVES

The goal of this lab is to demonstrate the process of setting up help desk procedures. After completing this lab, you will be able to:

- ⊿ Identify problems that would prevent users from browsing the network
- ⊿ Decide which types of problems can be solved over the telephone
- ⊿ Decide which types of problems require administrative intervention
- ⊿ Create a support matrix for telephone instruction

MATERIALS REQUIRED

This lab requires the following:

- ⊿ Windows Vista/XP operating system
- ⊿ A PC connected to a working TCP/IP network
- ⊿ Optional: An Internet connection
- ⊿ Two workgroups with 2 to 4 students in each group

LAB PREPARATION

Before the lab begins, the instructor or lab assistant needs to do the following:

- ⊿ Verify that Windows starts with no errors.
- ⊿ Verify that the network connection is available.

ACTIVITY BACKGROUND

When a company sets up a help desk for computer users, it establishes a set of procedures to address common troubleshooting situations. These procedures should include instructions that the average user can be expected to carry out with telephone support. In this lab, you design and create help desk procedures for a common problem: the inability to connect to a network. Assume you're working at the company help desk. If you can't solve the problem, you escalate it to the network administrator or another technician who actually goes to the computer to fix the problem.

ESTIMATED COMPLETION TIME: 60 Minutes

 Activity

1. Assume that your company network is designed according to the following parameters. (Note that your instructor might alter these parameters so that they more closely resemble your network's parameters.)

   - ⊿ Ethernet LAN is using only a single subnet.
   - ⊿ TCP/IP is the only protocol.
   - ⊿ The workgroup name is ATLGA.
   - ⊿ The DHCP server assigns IP information.

2. Assume that all users on your company network use computers with the following parameters. (Note that your instructor might alter these parameters so that they more closely resemble your PC.)

   ◢ Pentium IV 2.8 GHz

   ◢ Windows Vista or XP operating system

   ◢ Internal NIC

   ◢ Category 5e cabling with RJ-45 connectors

3. As a group, discuss the reasons a user might not be able to connect to the network, and then make a list of the four most common reasons. If your group has trouble completing the list, feel free to ask your instructor or search the Internet. List the source of these problems, both hardware and software, on the following lines. In your list, include at least one problem that's difficult to solve over the phone and requires the network administrator or another technician to go to the computer to solve the problem. Order the four problems from the least difficult to solve to the most difficult to solve. Write the one problem that requires administrator intervention at the bottom of the list.

   ◢ Source of Problem 1, which is the least difficult to solve:

   _____

   ◢ Source of Problem 2, which is more difficult to solve:

   _____

   ◢ Source of Problem 3, which is even more difficult to solve:

   _____

   ◢ Source of Problem 4, which is so difficult to solve that it requires an administrator or another technician to get involved:

   _____

For each problem, describe the symptoms as a user would describe them:

   ◢ Symptoms of Problem 1:

   _____

   _____

   ◢ Symptoms of Problem 2:

   _____

   _____

   ◢ Symptoms of Problem 3:

   _____

   _____

   ◢ Symptoms of Problem 4:

   _____

   _____

As a group, decide how to solve each problem by following these steps:

1. On separate sheets of paper, list the steps to verify and solve the problems. (This list of steps is sometimes referred to as a procedure, support matrix, or job aid.)

2. Double-check the steps by testing them on your computer. (In real life, you would test the steps using a computer attached to the network you're supporting.) When making your list of steps, allow for alternatives, based on how the user responds to your questions. For example, you might include one list of steps for situations in which the user says others on the network are visible in My Network Places and another list of steps for situations in which the user says no remote computers can be seen in My Network Places. Well-written help desk procedures ensure that help desk workers know exactly what steps to perform, which results in quicker support and users feeling more confident about getting help.

3. For any problem that can't be solved by the procedure, the last step should be for help desk personnel to notify the administrator. In your procedure, include questions to the user when appropriate. As you work, you might find it helpful to use a diagram or flowchart of the questions asked and decisions made.

Here's an example of one step that involves a question:

◢ **Question:** Is your computer on?

◢ **Answer:** Yes, go to Step 3; no, go to Step 2.

Now it is time to test your help desk procedures by using them on another workgroup, as follows:

1. Introduce one of your four problems on a PC connected to a network.

2. Have someone from another workgroup sit at your PC. The remaining steps in this step sequence refer to this person as "the user."

3. Sit with your back to the user so that you can't see what he or she is doing. Place your step-by-step procedures in front of you, on paper or on-screen. (It's helpful if you can sit at a PC connected to the network so that you can perform the same steps you ask the user to perform. However, make sure you can't see the other PC or see what the user is doing.)

4. The user should attempt to access the network and then "call" your help desk for assistance.

5. Follow your procedure to solve the problem.

6. Revise your procedure as necessary.

7. Test all four help desk procedures.

REVIEW QUESTIONS

1. Can all users' computer problems be solved with help desk support? Why or why not?

   _____

   _____

2. After you design and write your help desk procedures to solve problems, what should you do next?

   _____

   _____

3. How should help desk procedures address complex problems that require administrative intervention?

_____

_____

_____

4. How should you alter your procedures based on your users' technical experience?

_____

_____

_____

5. Why do you need to consider what the network and computer are like when creating your procedures?

_____

_____

_____

6. What has been your experience when calling a help desk? How well did the technician walk you through the process of solving your problem?

_____

_____

Form Factors, Power Supplies, and Working Inside a Computer

Labs included in this chapter:

- **Lab 4.1:** Identify Form Factors
- **Lab 4.2:** Take a Computer Apart and Put it Back Together
- **Lab 4.3:** Measure the Output of Your Power Supply
- **Lab 4.4:** Find Documentation on the Internet
- **Lab 4.5:** Choose the Right Power Supply
- **Lab 4.6:** Upgrade a Power Supply

LAB 4.1 IDENTIFY FORM FACTORS

OBJECTIVES

The goal of this lab is to give you experience in identifying form factors. After completing this lab, you will be able to:

◢ Identify the form factor of the case, motherboard, and power supply

◢ Select appropriate components to match an existing form factor

MATERIALS REQUIRED

This lab requires the following:

◢ A PC designated for this lab

◢ A PC toolkit with antistatic wrist strap

◢ Internet access

LAB PREPARATION

Before the lab begins, the instructor or lab assistant needs to do the following:

◢ Verify that Windows starts with no errors.

◢ Verify that Internet access is available.

ACTIVITY BACKGROUND

The form factor is a set of specifications about the size, shape, and configuration of the components that make up a computer system. Sharing a common standard allows components such as the case, motherboard, and power supply to fit together and function properly. There are three common types of form factors: ATX, BTX, and NLX. Each comes in several variations that determine characteristics such as size and shape. In this lab, you identify your system's form factor and research some identifying characteristics of common form factors.

ESTIMATED COMPLETION TIME: 30 Minutes

Activity

1. Open your browser and go to your favorite search engine, such as *www.google.com*.

2. Use the Internet to research the main differences between ATX and BTX and list them here:

_____

_____

3. Now *explain* the main differences between ATX and NLX:

_____

_____

4. Each form factor comes in several sizes. How could you tell whether a system was Regular BTX, Micro BTX, or Pico BTX?

_____

_____

5. Form factors are also available in various shapes. What slimline form factor is similar to ATX?

_____

6. Now turn the computer off and unplug the power cord.

7. Disconnect all peripherals and remove the case cover. Remove the cover from your desktop PC.

8. Examine the case, motherboard, and power supply.

9. What is the form factor of this system?

_____

10. Close the case, reattach the peripherals, and test the system to make sure it boots without errors.

REVIEW QUESTIONS

1. Why is it important that your case and motherboard share a compatible form factor?

_____

2. When might you want to use a slimline form factor?

_____

3. What advantages does ATX have over Micro ATX?

_____

4. Where is the CPU located on the BTX motherboard? Why?

_____

5. Is it possible to determine the form factor without opening the case?

_____

LAB 4.2 TAKE A COMPUTER APART AND PUT IT BACK TOGETHER

OBJECTIVES

The goal of this lab is to help you get comfortable working inside a computer case. After completing this lab, you will be able to:

⊿ Take a computer apart

⊿ Recognize components

⊿ Reassemble the computer

MATERIALS REQUIRED

This lab requires the following:

⊿ A computer designated for disassembly

⊿ A PC toolkit with an antistatic wrist strap and mat

⊿ A marker and masking tape

⬗ Small containers, such as paper cups, to hold screws as you work

⬗ A workgroup of 2 to 4 students; an individual student can work this lab as well

LAB PREPARATION

Before the lab begins, the instructor or lab assistant needs to do the following:

⬗ Verify that a computer designated for disassembly is available to each student or workgroup.

ACTIVITY BACKGROUND

If you follow directions and take your time, there's no reason to be intimidated by working inside a computer case. This lab takes you step by step through the process of disassembling and reassembling a PC. Follow your computer lab's posted safety procedures when disassembling and reassembling a PC, and remember to always wear your antistatic ground strap. Also, never force a component to fit into its slot. Doing so might damage the card or the motherboard.

You begin this lab by removing the cover of your PC and then removing the components inside. Next, you reassemble the components and replace the cover. This lab includes steps for working with a desktop PC and a tower PC. Follow the steps that apply to your computer.

Also, in this lab, you're instructed to disassemble your PC in this order: case cover, interior cables and cords, expansion cards, motherboard, power supply, case fans, and drives. Because some systems are designed so that the disassembly order is different from this one, your instructor might change the order. For example, you might not be able to get to the power supply to remove it until drives or the motherboard are out of the way. Be sure to follow any specific directions from your instructor.

> **Notes** In a lab environment, the instructor might consider giving a demonstration of tearing down a PC and putting it back together before students begin this lab.

As you work, when you remove a screw, place it in a paper cup or on a piece of paper so that you can keep different size screws separated. Later, when you reassemble your computer, having the screws organized in this way makes it easier to match the right screw to the hole.

ESTIMATED COMPLETION TIME: 60 Minutes

 Activity

Follow the procedure outlined in the following steps to remove the case cover and expansion cards. (If you're working with a tower case, lay it on its side so that the motherboard is on the bottom.)

1. Remove the cover from your PC and attach your antistatic wrist strap to the side of the case, as shown in Figure 4-1.

2. To make reassembly easier, take notes or make a sketch (or take a picture) of the current placement of boards and cables and identify each board and cable. You can mark the location of a cable on an expansion card or the motherboard with a marker, if you like. Note the orientation of the cable. Each cable for an ATA hard drive, CD/DVD-ROM drive, or a floppy drive has a colored marking on one side of the cable called the "edge color." This color marks pin 1 of the cable. On the board, pin 1 is marked with the number 1 or 2 beside the pin or with a square soldering pad on the back side of the board, as shown in Figure 4-2. You might not be able to see this soldering pad now.

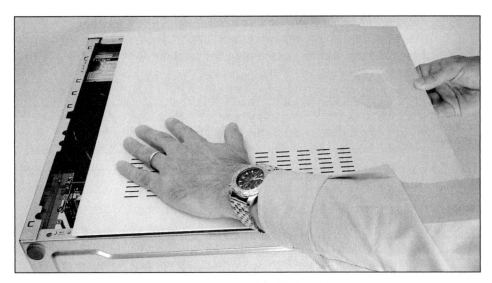

Figure 4-1 Slide the side panel to the rear and then lift it off the case
Courtesy: Course Technology/Cengage Learning

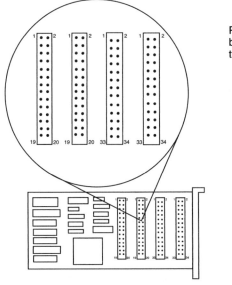

Pin 1 is shown
by a stencil on
the circuit board.

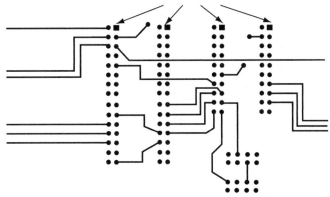

Pin 1 is shown by square solder
pads on the reverse side of the circuit board.

Figure 4-2 How to find pin 1 on an expansion card
Courtesy: Course Technology/Cengage Learning

3. Remove any cables from the expansion cards. There's no need to remove the other end of the cable from its component (hard drive, CD/DVD-ROM drive, or floppy disk drive). Lay the cable over the top of the component or case.

4. Remove the screw holding the card to the back of the case.

5. Grasp the card with both hands and remove it by lifting straight up and rocking the card from end to end (not side to side). Rocking the card from side to side might spread the slot opening and weaken the connection. To avoid causing ESD damage, when you remove the card, be sure you don't touch the edge connectors on the card.

6. If the card had a cable attached, examine the card connector for the cable. Can you identify pin 1? Lay the card aside on a flat surface.

7. Remove any other expansion cards in the same way.

8. In some proprietary systems, a riser card assembly attaches to the motherboard, with each card attached to the assembly. If your system has this arrangement, remove it now. It's probably held in place by screws or clips and may or may not have a rail guide you can use to locate the assembly in the case.

9. To remove the power supply, first remove the power cables to the motherboard, case fans, other remaining components, and the power switch, if necessary. Make notes about which cable attaches to what hardware. After the cables are removed, support the power supply with one hand, and remove the screws attaching it to the case.

10. Unplug any case fans.

In some systems, it's easier to remove the drives first and then the motherboard. In other systems, it's easier to remove the motherboard first. In these instructions, to make sure you don't risk dropping a drive on the motherboard when removing the drive, you're directed to remove the motherboard first and then the drives. Your instructor, however, might prefer that you remove the drives first and then the motherboard.

1. Begin removing the motherboard by removing any remaining wires or cables such as power cables, audio wires, or wires from the front of the case. Be sure to make notes or label the cables so that you can reinstall them correctly.

2. Finish removing the motherboard by removing the screws holding the board to the spacers or stand-offs. Usually six to nine screws attach the motherboard to the case. Be careful not to gouge the board or damage components with the screwdriver. Because the screws on the motherboard are often located between components, they can be hard to reach. Be very careful not to damage the motherboard. See Figure 4-3.

3. The motherboard should now be free and you can carefully remove it from the case. See Figure 4-4.

4. To remove drives, remove the data cable if it's still attached. Many cases have a removable drive bay. The drives are attached to this bay, and the bay can be removed with all the drives attached. This arrangement gives you easier access to drive-mounting screws than from inside the case. If your case has a removable drive bay, this removal method is preferred. Otherwise, remove each drive separately. Be careful not to jar the drive as you remove it from the case.

5. If your system has a removable drive bay, the floppy drive likely came out with the removable bay. If the floppy drive is still in the system, remove the screws holding the drive in place, and slide the drive out of the case.

6. Remove any CD-ROM, DVD, or tape drives from the case. These drives are usually in the five-inch drive bays and are normally held in place by four to eight screws. After the screws are removed, the drive slides out the front of the case.

7. Remove any other components.

Figure 4-3 Remove the screws that hold the motherboard to the case
Courtesy: Course Technology/Cengage Learning

Figure 4-4 Carefully remove the motherboard from the case
Courtesy: Course Technology/Cengage Learning

Now that you have removed all the components, you're ready to reassemble the PC. Replace each component carefully. Take care to install each component firmly without overtightening the screws. Don't force components to fit. If a component won't fit easily the way it should, look for some obstruction preventing it from falling into place. Look carefully for the reason the component won't fit correctly, and make any small adjustments as necessary. The following steps outline the assembly procedure, which is essentially the reverse of the disassembly procedure:

1. Install the drives in their bays and then install the motherboard, unless your instructor prefers that you install the motherboard first.

2. Install the power supply and replace the screws holding it in position.

3. Connect the power cables from the power supply to the drives and the motherboard. Double-check to make sure all the power supply connectors to the motherboard are connected correctly.

4. Place each card in its slot (it doesn't have to be the same slot, just the same bus), and replace the screw. Don't place a PCI video card near the power supply; otherwise, electromagnetic interference (EMI) from the power supply might affect the video picture.

5. Replace the cables, being sure to align the colored edge with pin 1. (In some cases, it might work better to connect the cable to the card before you put the card in the expansion slot.)

6. Check to make sure no cables are interfering with any fan's ability to turn. A common cause of an overheated system is a fan that can't move air because a cable is preventing it from spinning.

7. When all components are installed, you should have refitted all the screws you removed earlier. If some screws are missing, it's important to turn the case upside down and *gently* shake the case to dislodge any wayward screws. Any screw left lying on a board has the potential to short out that board when power is applied. Don't use a magnet to try to find missing screws in the case because you might damage data on hard drives and floppy disks left in the floppy disk drives.

8. Plug in the keyboard, monitor, and mouse.

9. In a classroom environment, have the instructor check your work before you power up.

10. Plug in the power cord to the PC and to the power outlet or surge protector. Verify that any power switches on the rear of the case are set correctly. Some cases have a power switch to close the AC voltage, and others have an on/off switch.

11. Using the power button on the front of the case, turn on the power and check that the PC is working properly before you replace the cover. Don't touch the inside of the case while the power is on.

12. If all is well, turn off the PC and replace the cover and its screws. If the PC doesn't work, don't panic. Turn off the power, and then go back and check each cable connection and each expansion card. You probably haven't seated a card solidly in the slot. After you have double-checked everything, try again.

REVIEW QUESTIONS

1. When removing the cover, why should you take care to remove only the screws that hold the cover on?

   _____

   _____

2. How should you rock a card to remove it from its slot? Why is it important to know how to rock a card correctly?

   _____

3. What should you do to help you remember which components connect to which cables?

   _____

4. What marking on a ribbon cable identifies pin 1?

   _____

5. What component(s) defines the system's form factor?

   _____

6. What form factor does your PC use?

   _____

7. Why would a PC technician ever have to change out a computer's motherboard?

   _____

   _____

LAB 4.3 MEASURE THE OUTPUT OF YOUR POWER SUPPLY

OBJECTIVES

The goal of this lab is to use a multimeter to measure the voltages provided by a power supply. After completing this lab, you will be able to:

- Use a multimeter
- Measure voltage provided by a power supply

MATERIALS REQUIRED

This lab requires the following:

- A computer designated for this lab
- A PC toolkit with antistatic ground strap
- A multimeter
- Access to the online content "Electricity and Multimeters," downloaded from the publisher's Web site
- A workgroup of 2 to 4 students

LAB PREPARATION

Before the lab begins, the instructor or lab assistant needs to do the following:

- Announce to students that before they come to lab, they should read the online content "Electricity and Multimeters." They also might like to bring this content to class in printed form.

ACTIVITY BACKGROUND

In most situations, if you suspect a problem with a power supply, you simply exchange it for a known good one. In a few instances, however, you might want to measure your power supply's output by using a multimeter.

A multimeter is an electrical tool that performs several tests. It can typically measure continuity, resistance, and voltage. It might have a digital or an analog meter that displays output. It also has two leads used to contact the component you're testing. The various models of multimeters work slightly differently. Follow the correct procedure for your specific multimeter. In this lab, you measure the electrical voltage supplied to the motherboard and hard drives. Follow your computer lab's posted safety procedures when completing this lab.

ESTIMATED COMPLETION TIME: 30 Minutes

 Activity

Using your multimeter, measure the power output to your system's motherboard and to the floppy drive, and then fill in the following charts that apply to your system. Note that the column headings "Red Lead" and "Black Lead" refer to the color of the probes.

> **⚡ Caution**   Be sure you have your multimeter set to measure voltage, not resistance (ohms) or current (amps). If the multimeter is set to measure current, you might damage the power supply, the motherboard, or both.

Again, detailed directions for using a multimeter can be found in the online content "Electricity and Multimeters." Be very careful as you work inside the computer case with the power on. Don't touch any components other than those described in the steps.

The following steps outline the basic procedure for using a multimeter:

1. Remove the cover from the computer case.
2. Set the multimeter to measure voltage in a range of 20 volts, and set the AC/DC switch to DC. Insert the black probe into the meter's − jack and the red probe into the meter's + jack.
3. Turn on the multimeter, and then turn on the computer.
4. Measure each circuit by placing a red probe on the lead and a black probe on ground (see Figure 4-5).

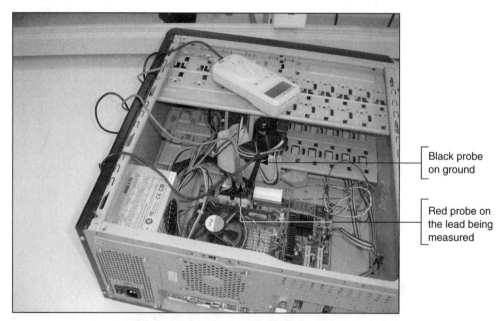

Black probe on ground

Red probe on the lead being measured

Figure 4-5   A multimeter measuring voltage on an ATX motherboard
Courtesy: Course Technology/Cengage Learning

5. If you're using an AT power supply, refer to Table 4-1 for the purposes of these 12 leads. If you're using an ATX power supply, refer to Table 4-2.

Connection	Lead	Description	Acceptable Range
P8	1	Power good	
	2	Not used or +5 volts	+4.4 to +5.2 volts
	3	+12 volts	+10.8 to +13.2 volts
	4	-12 volts	-10.8 to -13.2 volts
	5	Black ground	
	6	Black ground	
P9	7	Black ground	
	8	Black ground	
	9	-5 volts	-4.5 to -5.5 volts
	10	+5 volts	+4.5 to +5.5 volts
	11	+5 volts	+4.5 to +5.5 volts
	12	+5 volts	+4.5 to +5.5 volts

Table 4-1　12 leads to the older AT motherboard from the AT power supply

Unnotched Side			Notched Side		
Lead	Description	Acceptable Range (Volts = V)	Lead	Description	Acceptable Range (Volts = V)
1	+3.3 volts	+3.1 to +3.5 V	11	+3.3 volts	+3.1 to +3.5 V
2	+3.3 volts	+3.1 to +3.5 V	12	-12 volts	-10.8 to -13.2 V
3	Black ground		13	Black ground	
4	+5 volts	+4.5 to +5.5 V	14	Power supply on	
5	Black ground		15	Black ground	
6	+5 volts	+4.5 to +5.5 V	16	Black ground	
7	Black ground		17	Black ground	
8	Power good		18	-5 volts	-4.5 to -5.5 V
9	+5 volts standby	+4.5 to +5.5 V	19	+5 volts	+4.5 to +5.5 V
10	+12 volts	+10.8 to +13.2 V	20	+5 volts	+4.5 to +5.5 V

Table 4-2　20 leads to the ATX motherboard from the ATX power supply

6. Complete the following chart for an AT motherboard. Write the voltage measurement for each connection in the Voltage measure column.

Red Lead	Black Lead	Voltage Measure
3	5	
3	6	
3	7	
3	8	

Red Lead	Black Lead	Voltage Measure
4	Ground	
9	Ground	
10	Ground	
11	Ground	
12	Ground	

7. The 20-pin P1 power connector on an ATX motherboard is shown in Figure 4-6. Refer to Table 4-2 for the purpose of each pin.

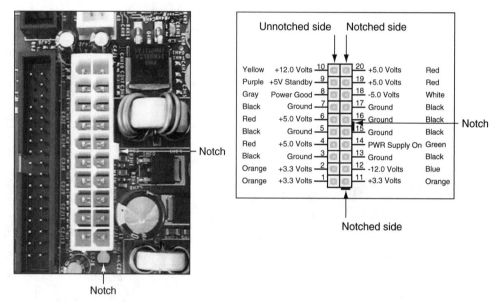

Figure 4-6 Power connection on an ATX motherboard
Courtesy: Course Technology/Cengage Learning

8. Complete the following chart for an ATX motherboard:

Red Lead (Positive)	Black Lead (Ground)	Voltage Measure
10	7	
10	5	
10	3	
10	17	
10	16	
10	15	
10	13	
9	Ground	
6	Ground	
4	Ground	
2	Ground	

Red Lead (Positive)	Black Lead (Ground)	Voltage Measure
1	Ground	
20	Ground	
19	Ground	
18	Ground	
12	Ground	
11	Ground	

9. The BTX motherboard and power supply are designed so that the power supply monitors the range of voltages provided to the motherboard and halts the motherboard if voltages are inadequate. Therefore, measuring voltage for a BTX system isn't usually necessary. However, in a lab environment, if you have access only to a BTX system, you can fill in the same chart that you did for the previous motherboards. Figure 4-7 shows the 24-pin power connector for a BTX motherboard, and the purposes of the pins are listed in Table 4-3.

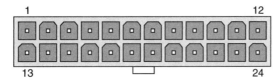

Figure 4-7   BTX 24-pin power connector on the motherboard
Courtesy: Course Technology/Cengage Learning

Lead	Signal	Acceptable Range (Volts = V)
1	+3+.3 volts	3.2 to 3.5 V
2	+3.3 volts	3.2 to 3.5 V
3	COM	
4	+5 volts	4.75 to 5.25 V
5	COM	
6	+5 volts	4.75 to 5.25 V
7	COM	
8	Power OK	Voltages are in acceptable range
9	+5 volts	Standby voltage always on
10	+12 volts	11.4 to 12.6 V
11	+12 volts	11.4 to 12.6 V
12	+3.3 volts	3.2 to 3.5 V
13	+3.3 volts	3.2 to 3.5 V
14	-12 volts	-10.8 to -13.2 V
15	COM	

Table 4-3   BTX 24-pin power connector

Lead	Signal	Acceptable Range (Volts = V)
16	COM	
17	COM	
18	COM	
19	NC	
20	+5 volts	4.75 to 5.25 V
21	+5 volts	4.75 to 5.25 V
22	+5 volts	4.75 to 5.25 V
23	COM	4.75 to 5.25 V
24		

Table 4-3   BTX 24-pin power connector (continued)

10. Complete the following chart for a BTX motherboard:

Red Lead (Positive)	Black Lead (Ground)	Voltage Measure
1	Ground	
2	Ground	
4	Ground	
6	Ground	
9	Ground	
10	Ground	
11	Ground	
12	Ground	
13	Ground	
14	Ground	
21	Ground	
22	Ground	
23	Ground	

11. The power connectors for a drive power cord were shown in Figure 4-3. Complete the following chart for the floppy drive:

Red Lead	Black Lead	Voltage Measure
1	3	
4	2	

12. Turn off the PC and replace the cover.

REVIEW QUESTIONS

1. What is the electrical voltage from the house outlet to the power supply?

2. What voltages are supplied by the power supply on your system?

_____

3. What model of multimeter are you using?

_____

4. List the steps to set your multimeter to measure resistance:

_____

_____

_____

5. Besides voltage and resistance, what else can your multimeter measure?

_____

LAB 4.4 FIND DOCUMENTATION ON THE INTERNET

OBJECTIVES

The goal of this lab is to show you how to locate documentation on the Internet so that you can determine how much power a component uses. After completing this lab, you will be able to:

◢ Find the manufacturer and model of a component

◢ Search for a product's documentation or manual

◢ Download and view a product manual

MATERIALS REQUIRED

This lab requires the following:

◢ A computer designated for disassembly

◢ Internet access

◢ Adobe Acrobat Reader

◢ A PC toolkit with antistatic ground strap

◢ A workgroup of 2 or 3 students or individual students

LAB PREPARATION

Before the lab begins, the instructor or lab assistant needs to do the following:

◢ Verify that a computer designated for disassembly is available for each student or workgroup.

◢ Verify that Internet access is available.

ACTIVITY BACKGROUND

Often the power specifications for a component aren't labeled on the component itself but are included in the documentation. When working with PCs, it's common to encounter a component for which you have no documentation on hand. In this lab, you learn how to find a component's make and model and, if possible, find online documentation for it.

ESTIMATED COMPLETION TIME: 30 Minutes

Activity

1. Open the PC's case and locate the component your instructor assigned to you (or select a component randomly). If you're in a workgroup, each person should be assigned a different component.

> **Notes** The manufacturer and model aren't marked clearly on every component. If you're having trouble finding this information on a component, such as a video card, try researching based on the component's chipset. The information identifying the chip is usually stenciled on the chip. For communication devices, such as a modem or network card, look for an FCC number printed on the card and use it for your search. If you need to find out how much power an unlabeled component uses, sometimes it's helpful to consult the documentation for similar components.

2. Examine the component until you find a sticker or stenciled label identifying its manufacturer and model number.

3. Take your notes to a computer that has Internet access.

4. If you already know the manufacturer's URL, go to that site and try to find documentation in these locations:

   ◢ The Support section of the site, as shown in Figure 4-8

   ◢ The Downloads section

   ◢ The Customer Service section

If you're not sure of the manufacturer's URL, try searching for the manufacturer or model number with a search engine. In fact, searching by model number can often get you to the information in the fewest steps. For example, if SD11 is imprinted on your motherboard, searching on "SD11" can take you right to

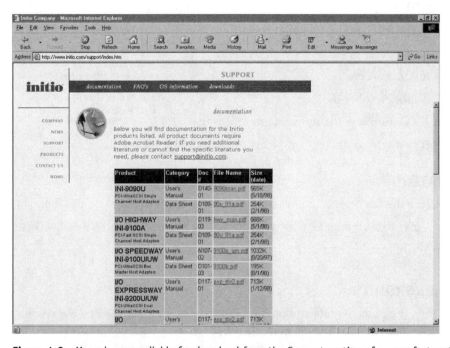

Figure 4-8 Manuals are available for download from the Support section of a manufacturer's Web site
Courtesy: Course Technology/Cengage Learning

the documentation you need. Keep in mind that most documentation is in PDF format, which means you might need Adobe Acrobat Reader or a browser plug-in to view the documentation.

5. Print or save the documentation, and file it as a reference for when you need information about that component.

6. Now determine what CPU your system uses, and list that CPU below:

   _____

7. Go to the manufacturer's Web site, and find and print the Web page showing the power consumption of your CPU expressed in watts.

REVIEW QUESTIONS

1. How is a computer component, such as a network card, commonly marked for identification?

   _____

   _____

2. In what sections of a Web site are manuals commonly found?

   _____

3. In what format are manuals usually provided?

   _____

4. What software do you need to view a PDF document?

   _____

5. Why would a PC repair technician need to know the power consumption of a peripheral component?

   _____

   _____

LAB 4.5 CHOOSE THE RIGHT POWER SUPPLY

OBJECTIVES

The goal of this lab is to show you how to locate documentation on the Internet so that you can determine how much power a system as a whole uses. You can use this information to decide the wattage rating of the power supply you need to purchase for a new or upgraded system. After completing this lab, you will be able to:

▲ Calculate the total wattage requirements for a system

▲ Choose the correct type and rating of a power supply

MATERIALS REQUIRED

This lab requires the following:

▲ A computer designated for disassembly

▲ *Optional*: Internet access

◢ A PC toolkit with antistatic ground strap

◢ A workgroup of 2 or 3 students or individual students

LAB PREPARATION

Before the lab begins, the instructor or lab assistant needs to do the following:

◢ Verify that a computer designated for disassembly is available for each student or work-group.

◢ *Optional*: Verify that Internet access is available.

ACTIVITY BACKGROUND

When selecting a power supply for a computer system, you must take many factors into account. It's important to look at the system's components as a whole and how the system will be used. You might be tempted to simply purchase a power supply that has a very high wattage rating, but this choice isn't always the most economical. The typical efficiency rating of a power supply is 60 percent to 70 percent. Usually, this rating means 30 percent to 40 percent of the power is blowing out of the case as wasted heat. You want to keep waste to a minimum. On the other hand, if you intend to upgrade your system, buying an overrated power supply might be wise.

Running a system with an inadequate power supply can cause the power supply to wear out faster than normal. Also, an inadequate power supply can cause a system to reboot at odd times and exhibit other types of intermittent errors. It pays to install a correctly rated power supply for a system.

ESTIMATED COMPLETION TIME: 45 Minutes

 Activity

1. The following chart shows the estimated power requirements for components inside a computer case. These estimates come from the Web site PC Power and Cooling, Inc. at *www.pcpowercooling.com/technology/power_usage*. Open the PC's case. Locate each component listed in the chart, and record how many components are present. Note that some entries will be zero.

Component	Wattage Requirement	Number Present	Total Wattage
AGP video card	30 W–50 W		
PCI Express video card	50 W–100 W		
Average PCI cards	5 W–10 W		
DVD or CD drives	20 W–40 W		
Hard drives	15 W–30 W		
Case fans and CPU fans	3 W (each)		
Motherboard	15 W–150 W		
RAM modules	15 W per 1 GB		
Processor	80 W–140 W		
PCIe	100 W–250 W		
DVD/CD	20 W–30 W		
Motherboard	50 W–150 W		

2. To fill in the Total wattage column, first check the manufacturer's Web site for each component to find the exact wattage amounts. If this information isn't available, use the estimate provided or the midpoint of the estimate. Add the wattage for all components to come up with the total wattage. Record the system's total wattage in the last row of the chart.

3. Multiply the total wattage by 1.3. This multiplier takes into account the overhead the system and a power supply need so that the system can run at about 30 percent to 70 percent of its maximum capacity. What is your calculated total wattage, taking into account the required overhead?

4. Now look at the power supply, and make sure it has the number and type of connectors needed for your system. Figure 4-9 can help you identify connectors. Many power supplies don't provide the new serial ATA (SATA) connector shown in Figure 4-10. However, you can use an adapter power cord like the one in the figure to accommodate SATA hard drives.

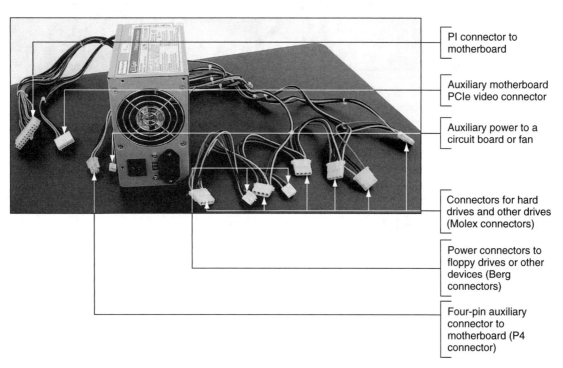

PI connector to motherboard

Auxiliary motherboard PCIe video connector

Auxiliary power to a circuit board or fan

Connectors for hard drives and other drives (Molex connectors)

Power connectors to floppy drives or other devices (Berg connectors)

Four-pin auxiliary connector to motherboard (P4 connector)

Figure 4-9 Power supply with connectors labeled
Courtesy: Course Technology/Cengage Learning

Figure 4-10 Adapter power cord can be used for a SATA hard drive
Courtesy: Course Technology/Cengage Learning

5. Fill in the following chart to show the available power connectors and how many are needed for your system:

Connector	Current Quantity	Quantity Needed
EIDE drive connectors (Molex)		
Floppy drive connectors (Berg)		
SATA connectors		
ATX connector (20 or 24 pins)		
Auxiliary power (4, 6, or 8 pins)		
PCIe connector		

6. Look on the power supply label for the peak load rating in watts. What is this value?

_____

7. Based on what you have learned in this lab, is the power supply adequate for the job? Why or why not?

_____

_____

CRITICAL THINKING (ADDITIONAL 30 MINUTES)

Suppose your power supply stops working, and you must buy a replacement. Search the Internet for a comparable power supply. The cost of power supplies varies widely. For example, a 400-watt power supply can cost from $15 to $75. The difference in quality can be judged partly by the weight of the power supply because, in general, the heavier it is, the more transistors it has and the more heavy-duty the transistors are, which makes for a better power supply. Another factor to consider is noise level; quiet power supplies can be more expensive than noisy ones. Print two Web pages showing a high-end and a low-end power supply that would meet your system's needs. Which power supply would you recommend purchasing for your system, and why?

_____

_____

REVIEW QUESTIONS

1. The estimated wattages for individual components were provided in the lab. How can you find the actual wattage for each component?

   _____

2. What is the typical efficiency rating for a power supply?

   _____

3. Are there any connectors your system needs that the power supply doesn't have? If so, what are they?

   _____

4. Are there any connectors provided by the power supply that your system isn't using? If so, what are they?

   _____

5. Why is it important to buy a power supply that's close to the requirements for your system instead of buying a higher wattage power supply?

   _____

   _____

LAB 4.6 UPGRADE A POWER SUPPLY

OBJECTIVES

The goal of this lab is to give you experience in replacing a power supply. After completing this lab, you will be able to:

▲ Identify the power supply

▲ Remove the power supply from the case

▲ Install a new power supply and new cabling

MATERIALS REQUIRED

This lab requires the following:

▲ A PC designated for this lab

◢ A PC toolkit with antistatic ground strap

◢ A workgroup of 2 to 4 students

LAB PREPARATION

Before the lab begins, the instructor or lab assistant needs to do the following:

◢ Verify that a computer designated for disassembly is available for each workgroup.

ACTIVITY BACKGROUND

This lab tests your ability to remove and replace a power supply. Power supplies, as a rule, are considered field replaceable units (FRUs). To save time and avoid the danger of working inside power supplies, PC technicians don't repair power supplies; they replace them. If you find that a power supply is faulty, replace it with a compatible power supply, and then send the original off to be reconditioned or recycled.

ESTIMATED COMPLETION TIME: 30 Minutes

 Activity

1. Turn the computer off and unplug the power cord.

2. Disconnect all peripherals and remove the case cover.

3. Examine the label on the power supply. What is the peak load rating of the power supply? A system requiring more power than the power supply provides can contribute to an early failure of the power supply.

   _____

4. What type of power connectors to the motherboard does the power supply provide? Possible answers are P8, P9, P1, and auxiliary power connectors.

   _____

5. What is the form factor of the power supply?

   _____

6. Remove the cabling and the power supply. Usually the power supply is held in place by four screws in the back of the case. Some proprietary systems might use other methods of securing the power supply.

7. Examine the power supply designated by your instructor, or swap your power supply with another workgroup.

8. What is the form factor of this new power supply?

   _____

9. What is the power rating of this new power supply?

   _____

10. Will this new power supply satisfy the needs of your system?

    _____

11. Install the new power supply. *Ask your instructor to check your work before you close the case.* This check is crucial because some older power supplies must be connected correctly so that they aren't damaged when they're turned on.

12. Close the case, reattach the peripherals, and test the system.

REVIEW QUESTIONS

1. How many connectors linked your original power supply to the motherboard?

   _____

2. How many watts of peak power could the original power supply provide?

   _____

3. Why is it important to be able to calculate the peak power required for all components? (You learned how to do this in Lab 4.5.)

   _____

   _____

4. What are two reasons that PC technicians don't usually repair a power supply?

   _____

   _____

5. What term is used to refer to components that are commonly replaced but not repaired?

   _____

6. What is the most efficient way to determine whether your power supply is bad?

   _____

All About Motherboards

Labs included in this chapter:

- **Lab 5.1:** Examine and Adjust CMOS Settings
- **Lab 5.2:** Use a Hardware Information Utility
- **Lab 5.3:** Identify Motherboard Components
- **Lab 5.4:** Identify a Motherboard and Find Documentation and Drivers on the Internet
- **Lab 5.5:** Remove and Replace a Motherboard
- **Lab 5.6:** Flash BIOS

LAB 5.1 EXAMINE AND ADJUST CMOS SETTINGS

OBJECTIVES

The goal of this lab is to help you explore and modify CMOS settings. After completing this lab, you will be able to:

- Enter the CMOS setup utility
- Navigate the CMOS setup utility
- Examine some setup options
- Save changes to setup options

MATERIALS REQUIRED

This lab requires the following:

- A Windows Vista/XP computer designated for this lab
- SiSoftware Sandra Lite, installed in Lab 1.3

LAB PREPARATION

Before the lab begins, the instructor or lab assistant needs to do the following:

- Verify that Windows starts with no errors.
- Verify that SiSoftware Sandra Lite has been installed (see Lab 1.3).

ACTIVITY BACKGROUND

When a system is powered up, the startup process is managed by a set of instructions called the Basic Input/Output System (BIOS). The BIOS, in turn, relies on a set of configuration information stored in CMOS that's refreshed continuously by battery power when the system is off. You can access and modify CMOS setup information via the CMOS setup utility in the BIOS. In this lab, you examine the CMOS setup utility, make some changes, and observe the effects of your changes.

Setup utilities vary slightly in appearance and function, depending on the manufacturer and version. The steps in this lab are based on the CMOS setup program for Award BIOS, which is a common BIOS. You might have to perform different steps to access and use the CMOS utility on your computer.

For most computers today, you seldom need to make changes in CMOS setup except to set the date and time for a new system or perhaps to change the boot sequence. The exception is if you're attempting to overclock a system, which is done by changing the default frequencies of the processor and/or motherboard. Overclocking isn't a recommended best practice, however, because of problems with overheating and possibly causing the system to become unstable.

ESTIMATED COMPLETION TIME: 30 Minutes

 Activity

Before you access the BIOS on your computer, you need to record the exact date and time indicated by your computer's internal clock. (You use this information later to confirm that you have indeed changed some CMOS settings.) After you record the date and time, you use the Sandra utility (installed in Lab 1.3) to determine which version of BIOS is installed on your computer. Follow these steps:

1. In Windows Vista, move your mouse over the clock (double-click the clock on the taskbar in XP), and record the time and date:

2. In XP, close the Date and Time Properties dialog box.
3. Start Sandra, and click the **Hardware** tab.
4. Double-click **Computer Overview** and wait for the scan to complete.
5. Record the manufacturer and version information for your BIOS:

6. Close Sandra.

Now that you know what BIOS your computer runs, you can determine how to enter the setup utility. In general, to start the setup utility, you need to press a key or key combination as the computer is booting. Some CMOS utilities are password protected with a supervisor password and a user password (also called a power-on password). The supervisor password allows full access to CMOS setup, and the user password allows you to view CMOS setup screens, but you won't be able to change any settings or sometimes you can change only certain settings. In addition, if the user password is also set to be a power-on password and you don't know this password, you won't be able to boot the system. When you attempt to access CMOS setup, if password protection has been enabled, you're asked for a password, and you must enter a valid password to continue.

> **Notes** CMOS setup supervisor, user, and power-on passwords are different from the Windows password required to log on to Windows. Also, if you're responsible for a computer and have forgotten the supervisor password, you can move a jumper on the motherboard to return all CMOS settings to their default values, which erases any CMOS passwords. Lab 5.5 covers how to find this jumper.

To learn more about entering the setup utility on your computer, follow these steps:

1. Using the information you recorded previously in Step 5, consult Table 5-1 to find out how to enter your system's setup utility. (Alternatively, when you first turn on your PC, look for a message on your screen, which might read something like "Press F2 to access setup.")

BIOS	Method for Entering CMOS Setup Utility
AMI BIOS	Boot the computer, and then press the Delete key.
Award BIOS	Boot the computer, and then press the Delete key.
Older Phoenix BIOS	Boot the computer, and then press the Ctrl+Alt+Esc or Ctrl+Alt+S key combination.
Newer Phoenix BIOS	Boot the computer, and then press the F2 or F1 key.
Dell Computers with Phoenix BIOS	Boot the computer, and then press the Ctrl+Alt+Enter key combination.
Some older Compaq computers, such as Deskpro 286 or 386	Place the diagnostics disk in the drive, reboot the system, and choose Computer Setup from the menu.
Some newer Compaq computers, such as Prolinea, Deskpro, DeskproXL, Deskpro LE, or Presario	Boot the computer, wait for two beeps, and when the cursor is in the upper-right corner of the screen, press the F10 key.
All other older computers	Use the setup program on the floppy disk that came with the PC. If the floppy disk is lost, contact the motherboard manufacturer to get a replacement.

Table 5-1 Methods for entering CMOS setup utilities by BIOS

> **Notes** The CMOS setup program for older Compaq computers is stored on the hard drive in a small, non-DOS partition of about 3 MB. If this partition becomes corrupted or the computer is an older model, you must run setup from a diagnostic disk. If you can't run setup by pressing F10 at startup, a damaged partition or a virus is likely taking up space in conventional memory.

Now you're ready to enter the CMOS setup utility included in your BIOS. Follow these steps:

1. If a floppy disk is necessary to enter the CMOS setup utility, insert it now.

2. Restart the computer.

3. When the system restarts, enter the setup utility using the correct method for your computer. If you weren't fast enough and the computer boots to the operating system, return to Step 2.

4. Notice that the CMOS utility groups settings by function. For example, all the power management features are grouped together in a Power Management section.

5. The main screen usually has a Help section that describes how to make selections and exit the utility. Typically, you can use the arrow keys or Tab key to highlight options. After you have highlighted your selection, usually you need to press Enter, Page Down, or the Spacebar. The main screen might display a short summary of the highlighted category. Look for and select a category called something like **Standard CMOS Features**.

6. In the Standard CMOS Setup screen, you should see some or all of the following settings. List the current setting for each of the following:

    ◢ Date: _____

    ◢ Time: _____

    ◢ For IDE hard drives, a table listing drive size; mode of operation; and cylinder, head, and sector information:

    _____ _____

    _____

    ◢ Floppy drive setup information, including drive letter and type:

    _____

    ◢ Halt on error setup (the type of error that halts the boot process):

    _____

    ◢ Memory summary (summary of system memory divisions):

    _____

    ◢ Boot sequence (drives the BIOS searches for an OS):

    _____

7. Exit the Standard CMOS Setup screen and return to the main page. Select a section called something like **Advanced Chipset Features**. This section may be split into North Bridge and South Bridge sections.

8. Record settings for the following as well as any other settings in this section:

    ◢ Setup options for memory or RAM:

    _____

    _____

◢ Setup options for expansion buses such as PCI or AGP:

_____

_____

◢ CPU-specific setup options:

_____

_____

◢ Settings for I/O ports such as USB:

_____

_____

◢ Provisions for enabling and disabling onboard drive controllers and other embedded devices:

_____

_____

_____

_____

9. Exit to the CMOS setup main screen. Explore the menus and submenus of the CMOS setup utility and answer the following questions. Note that most of the CMOS settings never need changing, so understanding every setting isn't necessary.

◢ Does CMOS setup offer the option to set a supervisor password? If so, what's the name of the screen where the password is set?

_____

_____

◢ Does CMOS setup offer the option to set a user password? Is so, what options can affect the way users can access and use CMOS setup?

_____

_____

_____

10. Exit to the CMOS setup main screen. You might see options for loading CMOS defaults (which restore factory settings and can be helpful in troubleshooting) as well as options for exiting with or without saving changes.

Now that you're familiar with the way the CMOS setup utility works, you can change the date and time settings. Then you reboot the computer, confirm that the changes are reflected in the operating system, and return the CMOS date and time to the correct settings. Follow these steps:

1. Return to the Standard CMOS Setup screen.

2. Highlight the time field(s) and set the time ahead one hour.

3. Move to the date field(s) and set the date ahead one year.

4. Return to the main CMOS setup screen, and click an option named something like **Save Settings and Exit**. If prompted, verify that you want to save the settings.

5. Wait while the system reboots. Allow Windows to load.

6. At the desktop, check the time and date. Are your CMOS setup changes reflected in Windows?

_____

7. Reboot the computer, return to CMOS setup, and set the correct time and date.

8. Verify again that the changes are reflected in Windows.

CRITICAL THINKING (ADDITIONAL 30 MINUTES)

Form workgroups of two to four people, and do the following to practice troubleshooting problems with CMOS:

1. Propose a change you could make to CMOS setup that would prevent a computer from booting successfully. What change did you propose?

_____

2. Have your instructor approve the change because some changes might cause information written to the hard drive to be lost, making it difficult to recover from the problem without reloading the hard drive. Did your instructor approve the change?

_____

3. Now go to another team's computer and make the change to CMOS setup while the other team makes a change to your system.

4. Return to your computer and troubleshoot the problem. Describe the problem as a user would:

_____

_____

5. What steps did you go through to discover the source of the problem and fix it?

_____

_____

6. If you were to encounter this same problem in the future, what might you do differently to troubleshoot it?

_____

_____

REVIEW QUESTIONS

1. Do all systems use the same method to enter CMOS setup? Can you enter CMOS setup after the system has booted?

_____

2. How are settings usually grouped in the CMOS setup utility?

_____

3. In what section do you usually find time and date setup in the CMOS setup utility?

_____

_____

4. What types of options are shown on the CMOS setup main screen?

_____

5. What happens automatically after you exit CMOS setup?

_____

6. What tool in Sandra can you use to find information on your version of BIOS?

_____

_____

7. Why does a computer need CMOS?

_____

_____

8. When troubleshooting a computer, why might you have to enter CMOS setup? List at least three reasons:

_____

_____

_____

LAB 5.2 USE A HARDWARE INFORMATION UTILITY

OBJECTIVES

The goal of this lab is to help you learn how to use a hardware information utility. After completing this lab, you will be able to:

◢ Download and install the HWiNFO32 utility by Martin Malik

◢ Use the HWiNFO32 utility to examine your system

MATERIALS REQUIRED

This lab requires the following:

◢ A computer designated for this lab

◢ Windows Vista/XP operating system

◢ Alternate boot device such as CD, floppy drive, or USB flash drive

◢ Internet access for file downloading only

LAB PREPARATION

Before the lab begins, the instructor or lab assistant needs to do the following:

◢ Verify that Windows starts with no errors.

◢ Verify that Internet access is available.

◢ For labs that don't have Internet access, download the following file to a file server or other storage media available to students in the lab: latest version of HWiNFO32 downloaded from *www.hwinfo.com*. At the time this lab was tested, the latest version was Version 2.40 and the filename was Hw32_240.exe. However, the version number and filename might have since changed.

ACTIVITY BACKGROUND

A hardware information utility can be useful when you want to identify a hardware component in a system without having to open the computer case. Also, a hardware information utility can help you identify features of a motherboard, video card, or processor installed in a system and establish benchmarks for these components. In this lab, you learn to use HWiNFO32 written by Martin Malik from Slovakia. The utility comes in a Windows version and a DOS version. You can use the Windows version on any Windows Vista or XP computer, and you can install the DOS version on a bootable floppy disk or CD-ROM so that the utility is available on any computer you're troubleshooting.

In this lab, you download a shareware Windows version of HWiNFO32 from the Internet and then learn how to use it. Web sites sometimes change, so as you follow the instructions in this lab, you might have to adjust for changes to the *www.hwinfo.com* site. If your lab doesn't have Internet access, ask your instructor for the location of the file downloaded previously for your use. Write the path to that file here: _____

ESTIMATED COMPLETION TIME: 30 Minutes

 Activity

1. Go to the HWiNFO32 Web site at **www.hwinfo.com**. Click **Download**. In the submenu under Download, click **HWiNFO32**. Select the **Self-installing EXE** from one of the download locations, and the File Download dialog box opens. If a yellow information bar opens across the top of your browser, click **Download File**. Next click **Save**. Select a folder on your computer to save the file, and click **Save**. What is the path and name of the downloaded file?

   _____

2. When the download is complete, click **Close**, close your browser, open Windows Explorer, and then double-click the filename to install HWiNFO32 for Windows. If the Security Warning dialog box opens, click **Run** to start setup. Follow the directions on the screen to install the software.

3. After the software is installed, use the Help feature to answer the following questions about the utility:

▲ Why does the utility's installation program install a driver running in kernel mode?

_____

_____

▲ What kind of rights are required to install the kernel-mode driver?

_____

▲ Why do you think it is necessary for the utility to be updated often?

_____

4. Close the HWiNFO32 Help window.

5. When the utility runs, it examines your system, and then the HWiNFO32 window shown in Figure 5-1 opens.

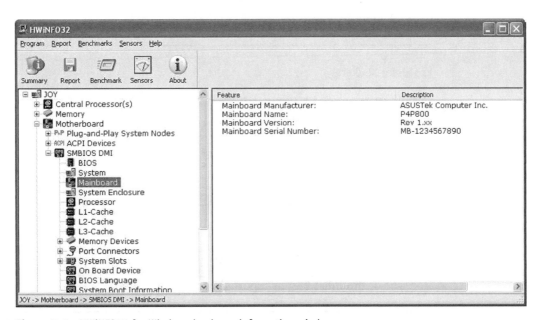

Figure 5-1   HWiNFO32 for Windows hardware information window
Courtesy: Course Technology/Cengage Learning

Many times you aren't given step-by-step directions when using utility software but must learn how to use it by exploring menus and using the software's help functions. The following steps give you practice in doing that:

1. Use the HWiNFO32 utility to find the following information about your system:

▲ Motherboard model and manufacturer:

_____

▲ Motherboard chipset:

_____

◢ Motherboard slots:

_____

◢ BIOS vendor:

_____

◢ BIOS version:

_____

◢ BIOS release date:

_____

◢ Processor manufacturer:

_____

◢ Processor version:

_____

◢ Current and maximum clock speed of the processor:

_____

◢ Processor socket:

_____

◢ Amount of L1 cache:

_____

◢ Amount of L2 cache:

_____

◢ Amount of L3 cache:

_____

◢ Slot type of the video bus, as reported by the video card:

_____

◢ Slot type of the video bus, as reported by the motherboard:

_____

◢ Amount of video RAM:

_____

2. To identify your motherboard's serial number, double-click **motherboard, SMBIOS DMI,** and then **Mainboard.** What is your motherboard's serial number?

_____

3. Exit the program.

CHALLENGE ACTIVITY (ADDITIONAL 30 MINUTES)

Martin Malik also offers a DOS-based utility for finding information about hardware. If you download and install this DOS version of HWiNFO on a Windows bootable CD, USB flash drive, or floppy disk, you can boot a system with this disk and run the utility without using Windows. This option can be useful when Windows isn't working or you don't want to take the time to install the utility's 32-bit version in Windows. Also, if you're servicing a customer's computer, you can use the DOS-based utility on a Windows startup disk to get information about the system quickly without installing software on a customer's computer.

Create a bootable disk. Download the DOS version of HWiNFO from the *www.hwinfo.com* Web site and copy it to the disk. Boot from the disk and start the utility on any Windows computer. Answer the following questions:

1. What is the name of the downloaded compressed file for HWiNFO for DOS?

2. List the steps you took to download the utility and install it on a bootable floppy disk:

3. Describe how the software works using this method:

REVIEW QUESTIONS

1. Why does a Windows driver need to run in kernel mode?

2. In your system, did the type of video slot reported by the video card differ from the type of video slot reported by the motherboard? If so, how can you explain this difference?

3. Using Windows XP, list the steps to create a bootable floppy disk:

4. Can you use a bootable floppy disk created in Windows XP to boot a Windows 98 computer?

5. What is an advantage of using the DOS version instead of the Windows version of the HWiNFO utility?

_____

6. List three reasons you might use HWiNFO or HWiNFO32 when troubleshooting or upgrading a PC:

_____

_____

_____

LAB 5.3 IDENTIFY MOTHERBOARD COMPONENTS

OBJECTIVES

The goal of this lab is to help you learn to identify motherboard form factors and components. After completing this lab, you will be able to:

◢ Identify a motherboard's CPU type

◢ Identify connectors

◢ Identify the form factor based on component type and placement

MATERIALS REQUIRED

Instructors are encouraged to supply a variety of motherboards, some common and others not so common. At the very least, this lab requires the following:

◢ Three different motherboards

> **Notes** If three motherboards aren't available, refer to the Web sites of three motherboard manufacturers.

LAB PREPARATION

Before the lab begins, the instructor or lab assistant needs to do the following:

◢ Gather an assortment of motherboards, with as many form factors as possible.

ACTIVITY BACKGROUND

As a PC technician, you should be able to look at a motherboard and determine what type of CPU, RAM, and form factor you're working with. You should also be able to recognize any unusual components the board might have. In this lab, you examine different motherboards and note some important information about them.

Activity

Fill in the following chart for your assigned motherboards. If you have more than three motherboards, use additional paper. When the entry in the Item column is a question (such as "AGP slot?") write a yes or no answer.

Item	Motherboard 1	Motherboard 2	Motherboard 3
Manufacturer/model			
BIOS manufacturer			
CPU type			
Chipset			
RAM type/pins			
How many PCI slots?			
How many PCIe X1 slots?			
How many PCIe X16 slots?			
How many AGP slots?			
Parallel ATA (IDE) connectors?			
Serial ATA (SATA) connectors?			
SCSI controller?			
Embedded audio, video, and so on			
Jumperless?			
Form factor			
Describe any unusual components			

REVIEW QUESTIONS

1. How can you determine whether a motherboard is an ATX or BTX board, based on the CPU's location in relation to the expansion slots?

   _____

   _____

2. How can you determine the chipset if it's not written on the board?

   _____

   _____

3. Of the motherboards you examined, which do you think is the oldest? Why?

   _____

   _____

   _____

4. Which motherboard best supports old and new technology? Why?

_____

_____

_____

5. Which motherboard seems to provide the best possibility for expansion? Why?

_____

_____

_____

6. Which motherboard is most likely the easiest to configure? Why?

_____

7. Which motherboard do you think is the most expensive? Why?

_____

8. What are some considerations a motherboard manufacturer has to contend with when designing a motherboard? (For example, consider room for large CPUs and cooling fans, where the power supply is located in relationship to the power connector, new technologies, and so forth.)

_____

_____

LAB 5.4 IDENTIFY A MOTHERBOARD AND FIND DOCUMENTATION AND DRIVERS ON THE INTERNET

OBJECTIVES

The goal of this lab is to learn to identify a motherboard and find online documentation for it. After completing this lab, you will be able to:

◢ Identify a motherboard by examining it physically

◢ Determine a motherboard's manufacturer and model

◢ Search the Internet for motherboard documentation

MATERIALS REQUIRED

This lab requires the following:

◢ A computer designated for disassembly

◢ SiSoftware Sandra Lite (installed in Lab 1.3)

◢ Internet access

◢ Adobe Acrobat Reader

◢ A PC toolkit with antistatic wrist strap

LAB PREPARATION

Before the lab begins, the instructor or lab assistant needs to do the following:

◢ Verify that Windows starts with no errors.

◢ Verify that Internet access is available.

◢ Verify that SiSoftware Sandra and Adobe Acrobat Reader are installed.

ACTIVITY BACKGROUND

Often a PC technician is asked to repair a PC, but the documentation is lost or not available. Fortunately, you can usually find documentation for a device online, as long as you have the device's manufacturer name and model number. In this lab, you learn how to find the manufacturer's name and model number on a motherboard, and then locate documentation for that device on the Internet.

ESTIMATED COMPLETION TIME: 30 Minutes

 Activity

1. Boot your PC and use SiSoftware Sandra (installed in Lab 1.3) to find out which type of CPU is installed on your computer. Record that information:

   _____

2. Following safety precautions, including using an antistatic ground strap, remove the PC's case cover, and then remove any components obscuring your view of the motherboard. In some cases, you might have to remove the motherboard itself, but this step usually isn't necessary.

3. Look for a stenciled or silkscreened label printed on the circuit board that indicates the manufacturer and model. Note that other components sometimes have labels printed on a sticker affixed to the component. On a motherboard, the label is usually printed directly on the circuit board. Common motherboard manufacturers include AOpen, ASUS, and Intel.

Also, note that the manufacturer name is usually printed in much larger type than the model number. Model numbers often include both letters and numbers, and many indicate a version number as well. Figure 5-2 shows an example of a motherboard label.

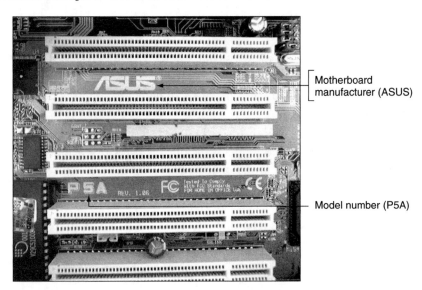

Figure 5-2 Label printed directly on a motherboard
Courtesy: Course Technology/Cengage Learning

4. Record the information on the motherboard label:

_____

5. Take your information to a PC with Internet access and open a browser.

6. If you know the manufacturer's URL, go directly to the Web site. (Table 5-2 lists the URLs for some motherboard manufacturers.) If you don't know the manufacturer's URL, search for the manufacturer or model with your favorite search engine, as shown in Figure 5-3. In the search results, click a link associated with the manufacturer. If this link doesn't take you directly to the documentation, it usually gets you within two or three links. Continue until you find the manufacturer's Web site.

> **Notes** For a listing of Web sites about motherboards, including motherboard manufacturers, diagnostics, and product comparisons and reviews, see *www.motherboards.org*.

Manufacturer	URL
American Megatrends, Inc.	*www.megatrends.com*
AOpen	*www.aopen.com*
ASUS	*www.asus.com*
Dell	*www.dell.com*
Diamond Multimedia	*www.diamondmm.com*
First International Computer, Inc.	*www.fica.com*
Gateway	*www.gateway.com*
Giga-Byte Technology Co., Ltd.	*www.giga-byte.com*
IBM	*www.ibm.com*
Intel Corporation	*www.intel.com*
Supermicro Computer, Inc.	*www.supermicro.com*
Tyan Computer Corporation	*www.tyan.com*

Table 5-2　URLs for major motherboard manufacturers

7. When you have found the site of your motherboard's manufacturer, look for a link to service or support. Click this link, and, if necessary, select a product category and model number. Sometimes knowing the type of CPU the board supports can be useful in finding the right board.

8. Continue working your way through the site until you find the motherboard documentation. The documentation might include a variety of documents covering technical specifications and installation instructions. Often the documentation includes a basic manual, which is usually a combination of technical and installation specifications.

9. When you find the documentation, you might also find a link to updated drivers. If you see such a link, click it and note the release date of these drivers. If they are newer than the current drivers, it's often advisable to update the drivers as well. If possible, record the release dates for updated drivers:

_____

Figure 5-3 Search results using manufacturer name and model number
Courtesy: Course Technology/Cengage Learning

10. Return to the main documentation page, and, if it's available, select the manual. If it's not available, select the installation instructions.

11. The manual is probably in PDF format, so you need to have Adobe Acrobat Reader installed. If you have the browser plug-in, you can open the document from the source location, or you can download the manual to your computer and then open it. Using your preferred method, open the document and print the motherboard documentation. Save this documentation for use in Lab 5.5.

REVIEW QUESTIONS

1. How is the label usually applied to a motherboard? How is it most often applied to other components?

2. On the label of a motherboard or other component, how can the manufacturer often be differentiated from the model number?

3. What type of link on a manufacturer's Web site usually leads you to manuals and other documentation?

4. What other information about your motherboard might you want to examine on the manufacturer's Web site?

5. In what format is documentation most often available for download?

_____

6. What information besides motherboard documentation, such as BIOS updates and drivers, can be found at the manufacturer's Web site?

_____

LAB 5.5 REMOVE AND REPLACE A MOTHERBOARD

OBJECTIVES

The goal of this lab is to familiarize you with the process of replacing an old or faulty motherboard. After completing this lab, you will be able to:

◢ Use SiSoftware Sandra to determine your CPU's specifications

◢ Remove a motherboard

◢ Configure a new motherboard according to its documentation

◢ Install a replacement motherboard

MATERIALS REQUIRED

This lab requires the following:

◢ A computer designated for this lab

◢ Motherboard manual (printed during Lab 5.4)

◢ SiSoftware Sandra (installed in Lab 1.3)

◢ A workgroup of 2 to 4 students

◢ A PC toolkit with antistatic ground strap

LAB PREPARATION

Before the lab begins, the instructor or lab assistant needs to do the following:

◢ Verify that Windows starts with no errors.

◢ Verify that SiSoftware Sandra has been installed.

ACTIVITY BACKGROUND

In this lab, you exchange a motherboard with another team to simulate the process of replacing a faulty motherboard. When you install the new motherboard, you must configure it for your system by adjusting jumper and CMOS settings according to the documentation you printed in Lab 5.4. Then you install the replacement motherboard.

Activity

In this lab, while you remove the motherboard, follow the safety precautions that were outlined in Lab 4.2 as well as those outlined in the motherboard's documentation. Be sure to use an antistatic wrist strap.

1. Launch Sandra (installed in Lab 1.3) and use the CPU & BIOS Information utility to examine the CPU in your system. Record the information listed in the Processor section:

   _____

   _____

   _____

2. Power the system down, unplug everything, and remove the case cover. Then remove the cabling and expansion cards from the motherboard. Take all necessary precautions (including using an antistatic ground strap), and make a sketch of cabling and component placement.

3. Six to nine screws usually attach the motherboard to the case via spacers or stand-offs. The spacers prevent the printed circuitry from shorting out on the metal case and provide space for air circulation. Also, it's important that the motherboard be securely attached to the case with enough spacers and screws so that the board won't crack when expansion cards are being inserted. Remove the screws attaching the motherboard, and set them aside in a cup, bag, or bowl so that you don't lose them.

> **Tip** In this lab, it's not necessary to remove the spacers from the holes in the computer case. However, sometimes you might have to move a spacer from one hole to another, such as when you're replacing a motherboard and the new board lines up over different holes in the computer case. To remove a plastic spacer held in place with barbs, use needlenose pliers to pinch the spacer and slide it out of the hole. To install it in a new hole, push the spacer into the hole until it pops in place. For metal spacers, carefully squeeze the spacer with pliers and remove it from the bracket holding it to the computer case.

4. Carefully lift the motherboard out of the case. You might have to tilt the board to clear the drive bays and power supply. In some cases, you might have to remove the drives to get the motherboard out.

5. Exchange the motherboard and motherboard documentation with that of another team. You might also exchange the CPU and memory, depending on whether your current CPU and memory modules are compatible with the new motherboard. Follow directions from your instructor on what to exchange. Be sure you have the new motherboard's documentation, which you should have found on the Internet in Lab 5.4.

Your instructor might ask you to remove jumpers and reset DIP switches on your motherboard before passing it to the other team. These modifications will make the other team's configuration more challenging. As an alternative, your instructor might have a display motherboard somewhere in the lab that uses jumpers and DIP switches for part of its configuration.

1. With the new motherboard in front of you, consult its documentation and find any jumpers that must be configured to match the system. Older boards use jumpers to adjust clock multipliers and memory speeds and to clear CMOS settings. Unless otherwise instructed, *do not* remove the jumper to clear CMOS settings. Note that newer boards are often "jumperless," with all configuration settings made in CMOS setup. The only jumper these boards have is the one to clear CMOS settings. Remove and replace the jumpers in the configuration specified to match your processor information.

2. Install the motherboard, cabling, expansion cards, and any other components you removed.

3. Have your instructor check your work before you turn on the power.

4. Boot the system and enter the CMOS setup utility. For jumperless motherboards, make any adjustments specified in the motherboard's documentation.

5. Save your settings and exit CMOS setup.

6. Reboot the system and verify that the system is functioning correctly. Describe any error messages:

   _____

7. What steps do you plan to take to troubleshoot this error?

   _____

CRITICAL THINKING (ADDITIONAL 30 MINUTES)

To learn more about motherboards, do the following:

1. After the PC is working, ask your instructor to configure a power-on password on your computer.

2. Without knowing the password, boot the computer.

3. List the steps required to boot the computer without the power-on password:

   _____

   _____

   _____

REVIEW QUESTIONS

1. How many screws usually attach the motherboard to the computer case?

   _____

2. What is the purpose of spacers?

   _____

3. Even a jumperless motherboard is likely to have one jumper. Which jumper is it?

   _____

4. Where can you access configuration settings for a jumperless motherboard?

   _____

LAB 5.6 FLASH BIOS

OBJECTIVES

The goal of this lab is to help you examine the process of flashing BIOS. After completing this lab, you will be able to:

- Gather motherboard information
- Gather BIOS string information
- Research correct BIOS update information
- Record current BIOS settings
- Flash your BIOS, if permitted by your instructor

MATERIALS REQUIRED

This lab requires the following:

- Windows Vista/XP operating system
- Motherboard documentation or SiSoftware Sandra, installed in Lab 1.3
- Internet access
- Some BIOS may require a floppy drive and a blank floppy disk

LAB PREPARATION

Before the lab begins, the instructor or lab assistant needs to do the following:

- Verify that Windows starts with no errors.
- Verify that Internet access is available.
- Determine if the Flash program will require a floppy drive.

ACTIVITY BACKGROUND

The BIOS on a motherboard controls many of the system's basic input/output (I/O) functions. You can update the BIOS programming by downloading the latest update from the BIOS or motherboard manufacturer's Web site and then following specific procedures to update (or "flash") the BIOS. Flashing a computer's BIOS is necessary when troubleshooting an unstable motherboard. You might also need to flash a computer's BIOS to provide support for new hardware (such as a processor, hard drive, or DVD-ROM drive) or an operating system you're about to install. For example, before upgrading your operating system to Windows XP Professional x64 edition, you might need to update your BIOS to support 64-bit drivers. In this lab, you gather information about your system, including what BIOS you're using and how to flash it. If your instructor permits, you also flash your BIOS.

Activity

Before making hardware, software, or BIOS changes to a system, it's important to know your starting point so that if problems occur, you know whether the problems already existed or you created them by what you did to the system. Do the following:

1. Verify that your computer can boot successfully to a Windows desktop with no errors.

2. How long does it take your PC to boot?

_____

When flashing the BIOS, using the correct BIOS update is critical. Using the wrong BIOS update can render your system inoperable. Follow these steps to gather information on the motherboard chipset and BIOS:

1. Use motherboard documentation or Sandra to find and record the following:

◢ Motherboard manufacturer:

_____

◢ Motherboard model number and version/revision:

_____

◢ Chipset manufacturer:

_____

◢ Chipset model number and version/revision:

_____

2. Next, you need to record the BIOS string and manufacturer information displayed during the boot process. To make it possible to record this information, for an older PC, turn off the PC, unplug your keyboard, and then turn on the PC. In most cases, the first screen contains video BIOS information from the video card and is identified by "VGA BIOS" or "Video BIOS." Ignore this screen and wait for the next screen, which indicates the start of POST. At this point, because you unplugged the keyboard, POST stops and reports the error about a missing keyboard. This freezes the screen so that you can read the BIOS information. For a newer PC, turn off the PC and then turn it on again while pressing the Pause/Break key, which causes POST to halt.

3. Usually, you can find the BIOS manufacturer and version at the top left of the POST screen. You might also see a release date, which is useful in determining whether newer versions of the BIOS are available. The motherboard identification string is usually located at the bottom left and often contains dozens of characters. Make sure you verify that this string is correct so that you get the correct BIOS update. Record your information on the following lines:

◢ BIOS manufacturer and version:

_____

◢ BIOS release date, if provided:

_____

◢ Motherboard identification string:

_____

If you have a name-brand PC that doesn't identify BIOS information during the boot process, you should be able to locate BIOS information on the manufacturer's Web site by computer model number and serial number. Alternatively, you can go to CMOS setup and look for the BIOS identifying information on the CMOS main menu screen.

Using the information you gathered, you can search the Web to determine what files you need to update your BIOS:

1. First, search the motherboard manufacturer's Web site and then the BIOS manufacturer's Web site in the Support section for information on updating your BIOS. Alternatively, search by motherboard model number or BIOS version number. Download the files to update your BIOS or, if your computer is running the latest version of the BIOS, download the files to refresh your existing BIOS. Answer the following questions:

   ◢ Did you download files to update or refresh your BIOS?

   _____

   ◢ Which manufacturer provided the BIOS: the BIOS manufacturer or motherboard manufacturer?

   _____

   ◢ What is the name of the file you downloaded?

   _____

   ◢ What is the release date of the latest version?

   _____

2. Search the manufacturer's Web site for the steps to flash your BIOS. Print this procedure so that you can use it during the upgrade. Does the procedure call for an additional BIOS utility or flash utility? If so, download this utility as well. Research flash utilities on *www.wimsbios.com*. Wim's BIOS is an excellent Web site for researching BIOS information in general. Print information on what BIOS utilities are available.

3. The next step is to record any changes you have made previously to CMOS settings. Generally, when BIOS is updated, settings are returned to their default state, so you probably need to return the settings to their present state after you have flashed BIOS. In addition, you might need to manually input settings for all hard drives (or allow these settings to be detected automatically). Record any settings you know you changed, any hard drive settings that might have to be reconfigured after you update the BIOS, and any additional settings specified by your instructor:

   ◢ Hard drive information:

   _____

   _____

   ◢ Settings you have changed:

   _____

   _____

   ◢ Settings specified by your instructor:

   _____

   _____

4. At this point, if your update procedure requires using a bootable floppy disk, verify that the boot order allows you to boot from drive A before drive C.

5. Prepare to update your BIOS. Uncompress any files, double-check procedures, read any Readme.txt files included in the upgrade files (which often contain last-minute adjustments to the procedure), and create the upgrade boot disk, if necessary.

6. If your instructor permits, follow the BIOS update procedure to flash your BIOS. During the procedure, if you're given the opportunity to save your old BIOS, do so. This information makes it possible to return to the previous BIOS version if you encounter problems with the new BIOS.

7. Reboot, verify CMOS settings, and verify that the computer boots to a Windows desktop successfully.

REVIEW QUESTIONS

1. At what point in the boot process is BIOS information displayed?

   _____

2. How can you freeze the screen during POST so that you can read the BIOS information?

   _____

   _____

3. Why is it so important to record BIOS and motherboard information correctly?

   _____

   _____

4. What files might contain last-minute adjustments to the upgrade procedures?

   _____

5. In what state are CMOS settings usually placed after a BIOS update?

   _____

6. If given the opportunity during an update, what should you always do and why?

   _____

Supporting Processors

Labs included in this chapter:

- **Lab 6.1:** Remove and Replace a CPU

- **Lab 6.2:** Benchmark and Burn-In a CPU

- **Lab 6.3:** Compare CPU Benchmarks

- **Lab 6.4:** Choose a CPU Cooling Solution

- **Lab 6.5:** Critical Thinking: Restoring an Overclocked PC

LAB 6.1 REMOVE AND REPLACE A CPU

OBJECTIVES

The goal of this lab is to help you learn the correct procedure for removing and reinstalling a CPU. After completing this lab, you will be able to:

◢ Remove the CPU from your system

◢ Install a CPU into your system

MATERIALS REQUIRED

This lab requires the following:

◢ A computer designated for this lab

◢ Windows Vista/XP operating system

◢ Flathead screwdriver

◢ An antistatic wrist strap

◢ Masking tape and marker or other method of labeling parts

◢ Another computer with an active Internet connection

◢ Alcohol wipe to remove thermal compound from the CPU

◢ Additional thermal compound (if necessary)

LAB PREPARATION

Before the lab begins, the instructor or lab assistant needs to do the following:

◢ Verify that Windows starts with no errors.

◢ Verify that Internet access is available.

ACTIVITY BACKGROUND

Removing and installing a CPU isn't difficult after you have done it a time or two. However, in today's systems, it's fairly rare for the CPU to be the source of a problem. Instead, a CPU replacement is usually done to increase the system's operating speed. In this lab, you remove the CPU and cooling unit (heat sink and fan or HFS) and then replace both. When you're considering upgrading the CPU in a system, be aware that if you upgrade the CPU, you might not realize the new processor's full potential if all the other components remain outdated.

Often, when disassembling or assembling parts to a system, you won't have step-by-step directions but must discover how to do so. Removing the heat sink and fan for the CPU is one of these tasks. Because of the overwhelming number of models on the market, you might need to refer to the manufacturer's documentation for exact details on how to remove the cooling unit.

An important note on electrostatic discharge (ESD): The CPU is an intricate and complicated array of wires and transistors. When you feel a static shock, you're feeling somewhere in the neighborhood of 3000 volts or more. The CPU can be damaged by a shock of 10 to 1000 volts, a discharge you would never feel. It's important to wear your ground strap while handling the CPU and memory, or you could easily damage components and never know that you have done so.

Activity

Because the CPU is a delicate component and is easily damaged, watch your instructor demonstrate how to remove and replace one before you attempt to do so. Then, answer the following questions about the demonstration:

1. What CPU did the instructor remove and replace?

   _____

2. What type of heat sink or cooler was attached to the CPU?

   _____

3. How was the heat sink or cooler attached to the motherboard?

   _____

4. What precautions did the instructor take to protect the CPU against ESD?

   _____

   _____

5. How did the instructor protect the CPU while it was out of its socket?

   _____

   _____

Do the following to remove the CPU from your system:

1. Power down the computer.

2. Unplug any cords or cables connected to it.

3. Remove the case cover.

4. Examine the inside of the case and decide what you need to remove so that you have easy access to the CPU. Next, remove and carefully label any wires or other parts that need to be removed to expose the CPU. With some system cases, the power supply needs to be removed to be able to proceed.

5. Disconnect the power cord from the heat sink and fan (HSF) to the motherboard.

6. Depending on the CPU that's installed, there are different methods for removing and installing an HSF unit. Some units can be removed by hand simply by opening the levers that attach them to the socket. Other units require using the eraser end of a pencil to carefully dislodge the unit from the retaining mechanism hooks. Typically, the HSF is latched on both sides. After the pressure is removed from the main latch, it unlatches easily from the opposite side. Rather than use a screwdriver or other metal object to unlatch a stubborn latch, the preferred method is to use the eraser end of a pencil. If you slip while releasing the latch mechanism and the motherboard is damaged, it might be beyond repair. Also, some heat sinks are permanently glued to the processor and aren't intended to be removed. In this case, leave the heat sink attached. Decide how to proceed and, if appropriate, remove the heat sink and fan unit carefully.

7. After you have removed the HSF unit, you can proceed to actually removing the CPU. Handling the CPU must be done with your full attention. Some CPUs have tiny pins on the bottom of the chip that can be bent easily and need to be handled with care.

Typically, CPUs and motherboards are shipped with antistatic foam that's an ideal surface to set CPU pins into for protection. If you don't have this shipping container, when you remove the CPU, lay it bottom-side up so that the pins aren't sitting on your work surface. Find the CPU shipping container or plan for a way to store the CPU safely.

8. You'll see a metal bar right next to the socket of the base of the CPU. This metal bar is the lever for the zero insertion force (ZIF) socket. Pull the lever out slightly and then up 90 degrees to release the CPU. In Figure 6-1, you can see the lever about to be released from an empty LGA775 socket.

Figure 6-1   Open the socket lever
Courtesy: Course Technology/Cengage Learning

9. Carefully grasp the sides of the CPU and pull up gently to remove it from the socket.

10. Using an alcohol wipe, carefully remove any thermal grease (also called thermal compound) that's smeared on the top of the CPU. You can now safely store the CPU.

Now you're ready to install the new CPU or, for this lab, replace the CPU. If you're actually upgrading to a new CPU, you need to make several checks before installing the new CPU into a motherboard. You need to verify that the socket type, clock speed, and multiplier match the new CPU.

In this lab, you're replacing the existing CPU; however, go through the following steps to practice as though you were installing a new upgraded CPU:

1. Remember that the CPU is a delicate piece of equipment. The pins on the processor can be bent easily, and if the heat sink isn't connected properly, you run the risk of allowing the CPU to overheat. Inspect the new CPU to verify that it has no bent pins. If you suspect the CPU has been damaged or if the pins are bent, you might need to replace the CPU.

2. Visually inspect the socket on the motherboard for any indication as to what type of socket it is. Usually it's clearly marked as to the type. Double-check that the CPU was manufactured for the type of socket on the motherboard. What is the CPU socket this motherboard is using?

3. Using the manual for the CPU, determine the correct front-side bus (FSB) speed, multiplier, and voltage for the CPU. If you don't have the manual, visit the manufacturer's

Web site. Although some motherboards configure this information automatically, as a technician you need to be able to determine that it was done correctly. Your CPU is most likely manufactured by Intel (*www.intel.com*) or AMD (*www.amd.com*). Go to the manufacturer's Web site and fill in these blanks:

◢ FSB speed:

_____

◢ Multiplier:

_____

◢ Voltage:

_____

4. You might need to set the FSB speed, multiplier, and voltage on the motherboard or in the BIOS. Again, read the manufacturer's documentation if you have it. If you don't have the documentation, visit the manufacturer's Web site and download it. Some motherboards require you to set this information by using DIP switches or jumpers, but others allow you to do so in CMOS setup. Still others detect the CPU and configure everything for you automatically. How does this motherboard recognize and configure the CPU?

_____

_____

5. Before you install the CPU in the socket, practice raising and lowering the socket lever so that you can feel how much force is necessary to close the lever.

6. Now you're ready to install the CPU. Verify that the power cable has been removed from the machine. Unlatch the ZIF lever and bring it to the up position. It should be pointing directly upward. The pins on the CPU are keyed to line up with the grid array on the socket. Gently align the CPU with the socket (see Figure 6-2) and allow it to fall into place.

Figure 6-2 Align the CPU over the socket
Courtesy: Course Technology/Cengage Learning

7. Carefully replace the socket lever so that force is applied to the top of the CPU and the CPU is installed securely in the socket. You need to place a little more pressure on the lever than you did when no CPU was present, but don't force it! If you have to force it, most likely the CPU isn't oriented in the socket correctly.

8. Now you're ready to install the heat sink. First, examine the underside of the heat sink for any foreign matter. It's common for a new heat sink to come with a thermal pad that's covered by a protective film of plastic. If this plastic isn't removed, you run the risk of damaging your CPU. If there's no thermal pad, put on latex gloves and gently apply a very thin layer of thermal grease to the portion of the heat sink that will come into contact with the CPU. Be careful not to apply thermal grease so that it later comes in contact with the edges of the processor or the socket. You don't want grease to get down into the CPU socket. Figure 6-3 shows just about the right amount of thermal grease applied.

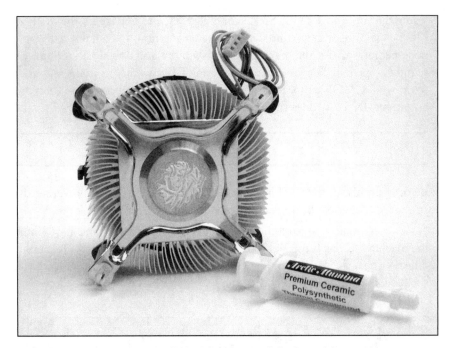

Figure 6-3　Thermal grease applied to the bottom of the heat sink assembly
Courtesy: Course Technology/Cengage Learning

9. Carefully align the bottom of the heat sink with the socket and attach the heat sink. Plug the heat sink fan's power cord into the motherboard.

10. Have your instructor inspect your work to make sure the heat sink is attached correctly. (Booting up a system with an incorrectly attached heat sink can cause damage to the processor because it will overheat.)

11. It's always a good idea to test the CPU operating temperature after replacing the heat sink. Most BIOS programs will display the current temperature of the CPU. Boot your machine to the CMOS Setup screen and make sure the CPU is not overheating.

REVIEW QUESTIONS

1. Why shouldn't you use a screwdriver to remove a heat sink?

2. What is the minimum voltage of an electrostatic discharge (ESD) that you can feel?

   _____

3. What is the voltage range in which ESD can affect components?

   _____

4. What was the operating temperature of the CPU?

   _____

5. Why is it important to double-check the bottom of the heat sink before attaching it to the CPU socket?

   _____

   _____

LAB 6.2 BENCHMARK AND BURN-IN A CPU

OBJECTIVES

The goal of this lab is to learn how to compare your CPU's performance in relation to other processors, to make sure the CPU is stable, and to ensure that the heat sink and fan are working correctly. After completing this lab, you will be able to:

◢ Benchmark a CPU

◢ Burn-in a CPU

◢ Monitor CPU temperature

MATERIALS REQUIRED

This lab requires the following:

◢ A computer running Windows Vista/XP

◢ An active Internet connection

◢ SiSoftware Sandra Lite (installed in Lab 1.3)

LAB PREPARATION

Before the lab begins, the instructor or lab assistant needs to do the following:

◢ Verify that Windows starts with no errors and the Internet connection is working.

◢ Verify that SiSoftware Sandra Lite is installed (see Lab 1.3).

ACTIVITY BACKGROUND

Today's CPUs are very reliable. In spite of this reliability, after completing a system build, you should test the CPU for stability before sending it out to the end user. This testing is known as burn-in testing or a stress test. Although performing burn-in testing can take up to 24 hours, it can still save you time in the long run by catching potential problems before they start.

Although an unstable system *might* boot without any errors, it usually shows problems when a load has been placed on the system. Any time you're running a stress test, it's crucial to monitor the temperature of the CPU so that you don't damage the CPU if there's a problem. SiSoftware Sandra Lite (installed in Lab 1.3) allows both burn-in testing and temperature monitoring.

ESTIMATED COMPLETION TIME: 60 Minutes to 24 Hours

 Activity

It's best to devote 24 hours to burning in a CPU for verification that it's truly stable. In a lab environment, however, this amount of time might not always be practical. Therefore, this lab allows for one hour of testing. Follow these steps:

1. First, you'll run a short test to make sure the CPU is not overheating. Start SiSoftware Sandra Lite. Click the **Tools** tab, and then double-click the **Burn-in Computer** icon. On the opening screen, click **Next** (the green forward arrow).

2. In the Configuration screen, select **Make choices and generate report** and then click **Next**.

3. In the Benchmarks screen, click to clear all check boxes except **Processor Arithmetic** and **Processor Multi-Media**. Click **Next**.

4. On the Count Down page, leave all the options at their default settings, and then click **Next**. How many times will the test run?

_____

5. On the Processor page, leave the Minimum Utilization setting at 100%, and then click **Next**.

6. On the Maximum Temperature(s) page, enter the maximum temperature that the CPU manufacturer recommends for the processor you're using. If you don't know this temperature, leave the entry blank. Click **Next**.

7. On the Minimum Fan Speed(s) page, leave all entries blank, and then click **Next**.

8. Next add any comments and select how you would like your report to be delivered. Click **Next** to proceed.

9. On the Burn, Baby, Burn! page, click **OK** (the green check mark) to begin the burn-in test. Figure 6-4 shows the completed burn test.

10. When the test has finished, verify that the CPU's temperature has stayed within the correct range. Are there any unusual results from this test?

_____

_____

11. If time permits, run SiSoftware Sandra again, but on the Count Down page, click to enable the **Run Continuously** radio button. This time, when the program runs, it won't stop running until you tell it to. This way, you can allow the program to run overnight, and then come back the next day to check for errors. If there are no errors, you can assume that the system is stable.

After you're sure the system is stable, you can see how the system's performance compares to other systems with similar configurations. Follow these steps:

1. Open SiSoftware Sandra. Click **Tools**, and then double-click **Performance Index** to run this module.

2. Click the **OK** (green check mark) to start the benchmark test. The system will appear to hang while the test is running. To show you that the test is still running, an animated pie chart at the top-right corner continues to move.

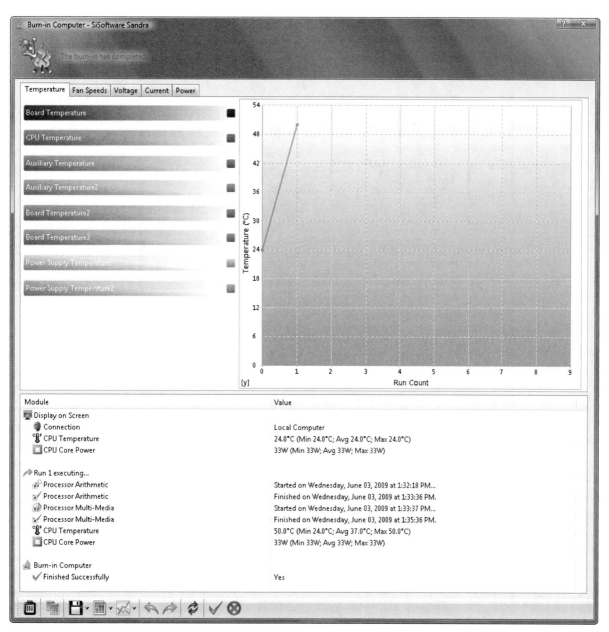

Figure 6-4 SiSoftware Sandra Lite showing a completed burn-in test
Courtesy: Course Technology/Cengage Learning

3. When the test is complete, your computer is then compared to other systems using the coverage matrix. The red color in the graphic represents your system, and the blue color represents the reference system. Figure 6-5 shows the results for one computer. Looking at this figure, you can deduce that this computer is strong on memory performance but weakest on network performance. Based on the results of your test, which area is strongest and which area is weakest on your system?

_____

_____

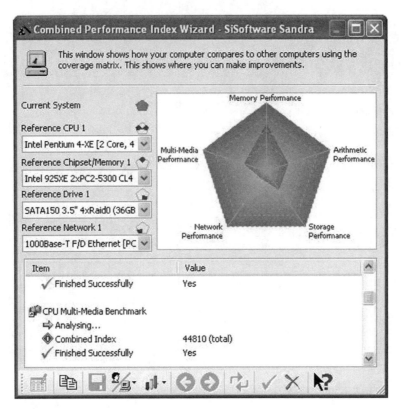

Figure 6-5   Results of the Performance Index Wizard in SiSoftware Sandra Lite
Courtesy: Course Technology/Cengage Learning

CHALLENGE ACTIVITY (ADDITIONAL 30 MINUTES)

Sometimes updating chipset drivers on a motherboard can improve a system's overall perform-ance. Use the Performance Index to test performance; then, download and install updated chipset drivers (see Lab 5.4), and retest the performance and note any improvements.

REVIEW QUESTIONS

1. Why do you place the system under a load to test for errors?

2. If the performance of your CPU is much lower than that of the reference comparables, how can you improve your CPU's performance?

3. Using the Burn-in Computer Wizard, if you decide to run the test 10 times, can you know for certain how long it will take? Why or why not?

4. When using the Burn-in Computer Wizard, what does it mean if the animation hangs while the test is being performed?

_____

_____

LAB 6.3 COMPARE CPU BENCHMARKS

OBJECTIVES

The goal of this lab is to allow you to compare different CPU choices and determine which is best for a given budget. After completing this lab, you will be able to:

◢ Find CPU benchmarks

◢ Compare CPU benchmarks

◢ Compare CPU performance and price

MATERIALS REQUIRED

This lab requires the following:

◢ A computer running Windows Vista/XP

◢ An active Internet connection

LAB PREPARATION

Before the lab begins, the instructor or lab assistant needs to do the following:

◢ Verify that Windows starts with no errors and the Internet connection is working.

◢ Verify each Web site to see whether the content has changed.

ACTIVITY BACKGROUND

When purchasing or building a computer system, you need to make many choices. The CPU is one of the most critical components in your system and has a major impact on the machine's overall performance. The CPU you select must match the motherboard you plan to use. If you have already selected the motherboard or you're buying a CPU to install in an existing motherboard, you're limited in selecting a CPU that matches the motherboard. A motherboard has a socket the CPU must fit into and supports only certain ranges of CPU speed and features. However, if you haven't yet selected a motherboard, you can select the CPU first and then choose a motherboard that supports this CPU. In this lab, you begin your purchasing decisions by first selecting the CPU.

CPU manufacturers used to label their products with the chip speed, so it was easy to compare a 400 MHz AMD with a 400 MHz Intel, for example. However, as the technologies used by competing manufacturers changed, the public relations (PR) system emerged. The AMD 1800+ was clocked at 1533 MHz, but benchmarks showed it to be a comparable product to Intel's 1800 MHz chip, hence the name 1800+. Today's market is full of many different naming conventions, with names such as Pentium, Core, Xeon, Celeron, and Phenom. To be able to make an informed decision on which CPU to purchase, you must be able to compare CPU benchmarks, which give a more objective measure of the CPU's performance.

Activity

Given a budget of $300 for a CPU, you'll compare different choices and decide on the best choice for a given situation. The first step is to see which CPUs fall into this specified price range. Follow these steps:

1. Use your Web browser to navigate to **www.pricewatch.com**. Under the heading CPUs & Motherboards, click **CPUs**. To make a valid comparison, you must look at several models. From this list of CPUs, make note of which four are closest to $300 (without going over $300), and write the model names here:

_____

_____

_____

_____

2. Now click the name of each CPU you have selected. In the following chart, make note of the socket type, number of cores, and speed (in GHz or MHz) of each. If, for example, you had picked an "Intel Core 2 Duo E8600, 3.33 GHz Processor, 1333 MHz FSB, 6 MB Cache, Socket LGA775, with 1 year warranty," the speed would be 3.33 GHz, there would be two cores, and the socket type would be LGA775.

CPU	Speed	# of Cores	Socket	Price

When choosing a benchmark for a CPU, it's important to consider the system's primary use. Different CPUs have different strengths and weaknesses, and there are several tests you can choose from to look at performance.

3. Go to the Tom's Hardware Guide (THG) Web site at **www.tomshardware.com**. Click the **Charts** tab, click **Processors**, and then select the most recent **Desktop CPU Charts**.

4. Examine the resulting page. It lists all of the available CPU benchmark tests in alphabetical order.

5. If you were building a computer for gaming purposes, the tests that would interest you most would be the game-related tests. This would give you the best possible comparison for how the system will be used. In the benchmark list, click **World in Conflict - 1680x1050**. If this benchmark is no longer available, choose a benchmark for another recent PC game.

6. The chart reflects the scores for the benchmark test you selected. What are the scores for the top two performing CPUs displayed?

   ◢ CPU 1:_____

   ◢ CPU 2:_____

7. Look at the price for CPU 1, and then look at the price for CPU 2. Based on the performance in this test, which one is a better value?

_____

8. You should make this type of comparison for each processor you're considering. It's important to choose a benchmark that's closest to the actual type of work you'll be performing on the system. Using what you've learned in the preceding steps, make comparisons for the **3DMark Vantage - CPU** and **Photoshop CS 3** benchmarks for the four CPUs you're considering. Complete the following chart with the information from the comparison charts and the two benchmark tests:

CPU	3DMark Vantage	Photoshop CS 3	Price

CHALLENGE ACTIVITY (ADDITIONAL 20 MINUTES)

In this lab, you used the Tom's Hardware Guide (THG) Web site (*www.tomshardware.com*), a long-standing and reliable Web site, to find reviews and comparisons of computer components. However, many other similar sites exist on the Web. Using a good search engine, locate three more Web sites that offer technical reviews of computer parts, and then complete the following table:

Web Site	Products Reviewed

REVIEW QUESTIONS

1. Why might your choice of CPUs change if you were building a computer system for encoding DivX home movies instead of for gaming?

   _____

   _____

2. Why shouldn't a technician simply put the lowest price CPU into a machine to save costs?

   _____

   _____

3. What is the purpose of choosing four models of CPUs for comparison?

   _____

   _____

4. It seems that for the best performance, you could simply choose the fastest model in each category. Why isn't this method a good way to choose a CPU?

   _____

   _____

   _____

5. How would the benchmark test results change if you had only a $100 budget?

_____

_____

_____

LAB 6.4 CHOOSE A CPU COOLING SOLUTION

OBJECTIVES

Years ago, you could run your 25 MHz computer all day long without a heat sink. Not so today. Because users continue to demand more speed from their CPUs and many hobbyists overclock their CPUs, their systems must constantly battle high temperatures. The most common solution for cooling a CPU is an air-cooled solution: a heat sink and fan (HSF). Although water cooling is effective and extremely quiet, it's still too expensive to be considered for typical computer systems. The heat sink is a metal unit that conducts heat away from the CPU and dissipates that heat into the air, typically with a fan forcing air over the top. Some fans are variable-speed fans that adjust their speeds according to the CPU's temperature. For these fans to work, they must be supported by the motherboard chipset.

If you purchase a retail CPU, the HSF likely will be included. If you purchase an original equipment manufacturer (OEM) CPU, you likely must purchase the HSF separately. Even with a retail CPU that comes with an HSF, you might want to buy a more effective HSF to accommodate overclocking the CPU.

After completing this lab, you will be able to:

◢ Choose a heat sink and fan

MATERIALS REQUIRED

This lab requires the following:

◢ A computer running Windows Vista/XP

◢ An active Internet connection

LAB PREPARATION

Before the lab begins, the instructor or lab assistant needs to do the following:

◢ Verify that Windows starts with no errors and the Internet connection is working.

ACTIVITY BACKGROUND

There are several factors to look for when choosing an HSF. First, the unit must fit the CPU and socket you're using. Next, the unit must provide adequate cooling at an acceptable noise level. Finally, the preferred unit should be easy to mount. In a perfect world, you would be able to test all these cooling units and make an educated decision based on performance.

One common model of CPU that's purchased OEM is the AMD Athlon series. AMD's weight limit for the HSF is 300 grams, which is light enough not to cause damage to a CPU, CPU socket, or motherboard components. In this lab, you'll read the tests Tom's Hardware has run on 55 coolers and make a decision based on those results.

Activity

It's essential to choose an HSF made specifically for the processor you're using. Just because a unit fits doesn't mean it will cool the CPU sufficiently. Follow these steps:

1. Go to the Tom's Hardware Guide (THG) Web site at **www.tomshardware.com.** In the SEARCH box on the top-right side of the home page, search for "Cool Stuff" and click **OK.**

2. Look for the article "Cool Stuff: How THG Tests Coolers." After reading it, answer these questions:

   ◢ How did THG measure the performance level of coolers?

   _____

   _____

   ◢ How did THG test the noise level of coolers?

   _____

   _____

   ◢ Why is it important to know the weight of a cooler when comparing coolers?

   _____

   _____

   ◢ What type of guarantee should you look for when comparing coolers?

   _____

   _____

   ◢ What are some factors to consider about the ease of installation and size of coolers?

   _____

   _____

   _____

3. Now do a search for the article "A Beginner's Guide For WaterCooling Your PC." After reading it, answer these questions:

   ◢ What are the two properties that matter most when comparing the effectiveness of cooling methods?

   _____

   _____

   ◢ What are the three basic types of water-cooled systems?

   _____

   _____

   _____

◢ Explain why it is good practice to split the liquid coolant lines into separate parallel paths:

_____

_____

_____

CHALLENGE ACTIVITY (ADDITIONAL 20 MINUTES)

Based on what you've learned in this lab, complete the following steps:

1. Using the AMD Web site (*www.amd.com*), select a processor for gaming, and then answer these questions:

   ◢ Which processor did you select?

   _____

   ◢ Describe the processor:

   _____

   _____

   ◢ Why did you select this processor?

   _____

   _____

2. Using other Web sites that sell or manufacture coolers, select the best cooler for the processor that you selected in Step 1. Answer these questions:

   ◢ What is the cooler manufacturer and model?

   _____

   _____

   ◢ Why did you select this cooler?

   _____

   _____

   _____

REVIEW QUESTIONS

1. List five factors mentioned in this lab that you should consider when selecting a cooler:

   _____

   _____

   _____

2. If you were in an office building and needed a very quiet system, which of the coolers tested would be a good choice?

_____

_____

3. If you have a CPU that gets very hot and will be used in a noisy industrial building, what effect would these conditions have on your choice of coolers? Would you choose a different cooler than the one you selected in Question 2? Which cooler would you choose?

_____

_____

4. When you purchase a boxed CPU with a cooler, the cooler is usually one with a blend of cooling performance and low noise level. Which of the units that you see in the charts would be a good unit for the manufacturer to include?

_____

_____

5. Can you see any reason that AMD wouldn't recommend the Alpha PAL8045 cooler?

_____

LAB 6.5 CRITICAL THINKING: RESTORING AN OVERCLOCKED PC

OBJECTIVES

Overclocking is when a CPU or motherboard is run at a faster frequency than the manufacturer recommends. Manufacturers discourage overclocking because the resulting higher speeds can cause overheating. This overheating can make the system less stable and/or damage the processor. To avert these dangers, some motherboards will not even allow overclocking. Despite the risks, some people choose to overclock their PCs anyway.

The frequency of a processor is determined by multiplying the CPU's multiplier by the motherboard's system bus frequency (SBF). A system can be overclocked by raising either value. It's generally safer to change only the CPU's multiplier because changing the SBF will also affect the speed of other motherboard components, such as the RAM and Northbridge, and may cause them to overheat.

After completing this lab, you will be able to:

◢ Overclock the CPU by changing its multiplier

MATERIALS REQUIRED

This lab requires the following:

◢ A computer designated for this lab

◢ Windows Vista/XP operating system

◢ SiSoftware Sandra Lite installed (in Lab 1.3).

LAB PREPARATION

Before the lab begins, the instructor or lab assistant needs to do the following:

◢ Verify that Windows starts with no errors and the Internet connection is working.

◢ Verify that the motherboard and BIOS being used support overclocking.

◢ Verify that SiSoftware Sandra Lite is installed (see Lab 1.3).

ACTIVITY BACKGROUND

Sometimes a little knowledge can be a dangerous thing. Often, amateur PC enthusiasts will damage their PCs by trying to overclock them. When overclocking a CPU, it is important to keep a close eye on the temperature and stability of the processor. Typically, experts slowly and incrementally raise the speed of a system while watching these factors for a problem. In this lab, we will pretend that the speed of the system has been increased by raising the CPU multiplier and has caused the system to become unstable. As a computer technician, you will fix the problem by undoing these changes. Then, the temperature and stability of the CPU will be examined for any change.

Because changing the frequency or multiplier carries some risk, this lab should be attempted only with the approval and supervision of your instructor.

ESTIMATED COMPLETION TIME: 45 Minutes

 Activity

Before changing the system, the current operating temperature of the CPU needs to be determined. Follow these steps:

1. Allow the computer to run for at least five minutes and then boot into the BIOS (see Lab 5.1) and explore the various menus to determine the current system temperature. Answer the following questions:

   ◢ What is the temperature of the CPU?

   _____

   ◢ What is the system temperature?

   _____

2. Check the CPU documentation or search the Internet to find the range of recommended operating temperatures.

   ◢ Is the CPU currently running within this range?

   _____

3. Next, use SiSoftware Sandra Lite to run the **Processor Arithmetic** benchmark for the CPU (see Lab 6.2). Look at the values under the Benchmark Results section near the bottom and determine the answers to the following measures of CPU performance:

   ◢ What is the current value for Dhrystone ALU (GIPS)?

   _____

   ◢ What is the current value for Whetstone iSSE3 (GFLOPS)?

   _____

6

4. Now boot into the Setup screen of the BIOS and find the section where the operating speed of the CPU can be set. The current setup is probably set to Autodetect the CPU. Change this setting to **Manual** or **User Define** and two subcategories will probably appear. One defines the frequency of the Front Side Bus (FSB) or External Clock; the other sets the CPU Multiplier. Answer these questions:

   ◢ What is the default setting for the front side bus?

   _____

   ◢ What is the default CPU multiplier?

   _____

   ◢ When the FSB and multiplier values are multiplied, what is the resulting speed of the CPU?

   _____

5. Now underclock the CPU by decreasing the value of the CPU Multiplier by the smallest decrease allowable. Save your settings, reboot the computer, and answer these questions:

   ◢ What is the new setting for the CPU multiplier?

   _____

   ◢ When you multiply this new multiplier by the frequency of the FSB, what is the new speed of the CPU?

   _____

   ◢ How is the temperature of the CPU affected by the change in frequency?

   _____

6. Use SiSoftware Sandra Lite and again run the CPU benchmark from Step 3. Then, answer these questions:

   ◢ How was the performance of the CPU affected by underclocking?

   _____

   ◢ What is the new setting for the CPU multiplier?

   _____

   ◢ When you multiply this by the frequency of the FSB, what is the new speed of the CPU?

   _____

7. Finally, go back into the BIOS setup and return the CPU frequency to its default values.

REVIEW QUESTIONS

1. What two factors determine the frequency of the CPU?

   _____

   _____

2. Why is overclocking not recommended by manufacturers?

   _____

   _____

3. Why might a specialized cooler be required to overclock a computer?

_____

_____

4. Why is it safer to overclock a CPU by changing the multiplier?

_____

_____

5. Based on your temperature and stability findings, do you think you could have over-clocked your system without a causing a problem?

_____

_____

CHAPTER 7

Upgrading Memory

Labs included in this chapter:

- **Lab 7.1:** Research RAM on the Internet
- **Lab 7.2:** Explore the Kingston Web Site
- **Lab 7.3:** Upgrade RAM
- **Lab 7.4:** Use Vista ReadyBoost
- **Lab 7.5:** Troubleshoot Memory Problems

LAB 7.1 RESEARCH RAM ON THE INTERNET

OBJECTIVES

The goal of this lab is to help you learn how to find important information about RAM that you need when upgrading memory. After completing this lab, you will be able to:

◢ Find documentation on your system's motherboard

◢ Read documentation for your system's RAM specifications

◢ Search the Internet for RAM prices and availability

MATERIALS REQUIRED

This lab requires the following:

◢ Windows Vista/XP operating system

◢ Internet access

◢ *Optional*: A workgroup of 2 to 4 students

LAB PREPARATION

Before the lab begins, the instructor or lab assistant needs to do the following:

◢ Verify that Internet access is available.

ACTIVITY BACKGROUND

In the past, RAM was literally worth more than its weight in gold. When building a system, most people made do with the minimum amount of RAM needed for adequate performance. These days, RAM is less expensive, which means you can probably buy all of the RAM you need to make your system perform at top speed. Graphics-editing software, in particular, benefits from additional RAM. In this lab, you research how to optimize RAM on a graphics workstation with a memory upgrade budget of $100.

ESTIMATED COMPLETION TIME: 30 Minutes

 Activity

1. Use Computer (My Computer in Windows XP) to determine the amount of RAM currently installed on your computer. Record the amount of RAM here:

_____

2. Using skills you learned in Lab 5.3, determine your motherboard's manufacturer and model. (If you don't have the motherboard documentation available, search for it on the Web and print it.)

Use the documentation for your motherboard or the Internet to answer these questions:

1. What type (or types) of memory does your motherboard support? Be sure to include categories such as speed, physical type (such as SDRAM or DDR3), and whether it is interlaced:

_____

_____

2. How many slots for memory modules are included on your motherboard?

_____

3. How many memory slots on your motherboard are used, and how much RAM is installed in each slot?

_____

_____

4. What is the maximum amount of memory your motherboard supports?

_____

5. How does the maximum memory supported by your motherboard compare to the maximum supported by your operating system?

_____

6. What size and how many memory modules would be needed to upgrade your system to the maximum amount of supported memory?

_____

Now that you have the necessary information about your system's memory, go to a local computer store that sells memory, or go to *http://pricewatch.com* or a similar Web site, and answer the following questions:

1. What is the price of the memory modules required to configure your system for maximum memory?

_____

2. Does your budget allow you to install the maximum supported amount of RAM?

_____

3. Can you use the existing memory modules to upgrade to the maximum amount of supported memory?

_____

_____

4. What is the most additional memory you could install and still stay within your budget? (Assume you'll use the existing memory modules.)

_____

Explore other types of memory on *http://pricewatch.com* or another similar Web site, and answer the following questions:

1. On average, what is the least expensive type of memory per MB you can find? What is its price?

_____

_____

2. On average, what is the most expensive type of memory per MB you can find? What is its price?

_____

3. Is SO-DIMM memory for a notebook computer more or less expensive than an equivalent amount of DDR2 memory for a desktop PC? Give specific information to support your answer:

_____

_____

REVIEW QUESTIONS

1. Why might you want to upgrade RAM on a system?

_____

_____

2. How many pins are on the different types of DIMMs?

_____

3. Which is more expensive: DDR-DIMM or RIMM?

_____

4. What is a disadvantage of using two 512 MB modules instead of a single 1 GB module in a system with three slots for memory modules?

_____

_____

5. What are two disadvantages of using only one 2 GB module rather than two 1 GB modules?

_____

_____

_____

LAB 7.2 EXPLORE THE KINGSTON WEB SITE

OBJECTIVES

The goal of this lab is to use the Kingston Web site to learn about RAM. After completing this lab, you will be able to:

◢ Identify types of RAM

◢ Determine appropriate memory types for a system

MATERIALS REQUIRED

This lab requires the following:

◢ Internet access

LAB PREPARATION

Before the lab begins, the instructor or lab assistant needs to do the following:

◢ Verify that Internet access is available.

ACTIVITY BACKGROUND

RAM comes in a variety of shapes, sizes, and speeds. Not every type of RAM works with every system. In this lab, you use the Kingston Technology (a major RAM manufacturer) Web site to learn about RAM and see how to make sure you have the right memory module to upgrade your system.

ESTIMATED COMPLETION TIME: 30 Minutes

 Activity

Do the following to begin learning about system memory:

1. Open your browser and go to **www.kingston.com**.

2. Notice that you can use the site's Memory Search section to search for memory based on the manufacturer of system you have. What other three ways can you search for memory?

_____

_____

_____

When you search the site based on your system information, the results include a list of compatible memory types with prices, maximum memory your system supports, processors supported, and number of expansion slots on your system for memory modules. Do the following to find information about a memory upgrade for a motherboard:

1. Select one of the motherboards you researched in Lab 5.3. Which motherboard did you select?

_____

2. Perform a memory search on the Kingston site for information on this motherboard. Answer the following questions:

◢ What types of memory modules can this board use?

_____

_____

◢ What types of processors does the board support?

_____

_____

◢ How many memory slots are on the board?

_____

◢ What is the maximum amount of memory the board supports?

_____

Now continue exploring the Kingston site by following these steps:

1. Return to the Kingston home page, if necessary.
2. Click the **Memory Tools** link. A new page opens displaying several tools, one being the Memory Assessor. With this tool, you specify which OS you're researching, and Kingston displays a recommended amount of physical RAM based on usage criteria.
3. Using these tools, and perhaps other areas of the site, answer the following questions:

   ◢ In general, do operating systems for desktops and workstations require more or less memory than operating systems for servers?

   _____

   _____

   ◢ How wide is the data path on a 168-pin DIMM?

   _____

   ◢ DDR is an extension of what older memory technology?

   _____

   _____

   ◢ What does the SO in SO-DIMM represent?

   _____

   ◢ What is an advantage of loading an application entirely into RAM rather than loading part of that application into virtual memory (a page file)?

   _____

   _____

   _____

   ◢ What is another term for "page file," and why are page files used?

   _____

   _____

   ◢ How many bits of information does a single cell of a memory chip on a 256 MB PC2700 DDR module hold?

   _____

◢ Why might you have problems with a system in which you installed three known good RIMMs?

_____

_____

_____

◢ One memory technology uses only a 16-bit path. What acronym is used for this type of memory?

_____

◢ What type of material is used to make a memory "chip"?

_____

_____

◢ What function(s) does the aluminum plate on a RIMM serve?

_____

_____

◢ Why might you not mind using slower memory if faster memory is available for a marginal price difference?

_____

_____

◢ What is the system's bank schema, and why is it important when installing RAM?

_____

_____

◢ What is a memory performance measurement in which the lower the number, the better the performance?

_____

◢ What memory technology achieves better performance by using both the rising and falling sides of the clock cycle?

_____

_____

◢ List five considerations when upgrading memory:

_____

_____

_____

_____

◢ If a motherboard can support SDRAM or EDO, which would result in better performance?

_____

◢ What memory technology uses a heat spreader?

_____

◢ What types of memory do notebook computers typically use?

_____

◢ Name two characteristics of a system using RAMBUS licensed memory:

_____

_____

REVIEW QUESTIONS

1. Is a DIMM or RIMM more expensive, given that both hold the same amount of memory? Why do you think the price varies?

_____

_____

2. Summarize why adding RAM offers a performance advantage:

_____

_____

3. Which tool on the Kingston Web site could you use to find Kingston modules for your system if you know the model number of your system's motherboard?

_____

4. If you were planning to buy a new system, would you choose a motherboard that uses DIMMs or RIMMs? Why?

_____

_____

LAB 7.3 UPGRADE RAM

OBJECTIVES

The goal of this lab is to learn how to plan a memory upgrade and then perform the upgrade. After completing this lab, you will be able to:

◢ Estimate how much free memory your system has available during typical and stressed use

◢ Determine how much and what kind of memory is needed for an upgrade

◢ Upgrade RAM in your system

MATERIALS REQUIRED

This lab requires the following:

◢ Windows Vista/XP operating system

◢ SiSoftware Sandra Lite, installed in Lab 1.3

◢ Internet access

◢ A PC designated for disassembly

◢ A PC toolkit and antistatic wrist strap

◢ Additional memory module compatible with your system

LAB PREPARATION

Before the lab begins, the instructor or lab assistant needs to do the following:

◢ Verify that a computer designated for disassembly and a compatible memory module are available to each student or workgroup.

◢ Verify that Internet access is available.

ACTIVITY BACKGROUND

In this lab, you examine your system, gather information on its memory subsystem, and establish a memory usage baseline. Using this information, you then determine through further research whether the system can support a RAM upgrade required to run a computer-aided design (CAD) application. Finally, you install an additional memory module, examine your system again, and compare it against the baseline.

> **ESTIMATED COMPLETION TIME: 45 Minutes**

 Activity

1. Start SiSoftware Sandra Lite, and use it to answer the following questions about your system:

   ◢ What OS are you running?

   _____

   ◢ What type of processor is your system using?

   _____

   ◢ What is your motherboard's manufacturer and model?

   _____

   ◢ How many MB of RAM are currently installed?

   _____

   ◢ What type of memory modules are installed? Be as specific as you can.

   _____

   ◢ At what speed does the memory bus operate?

   _____

To establish a memory usage baseline, follow these steps:

1. Leaving Sandra open, launch one instance each of Windows Explorer, Paint, and Internet Explorer.

2. Use the Memory Usage tool under the Software tab in Sandra and record the amount of free physical memory. This is your memory baseline. How much memory is free?

_____

3. Open six more instances of Internet Explorer, browsing to a different site on each instance. Try to view a movie trailer or video, because this activity is memory intensive compared with displaying a static Web page.

4. Refresh the information in the Memory Usage tool by clicking **Next** (the green arrow). Record the free physical memory. How much memory is free now?

_____

The change is the result of the demands of running and displaying six additional Web pages.

Suppose your employer's Engineering Department is interested in deploying a CAD program that requires 1 GB of RAM more than what is currently in your system. Use your investigating skills to gather information on supporting the additional required RAM:

1. Can you upgrade your system's RAM without removing any of the current memory modules?

_____

2. What would be the least expensive upgrade to meet the new requirements?

_____

3. How would your answers to Questions 1 and 2 change if the CAD program required an additional 4 GB of RAM?

_____

_____

_____

_____

Next, you upgrade the memory by following these steps:

1. Shut down your system and remove all exterior cabling.

2. Be sure you're wearing your antistatic ground strap. Open the system case and locate the slots for memory modules.

3. Remove any data cabling and other devices preventing you from getting at the slots. Answer the following questions:

⊿ How many modules are currently installed?

_____

⊿ Are there any empty slots in which to install an additional module?

_____

4. Notice that the slots have a retaining mechanism at each end to secure the modules in the slot. Typically, these mechanisms are plastic levers that you spread outward to unseat and remove modules. Modules are inserted and removed straight up and down. Spread the plastic levers apart before inserting or removing the memory modules.

5. Examine an empty slot and note the raised ridges that line up with notches on the memory module's pin edge. Because modules are designed to be inserted in only one orientation, these ridges prevent them from being inserted incorrectly.

6. With the module oriented correctly, insert the module and gently but firmly push it in.

7. Reassemble your system.

Although purchasing a bad memory module is extremely rare, it's a good idea to give the system every opportunity to detect faulty memory. BIOS tests physical memory each time the system is booted. If a module is drastically flawed, usually the system won't boot. Instead, it issues a beep code indicating memory problems. Assuming that the module is in fairly good shape and the video has initialized, the system BIOS's POST routine typically displays a memory count in bytes as it tests memory.

Most POST routines run through the test three times before proceeding. You can usually skip this redundant testing by enabling a Quick POST in CMOS setup. Quick POST skips some parts of the POST test and is great for cutting down bootup time during normal use, but when installing new RAM, it's best to give the system every opportunity to detect a problem. Therefore, you should disable Quick POST until you're confident the module has no obvious problem. With this in mind, follow these steps to verify that the system recognizes the upgrade:

1. Boot the system and enter CMOS setup.

> **Notes** The first time you boot after a memory upgrade, the BIOS might display a memory mismatch error to let you know the memory has been changed.

2. Verify that Quick POST is disabled, and specify that you have installed additional memory, if necessary. (Telling CMOS about new memory isn't necessary unless you have a very old motherboard.)

3. Save your settings and reboot. Record whether the additional memory was recognized and how many times it was tested:

_____

4. Now perform the same memory usage baseline tests that you did earlier in this lab with the Memory Usage tool in Sandra. Record the results here:

   ◢ Amount of free memory with Sandra, Windows Explorer, Paint, and Internet Explorer open:

   _____

   ◢ Amount of free memory with the system heavily used:

   _____

5. When you have finished, remove the additional memory and return the system to its previous configuration.

REVIEW QUESTIONS

1. What is the minimum and recommended memory requirement for the OS your system is running?

_____

_____

2. What are at least two ways you can determine how much RAM is installed?

_____

_____

3. Which Sandra module(s) can be used to display information about system memory?

_____

_____

4. What feature is used on memory slots and modules to prevent modules from being inserted incorrectly?

_____

_____

5. In what situation might you want to disable Quick POST, and why?

_____

_____

LAB 7.4 USE VISTA READYBOOST

OBJECTIVES

The goal of this lab is to use ReadyBoost to increase the performance of Vista. After completing this lab, you will be able to:

◢ Enable ReadyBoost on a computer running Windows Vista

◢ Configure ReadyBoost for optimum performance

MATERIALS REQUIRED

This lab requires the following:

◢ Windows Vista operating system

◢ A 256 MB (or larger) USB flash drive that is ReadyBoost compliant

LAB PREPARATION

Before the lab begins, the instructor or lab assistant needs to do the following:

◢ Verify that a computer boots successfully to Windows Vista.

◢ Verify that the USB flash drive supports ReadyBoost.

ACTIVITY BACKGROUND

Most versions of Windows supplement their RAM by creating a paging file on the hard drive that acts as virtual memory. If a machine has too little RAM for the applications it's trying to support, the system performance can suffer since the access time of a hard drive is typically much slower than RAM. Because solid state flash drives typically have a faster access time than hard drives, Vista can speed up a system by caching some of the files on a flash drive instead of on a hard drive.

ESTIMATED COMPLETION TIME: 20 Minutes

 Activity

Systems with less RAM (512 MB or less) will experience the most noticeable gains with ReadyBoost because they rely more on the hard drive than systems with enough RAM to run all of their applications. Do the following to set up ReadyBoost on a computer running Windows Vista:

1. Begin by determining how much RAM is installed on your system (see Lab 7.1).

2. Now plug in a flash drive to the computer's USB port. If this is the first time this flash drive has been attached, the drivers will have to be automatically installed. When the installation is complete, the Autoplay dialog box will appear. See Figure 7-1.

Figure 7-1 Autoplay dialog box in Vista
Courtesy: Course Technology/Cengage Learning

3. If the Autoplay dialog box does not appear, go to **Computer**, right-click your flash drive, and select **Open AutoPlay**.

4. Select **Speed up my system**, and the ReadyBoost configuration page will be displayed. See Figure 7-2.

5. Select **Use this device** if it is not already selected. How much memory does Windows recommend reserving for optimal performance?

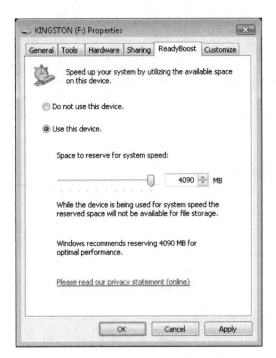

Figure 7-2   ReadyBoost configuration page
Courtesy: Course Technology/Cengage Learning

6. Click **OK**; from now on, a portion of the device will be used for ReadyBoost.

7. Now without removing the flash drive, reboot the system and answer the following questions:

   ◢ Based on the initial amount of RAM and the size of the flash drive, did you expect to see any change in performance? Why?

   _____

   _____

   ◢ Was the actual change in performance noticeable?

   _____

   ◢ How much space was left on the flash drive for saving files?

   _____

8. Finally, remove the flash drive and reboot the system again.

REVIEW QUESTIONS

1. Why does ReadyBoost increase the performance of a Windows Vista machine?

   _____

   _____

2. Do you think ReadyBoost would help a system that was already running the maximum RAM supported by the operating system? Why?

   _____

   _____

3. Which of the following would give a better increase in performance: adding more RAM or adding an equal amount of reserved space on a flash drive? Why?

_____

_____

4. Why do you think this feature would be particularly useful on an older laptop running Vista?

_____

_____

LAB 7.5 TROUBLESHOOT MEMORY PROBLEMS

OBJECTIVES

The goal of this lab is to give you hands-on experience in troubleshooting memory problems. After completing this lab, you will be able to:

◢ Identify some symptoms that indicate memory problems

◢ Identify a faulty module

◢ Use Memtest86 to test installed RAM

MATERIALS REQUIRED

This lab requires the following:

◢ Internet access (to download files)

◢ Windows Vista/XP operating system

◢ SiSoftware Sandra Lite, installed in Lab 1.3

◢ Burnable CD or blank floppy disk

◢ A PC designated for disassembly

◢ A PC toolkit and antistatic ground strap

LAB PREPARATION

Before the lab begins, the instructor or lab assistant needs to do the following:

◢ Verify that a computer designated for disassembly and a printer are available to each student or workgroup.

◢ Verify that Internet access is available. For labs that don't have Internet access, download the latest image of Memtest86 for the boot media selected from *www.memtest86.com* to a file server or other storage media available to students in the lab.

ACTIVITY BACKGROUND

The symptoms of faulty RAM are many and varied. Faulty memory can cause a complete failure to boot, fatal exception errors while working with an application, or catastrophic data loss. However, sometimes faulty memory is noticeable only as annoying interruptions while you're working. RAM that's outright dead is fairly easy to identify. If the dead module is the only module installed, the system won't boot. If it's one of several modules, you'll notice that the system reports less memory than you expected.

However, it's not common for a module to fail absolutely. More often, a module develops intermittent problems that cause data corruption, applications hanging at unexpected times, the system rebooting, or Windows Vista/XP hanging and displaying the "Blue Screen of Death" (which is an error message displayed on a blue background). In this lab, you learn how to detect and isolate faulty memory modules to prevent these problems.

ESTIMATED COMPLETION TIME: 60 Minutes

 Activity

Reliable memory function is essential to system operation. Therefore, when the system is booted, if memory isn't detected or if it has major problems, the startup BIOS begins emitting a beep code to define a general or particular memory problem. The memory testing on a computer is quite extensive. After POST startup does an initial test, the BIOS does a more thorough test of physical memory, which is usually repeated three times before the system summary is displayed and booting continues. Then while Windows is loading, it tests memory again.

These tests are all completed at startup, but often partially corrupted modules don't show a problem until they're running at certain temperatures. When problems do show up at certain temperatures, these problems are referred to as "thermal intermittents." Although thermal intermittents are difficult to nail down and document, they are actually fairly easy to remedy if the fault is on the memory module instead of on the motherboard.

Memtest86 is a utility that allows you to test the memory from a bootable CD or floppy disk. This kind of test is particularly useful in discovering a thermal intermittent fault.

In the following steps, you use Memtest86 to test installed RAM. First, you create a bootable CD or floppy disk with the Memtest86 software on it; you then use the boot disk to boot a PC and test memory on that PC. Follow these steps:

1. Open your browser, and go to **www.memtest86.com**. Click the **Free Download** link and then click either the **ISO image for creating a bootable CD** or the **Floppy disk package** for creating a bootable floppy disk.

2. Save the zipped image to your desktop.

3. To extract the compressed ISO file, double-click the downloaded folder and drag the uncompressed file to your desktop. The ISO contains a complete image of the files that will be copied to your blank CD. Copying these files requires a separate program. In this lab, we will use a free tool called ISO Recorder.

4. Open your browser and go to **http://isorecorder.alexfeinman.com** and download and install the version recommended for your particular OS.

5. Once ISO Recorder is installed, close any open windows and double-click the ISO file that was extracted in Step 3. The **CD Recording Wizard** will run automatically.

6. Insert a blank CD in your CD burner and click **Next** to begin recording. See Figure 7-3. When the recording is complete, click **Finish**.

7. The disk is now ready to be used on any computer. For the purpose of this lab, leave the disk in the system and reboot.

8. The system boots into the Memtest86 utility. From the boot menu, select the option appropriate to your computer hardware.

9. Allow the test to finish one pass and then press **Esc** to exit and reboot to Windows. Did the test detect any errors?

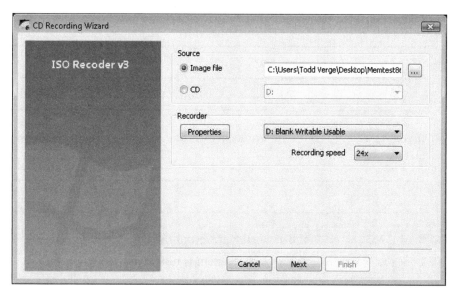

Figure 7-3 ISO Recorder's CD Recording Wizard
Courtesy: Course Technology/Cengage Learning

10. Return to the Memtest86 Web site, select **Technical Info**, and answer the following questions:

◢ What three options does Memtest86 have for reporting errors?

_____

_____

_____

◢ What is the first test (Test 0) performed by Memtest86?

_____

_____

◢ Why does Memtest86 not require operating system support to run?

_____

_____

Follow these steps to observe the effects of a faulty memory module and interpret beep codes:

1. Use Sandra to determine the BIOS manufacturer for your system, and record it here:

_____

2. Search documentation or the Internet for a list of beep codes for that manufacturer.

3. Shut down the system and remove all external cabling.

4. Put on your antistatic ground strap, open the case, remove all memory modules, and set them aside in an antistatic bag.

5. Reassemble the system, leaving out the memory.

6. Power up the system and describe the outcome, including any beep codes:

_____

_____

_____

7. If you heard beep codes, interpret their meaning using the information you found in Step 2:

_____

_____

8. Shut down the system, disassemble it, install the RAM, and reassemble.

9. Boot the system to verify that the system is functional.

REVIEW QUESTIONS

1. What are some common symptoms of a thermal intermittent?

_____

_____

2. How many times does POST usually test memory?

_____

3. Why must the Memtest86 software run from a boot disk?

_____

_____

4. Describe the symptoms caused by a dead memory module:

_____

_____

_____

5. Why would a continuous test be ideal for diagnosing a thermal intermittent?

_____

Supporting Hard Drives

Labs included in this chapter:

- **Lab 8.1:** Test Hard Drive Performance Using Sandra
- **Lab 8.2:** Use Disk Management
- **Lab 8.3:** Install a Second Hard Drive
- **Lab 8.4:** Use Hard Drive Utilities
- **Lab 8.5:** Troubleshoot Hard Drives
- **Lab 8.6:** Critical Thinking: Use Debug to Examine Disk Information
- **Lab 8.7:** Critical Thinking: Troubleshoot and Repair a Hard Drive

LAB 8.1 TEST HARD DRIVE PERFORMANCE USING SANDRA

OBJECTIVES

The goal of this lab is to help you use Sandra to compare the performance of your system's drives against similar drives. After completing this lab, you will be able to:

◢ Use Sandra to test your drives' performance

◢ Use Sandra to compare your system's drives with similar drives

MATERIALS REQUIRED

This lab requires the following:

◢ Windows Vista/XP operating system

◢ SiSoftware Sandra Lite, installed in Lab 1.3

LAB PREPARATION

Before the lab begins, the instructor or lab assistant needs to do the following:

◢ Verify that Windows starts with no errors.

ACTIVITY BACKGROUND

You can use Sandra to run a routine of several tests on your drive, report the results, and compare your drive to a selection of comparable drives. This lab gives you an indication of how your drive is performing and whether another product is available that better meets your performance needs. Some tasks, such as video editing, are demanding on the drive where files are stored; a faster drive can increase productivity. When making an upgrade decision, it's helpful to compare results reported by Sandra to information on other hard drives. In this lab, you use Sandra to test your drive.

ESTIMATED COMPLETION TIME: 30 Minutes

 Activity

Follow these steps to test your drive:

1. Start Sandra.

2. Click the **Benchmarks** tab to open the Benchmarks window.

3. Double-click the **Physical Disks** icon in the Storage Devices section, and then select the drive you're testing from the drop-down menu at the top. How is this drive displayed in the drop-down menu?

   _____

4. Click the **Next** button (green arrow) to initiate the scan and wait until Sandra has finished testing your drive before moving your mouse or doing anything else with the system. After the test is finished, a summary is displayed. Use the summary to answer the following questions:

   ◢ In the Current Drive field, what drive index is reported?

◢ What drives were compared to the current drive?

_____

_____

5. You can select other drives for comparison by choosing them from the drop-down menu under each of the reference drives. Select four reference drives that are closest in size to your drive and note their performance ratings. List two drives with a similar performance rating to the current drive:

_____

_____

6. Click the **Compare Prices** tab at the top. Which drive do you think is the best value and why?

_____

_____

7. Use the bottom field of the Physical Disks window to fill in the following chart. (Scroll down as necessary to display the information you need.)

Parameter	Value
Drive Index (MB/s)	
Random Access Times (ms)	
Capacity (GB)	
Interface	
Rotational Speed (rpm)	
Model	
Serial Number	
Windows Experience Index	

8. Once you are finished, exit Sandra and close all open windows.

REVIEW QUESTIONS

1. Why might you want to test your drive with Sandra?

_____

_____

2. Based on the drive ratings information you got from Sandra, does a drive perform better if it spins faster or slower?

_____

3. Based on the drive ratings information you got from Sandra, does a drive perform better if it reads data randomly or sequentially?

_____

4. Why shouldn't you use the system when Sandra is testing a drive?

_____

_____

LAB 8.2 USE DISK MANAGEMENT

OBJECTIVES

The goal of this lab is to help you use Disk Management to work with local hard drives. After completing this lab, you will be able to:

◢ Create a partition from unused disk space

◢ Specify a file system

◢ Format a partition

◢ Delete a partition

MATERIALS REQUIRED

This lab requires the following:

◢ Windows Vista/XP operating system

◢ A printer

◢ Windows Vista/XP installation CD or installation files

◢ Unallocated disk space

LAB PREPARATION

Before the lab begins, the instructor or lab assistant needs to do the following:

◢ Verify that Windows starts with no errors.

◢ Provide each student with access to the Windows Vista/XP Professional installation files, if needed.

◢ Verify that there is unallocated space on the hard drive.

ACTIVITY BACKGROUND

Disk Management is a Microsoft Management Console (MMC) snap-in and an administrative tool installed in the Computer Management console by default. To start Disk Management, you need to start Computer Management first. Unlike command-line utilities such as Diskpart or Fdisk, Disk Management allows you to partition and format disk space from within Windows. In this lab, you create and delete two different partitions using unallocated disk space.

ESTIMATED COMPLETION TIME: 30 Minutes

 Activity

To work with your local hard drive using Disk Management, follow these steps:

1. Log on with an administrator account. Open Control Panel, click **System and Maintenance** (**Performance and Maintenance** in XP), and then click **Administrative Tools**. The Administrative Tools window opens.

2. Double-click **Computer Management**. If Windows opens a User Account Control window, click **Continue**. The Computer Management snap-in opens in an MMC. In the left pane, click **Disk Management**. The Disk Management interface opens in the middle pane (the right pane in XP) (see Figure 8-1).

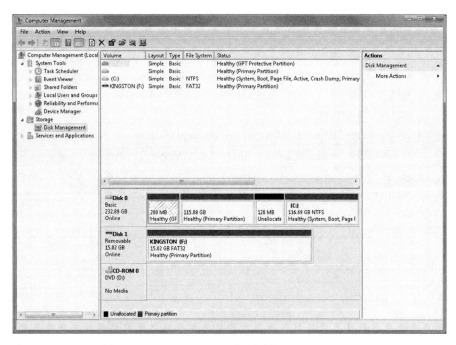

Figure 8-1 Use Disk Management to manage hard drives
Courtesy: Course Technology/Cengage Learning

3. Use the information at the top of the right pane to complete the following chart:

Volume	Layout	Type	File System	Status	Capacity

4. Information about each physical drive is displayed in the bottom section of the middle pane. In addition, a graphic shows each drive's space distribution. Note that drives are labeled with numbers (0, 1, and so forth) and logical drives or volumes are labeled with letters (C, D, E, and so forth). If a hard drive has just been installed and not yet partitioned, the graphic shows all unallocated (unpartitioned) space. What drive letters are used on your system?

5. Right-click a blank area of the C drive space in the Disk Management interface. A shortcut menu opens with the following options:

   ◢ *Open*—Displays the drive's contents in a window similar to Computer.

   ◢ *Explore*—Displays the drive's contents in a window similar to Windows Explorer.

   ◢ *Mark Partition as Active*—Marks the current partition as the partition from which Windows is loaded.

◢ *Change Drive Letter and Paths...*—Allows you to select a new letter for the drive. For instance, you can change the drive letter from C to F.

◢ *Format . . .* —Allows you to format a partition and make partition-related choices, including specifying the file system and sector size. (*Note*: Windows protects itself by disabling Format on the (System) partition.)

◢ *Extend Volume . . .* (Vista Only) —Allows you to increase the size of a volume on a drive.

◢ *Shrink Volume . . .* (Vista Only)—Allows you to decrease the size of a volume on a drive.

◢ *Delete Volume . . . (Delete Partition in XP)*—Allows you to delete an entire volume and all its contents.

◢ *Properties*—Displays information about the partition, such as how it's formatted.

◢ *Help*—Provides information about Disk Management.

6. Right-click the unpartitioned area of the disk drive, which is labeled Unallocated. List the differences between the options in this shortcut menu and the menu you examined in Step 5:

_____

_____

In the next set of steps, you create a new partition from unpartitioned space. Note that the partition you're creating should use only *currently unpartitioned* space. Follow these steps:

1. Using only *unpartitioned space*, create and format a new partition using the FAT32 file system and drive letter S. (If S is not available, choose another letter that isn't being used.) List the steps to perform this task:

_____

_____

_____

_____

2. Print a screen shot of the Disk Management window showing the FAT32 drive S.

3. Delete the partition you just created. List the steps to perform this task:

_____

_____

4. Using only *unpartitioned space*, create and format a new NTFS partition using the drive letter H or a different letter if H is not available. List the steps to perform this task:

_____

_____

_____

5. Print a screen shot of the Disk Management window showing the NTFS drive H.

6. Close the Computer Management window.

CRITICAL THINKING: MANAGING PARTITIONS FROM THE WINDOWS XP RECOVERY CONSOLE (ADDITIONAL 60 MINUTES)

Note: In Windows Vista, Recovery Console has been replaced by a command prompt that can be accessed from the installation disk. Working at the command prompt in Vista will be covered in Chapter 15.

Do the following to practice managing partitions from the Recovery Console:

1. Open the Windows XP Recovery Console. List the steps to perform this task:

_____

_____

_____

2. Open Help and display information about the Diskpart command, including possible command-line options. List the steps to perform this task:

_____

_____

_____

3. Delete the NTFS partition you created earlier using Disk Management. List the steps to perform this task:

_____

_____

_____

4. Create and format a new NTFS partition, using the drive letter R. List the steps to perform this task:

_____

_____

_____

5. Delete the newly created partition. List the steps to perform this task:

_____

_____

_____

REVIEW QUESTIONS

1. Name an advantage that Disk Management has over Diskpart:

_____

2. Name an advantage that Diskpart has over Disk Management:

_____

3. What happens to all the information in a partition if you delete the partition?

_____

_____

4. What feature opens if you choose Explore from a shortcut menu in Disk Management?

_____

5. Is it possible to create two partitions from one area of unallocated disk space and to do so using different file systems? Explain:

_____

_____

_____

LAB 8.3 INSTALL A SECOND HARD DRIVE

OBJECTIVES

The goal of this lab is to install a second internal hard drive. After completing this lab, you will be able to:

◢ Physically install a new hard drive

◢ Configure hard drive jumpers for proper operation

◢ Configure a hard drive in the BIOS setup

MATERIALS REQUIRED

This lab requires the following:

◢ A computer that can be disassembled

◢ A second internal hard drive that can be installed

◢ A PC toolkit with antistatic wrist strap

◢ A workgroup of 2 to 4 students

LAB PREPARATION

Before the lab begins, the instructor or lab assistant needs to do the following:

◢ Verify that Windows starts with no errors.

◢ Verify that a second compatible hard drive is available for installation.

ACTIVITY BACKGROUND

Over time, users often find that the original hard drive in a system is no longer large enough to meet their needs. To avoid the trouble of replacing the hard drive and reinstalling the operating system, many people add a second hard drive. Although external USB or network drives are easier to install, internal drives generally offer better performance.

Activity

1. Examine the new hard drive to determine the answers to the following questions:

   ◢ What is the manufacturer and model of the hard drive?

   _____

   ◢ What size is the hard drive?

   _____

   ◢ What interface does the hard drive use (ATA or SATA)?

   _____

2. Determine if the new drive will be sharing a data cable with an existing drive or if it will have a data cable of its own. Record your determination below:

   _____

If the drive is sharing a data cable, the jumpers on both drives may need to be configured so that both drives are set to cable select (CS) or one drive is set as master (MA) and one is set as slave (SL). If the jumpers are not set properly, the BIOS may not be able to detect the new drive. If you're unsure about how to set the jumpers, you can either consult the hard drive's documentation or ask your instructor. Most ATA drives are labeled with a diagram showing the proper master and slave jumper settings, as shown in Figure 8-2.

3. Install the new hard drive in a free bay and attach both the data and power cables, as shown in Figure 8-3. (See Lab 4.2 if you need a refresher on how to execute this step.)

4. Boot the computer into the CMOS setup screen (see Lab 5.1 for supplemental information) and ensure that the BIOS autodetects the new hard drive. Is the size reported by the BIOS exactly the same as the size written on the drive?

   _____

5. Boot the computer into Windows and use the Disk Management utility to examine the drive (see Lab 8.2, if necessary).

6. Answer the following questions:

   ◢ Is the new drive formatted? If so, what file system is being used?

   _____

   ◢ Does the new drive contain any unpartitioned space?

   _____

   ◢ How does the size reported by Windows compare with the size reported by the BIOS or written on the drive?

   _____

   _____

7. Now remove the drive and return the computer to its original state.

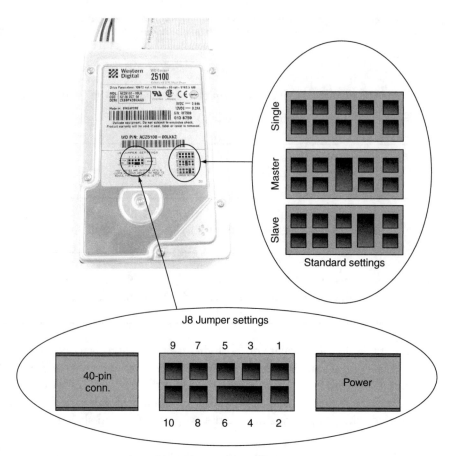

Figure 8-2   Jumper settings are usually printed on the drive housing
Courtesy: Course Technology/Cengage Learning

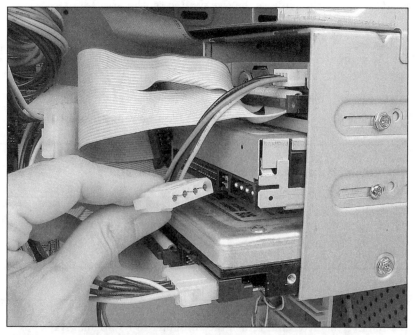

Figure 8-3   Attach the data and power cables
Courtesy: Course Technology/Cengage Learning

REVIEW QUESTIONS

1. Why might someone need to install a second hard drive?

   _____

   _____

2. What is one way to determine how to set the jumpers on a hard drive?

   _____

   _____

3. What can happen if the jumpers on both drives are not configured properly?

   _____

   _____

4. Why do you think the drive label, the BIOS, and the operating system sometimes report slightly different sizes for a hard drive?

   _____

   _____

5. List the steps used in installing a second hard drive:

   _____

   _____

   _____

   _____

   _____

LAB 8.4 USE HARD DRIVE UTILITIES

OBJECTIVES

The goal of this lab is to give you an opportunity to work with utilities from hard drive manufacturers that examine and diagnose hard drive problems. After completing this lab, you will be able to:

▴ Identify your hard drive manufacturer

▴ Evaluate utilities that hard drive manufacturers provide for their drives

▴ Test for hard drive problems

MATERIALS REQUIRED

This lab requires the following:

▴ Windows Vista/XP operating system

▴ SiSoftware Sandra Lite, installed in Lab 1.3

◢ Internet access

◢ A printer

◢ A blank floppy disk or burnable CD and drive

LAB PREPARATION

Before the lab begins, the instructor or lab assistant needs to do the following:

◢ Verify that Windows starts with no errors.

◢ Verify that Internet access is available.

ACTIVITY BACKGROUND

Hard drive problems can manifest themselves in different ways. The drive might exhibit immediate and total failure so that it doesn't operate at all. If the failure is caused by a problem with the platters, you might not be able to boot at all if the area where system files are stored is affected. If system files aren't affected, you might be able to boot and work normally but could have file loss or file corruption. Then again, you might never realize you have a hard drive problem if your hard drive has bad sectors because data might not be saved to that particular physical area of the disk. More often, however, when a disk begins to fail, you notice errors. One tool you can use to diagnose hard drive problems is diagnostic software that your hard drive manufacturer supplies. In this lab, you identify your drive manufacturer and use its software to examine your drive.

ESTIMATED COMPLETION TIME: 60 Minutes

 Activity

When you need to use a hard drive diagnostic utility, first you must identify your hard drive's manufacturer and model number.

1. Use Sandra to find the following information on the hard drive you wish to test (see Lab 8.1, if necessary):

   ◢ Manufacturer:

   _____

   ◢ Model number:

   _____

2. Remove the case cover and physically examine the hard drive for a label.

3. How does the label information compare to what you learned using Sandra?

   _____

   _____

4. When you're finished examining the hard drive, be sure to replace the case cover.

Next, you find out about hard drive utilities supplied by several hard drive manufacturers.

The Hitachi line of hard drives provides a Drive Fitness Test (DFT) for its hard drives. Do the following to find out about this software:

1. In your Web browser, go to **www.hitachigst.com**. Point to **Support**, and then click **Downloads**.

2. Click **Drive Fitness Test** and open **Drive Fitness Test User's Guide**. Search the information about the product, and answer the following questions:

   ◢ What two types of boot media are supported by DFT?

   _____

   _____

   ◢ Does DFT support drives manufactured by other OEM manufactures? Are any features not tested?

   _____

   _____

   ◢ If you have Linux installed on your system, how can you still create a bootable floppy disk to use the utility?

   _____

   _____

3. If you have an IBM or Hitachi drive, click the link to download the Drive Fitness Test utility and save it in its own folder. What is the filename and path to the file?

   _____

Western Digital provides Data Lifeguard Tools. Do the following to find out about this software:

1. In your Web browser, go to **http://support.wdc.com** and search for the **Data Lifeguard Tools User Manual** using the Search box in the upper-right side of the Web page. Click the appropriate link in the search results to open the user manual in PDF format.

2. Examine the information and answer these questions:

   ◢ What are the four basic functions of this software?

   _____

   _____

   _____

   _____

   ◢ Which forms of boot media are supported by Data Lifeguard Tools?

   _____

   _____

3. If you have a Western Digital drive, click the link appropriate to your model of hard drive in the Downloads section to download the utility and save it to its own folder. What is the filename and path to the file?

   _____

Seagate offers SeaTools. Do the following to find out about this software:

1. In your Web browser, go to **http://www.seagate.com/www/en-us/support/downloads/seatools** and click the **Learn More** link for SeaTools for Windows.

2. Examine the information and answer these questions:

◢ Give three reasons why a perfectly good drive might be considered damaged and in need of being returned to the manufacturer:

_____

_____

_____

◢ Why should you close all other applications before running SeaTools?

_____

_____

3. If you have a Seagate or Maxtor drive, click the link to download this utility and save the file to its own folder. What is the filename and path to the file?

_____

Next, follow these steps to use a manufacturer's utility to test your drive:

1. If your drive is from one of the previous manufacturers, follow the instructions on your drive manufacturer's Web site to create a bootable CD or floppy disk and use it to perform the test for your hard drive.

2. Summarize the process and results:

_____

_____

_____

_____

3. If your hard drive isn't made by one of the previous manufacturers, go to your manufacturer's Web site and search for diagnostic software. What software did you find?

_____

REVIEW QUESTIONS

1. What are some symptoms of hard drive problems listed on the hard drive manufacturers' Web sites? List three in order of seriousness:

_____

_____

_____

2. Which hard drive manufacturer's Web site was the most informative and easiest to use? Why?

_____

_____

_____

3. Which utility from a hard drive manufacturer seemed to be the most powerful? Why?

_____

_____

_____

4. What was the most common method used to run the utilities?

_____

5. Why is it useful to run the utility from a bootable CD or floppy disk rather than from Windows?

_____

6. What operating system is used on the bootable CD or floppy disk?

_____

7. How do you determine that your system is set to boot from a CD or floppy disk?

_____

LAB 8.5 TROUBLESHOOT HARD DRIVES

OBJECTIVES

The goal of this lab is to help you troubleshoot common hard drive problems. After completing this lab, you will be able to:

▲ Simulate common hard drive problems

▲ Diagnose and repair common hard drive problems

▲ Document the process

MATERIALS REQUIRED

This lab requires the following:

▲ A computer with a hard drive subsystem that you can sabotage

▲ Windows Vista/XP operating system

▲ A bootable floppy disk or CD

▲ A PC toolkit with antistatic ground strap

▲ A workgroup of 2 to 4 students

LAB PREPARATION

Before the lab begins, the instructor or lab assistant needs to do the following:

▲ Verify that Windows starts with no errors.

▲ Verify that a computer with a hard drive that can be sabotaged is available for each student or workgroup.

ACTIVITY BACKGROUND

This lab gives you practice diagnosing and remedying common hard drive problems.

ESTIMATED COMPLETION TIME: 45 Minutes

Activity

1. Verify that your hard drive is working by using a command prompt window or Windows Explorer to display files on the drive.

2. Switch computers with another team.

3. Sabotage the other team's computer by doing one of the following:

   ◢ Remove the power connector from the drive.

   ◢ Remove, loosen, or incorrectly configure the data cable.

   ◢ Remove, loosen, or incorrectly configure the drive jumpers.

4. Return to your computer and examine it for any symptoms of a problem.

5. On a separate piece of paper, answer the following questions about the problem's symptoms:

   ◢ What symptoms would a user notice? (Describe the symptoms as a user might describe them.)

   ◢ Does the system boot from the hard drive?

   ◢ Does POST display the hard drive?

   ◢ Can you boot from an alternative boot device such as a bootable CD or floppy disk and change to the drive in question?

   ◢ Does the CMOS HDD Autodetect option detect the hard drive?

6. On a separate piece of paper, before you actually begin your investigation, state your initial diagnosis.

7. Diagnose and repair the problem.

8. On a separate piece of paper, list the steps to confirm your diagnosis and solve the problem.

9. Answer the following questions about your final conclusions:

   ◢ What was the problem?

   _____

   ◢ What did you do to correct the problem?

   _____

   _____

   _____

   ◢ Was your preliminary diagnosis correct?

   _____

10. Repeat Steps 1 through 9, choosing actions at random from the list in Step 3, until your team has performed all the actions. Be sure to write down the relevant information (as instructed in the steps) for each problem.

REVIEW QUESTIONS

1. What was the first indication that the power was disconnected from your drive?

_____

_____

2. In what incorrect drive configuration would you be able to access files on the hard drive by booting from the CD or floppy drive?

_____

_____

3. What incorrect configurations have similar symptoms?

_____

_____

4. What problem resulted in no drives being detected except for the CD or floppy drive?

_____

_____

5. List the steps to use a drive whose partitions have been deleted:

_____

_____

_____

_____

_____

LAB 8.6 CRITICAL THINKING: USE DEBUG TO EXAMINE DISK INFORMATION

OBJECTIVES

The goal of this lab is to help you use the Debug utility to examine the beginning of a floppy drive. After completing this lab, you will be able to:

◢ Use Debug commands

◢ Explain how Debug displays information

◢ Examine the boot record on a floppy disk

MATERIALS REQUIRED

This lab requires the following:

◢ Windows Vista/XP operating system

◢ A blank floppy disk

LAB PREPARATION

Before the lab begins, the instructor or lab assistant needs to do the following:

◢ Verify that Windows starts with no errors.

ACTIVITY BACKGROUND

In this lab, you use the Debug tool to examine the boot record of a startup floppy disk. The file system on a floppy disk is similar to that of a hard drive, so the concepts you learn here about floppy disks can be applied to hard drives.

Using Debug, you can view the contents of a disk or memory location. This information helps you gain the strong technical insight you need to take advantage of more user-friendly data-recovery software and to be confident that you understand how these products work. The better you understand how data is constructed on the disk and exactly what problems can happen, the better are your chances of recovering lost or damaged data.

ESTIMATED COMPLETION TIME: 45 Minutes

 Activity

Follow these steps to create a Windows startup disk:

1. Boot your PC into Windows and then insert a blank floppy disk.

2. Go to a third-party Web site such as **www.bootdisk.com** to create a bootable floppy. Follow the on-screen instructions to create a bootable 98SE floppy. After the formatting is completed, you'll have a bootable startup disk

3. Click **Start**, type **cmd,** and press **Enter** in the Start Search box to open a command prompt window. (In XP click **Start, Run.** Type **cmd** and click **OK.**) At the command prompt, type **debug** and press **Enter.** The Debug utility starts, and the prompt changes to a dash (–).

The Debug utility can be used to examine and change the contents of a location in memory. Although Debug can't edit storage devices directly, it can also be used to view data on a storage device, such as a floppy disk or hard drive, by copying the data into memory first. To examine the startup disk you just created, first you have to copy some of its contents into memory. Follow these steps:

> **Notes** You can see a full list of Debug commands by typing ? at the prompt.

1. To view information, you're going to use the D command (which stands for "dump"). Type **D** and press **Enter.**

2. Observe the output of the D command, which shows the contents of memory beginning with a memory address (see Figure 8-4). Note that this command displays memory 128 bytes at a time. The information is in lines of 16 bytes each, with the start address at the left side, the hex value of each byte in the middle, and the ASCII interpretation (if any) of each byte at the right side.

3. Each time you dump memory, the pointer in memory moves to the next group of 128 bytes. By using successive dump commands, you can move through memory consecutively, dumping 128 bytes of memory to the screen with each command. To view the next 128 bytes, simply type **D** and press **Enter** again.

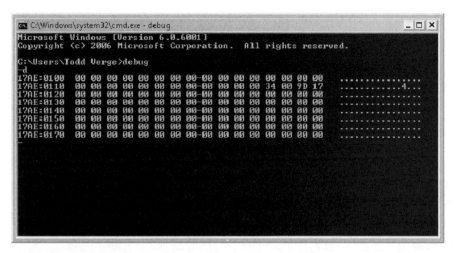

Figure 8-4 Results of the Debug D command showing the contents of 128 bytes of memory
Courtesy: Course Technology/Cengage Learning

8

4. If the contents of memory aren't ASCII text, the attempt to display the ASCII interpretation looks like gibberish in that section. Continue to scan each 128-byte section until you've examined the next 1 KB of memory (8 x 128 B = 1 KB). The content of the memory will depend on your system but will most likely be empty. Did you find anything but empty space in the 1 KB that you examined?

_____

_____

5. The next step is to copy, or load, the boot record from the floppy disk into memory. Type **L0 0 0 1** and press **Enter**. You should hear the floppy drive run. Type **?** and press **Enter** for help and answer these questions to decipher the command:

◢ What does "L" stand for?

_____

◢ What does the first 0 indicate?

_____

◢ What does the second 0 indicate?

_____

◢ What does the third 0 indicate?

_____

◢ What does the 1 indicate?

_____

6. The information from this sector of the floppy disk is now loaded in system memory. To view this information, type **D0** and press **Enter**. Can you see any indication of which file system is used to format the floppy disk? Explain:

_____

_____

7. Table 8-1 lists the items in the boot record. You can see from the table that the seventeenth byte (which is at the start of line two) indicates the number of File Allocation Tables (FATs). How many FAT tables are used on the floppy?

8. Continue to scroll through the content of the disk for several more screens with the D command. What error message do you see written out in ASCII text?

Description	Number of Bytes
Machine code	11
Bytes per sector	2
Sectors per cluster	1
Reserved	2
Number of FATs	1
Number of root directory entries	2
Number of logical sectors	2
Medium descriptor byte	1
Sectors per FAT	2
Sectors per track	2
Heads	2
Number of hidden sectors	2
Total sectors in logical volume	4
Physical drive number	1
Reserved	1
Extended boot signature record	1
32-bit binary volume ID	4
Volume label	11
Type of file system (FAT12, FAT16, or FAT32)	8
Program to load operating system (bootstrap loader)	Remainder of the sector

Table 8-1 Layout of the boot record of a floppy disk or hard drive

9. To exit Debug, type **Q** and press **Enter**. You return to the command prompt.

REVIEW QUESTIONS

1. Why do storage devices have to be copied into memory before their contents can be viewed in Debug?

2. What Debug command dumps data at the beginning of the memory address space?

3. What command loads two sectors from the C drive, starting at the sixth sector?

   _____

   _____

4. Debug displays data _____ bytes at a time.

5. Why do you think it's important to be careful when tinkering with the Debug utility?

   _____

   _____

LAB 8.7 CRITICAL THINKING: TROUBLESHOOT AND REPAIR A HARD DRIVE

OBJECTIVES

The goal of this lab is to learn to troubleshoot a more complicated hard drive by repairing a sabotaged system.

MATERIALS REQUIRED

This lab requires the following:

- A PC designated for sabotage (and containing no important data)
- Windows Vista/XP operating system
- Nonworking hard drive (optional)
- Nonworking hard drive data cable (optional)
- A workgroup of 2 to 4 students

LAB PREPARATION

Before the lab begins, the instructor or lab assistant needs to do the following:

- Verify that Windows starts with no errors.
- Verify that a PC that can be sabotaged is available for each student or workgroup.

ACTIVITY BACKGROUND

You have learned about several tools and methods for troubleshooting and recovering from a hard drive failure. This lab gives you the opportunity to use these skills in a troubleshooting situation. Your group will work with another group to sabotage a system, and then you recover your own sabotaged system.

ESTIMATED COMPLETION TIME: 45 Minutes

 Activity

1. If your system's hard drive contains important data, back it up to another medium. Is there anything else you would like to back up before another group sabotages the system?

   _____

2. Trade systems with another group and sabotage the other group's system while that group sabotages your system. Do something from the list below that will cause the hard drive to fail to work or return errors after the boot. For an extra challenge, try introducing more than one problem.

3. Use any of the problems suggested in Lab 8.5, or do one of the following:
   ◢ Replace the data cable with a nonworking one (if available).
   ◢ Replace the hard drive with a nonworking model (if available).
   ◢ Disable the hard drive or hard drive controller in CMOS setup.
   ◢ Remove the hard drive from the boot order.

   What did you do to sabotage the other group's system?

   _____

   _____

4. Return to your system and troubleshoot it.

5. Describe the problem as a user would describe it to you if you were working at a help desk:

   _____

   _____

6. What is your first guess as to the source of the problem?

   _____

7. List the steps you took in the troubleshooting process:

   _____

   _____

   _____

   _____

   _____

   _____

8. What did you do that finally solved the problem and returned the system to good working order?

   _____

   _____

9. Repeat Steps 1 through 8 for each of the members in your group.

REVIEW QUESTIONS

1. Now that you have been through this troubleshooting experience, what would you do differently the next time the same symptoms were exhibited?

   _____

2. What operating system utilities did you use or could you have used to solve the problem?

_____

3. Is there any third-party software that might have been useful in solving this problem?

_____

4. In a real-life situation, what might happen that would cause this problem to occur? List three things:

_____

_____

_____

Installing and Supporting I/O Devices

Labs included in this chapter:

LAB 9.1 GATHER INFORMATION ON I/O DEVICES

OBJECTIVES

The goal of this lab is to use various sources to compile information on your system's I/O devices, drivers, and the resources they use. After completing this lab, you will be able to:

- ◢ Use various Sandra modules to gather additional information about your system
- ◢ Use Control Panel applets to get information about your system
- ◢ Compile a documentation notebook

MATERIALS REQUIRED

This lab requires the following:

- ◢ Windows Vista/XP operating system
- ◢ Documentation you collected about your computer in Lab 1.3
- ◢ SiSoftware Sandra Lite, installed in Lab 1.3

LAB PREPARATION

Before the lab begins, the instructor or lab assistant needs to do the following:

- ◢ Verify that Windows starts with no errors.
- ◢ Verify that Sandra is installed or available.

ACTIVITY BACKGROUND

As you continue to work with different kinds of computers, you'll find it extremely useful to maintain a report listing the components installed on each computer. This report is especially important if you're responsible for many computers. In this lab, you create such a report. (Note that you may wish to refer to this document in future labs.) You can also use Sandra in this lab, which you installed in Lab 1.3.

ESTIMATED COMPLETION TIME: 45 Minutes

 Activity

Fill in Tables 9-1 through 9-3, which will become part of the total documentation you keep about your PC. If you're using the same system that you used in earlier labs, you can refer to the documentation about your computer that you've already collected. Otherwise, use the applets in the Control Panel and the Sandra software to compile new information. If you aren't sure which menus and applets to use in the Control Panel or Sandra, experiment to find the information you need. Some information can be found in more than one place. If you can't find some information or the entry doesn't seem to apply, just leave the section empty.

   After you have finished filling in the tables, make copies and attach them to the computer or place them in a documentation notebook for the lab.

Information Type	Your Information
Location of computer	
Owner	
Date purchased	
Date warranty expires	
Operating system (type and version)	
Size and speed of CPU	
Type of motherboard	
Type and amount of RAM	
Type of monitor	
Type of video card	
Hard drive(s) type and size	
Type of keyboard and mouse	
Other internal I/O card	
Other external I/O devices	

Table 9-1   Computer fact sheet

Software Install Name	Version	Installed By	Date

Table 9-2   Software installed

Name of Device	IRQ Channel	I/O Address Range	DMA Channel	Driver File Name and Location
USB port(s)				
Serial port(s)				
Parallel port(s)				
Mouse				
Keyboard				
Modem				
CD/DVD-ROM drive(s)				
Display adapter(s)				
Network card				
Other				

Table 9-3   Other devices

REVIEW QUESTIONS

1. What steps did you use to determine the CPU type?

_____

_____

_____

_____

2. List the steps you used to determine what driver is used by your display adapter:

_____

_____

_____

_____

3. List two ways to determine the amount of RAM installed on a system:

_____

_____

4. Suppose you want to add a legacy sound to your system that uses IRQ 5. What, if anything, is currently using this resource?

_____

5. Why is it important for PC technicians to keep documentation on computers for which they are responsible?

_____

_____

LAB 9.2 IDENTIFY HARDWARE CONFLICTS USING DEVICE MANAGER

OBJECTIVES

The goal of this lab is to help you learn to use Device Manager to identify hardware conflicts. After completing this lab, you will be able to:

◢ Use Device Manager to investigate your system specifications

◢ Detect hardware conflicts using Device Manager

◢ Use Device Manager properties to determine which resources are causing a conflict

MATERIALS REQUIRED

This lab requires the following:

◢ Windows Vista/XP operating system

⊿ A PC with no hardware resource conflicts

⊿ A hardware device, such as a sound card, you can install to create a hardware resource conflict

⊿ Windows installation CD/DVD or installation files

LAB PREPARATION

Before the lab begins, the instructor or lab assistant needs to do the following:

⊿ Verify that Windows starts with no errors.

⊿ Verify that the system is free of resource conflicts.

⊿ Provide a device that can be used to create a resource conflict.

⊿ Provide each student with access to the Windows installation files, if needed.

ACTIVITY BACKGROUND

Device Manager is an excellent tool for finding information about hardware specifications. You can also use it to diagnose problems with hardware devices, including those caused by two or more devices attempting to use the same system resources (a situation called a hardware resource conflict). Among other things, Device Manager can identify faulty or disabled devices, conflicting devices, and resources currently in use. This lab teaches you how to use Device Manager to find this information. You start by examining your system and verifying that no hardware resource conflicts currently exist on your system. Then you install a device that creates a resource conflict and observe the effects.

9

ESTIMATED COMPLETION TIME: 30 Minutes

 Activity

You can use Device Manager to find information about your system. Recording this information when your system is working correctly is a good idea because you can use that report later as a baseline comparison when troubleshooting conflicts or other problems.

Follow these steps to gather information with Device Manager:

1. Click **Start**, and then click **Control Panel**.

2. Click **System and Maintenance**, and then click **Device Manager**.

3. If Windows needs permission to continue, click **Continue**. The Device Manager console opens, as seen in Figure 9-1.

4. In Windows XP, click **Start, Control Panel, Performance and Maintenance**, and **System**. Then, click **Device Manager** on the Hardware tab.

5. Spend some time exploring Device Manager and then answer the following:

⊿ In the View menu, what is the default way that devices are organized?

_____

⊿ Which category most likely contains information about your video card?

_____

⊿ List two input devices displayed in the Device Manager window:

_____

_____

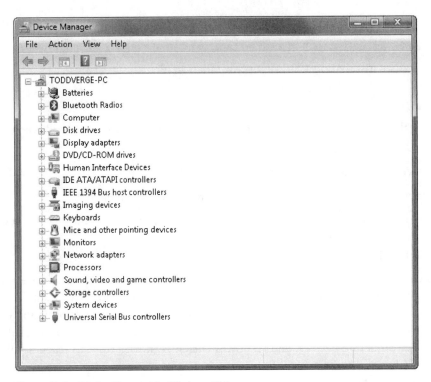

Figure 9-1 Device Manager in Windows Vista
Courtesy: Course Technology/Cengage Learning

Next, you use Device Manager to verify that there are no hardware conflicts:

1. Using Device Manager, check for conflicts among devices. Conflicts are indicated by a yellow triangle with an exclamation point. A gray circle with a white down arrow indicates that a device has been disabled and isn't working at all. (In XP, it's indicated by a red X.)

2. Shut down the system, and install the component and its drivers that your instructor supplied. This component should conflict with another component already installed on the system. If you don't have a device that causes a conflict, remove a nonessential device, such as a modem card or sound card, which at least causes Device Manager to report an error.

3. Reboot and install drivers if prompted. You might be asked to provide access to Windows setup files. Did you see a message indicating a conflict or other error? If so, record it here:

_____

_____

4. Open Device Manager. Does Device Manager report any conflicting devices? Describe the problem as Device Manager reports it, listing all devices causing conflicts:

_____

_____

5. For each device reporting a conflict, open the device's Properties dialog box by right-clicking the device and clicking **Properties** in the shortcut menu. What messages do you see in the Device status section?

_____

_____

6. Next, click the **Resources** tab in the Properties dialog box. What message do you see in the Conflicting device list section?

_____

7. Examine the information in the Resource type and Setting columns. What resources is the device using?

_____

8. Does it seem that you might be able to change settings for this device?

_____

9. Close the device's Properties dialog box, but leave Device Manager open if you're doing the Critical Thinking Activity.

CRITICAL THINKING (ADDITIONAL 15 MINUTES)

When you physically remove a device from your system that is not hot swappable, you should also remove it in Device Manager. If you don't, when you want to install a similar or the same device later, you end up with two devices installed under Device Manager, which can cause the new device not to work.

Follow these steps to uninstall the device in Device Manager and then remove it:

1. In Device Manager, right-click the device, and then click **Uninstall** in the shortcut menu. In the Confirm Device Uninstall dialog box that opens, click **OK**. If prompted to restart the computer, click **No**.

2. Close Device Manager and shut down the system.

3. Remove the device you installed earlier.

4. Restart the computer, open Device Manager, and verify that no conflicts exist before exiting from Device Manager.

REVIEW QUESTIONS

1. What symbol in Device Manager indicates that a component isn't working correctly?

_____

2. What two devices in your system were in conflict?

_____

3. What resources were causing a conflict?

_____

_____

4. Before physically removing a device from a system, what should you do?

_____

5. What would happen if you didn't uninstall the device before removing it from your system?

_____

LAB 9.3 RESEARCH HIGH-END VIDEO CARDS

OBJECTIVES

The goal of this lab is to help you gather information about new video cards. After completing this lab, you will be able to:

◢ Research video cards on the manufacturer's Web site

◢ Choose a video card to meet your needs

MATERIALS REQUIRED

This lab requires the following:

◢ A working computer with Internet access

◢ Adobe Acrobat Reader

LAB PREPARATION

Before the lab begins, the instructor or lab assistant needs to do the following:

◢ Verify the Internet is available.

ACTIVITY BACKGROUND

The choice of video card can have a profound effect on your computer's performance, especially with applications that use 3-D effects such as CAD software or games. To meet the ever-increasing requirements of some new programs or operating systems, many people choose to upgrade their video card. In this lab, you will research several new video cards on the Internet.

ESTIMATED COMPLETION TIME: 30 Minutes

 Activity

In this scenario, you have been asked to upgrade the video cards in several systems according to specific criteria. All the systems currently use on-board video, but each has a free PCIe 2.0 x16 slot. In each case, you will be working within a limited budget. You have already decided to limit your search to the two largest manufacturers of video cards, ATI/AMD (*www.amd.com*) and NVIDIA (*www.nvidia.com*). Both sites offer a method of comparing products:

1. Go to **www.amd.com**. In the Compare Products section, select **Desktop** as the System Type and **Graphics** as the Component Category. Click the **View Results** button.

2. Use the check boxes to select five of the products and click **Compare Selected Items**. Do they all use the same GPU? Which one(s) do they use?

_____

_____

3. Which card(s) support the most video memory?

_____

_____

4. AMD/ATI sells manufacturing rights to several different companies. What manufacturers produce these cards?

_____

_____

5. Which card(s) support the HDMI connection type?

_____

6. Which of these ATI video cards would you choose for a gaming machine? What criteria influenced your choice?

_____

_____

7. Now go to **www.nvidia.com** and click **Choose. Compare. Buy.** in the **Enjoy** section.

8. Follow the on-screen instructions to select four video cards and click **Compare.** Which card offered the best graphics performance?

_____

9. What was the maximum DVI resolution of the best card?

_____

10. Which card(s) was SLI ready?

_____

_____

11. What was the minimum power requirement of the fastest card?

_____

12. Which of these NVIDIA video cards would you choose for a gaming machine? What criteria influenced your choice?

_____

_____

Now use these two Web sites to find the best new video card for each of the systems below. Be sure to include the model number and price.

1. A Vista-certified video card for under $100:

_____

_____

2. A card that supports Direct X 10 and uses less than 300W for less than $200:

_____

_____

3. A card that incorporates a TV tuner and DVI outputs for less than $250:

_____

_____

4. A 1 GB or better high-end gaming system for less than $300:

_____

_____

5. A pair of SLI or CrossFire cards for less than $800 total:

_____

_____

REVIEW QUESTIONS

1. When might you choose not to upgrade your video card?

_____

2. Which manufacturer had the largest selection of video cards?

_____

3. When upgrading a video card, why might you also have to upgrade your power supply?

_____

_____

4. Which Web site did you find most informative? Why?

_____

_____

LAB 9.4 INSTALL AND TEST A SCANNER

OBJECTIVES

The goal of this lab is to give you experience installing and testing a scanner. After completing this lab, you will be able to:

◢ Install a scanner on a computer

◢ Test the scanner for functionality

MATERIALS REQUIRED

This lab requires the following:

◢ Windows Vista/XP operating system

◢ Windows installation CD or installation files

◢ An administrator account and password, if applicable

⊿ A USB scanner

⊿ Any necessary installation software or drivers for the scanner

LAB PREPARATION

Before the lab begins, the instructor or lab assistant needs to do the following:

⊿ Verify that Windows starts with no errors.

⊿ Provide each student with access to the Windows installation files, if needed.

ACTIVITY BACKGROUND

A scanner is a popular peripheral device used to digitize images, such as pages from a book or photographs. The images can be saved as an uncompressed bitmap or, because the files are often quite large, saved in a compressed file format, such as .jpg or .gif. Scanners can be purchased separately or combined with a printer in a single device that prints, scans, and copies. Most scanners use a USB connection, but other interface types, such as FireWire, parallel, and SCSI, are available. In this lab, you install and then test a USB scanner.

ESTIMATED COMPLETION TIME: 30 Minutes

9

 Activity

It's best to follow the manufacturer's directions when installing a scanner. You can get the directions and any required software from the CD/DVD that comes with the scanner or from the manufacturer's Web site. If the instructions tell you to use the Scanner and Camera Installation Wizard, you can use the following steps:

> **Notes** Most USB scanners come bundled with their own installation software. It's important to run this software *before* attaching the scanner.

1. Log on to an administrative account in Windows, and make sure all unnecessary programs are closed.
2. Attach the scanner to your computer, and then power on the scanner.
3. Because most scanners are Plug and Play, the Scanner and Camera Installation Wizard should launch automatically. If it doesn't, click **Start, Control Panel, Hardware and Sound, (Printers and Other Hardware** in XP), and **Scanners and Cameras**. In the Scanners and Cameras window, click the **Add Device** (**Add an imaging device** in XP) link.
4. Click **Next** in the Scanner and Camera Installation Wizard.
5 If Windows asks you to click Continue to continue, click **Continue**.
6. Click to select the manufacturer and model of your scanner (or click **Have Disk** if your scanner came with separate drivers), and then click **Next**.
7. Click to select the correct port (if required), and then click **Next**.
8. Enter a name for your scanner, and then click **Next**. Write the name of your scanner in the following space:

_____

9. Finally, click **Finish** to begin installing the drivers.
10. Once the drivers have finished installing, close any open windows.

To test that your scanner is working correctly, do the following:

1. Click **Start, Control Panel, Hardware and Sound (Printers and Other Hardware** in XP), and **Scanners and Cameras.**

2. Select the scanner you want to test (right-click in XP) and click **Properties.**

3. Click the **General** tab (if necessary) and click the **Test Scanner** button.

4. What message did you get after the test was completed?

   _____

   _____

5. What message do you get if you turn off the scanner and then go through Steps 1 through 3 again?

   _____

   _____

REVIEW QUESTIONS

1. What are some advantages and disadvantages of combining your printer and scanner into a single device?

   _____

   _____

2. Why does the Scanner and Camera Installation Wizard usually launch automatically the first time a scanner is attached to a computer?

   _____

3. When might you want to save images as .jpg files?

   _____

   _____

4. What are some reasons that a scanner might not work correctly after it has been installed?

   _____

   _____

   _____

LAB 9.5 CRITICAL THINKING: TROUBLESHOOT VIDEO PROBLEMS

OBJECTIVES

The goal of this lab is to help you learn to troubleshoot video problems. After completing this lab, you will be able to:

◢ Solve problems with the video subsystem

◢ Investigate and update video card drivers

MATERIALS REQUIRED

This lab requires the following:

◢ A working computer with Internet access

LAB PREPARATION

Before the lab begins, the instructor or lab assistant needs to do the following:

◢ Verify the computer for each student or workgroup is working and has Internet access, and a monitor is available.

ACTIVITY BACKGROUND

The video subsystem includes the video card, video cable, and monitor. When solving problems with video, always check the simple things first. Monitor settings might be wrong or the video cable might be loose. Check these things before opening the case to check the video card. Some applications, especially games and graphics programs, rely heavily on video. If an application is giving problems, one thing you can do is make sure the video card is using the latest drivers available for it. Also, if video is showing incorrect colors, streaks, or lines or is not working at all, you can try updating the video drivers. In this lab, you will find out what video drivers you are using and update them if an update is available.

ESTIMATED COMPLETION TIME: 60 Minutes

 Activity

In this scenario, you are the PC technical support person for a small accounting firm, and spend about one day a week at the firm addressing any technical problems that arise with computers, printers, scanners, fax machines, copiers, the network, and Internet access. One morning when you arrive at the firm, Larry, the owner, meets you at the door. He installed a new game on his desktop over the weekend, but notices that the game jumps and halts as he plays it. You know that gaming is generally not allowed on computers in the firm, but, oh well, this is the boss, so you get down to business in solving his problem. The first thing you suspect is the video drivers. Sometimes the latest video driver is sufficient to solve a problem with a poorly responding game.

TROUBLESHOOTING

A PC support technician needs to know more than one way to do something. Complete the following to show two methods of viewing video driver files.

1. List the steps to view the details about video driver files (see Lab 9.2).

_____

_____

_____

2. How many video driver files are listed?

_____

3. List the path and filename of three video driver files:

_____

4. List the steps of a second method to view the list of video driver files:

_____

5. List the path and filename of three more of the video driver files:

_____

6. What is the name of your video card, as shown in Device Manager?

_____

7. Identify the video card manufacturer and the URL of the manufacturer's Web site:

_____

8. Search the Web site of the video card manufacturer for the latest drivers for this video card and download the drivers to a folder on your hard drive.
   What is the path and filename of the downloaded file?

_____

   What is the version number of the video drivers?

_____

9. Check the Web site for any special instructions for updating the drivers. For example, one site says to stop all antivirus software and uninstall the current driver. What special instructions apply to your video card?

_____

_____

10. Follow the instructions to update the video drivers. List the steps you used here:

_____

_____

11. After the new video drivers were installed, what display settings did you have to reset?

_____

12. Compare the filenames of the video drivers that you just installed to the older drivers previously installed. What differences do you see? How might this information be useful when troubleshooting video problems?

_____

13. You might later decide to roll back the drivers. List the steps to do this:

_____

_____

On another day at the accounting firm, Jason, one of the staff accountants, asks for help with his monitor. He complains that his new LCD monitor is making it difficult for him to read large spreadsheets. He's tried adjusting the monitor settings, but still can't find the right combination of settings. Using an LCD monitor in your lab, complete the following tasks:

1. Using hardware settings on the monitor, describe how to adjust the monitor brightness:

_____

_____

2. Using hardware settings on the monitor, describe how to adjust the monitor contrast:

_____

_____

3. Using hardware settings on the monitor, describe how to adjust the monitor color:

_____

_____

4. List the steps in Windows to smooth the edges of screen fonts to make the text sharper on-screen.

_____

_____

5. List the screen resolutions the video drivers for this monitor support:

_____

_____

6. Can you adjust the screen settings so that text appears larger on the screen? If so, how?

_____

While helping Jason, you notice his old CRT monitor sitting on the floor beside his desk collecting dust. You check the back of Jason's computer and find a video card with two ports, one a digital DVI port and the other a 15-pin analog port. The LCD monitor is connected to the 15-pin analog port using an analog video cable. The old CRT monitor also has an analog cable. List the steps and parts you would need to hook up the old monitor for a dual monitor system to help give Jason a little more Windows desktop space:

_____

_____

_____

_____

REVIEW QUESTIONS

1. Which expansion slot is faster, AGP 8x or PCI Express x16?

_____

2. Before updating video drivers, you are asked to uninstall the current video drivers and restart the system. Why does the Found New Hardware Wizard launch when you restart the system?

_____

3. What is one way to install the video drivers downloaded from the Internet?

_____

4. List three situations where you might find it useful to update the video drivers:

_____

_____

_____

5. List the steps you can use to find the filenames of the video driver files:

_____

_____

_____

6. What button on the tab in Question 5 do you use to access the video driver filenames?

_____

CHAPTER 10

Multimedia Devices and Mass Storage

Labs included in this chapter:

- Lab 10.1: Install a Sound Card
- Lab 10.2: Install a PC Video Camera
- Lab 10.3: Compare CD, DVD, and Blu-ray Technologies
- Lab 10.4: Install Dual Displays in Windows
- Lab 10.5: Research Digital Cameras
- Lab 10.6: Explore Windows Audio Features

LAB 10.1 INSTALL A SOUND CARD

OBJECTIVES

The goal of this lab is to help you learn how to install a sound card. After completing this lab, you will be able to:

- Physically install a sound card
- Install device drivers
- Test the card and adjust the volume

MATERIALS REQUIRED

This lab requires the following:

- Windows Vista/XP operating system
- Windows installation CD or installation files
- An empty expansion slot
- A compatible sound card with speakers or headphones
- Sound card device drivers
- Motherboard documentation, if your system uses embedded audio
- A PC toolkit with antistatic wrist strap
- *Optional*: Internet access

LAB PREPARATION

Before the lab begins, the instructor or lab assistant needs to do the following:

- Verify that Windows starts with no errors.
- Verify access to motherboard and sound card documentation.
- *Optional:* Verify that Internet access is available.
- Provide each student with access to the Windows installation files, if needed.

ACTIVITY BACKGROUND

Two of the most popular multimedia devices are the sound card and the embedded audio device. A sound card enables a computer to receive sound input and to output sound, as when playing a music CD. Many newer systems have audio embedded on the motherboard. As an A+ computer technician, you need to know how to install a sound card, whether you're putting together a computer from scratch, repairing a failed device, or upgrading components on an existing system. In this lab, you install, configure, and test a sound card.

ESTIMATED COMPLETION TIME: 45 Minutes

 Activity

First, you need to find out whether your system has a sound card, an embedded audio device, or perhaps both or neither. Use the skills you have learned to discover and describe what audio configuration your system currently has. Describe the configuration, and then work through the steps to complete the lab in the following general order:

- Disable any existing audio devices in Windows.
- Remove or disable the hardware device(s).
- Verify that the audio is disabled.
- Physically install the sound card.
- Install the drivers in Windows.
- Verify the function of audio features.
- Return the system to its original state (optional, per instructor's directions).

Follow these steps to uninstall a sound card or embedded audio device in Windows:

1. After you have logged on as an administrator, open Control Panel.
2. Click **System and Maintenance**, and then scroll down and select **Device Manager**.
3. If Windows needs permission to continue, click **Continue**.
4. Click the **+** sign next to **Sound, video and game controllers** and select your audio device.
5. Right-click your device and click **Uninstall**.
6. If necessary, check the **Delete the driver software for this device** box, as shown in Figure 10-1, and click **OK**.

Figure 10-1   Confirm that this device should be uninstalled
Courtesy: Course Technology/Cengage Learning

7. Close any open windows, log off, and shut down your computer.

Next, you will either physically remove the sound card from your system or disable an audio device that's embedded in the motherboard.

Follow these steps to remove the sound card:

1. Disconnect all external cables from the case.
2. Remove the case cover and locate the sound card. List any cables connected to the sound card:

_____

_____

_____

3. Disconnect any cables from the sound card and secure them. Remove the sound card and place it in a safe place.

4. Reassemble the system and boot to Windows to verify that the audio doesn't function.

Follow these steps to disable the embedded audio device:

1. Consult the motherboard documentation to learn how to disable the embedded audio device. Also, take note of any internal audio cables. The way to disable the device is often a jumper setting, but sometimes you might have to disable the device in the CMOS setup utility. If you must disable the device in CMOS, describe the steps you took on the following lines, and then complete Steps 2 and 3:

_____

_____

_____

2. Disconnect all external cables. Remove the case cover and locate the way to disable the embedded audio (if applicable). List the steps, and then remove and secure any internal audio cables:

_____

_____

3. Reassemble the system and boot to Windows to verify that the audio doesn't function.

Now you are ready to physically install a new sound card. Follow these steps:

1. Shut down the computer and disconnect all external cables from the case.

2. Remove the case cover.

3. Locate an empty expansion slot that you can use for the sound card. On some systems, expansion cards are attached to a riser card, which you might have to remove at this time. If necessary, remove the expansion slot faceplate on the case so that the sound card fits into the expansion slot.

4. Insert the sound card into the expansion slot on the motherboard (or insert the sound card into the riser card and the riser card into the motherboard). Line up the sound card on the slot and press it straight down, making sure the tab on the backplate (the metal plate on the rear of the card where sound ports are located) fits into the slot on the case. Normally, seating the card requires a little effort, but don't force it. If you can't insert the card with just a little effort, something is preventing it from seating. Check for obstructions and try again, removing components that are in the way, if needed.

5. After the card is installed, secure it with a screw. The screw goes through a hole in the card's backplate, securing the backplate to the case.

6. Attach any cable required to carry an audio signal from other multimedia devices, such as a CD-ROM drive.

7. Replace any components you removed while installing the sound card, and replace and secure the cover on the case.

8. Reattach all cables from external devices to the correct ports. Attach speakers or headphones. (Some speakers receive power from the computer, and others have to be plugged into an external power source, such as a wall outlet.)

Next, you configure the drivers and other software for your sound card. If you have the documentation for your sound card, follow those instructions. Otherwise, follow these general steps to install software for most sound cards, keeping in mind that your sound card might require a slightly different procedure:

1. Start the computer, and log on as an administrator. If an "Installing device driver software" balloon pops up, you can wait for the drivers to install and then skip ahead to Step 10.

2. In Windows XP, the Found New Hardware dialog box opens, attempts to determine what type of new hardware is present, and displays the result.

3. The New Hardware Wizard launches, informing you that it will help you install a driver. Click **Next** to continue.

4. The New Hardware Wizard displays a message asking how you want to install the software. Click the **Search for a suitable driver for my device (Recommended)** option button, and then click **Next** to continue.

5. The New Hardware Wizard displays a message asking where the drivers for the new device are located (see Figure 10-2). Insert the CD containing the drivers, and click the check box to indicate the location of the drivers. (If the CD Autorun program launches when you insert the CD, close it.) Click **Next** to continue. If your files aren't located on removable media, click the **Specify a location** check box. A dialog box opens, prompting you to type the path or browse to the file location. Use either method you prefer, and when you finish, click **OK** to continue.

6. If the New Hardware Wizard can locate the correct driver, it displays a message identifying the sound card model name, driver location, and driver filename. Click **Next** to continue and then skip to Step 8. If the wizard reports that it is unable to find the drivers, proceed to Step 7.

7. If the New Hardware Wizard reports that it was unable to locate the drivers, click **Back** and repeat Step 4, but this time click the **Specify Location** option, and then click **Browse** to open the Browse for a Folder dialog box.

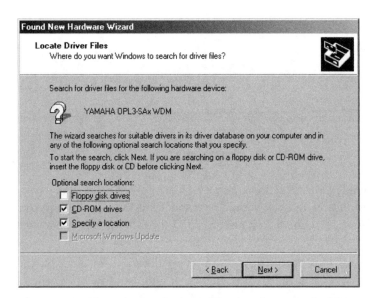

Figure 10-2 Direct the New Hardware Wizard to the correct location of the drivers
Courtesy: Course Technology/Cengage Learning

Browse to the location of the setup files, expanding folders as needed, and look for a folder named Vista, WinXP, or similar. (If you aren't sure which .inf file to choose, consult the Readme.txt file, which should include instructions and last-minute information.) After you select the correct folder, click **OK** to close the Browse for a Folder dialog box, and then click **Next** in the New Hardware Wizard. If the wizard finds the driver, continue to Step 8; otherwise, consult the documentation again for the correct installation procedure.

8. After locating and installing the drivers, the New Hardware Wizard displays a message notifying you that the device installation is completed. Click **Finish** to close the wizard. At some point, you might be required to supply the location of the i386 directory holding Windows installation files.

9. After the sound card is completely installed, Windows might detect additional devices. Sound cards sometimes include embedded features, such as MIDI Wave Audio, SB16 Emulation, Game Port, and so on. The New Hardware Wizard launches as needed to install these devices separately. Follow the preceding steps to install each device.

10. When Windows finishes installing software, you might be prompted to reboot. If so, go ahead and reboot. You should hear the Microsoft sound (the default sound played on startup) after you log on.

Follow these steps to test the sound card and adjust the volume in Windows:

1. Open Control Panel. Click **Hardware and Sound**, and then click **Sound**. The Sound dialog box opens, as shown in Figure 10-3.

Figure 10-3   Check the settings in the Sounds tab
Courtesy: Course Technology/Cengage Learning

2. Click the **Sounds** tab. Scroll down and select **Windows Logon** in the Program section. Click the **Test** button and you should hear the Windows logon sound from your speakers. Click **OK** to close the dialog box, close Control Panel, and reboot the system and log on as administrator.

3. On the right side of the taskbar, you should see the speaker volume setting represented by a speaker icon. Click the **speaker** icon. A pop-up window opens with a slider for adjusting speaker volume.

4. Drag the volume slider all the way to the top, and then click the desktop to close the pop-up window.

5. Right-click the **speaker** icon and click **Open Volume Mixer** (**Open Volume Control** in XP). The Volume Mixer window (Volume Control in XP) gives you more control than the pop-up window you used in Step 4. On the following lines, list the volume controls from left to right, and identify any settings (other than volume) that can be changed:

_____

_____

6. Set the Speakers volume slider to half volume, and then close the Volume Mixer window.

7. Next, if you have Internet access, you can do a further test of your sound card. Use a search engine, locate a Lion.wav file, and play it to hear a lion's roar. What was the Web site where you found the file?

_____

REVIEW QUESTIONS

1. Was Windows able to find and install the drivers for your new device automatically? If not, what steps did you have to follow?

_____

_____

2. What other devices embedded on the sound card might Windows detect after the sound card installation is finished?

_____

_____

3. Why might you wish to mute the Windows Sounds but not mute the speakers?

_____

_____

4. Why might someone need to remove and then reinstall the drivers for his or her sound card?

_____

_____

5. Why might someone choose to disable an embedded sound device and then add a sound card instead?

_____

_____

10

LAB 10.2 INSTALL A PC VIDEO CAMERA

OBJECTIVES

The goal of this lab is to help you complete the process of installing and testing a PC camera. After completing this lab, you will be able to:

◢ Install a PC video camera

◢ Use Windows Movie Maker to test your PC camera

MATERIALS REQUIRED

This lab requires the following:

◢ Windows Vista/XP

◢ Windows installation CD/DVD or installation files

◢ A USB-connected PC camera compatible with your system

◢ A spare USB port on the system

◢ Device drivers for the camera

◢ Sound card, speakers, and optional microphone

◢ *Optional*: Internet access

LAB PREPARATION

Before the lab begins, the instructor or lab assistant needs to do the following:

◢ Verify that Windows starts with no errors.

◢ Provide each student with access to the necessary installation files or drivers.

◢ *Optional:* Verify that Internet access is available.

ACTIVITY BACKGROUND

PC cameras are becoming increasingly popular. Using these cameras, you can set up a video conference, record or send video images to your family and friends, and monitor your house over the Internet. You can even detach some PC cameras and use them to take still pictures while away from your system, uploading them to the computer when you return. Most PC cameras install via the USB port, making physical installation fairly simple. In this lab, you install, configure, and test a basic PC camera.

> **ESTIMATED COMPLETION TIME: 45 Minutes**

 Activity

Follow these steps to install a PC camera:

1. Start the computer and, if necessary, log on as an administrator.

2. Locate an unused USB port. Insert the PC camera's cable into the USB port. (Don't force the cable. If you can't insert it easily, flip the connector over, and try again; it should insert easily.)

3. Windows detects the new USB device and installs the drivers automatically. In Windows XP, the Found New Hardware icon appears in the taskbar's notification area. A balloon

tip above the icon informs you that new hardware has been found. Next, the balloon tip identifies the hardware as a camera, and then notifies you that it has identified the particular camera model. Finally, the balloon tip notifies you that the camera has been installed successfully. If requested, insert the camera installation CD. (If the Autorun program launches, close it.)

Next, you use Control Panel to collect information about your camera by following these steps:

1. Open **Control Panel** and click **Hardware and Sound** (**Printers and Other Hardware** in XP).

2. Click **Scanners and Cameras** and select (right-click in XP) the camera you just installed. Click **Properties** and the camera properties dialog box opens. Select the General tab. What types of information are available in this section?

_____

_____

_____

3. In XP, click the **Test Camera** button in the Diagnostics section. On the following lines, describe the results reported in the message box that opens, and then click **OK** to close the message box. Click **OK** again to close the camera properties dialog box.

_____

_____

4. Now double-click the camera icon in Computer (**My Computer** in XP). Record what happens and what tasks are available in the Camera Tasks section:

_____

_____

5. Use what you know about Windows and list two ways, other than Computer or Windows Explorer, where you can find information about the camera. Briefly describe any differences from Computer on the amount of information available or the way it's presented:

_____

_____

_____

Most digital cameras will also record some video and audio. Put your camera to use with Windows Movie Maker by completing the following steps:

1. Click **Start**, point to **All Programs** (in XP point to **Accessories**, and then point to **Entertainment**), and then click **Windows Movie Maker**. Windows Movie Maker opens, as shown in Figure 10-4.

2. Depending on your hardware configuration, you may be able to record video directly from your camera. If this is not the case, you can still take pictures or video with your camera and import them into Windows Movie Maker as files.

3. Does your configuration allow you to record video directly?

_____

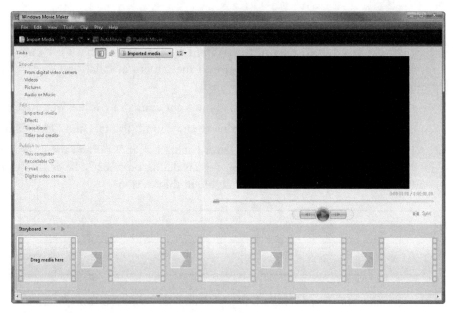

Figure 10-4 The Windows Movie Maker main window
Courtesy: Course Technology/Cengage Learning

4. In Windows Movie Maker, select **Import Media Items** (**Import into Collections** in XP) from the **File** menu.

5. Import at least three images or videos taken with your camera. List the media files being used:

_____

_____

_____

6. Drag your media files onto the storyboard at the bottom. Right-click the media files and add effects to each file. Which effects did you choose?

_____

_____

7. Add transitions between the media files. Which transitions did you choose?

_____

_____

8. Press play to view your creation. Take a few minutes to explore Windows Movie Maker before exiting the program.

CHALLENGE ACTIVITY (ADDITIONAL 60 MINUTES)

Use your digital camera and Windows Media Player to create a step-by-step tutorial on how to accomplish a task from an earlier chapter. Tasks could include upgrading RAM or adding a second hard drive.

REVIEW QUESTIONS

1. Typically, via what type of port do PC cameras attach to a system?

2. Do you have to power down the system before connecting a USB camera? Why or why not?

3. What kinds of media files can Windows Movie Maker import?

4. In what ways can you publish your movie?

5. Would Windows Movie Maker still be useful even if your digital camera only took still shots?

10

LAB 10.3 COMPARE CD, DVD, AND BLU-RAY TECHNOLOGIES

OBJECTIVES

The goal of this lab is to help you use the Internet to research CD, DVD, and Blu-Ray standards. After completing this lab, you will be able to:

◢ Recognize CD, DVD, and Blu-ray specifications

MATERIALS REQUIRED

This lab requires the following:

◢ Internet access

LAB PREPARATION

Before the lab begins, the instructor or lab assistant needs to do the following:

◢ Verify that Internet access is available.

ACTIVITY BACKGROUND

Many multimedia PCs include an optical drive such as a CD, DVD, or Blu-ray. These drives can be of three types: read-only (ROM), write/record (R), or write/record and rewrite (RW or RAM). (The last two types can write and record only to specialized discs.) You research the features and limitations of these optical standards in this lab.

ESTIMATED COMPLETION TIME: 60 Minutes

 Activity

Use the Internet and your favorite search sites, such as Google (*www.google.com*) or Yahoo! (*www.yahoo. com*), to answer the following questions on CD standards. Print the source page or pages supporting your answers.

1. What is the maximum storage capacity of a CD?

   _____

2. Briefly, how is information recorded on a CD-ROM disc?

   _____

   _____

3. Are CDs capable of storing data on both sides of the disc?

   _____

4. What type or color of laser is used in a CD drive?

   _____

5. What is a limitation of a CD-R drive that isn't an issue with a CD-RW drive?

   _____

6. What kind of problems might occur if you tried to use an older CD-ROM drive or a CD player to play a CD-R or CD-RW disc?

   _____

   _____

7. Define "constant angular velocity" and explain how it applies to CD standards:

   _____

   _____

8. Define "constant linear velocity" and explain how it applies to CD standards:

   _____

   _____

9. What term is used for the process of writing data to a disc?

   _____

10. Can any CD hold video data? Explain:

   _____

11. On a CD, is data written in concentric circles or a continuous spiral track?

   _____

12. What are three common standards CD drives use to interface with a system?

   _____

   _____

13. What does the X factor of a drive indicate? What is the specification of one X?

   _____

   _____

14. Briefly describe how a CD-RW writes data to a disc and how it's able to rewrite data:

   _____

   _____

   _____

   _____

15. How much would you pay for a package of CD-Rs? How much for a package of CD-RWs? How many discs are in a package of each type?

   _____

   _____

Use the Internet and your favorite search sites to answer the following questions on DVD standards. Print the source page or pages supporting your answers.

1. What is the maximum storage capacity of a DVD?

   _____

2. What two characteristics give a DVD more storage capacity than a CD?

   _____

   _____

3. Describe the difference between DVD-R and DVD-RAM:

   _____

   _____

   _____

4. Besides DVD-R, what other standards are available for burning DVDs?

_____

_____

5. Explain how DVD audio and CD audio differ:

_____

_____

_____

6. How many CDs worth of data can a single DVD hold?

_____

7. Are most DVD Players able to play CDs?

_____

8. How many layers of data can be stored on one side of a DVD?

_____

9. How many data areas are on a single side of a DVD-R?

_____

10. List the versions and maximum capacities of DVD-RAM:

_____

_____

11. Can DVDs be used in CD devices? Explain:

_____

12. Explain the use of the UDF file system and how it applies to a DVD:

_____

_____

_____

_____

Use the Internet and your favorite search sites to answer the following questions on Blu-ray standards. Print the source page or pages supporting your answers.

1. What is the maximum storage capacity of a Blu-ray disc?

_____

2. How much more information can be stored on a Blue-ray disc (BD) than a standard DVD? How much more than a CD?

_____

_____

3. Are most Blu-ray players able to play DVDs and CDs?

_____

_____

4. What are the most common CODECs used to store video on BD-ROM?

_____

_____

_____

5. How many layers of data can be stored on one side of a BD-ROM?

_____

6. Why do you think many motion pictures are still released on DVDs instead of BD-ROM?

_____

_____

7. Explain the use of digital rights management and how it applies to a BD:

_____

_____

_____

_____

_____

REVIEW QUESTIONS

1. What factors, other than storage capacity, would you consider when choosing an optical drive?

_____

_____

_____

2. What characteristics do DVD and BD drives share?

_____

_____

3. If you wanted to create a disc that would never need to be altered and would be compatible with the most systems, what type of disc would you use and why?

_____

_____

4. Why is BD-ROM a better media for high-resolution video than DVD?

_____

_____

LAB 10.4 INSTALL DUAL DISPLAYS IN WINDOWS

OBJECTIVES

The goal of this lab is to help you set up a second monitor on a system. After completing this lab, you will be able to:

◢ Install a second display adapter and its drivers

◢ Attach a second monitor or LCD projector

◢ Configure the system to use both monitors at the same time

MATERIALS REQUIRED

This lab requires the following:

◢ Windows Vista/XP operating system

◢ A PC toolkit with antistatic ground strap

◢ A second display adapter with drivers

◢ A second monitor or LCD projector

LAB PREPARATION

Before the lab begins, the instructor or lab assistant needs to do the following:

◢ Verify that Windows starts with no errors.

ACTIVITY BACKGROUND

Having two displays on a system is often quite handy. For instance, you can have two monitors giving you more desktop space and making it easier to work with multiple applications simultaneously. You might keep tabs on your e-mail in one screen while surfing the Internet on the other. Alternatively, your second display could be something else like an LCD display for presentations or a television for watching movies. In this lab, you install and configure a second display on a computer.

ESTIMATED COMPLETION TIME: 45 Minutes

 Activity

It's important to verify that the original hardware is working correctly before you try to add a second display adapter and monitor. That way, if a problem comes up after you install new hardware, you can be fairly sure something is amiss with the newly added components rather than the original equipment. Also, you should make sure the hardware is on the Windows Hardware Compatibility List (HCL) or, at the very least, the device manufacturer offers drivers and specific instructions for use with your version of Windows.

Follow these steps to physically install the second display adapter:

1. Check to see if the original display adapter uses a PCI, AGP, or PCIe standard, and decide whether it will be the primary or secondary display.

2. Determine which standard the new video card follows (PCI or PCIe) and install the second adapter card in the closest available slot to the original video card. If you need additional guidance on installing an I/O card, refer to Lab 10.1.

3. Attach the second display to the port on the back of the display adapter.

4. Boot your PC and enter CMOS setup. If your setup has display settings for dual monitors, adjust them so that the card you've chosen as your primary display adapter is initialized first.

5. If your system has an AGP adapter, make sure that it is selected as the primary adapter and the PCI adapter as the secondary adapter. For a system that uses two PCIe adapters, it doesn't matter which adapter is the primary one; you can leave the setting as is. For additional guidance on adjusting BIOS settings, refer to Lab 5.1.

6. If you don't see this setting, your BIOS doesn't support it, so you can exit CMOS setup and wait for your system to reboot.

Follow these steps to install device drivers and adjust Windows display settings:

1. When the system reboots, log on as an administrator. Windows recognizes the new adapter and displays a Driver Software Installation icon (Found New Hardware in XP) in the taskbar's notification area. Above the icon, a balloon tip appears with a notification about the driver installation.

2. At this point, Windows might install the drivers automatically for you (if the drivers were available when your version of Windows was published) or launch the Found New Hardware Wizard if the adapter is new enough that Windows isn't aware of the correct drivers. Complete the steps in the wizard to install the adapter. When the installation is completed, reboot. Refer to Lab 10.1 if you need additional information on using the wizard.

Before you use a second display, you must activate it. To do so, follow these steps:

1. Log on as an administrator, open Control Panel, click **Appearance and Personalization**, and then click **Personalization**. Click the **Display Settings** link to open the Display Settings dialog box.

2. The area at the top of Display Settings now displays two monitors (see Figure 10-5). Click the image of the monitor with the number 2.

3. Adjust the resolution and color settings to your preference, and then click the **Extend the desktop onto this monitor** (**Extend my Windows desktop onto this monitor** in XP) check box.

4. Click **Apply** to apply the settings. The second monitor displays the desktop.

Follow these steps to test your dual-display configuration:

1. Open Paint, and then drag it to the second display. Does your desktop extend to the second display as expected?

2. Open Windows Explorer, and maximize it on the original display. Can you see your mouse move as expected from one display to the next? Does the mouse interact with applications on each display?

3. Close Paint and Windows Explorer, and open Device Manager.

4. Does adjusting the settings of one display affect the settings of the other?

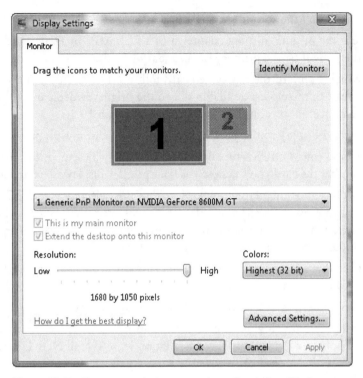

Figure 10-5 You must activate a second monitor before Windows can use it
Courtesy: Course Technology/Cengage Learning

Follow these steps to remove the second adapter and return to a single-monitor configuration:

1. Open Device Manager, find the second display adapter, and click to select it. (Make sure you're looking at the second adapter, not the first.)

2. Click **Uninstall**. If prompted, verify that you do want to remove the device, and when asked if you want to restart the computer, click **No**.

3. Shut down the computer. Don't restart the computer at this time.

4. Remove the second display and adapter card. If necessary, reverse any BIOS changes you made that affect the display initialization sequence, and reboot the system to verify that the system no longer recognizes the adapter card.

CRITICAL THINKING (ADDITIONAL 20 MINUTES)

Use the Internet to compare the costs of two sample systems: One with dual 17-inch LCD displays and one with a single 24-inch LCD display. Don't forget about the video card.

1. Which is less expensive?

_____

2. Which is a better value? Why?

_____

_____

REVIEW QUESTIONS

1. Before installing a second monitor, why is it important to know whether your existing configuration is working correctly?

2. Why do you think it is necessary to set the sequence in which the system initializes display adapters so that the primary display is initialized first?

3. In Display Settings, what is one way to select the monitor you want to adjust?

4. What would probably happen if the new adapter was on the Windows HCL and was in production before the release of Windows?

5. Why might you want to install multiple monitors on a system?

LAB 10.5 RESEARCH DIGITAL CAMERAS

OBJECTIVES

The goal of this lab is to help you research digital cameras and learn how you can integrate them with a multimedia PC. In this lab, you will research:

◢ Camera picture quality and compatibility

◢ Camera storage technology

◢ Methods of transferring images to a PC

MATERIALS REQUIRED

This lab requires the following:

◢ Internet access

LAB PREPARATION

Before the lab begins, the instructor or lab assistant needs to do the following:

◢ Verify that Internet access is available.

ACTIVITY BACKGROUND

As digital cameras have become more common and popular, they have also become more sophisticated. Their special features, image quality, methods of file storage, and methods of transferring image data to the PC have improved over earlier models. Also, the prices of digital cameras have decreased dramatically. In this lab, you research digital cameras and learn how they are used with multimedia PCs.

ESTIMATED COMPLETION TIME: 60 Minutes

 Activity

Research digital photography on the Internet. Try searching for "digital camera" or "digital photography" on your favorite search engine. Be sure to have the appropriate filters enabled to block adult content. Then, answer the following questions about general camera topics. Print the Web page or pages supporting your answers.

1. How is image quality measured? Do all digital cameras produce the same image quality?

   _____

   _____

2. What are three storage technologies that digital cameras might use to store images in a camera?

   _____

   _____

   _____

3. Name four technologies a camera might use to transfer images to a PC. What requirements must a PC meet for each?

   _____

   _____

   _____

   _____

4. Find and print information about at least two digital cameras that offer features such as changeable lenses, manual focus, aperture settings (f-stops), and shutter-speed settings (exposure). List the two digital cameras you selected on the following lines:

   _____

   _____

5. What are three advantages of a digital camera over a 35mm film camera?

   _____

   _____

   _____

Answer these questions on basic image characteristics:

1. What three file types might a digital camera use to store images?

   _____

2. Name three factors that affect the number of images that a camera can store on a single storage device:

   _____

   _____

   _____

3. Do most digital cameras offer the capability to control image quality? Why would you ever want to take lower-quality images?

   _____

   _____

   _____

4. Can you remove an image you don't like from a camera without transferring the image to a PC? Explain:

   _____

   _____

5. What are three means of printing a photo taken by a digital camera?

   _____

   _____

   _____

6. Would all 10-megapixel cameras have the same picture quality? Why or why not?

   _____

   _____

7. Can digital cameras record images other than still shots?

   _____

Answer these questions about how cameras transfer images to a PC:

1. Which transfer method offers the highest transfer speed? What is that speed?

   _____

2. Which transfer method requires the least specialized hardware on a PC?

   _____

10

3. Which storage technologies allow direct image transfer by removing the storage device from the camera and inserting it into the PC?

_____

_____

4. What image transfer method doesn't require removing a device from the camera or using cabling to the PC?

_____

5. Does image resolution have any effect on transfer speed? Explain:

_____

_____

_____

There are many factors that you need to consider when purchasing a photo printer. To consider the factors, answer these questions:

1. What resolution would you recommend for a printer capable of reproducing digital pictures?

_____

2. Do you need special paper to get the best quality in photo printing? Explain:

_____

3. Describe one way you could get pictures from your digital camera to the printer:

_____

_____

4. Do all photo printers have to be used with a computer? Explain:

_____

_____

5. What do you need to consider if you need your photos to last a long time?

_____

REVIEW QUESTIONS

1. Are there any advantages of a 35mm film camera over digital?

_____

_____

2. What are some features you would like on a digital camera? Explain your choices:

_____

_____

_____

3. What can you do to maximize the number of images stored on a camera without modifying the storage device capacity?

_____

_____

_____

4. Why is megapixel count not the only measure of image quality?

_____

_____

5. What factors should you consider when purchasing a photo printer?

_____

_____

LAB 10.6 EXPLORE WINDOWS AUDIO FEATURES

10

OBJECTIVES

The goal of this lab is to give you the opportunity to experiment with different audio features and capabilities of Windows. After completing this lab, you will be able to:

◢ Identify audio media types

◢ Download and install Nullsoft Winamp, a third-party sound application

◢ Control audio CD playback with Windows Media Player and Nullsoft Winamp

◢ Customize sounds that Windows plays for events

MATERIALS REQUIRED

This lab requires the following:

◢ Windows Vista/XP operating system

◢ Windows installation CD or installation files

◢ Internet access

◢ CD-ROM-compatible drive and an audio CD

LAB PREPARATION

Before the lab begins, the instructor or lab assistant needs to do the following:

◢ Verify that Windows starts with no errors.

◢ Provide each student with access to the Windows installation files, if needed.

◢ Verify that Internet access is available.

ACTIVITY BACKGROUND

Windows offers features that let you use audio files in different ways. For example, Windows events can be configured to play a certain sound when the event occurs. These features can be used simply to make using Windows more enjoyable for average users, but to a sight-impaired user, they can be vital tools.

Windows provides Windows Media Player to play audio CDs as well as other multimedia types. Some people also install third-party media players with additional features, such as built-in codecs that can play additional types of media files. In this lab, you experiment with Windows audio capabilities and use Nullsoft Winamp, a third-party sound application.

ESTIMATED COMPLETION TIME: 40 Minutes

Activity

Follow these steps to control which sounds play for certain Windows events:

Notes Refer to Lab 10.1 for a reminder on how to adjust the volume level in Windows.

1. Open Control Panel, click **Hardware and Sound,** and then click **Sound.** The Sound dialog box opens. Click the **Sounds** tab, and scroll down the Program list box; note that each event with a speaker icon has a sound assigned that plays when the event occurs, as shown in Figure 10-6.

Figure 10-6 A speaker icon indicates which events have sounds associated with them
Courtesy: Course Technology/Cengage Learning

2. Fill in the following chart by clicking each event in the table and writing down the sound associated with it. (The sound file associated with the selected event is displayed in the Sounds drop-down box.) Also, note that not all Windows events are assigned a sound.

Event	Sound Name
Critical Stop	
Exit Windows	
Empty Recycle Bin	

3. Click **Windows Logon** in the Program list box, and then click the **Test** button. The Windows Logon Sound file plays. If you don't hear the sound, check your volume levels and make sure the volume is not muted.

4. In the Sounds drop-down list, select and play several different sounds for Windows Logon until you find one you like better than the Windows default. Click the **Save As** button at the top, type **Custom** in the dialog box that opens, and click **OK** to save the new settings.

5. Click **OK** to apply and save the sound properties. To test the new sound, restart Windows and log on to the same account.

6. After you have verified that the new sound plays, repeat the process and return the sound to the original settings. (You could also apply the Windows Default scheme by selecting it in the Sound scheme drop-down list.)

Follow these steps to play an audio CD with Windows Media Player:

1. Insert the audio disc in the CD/DVD-ROM drive. If the Audio CD dialog box opens, click **Play Audio CD using Windows Media Player**, and then click **OK** to close the dialog box.

2. Windows Media Player should start and begin playing the CD automatically. Adjust the volume so that it's not distracting to others.

3. If another application is set to automatically play your CD, right-click the CD and select **Play audio CD** using Windows Media Player.

4. The right pane of Windows Media Player lists the tracks on the CD. The center section displays different images to accompany the audio output. Experiment with customizing this image by right-clicking this section and selecting another choice in the shortcut menu. List three of your favorite selections:

_____

_____

_____

5. Windows Media Player has the standard set of control features you would expect with a CD player. Experiment with Windows Media Player and answer the following questions:

◢ What happens when you click the Now Playing tab?

_____

◢ In what ways can you sort music in the library?

_____

◢ Other than music, what other information is available via the Media Guide?

_____

Follow these steps to install Winamp and use it to play the audio CD. Bear in mind that new versions of software are released often, so these directions might differ slightly, depending on the latest release:

1. Open your Web browser, and go to **www.winamp.com**. Click the **Free Download** button, and download the free version of Winamp. What is the name of the file you found to download?

   _____

2. Open Windows Explorer, find your download location, and double-click the file you downloaded to launch Winamp. Set up and begin the installation process. Winamp Setup is similar to other installation wizards you have used. Step through the installation without installing any additional features, but use default settings for everything else.

3. Note that when the installation is complete, Winamp should run automatically.

4. Experiment with Winamp to answer these questions:

   ◢ Does Winamp have the same basic features as Windows Media Player?

   _____

   ◢ What feature does Winamp have for customizing the sound tone?

   _____

   ◢ Name three popular music file types that Winamp supports:

   _____

   ◢ Could you set up a playlist for playing files on your CD in an order you choose, instead of first to last? Explain your answer:

   _____

   _____

   _____

REVIEW QUESTIONS

1. What Control Panel applet do you use to change the sound that plays for an event?

   _____

2. Does Windows Media Player enable you to listen to streaming audio content?

   _____

3. What is the default sound played during Windows startup?

   _____

4. Which audio player provided more features, and which was easier to use? Explain your answers:

_____

_____

_____

PC Maintenance and Troubleshooting Strategies

Labs included in this chapter:

LAB 11.1 INTELLECTUAL PROPERTY

OBJECTIVES

The goal of this lab is to build awareness of intellectual property and software copyright infringement. After completing this lab, you will be able to:

◢ Understand when software cannot be copied

◢ Identify signs that software might not be legal

◢ Find open source alternatives to some programs

MATERIALS REQUIRED

This lab requires the following:

◢ Windows Vista/XP operating system with access to the Internet

LAB PREPARATION

Before the lab begins, the instructor or lab assistant needs to do the following:

◢ Verify that Windows starts with no errors.

◢ Verify that the network connection is available.

ACTIVITY BACKGROUND

Most software is not free. Copying software beyond the terms of its software license agreement is illegal and can lead to stiff penalties or imprisonment. Computer technicians are often responsible for purchasing software and monitoring the use of company equipment. In this activity, you will research software piracy and test to see if your copy of Windows is legal.

ESTIMATED COMPLETION TIME: 30 Minutes

Activity

1. Go to the Software & Information Industry Association's home page at **www.siia.net**. Select the **Anti-Piracy** link and click the **Internet Anti-Piracy** program link. Answer the following questions:

2. What does the SIIA do to generate a list of potential pirated sites?

_____

_____

_____

3. What types of applications or protocols are monitored by the SIIA for piracy? Which do you think poses the greatest risk and why?

_____

_____

_____

Your Windows operating system is subject to a software license that must be purchased. You can check to see if your copy of Windows is genuine by following the steps below:

1. Go to **www.microsoft.com/genuine** and click the **Validate Windows** button. The steps may vary slightly depending on the version of Windows you're using and you may be asked to install Windows validation software. Follow the steps and after a short time, the validation will return with your answer.

2. Was your copy of Windows legal?

   _____

3. What are the advantages listed for using genuine Microsoft software?

   _____

Some software actually is free. The license for open source software (OSS) does not restrict free distribution but rather, encourages people to copy, use, modify, and improve the software as long as they follow certain rules. Many open source titles such as Apache, Firefox, and VLC are quite well known.

1. Go to the Open Source Initiative's home page at **http://opensource.org** and select **The Open Source Definition** link and read through the definition of open source.

2. Are you allowed to download the source code for an open source program, modify it to better meet your needs, and then install it on your computer?

   _____

3. Do you think allowing people to modify an open source program is more likely to cause problems or to fix them?

   _____

   _____

   _____

4. Next, go to **www.openoffice.org** and click the link called **I want to learn more about OpenOffice.org**. What would you consider to be the biggest advantage to switching to an open source office suite? Can you think of any disadvantages?

   _____

   _____

5. What format standard does Open Office use to save files? Can it also open files from other popular office programs?

   _____

   _____

6. Use the Internet to search for an OSS example of the following types of programs:

   ◢ Web Browser _____

   ◢ E-mail Client _____

   ◢ Photo Editor _____

   ◢ Media Player _____

11

7. Why do you think so many people illegally copy software when free alternatives are often available?

_____

_____

_____

REVIEW QUESTIONS

1. If open source software is free, why do you think it isn't more common?

_____

_____

2. What are some of the risks associated with pirating software?

_____

_____

3. Could you run a computer with nothing but open source software?

_____

4. If your copy of Windows was not found to be genuine, would you still have access to all the updates and downloads available through Microsoft?

_____

5. What is the difference between product activation and validation with Microsoft Windows?

_____

_____

_____

LAB 11.2 LEARN ABOUT SAFETY ISSUES

OBJECTIVES

The goal of this lab is to help you learn about safety issues while working on computers and repairing them. After completing this lab, you will be able to:

◢ Describe safety concerns of computer users

◢ Describe how to protect yourself and the equipment as you repair a computer

MATERIALS REQUIRED

◢ No equipment is necessary.

LAB PREPARATION

◢ No lab preparation is necessary.

ACTIVITY BACKGROUND

A PC support technician is expected to know how to support computer users and keep the computers in good repair. Part of that support includes knowing about safety and environmental issues and making users aware of these issues. This lab covers such concerns.

ESTIMATED COMPLETION TIME: 30 Minutes

Activity

Working at a computer for hours on end can be dangerous to your health! IT professionals often complain of strained eyes, wrists, backs, and shoulders, resulting from hours in front of a computer. Here are some useful tips for protecting yourself against these kinds of injuries:

- To prevent carpal tunnel syndrome, keep your wrists straight and your elbows about even with your keyboard. Occasionally stop, relax, and flex your hands, wrists, and arms.

- If you must talk on the phone as you work, you can prevent neck and back strain by using a headset that frees your hands from the phone and keeps you from having to tilt your head to the side.

- To protect your mental health and keep a positive and friendly attitude, don't face the wall as you work. If you can, turn your desk toward a window or toward the center of the room.

- To help prevent eyestrain as you work, occasionally look away from your monitor, focus on something in the distance, and blink your eyes rapidly. (People who stare at a monitor blink less often than normal, which can dry out their eyes.)

- Keep your head and neck upright and in line with your torso, not bent down or bent backward.

- Keep your torso upright, not bending down. Avoid hunching over your keyboard.

- Position your monitor directly in front of you, not to the left or right, and not so high or low that you have to bend your head or neck.

- Draw your keyboard close enough to your body that you don't need to extend your arms outward. Keep your elbows close to your body.

- Your chair needs support for your back (lumbar area). The seat should be comfortable, with rounded edges for your knees.

- If you are working for long hours at a computer, use a desktop rather than a laptop. A laptop screen is too close to the keyboard for comfort. If you must use a laptop, also use an external keyboard and/or monitor.

- Take breaks! Every 30 to 60 minutes, stand up, walk about, and get a drink. Every one to two hours, do some light exercise such as stretching and bending.

PC support technicians need to know how to protect themselves and their equipment as they work. Here are some useful tips:

- Use an antistatic ground bracelet. Attach the bracelet to any grounded surface. If you attach it to the computer case, all static electricity between you and the case will dissipate. You can then work safely inside the case. For added protection, use a ground mat.

- To protect yourself when working inside devices that contain highly charged capacitors, don't ground yourself. Such devices include laser printers, power supplies, and CRT monitors.

Notes You should not work inside a CRT monitor or power supply unless you understand the circuitry inside them. They can store a dangerous electrical charge even when they are unplugged. Although they are field replaceable units, working inside these devices is not considered a skill for A+ repair technicians.

▲ As you work on computer hardware, keep a Class C fire extinguisher close by your workbench.

▲ Manufacturers of cleaning solutions and pads provide a material safety data sheet (MSDS) that explains how to properly handle and store chemical solvents. The MSDS also includes information about health and first aid for the product. Keep the MSDS on hand in your lab or office. If you have an accident with chemicals, your organization might require you to fill out an incident report.

▲ Keep water away from electrical equipment, including computers. Don't turn on or service a computer in a wet area.

▲ Dispose of used equipment according to local government regulations. This equipment includes batteries, battery packs, toner cartridges, power supplies, monitors, cases, and chemical solvents.

REVIEW QUESTIONS

1. If you use a chemical solvent in your lab, what document should you keep on hand that describes the solvent's health effects, first aid, proper handling, and storage procedures?

_____

_____

2. How could you determine the correct disposal regulations for used toner cartridges?

_____

_____

3. Why is it best not to use a laptop computer for long hours of work?

_____

_____

4. Why is it important not to open a CRT monitor even when it is unplugged?

_____

_____

5. How can a user prevent eyestrain when using a monitor for a long time?

_____

_____

LAB 11.3 SAFELY CLEAN COMPUTER EQUIPMENT

OBJECTIVES

The goal of this lab is to help you learn about safety issues while cleaning and maintaining computers. After completing this lab, you will be able to:

◢ Clean a computer and other computer parts without damage to yourself or the computer

MATERIALS REQUIRED

This lab requires the following:

◢ Computer designed for this lab

◢ Can of compressed air and/or antistatic vacuum

◢ Contact cleaner

◢ Cotton swab

◢ Isopropyl alcohol (not rubbing alcohol) or liquid soap

◢ Sticky tape or duct tape

◢ Soft cloth or antistatic monitor wipes

◢ Antistatic wrist strap

◢ Plastic cable ties

◢ Additional faceplates (if any are missing)

LAB PREPARATION

Before the lab begins, the instructor or lab assistant needs to do the following:

◢ Verify that a computer is available for each student or workgroup.

◢ Verify that the cleaning materials listed above are available. These items can be shared among workgroups.

> **Notes** In this lab, students clean a computer. The instructor might consider taking the students to an office or computer lab on campus where computers are in need of cleaning.

ACTIVITY BACKGROUND

A PC support technician is expected to know how to maintain a computer and its peripherals. You need to know how to clean a monitor, mouse, keyboard, and computer system without damaging the equipment or yourself. This lab covers such concerns.

ESTIMATED COMPLETION TIME: 30 Minutes

 Activity

Table 11-1 lists guidelines to maintain and clean computer equipment. Following the guidelines in Table 11-1, do the following to clean a computer:

1. Ensure the computer is shut down and unplug it.

2. Clean the keyboard, monitor, and mouse.

Component	Cleaning and Maintenance	How Often
Keyboard	◢ Turn the keyboard upside down and lightly bump the keys to dislodge dirt, food, and trash. ◢ Use a damp cloth to clean the surface. ◢ Use compressed air or an antistatic vacuum to blow out dust and dirt. ◢ If a few keys don't work, remove the key caps and spray contact cleaner into the key well. Repeatedly depress the contact to clean it.	Monthly
Mouse	◢ To clean a mechanical mouse, first remove the cover of the mouse ball from the bottom of the mouse. ◢ Use compressed air to blow out the ball cavity. ◢ Clean the rollers with a cotton swab dipped in a very small amount of liquid soap or isopropyl alcohol (not rubbing alcohol). For really dirty rollers, use a toothpick or the end of a paper clip to pick dirt off the rollers. ◢ Use sticky tape to clean the mouse ball.	Monthly
Monitor	◢ Make sure monitor vents are not obstructed. ◢ If the vents look clogged with dust, use a vacuum to suck out the dust. (Don't open the monitor case.) ◢ Clean the outside of the monitor case with a damp cloth. ◢ Clean the screen with a soft dry cloth. For especially dirty screens, use antistatic monitor wipes, which contain a small amount of isopropyl alcohol and are safe for laptop LCD screens.	At least monthly
Inside the case	◢ Make sure the computer case is sitting in a location where air vents are not obstructed and the case will not be kicked. ◢ Use compressed air to blow the dust out of the case, or use an antistatic vacuum to clean vents, power supply, and fans. Be sure all fans and vents are dust free. ◢ Ensure that memory modules and expansion cards are firmly seated. ◢ Use plastic cable ties to tie cables out of the way of airflow. ◢ Be sure all empty bays and empty expansion slots have faceplates installed.	Yearly or whenever you open the case for repairs or installations
Written records of hardware maintenance	◢ Keep an MSDS on file for each chemical you use in your computer lab. ◢ Record when and what preventive maintenance is performed. ◢ Record any repairs done to the PC.	Whenever changes are made

Table 11-1   Guidelines for cleaning computer equipment

3. Clean the outside of the computer case.

4. Open the computer case. Connect the ESD bracelet to the side of the computer case. Be sure to connect the clip to case metal, not plastic.

5. Clean the dust from inside the case. Verify case fans can turn freely.

6. Verify that cables are out of the way of airflow. Use cable ties as necessary.

7. Check that each expansion card and memory module is securely seated in its slot. Remove and reseat the card or memory module as needed.

8. Close the case and plug in the power cord.

9. Power up the system and verify that all is working.

10. Clean up around your work area. If you left dust on the floor as you blew it out of the computer case, be sure to clean it up.

REVIEW QUESTIONS

1. Why is it necessary to use an ESD bracelet when you work inside a computer case?

2. Why is it necessary to have an MSDS on file in a computer lab?

3. Why should monitor vents not be obstructed?

4. Why is it important that computer fans not be clogged with dust?

5. What is the purpose of installing faceplates on empty bays and expansion slots?

6. How do you think restricted air flow affects a computer's performance? Why?

11

LAB 11.4 DIAGNOSE SIMPLE HARDWARE PROBLEMS

OBJECTIVES

The goal of this lab is to give you practice diagnosing and repairing simple hardware problems. After completing this lab, you will be able to:

◢ Start with a functioning PC, introduce a problem, and remedy the problem

◢ Diagnose a problem caused by someone else

◢ Record the troubleshooting process

MATERIALS REQUIRED

This lab requires the following:

◢ Computer designated for this lab

◢ Windows Vista/XP operating system

◢ A PC toolkit, including screwdrivers and an antistatic wrist strap

◢ Pen and paper

◢ The documentation notebook you began creating in Lab 9.1

◢ A workgroup of 2 to 4 students

LAB PREPARATION

Before the lab begins, the instructor or lab assistant needs to do the following:

◢ Verify that Windows starts with no errors.

ACTIVITY BACKGROUND

If you have worked in a computer repair shop dealing with the general public, you know that about half the problems you see are the result of an inexperienced person making a slight mistake when configuring a system and lacking the knowledge to diagnose and remedy the problem. Unless you're very skilled and lucky, you'll make many of the same mistakes from time to time. Your advantage is that you'll have the experience to narrow down and identify the problem and then fix it. This lab gives you experience troubleshooting and repairing simple problems. Before you begin, team up with another workgroup in your class. Your team works with this other group throughout the lab.

ESTIMATED COMPLETION TIME: 60-90 Minutes

 Activity

1. Verify that your team's system is working correctly. Also, verify that you have the completed tables for your system from Lab 9.1.

2. Make one of the following changes to your team's system:

   ◢ Remove the power cable from the hard drive on the primary interface or highest SCSI ID.

   ◢ Reverse the data cable for the floppy drive (if available).

◢ Remove the RAM and place it safely inside the case so that the other team can't see it.

◢ Disable IDE, SCSI, or serial ATA controllers in CMOS.

◢ Remove the power-on wire from the motherboard connection.

◢ Partially remove the data cable from the hard drive.

◢ For IDE drives, swap master/slave jumper assignments or set both drives to the same setting.

3. Switch places with the other team, and then diagnose and remedy the problem on your team's PC. Record the troubleshooting process on a separate sheet of paper, making sure you answer the following questions:

◢ Describe the problem as a user would describe it to you if you were working at a Help desk.

◢ What is your first guess as to the source of the problem?

◢ What did you do that solved the problem and returned the system to good working order?

4. Repeat Steps 1 through 3, choosing items at random from the list in Step 2. Continue until your team has made all the changes listed in Step 2 that are possible for your system.

CRITICAL THINKING (ADDITIONAL 30 MINUTES)

If time permits, try introducing two changes at a time. This procedure can prove much more difficult.

REVIEW QUESTIONS

1. What problems resulted in a "non-system disk" error?

_____

2. Typically, what's the first indication that RAM has been removed?

_____

3. What was the first indication of a problem with drive assignments?

_____

_____

4. Name three problems resulting in symptoms similar to those for a problem with the primary slave drive:

_____

_____

_____

5. What was the first indication of improper hard drive jumper assignments?

_____

LAB 11.5 TROUBLESHOOT A HARDWARE PROBLEM

OBJECTIVES

The goal of this lab is to help you learn how to solve hardware-related PC problems. After completing this lab, you will be able to:

◢ Troubleshoot boot problems caused by hardware

MATERIALS REQUIRED

This lab requires the following:

◢ A computer designated for this lab

◢ Windows Vista/XP operating system

◢ Internet access

LAB PREPARATION

Before the lab begins, the instructor or lab assistant needs to do the following:

◢ Make available a Windows Vista/XP computer and verify that Internet access is available.

SCENARIO BACKGROUND

When a PC does not boot or boots with errors, the problem might be software or hardware related. After you have observed the problem, the next step is to make your best educated guess: Is the problem caused by hardware or software? Then begin troubleshooting from there. Sometimes as you work, you can accidentally create a new problem, so you need to always be aware that the problem might have more than one source. This lab takes you through some real-life troubleshooting situations to help build your troubleshooting skills.

ESTIMATED COMPLETION TIME: 60 Minutes

 Activity

Katie, a PC support technician, is in the habit of leaving her computer turned on when she leaves the office in the evening. Each morning, pressing a key returns the computer to activity from standby mode and she's good to go. However, one morning she sits down at her desk to discover a window with this information on-screen:

P4P800 Asus Motherboard

Press DEL to run Setup

She recognizes the system is stuck at the very beginning of a restart, and the information on the screen is from startup BIOS. Follow along as Katie troubleshoots the problem.

1. She presses the Delete key and nothing happens. She tries other keys, but still no action. She tries pressing the power button on the front of the computer case, but that doesn't work either.

2. Katie unplugs the power cord to the system, plugs it back in, and presses the power button. The system powers up and hangs with the text shown in Figure 11-1 on-screen.

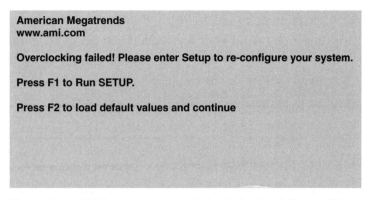

American Megatrends
www.ami.com

Overclocking failed! Please enter Setup to re-configure your system.

Press F1 to Run SETUP.

Press F2 to load default values and continue

Figure 11-1   Katie's system hangs early in the boot and displays this screen
Courtesy: Course Technology/Cengage Learning

3. Katie knows she has not overclocked her system and does not want to use BIOS default settings unless she has no other option. She presses F1 and the system enters CMOS setup.

4. In CMOS setup, she notices the date and time are correct and exits without saving changes. The Windows XP desktop loads normally. In the lower-right corner of the screen, she sees the bubble shown in Figure 11-2.

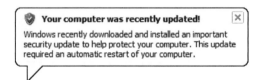

Your computer was recently updated!   [×]
Windows recently downloaded and installed an important
security update to help protect your computer. This update
required an automatic restart of your computer.

Figure 11-2   This bubble appeared on the Windows desktop
Courtesy: Course Technology/Cengage Learning

5. Katie is not satisfied that all is well, so she reboots the system. As the startup BIOS performs POST, she hears a single beep followed by two beeps, and the Windows desktop again loads normally.

6. Katie looks up the beep codes in AMI documentation and finds that one, two, and three beeps are all memory-related errors.

7. She powers down the system and reseats the two memory modules. As a preventive measure, she uses a can of compressed air to blow dust out of the case. And, because she suspects she might later need to replace the DIMMs, she records this information printed on each DIMM:

Elixir 256 MB DDR-400 MHz CL3 PC3200

8. She replaces the front panel and side panel of the PC case and powers up the system. When she does, the monitor screen is totally blank and she hears no beeps. She does hear the fans spinning.

9. She powers down the system again, reseats the DIMMs again, replaces the front panel, and powers up the system. The system boots to the Windows desktop.

10. Katie decides to perform a memory test using third-party memory-testing software. Memory failed the first test, but when she tried it a second time, memory passed with no errors.

TROUBLESHOOTING

Answer the following questions about what Katie did, the source of the problem(s), and what to do next.

◢ Why did Katie's computer reboot during the night?

_____

_____

◢ How can you be certain that Katie's problem is hardware related rather than software related?

_____

_____

◢ What do you think is the source of the original problem?

_____

◢ In Step 4, Katie discovers the date and time are correct. What does this indicate?

_____

◢ In Step 8, why do you think the monitor was blank?

_____

◢ What are four things you would suggest that Katie do next? List the four things in the order Katie should do them:

_____

_____

_____

_____

The motherboard documentation does not normally contain the beep codes needed for troubleshooting, but you should be able to download them from the BIOS manufacturer Web site.

◢ What is the name of the document that contains the explanation of beep codes downloaded from the AMI Web site?

_____

◢ Using the Internet as your source, list the names and Web sites of two diagnostic software applications that can test memory.

_____

_____

For more troubleshooting practice, answer this question about another PC problem that Katie encountered:

◢ Later, Katie complains that the window shown in Figure 11-3 appears each time she restarts her PC. She does not use a RAID controller even though her motherboard has that feature. How can you prevent the window from appearing without installing the controller in Windows?

_____

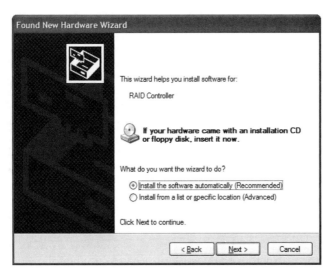

Figure 11-3 The Found New Hardware wizard is attempting to install a RAID controller
Courtesy: Course Technology/Cengage Learning

REVIEW QUESTIONS

1. In troubleshooting a boot problem, what is the advantage of restoring all CMOS settings to their default values?

2. In troubleshooting a boot problem, what is the disadvantage of restoring all CMOS settings to their default values?

3. In troubleshooting a boot problem, what would be the point of disabling the quick boot feature in CMOS setup?

4. What is the MHz rating of a memory module that is rated at PC3200?

5. What made Katie suspect she might be dealing with a memory problem?

LAB 11.6 TROUBLESHOOT GENERAL COMPUTER PROBLEMS

OBJECTIVES

The goal of this lab is to troubleshoot and remedy general computer problems. After completing this lab, you will be able to:

▲ Diagnose and solve problems with various hardware devices

▲ Document the troubleshooting process

MATERIALS REQUIRED

This lab requires the following:

- A computer designated for this lab
- Windows Vista/XP operating system
- Windows installation CD or installation files
- Drivers for all devices
- A pen and paper for taking notes
- A PC toolkit with antistatic ground strap
- A workgroup partner

LAB PREPARATION

Before the lab begins, the instructor or lab assistant needs to do the following:

- Verify that Windows starts with no errors.
- Provide each student with access to the Windows installation files, if needed.

ACTIVITY BACKGROUND

In previous labs, you have learned to troubleshoot specific problems of a PC. This lab takes a comprehensive approach to troubleshooting an entire system, so the problem might relate to any subsystem. Troubleshooting a general problem is no different from troubleshooting a specific subsystem. You simply apply your troubleshooting techniques to a wider range of possibilities.

ESTIMATED COMPLETION TIME: 60-90 Minutes

 Activity

1. Verify that your computer and your partner's computer are working by checking that the system runs smoothly and all drives are accessible. Browse the network and connect to a Web site.

2. Randomly pick one of the following hardware or software problems and introduce it on your PC:
   - Change the boot sequence to boot from a nonexistent device.
   - If both the mouse and the keyboard have PS/2 connectors, switch the connectors at the case.
   - Using Control Panel, install a nonexistent device.
   - Remove the data cable from the primary master hard drive.
   - Change the display settings to two colors that are hard to read.
   - Remove the RAM from the system. (Be sure to store all memory modules in an antistatic bag while they're outside the case.)
   - Unplug the monitor from the video adapter.
   - Use Control Panel to switch the primary and secondary buttons on the mouse.
   - In BIOS, manually add information for a fictitious hard drive.
   - Unplug the network cable from the wall or hub.
   - Use Control Panel to disable your current network connection.

3. Troubleshoot your partner's PC while your partner troubleshoots your computer. Verify that you can accomplish all the tasks you could before the computer was sabotaged.

4. On a separate sheet of paper, answer these questions:

   ◢ What is the initial symptom of the problem as a user would describe it?

   ◢ How did you discover the source of the problem?

   ◢ How did you solve the problem?

   ◢ If you were working at a help desk and someone called with this problem, could the problem have been solved over the phone, or would it have required a visit from a technician? Explain your answer.

5. Return to your computer and repeat Steps 2 through 4. Continue until you have solved all the problems listed in Step 2. For each problem, make sure to answer the questions in Step 4.

6. Which problem was the most difficult to repair? Why?

   _____

   _____

   _____

7. Of those problems that *allowed* the computer to boot, which problem was easiest to detect? Why?

   _____

   _____

   _____

8. Of those problems that *prevented* the computer from booting, which problem was easiest to detect? Why?

   _____

REVIEW QUESTIONS

1. Which problems caused the computer to halt during the boot process?

   _____

   _____

   _____

2. Was the solution to the problem usually obvious once you had discovered its source?

   _____

   _____

   _____

3. What did you usually check first when you were troubleshooting? Why?

_____

_____

_____

4. What general steps did you take in troubleshooting the computer?

_____

_____

_____

LAB 11.7 OBSERVE THE BOOT PROCESS

OBJECTIVES

The goal of this lab is to give you the opportunity to observe the sequence of events in a PC's boot process. After completing this lab, you will be able to:

◢ Describe the boot process in detail

◢ Halt the boot process

◢ Diagnose problems in the boot process

MATERIALS REQUIRED

This lab requires the following:

◢ Windows Vista/XP operating system

◢ A blank floppy disk and drive

◢ A pen and paper for taking notes

◢ A workgroup of 2 to 4 students

LAB PREPARATION

Before the lab begins, the instructor or lab assistant needs to do the following:

◢ Verify that Windows starts with no errors.

◢ Make sure that in CMOS setup, the boot sequence is the floppy drive first and then the hard drive.

ACTIVITY BACKGROUND

This lab familiarizes you with the boot process and gives you some practice recognizing when the boot process halts and observing the resulting information displayed on the screen. Working in teams, you begin by observing a PC booting up and noting every step, from turning on the power to the appearance of the Windows desktop. When you're familiar with all the steps in the boot process, your team then intentionally introduces problems that cause the boot process to fail on your PC and then observes the results. Next, you introduce one problem on your PC, and your team switches PCs with another team's PC and attempts to figure out why that team's PC failed to boot.

Activity

Boot your team's PC and then, using the information on the screen as a guide, record every step in the process. (List this information on a separate piece of paper.) For example, you're looking for RAM initialization, display of CPU speed, a list of devices that are detected, what happens when the screen turns from black to another color, and other similar events. You might have to boot the PC several times to record all the steps. Also, sometimes you can use the Pause key to pause what's on the screen so that you can read it before it flies by.

Perform the following steps to introduce a problem in the boot process of your team's PC. For each problem, boot the PC and describe the problem as a user unfamiliar with PC technology might describe it. List any error messages you see.

1. First boot the computer normally. What is the first message displayed on the screen after you turn on the power?

_____

_____

2. What devices are detected during the boot process?

_____

_____

3. Insert a blank floppy disk into the floppy drive. Describe the problem as a user sees it, including error messages:

_____

_____

4. Unplug the keyboard. Describe the problem. Does the computer still boot into Windows?

_____

_____

5. Unplug the mouse. Describe the problem. Does the computer still boot into Windows?

_____

_____

6. Unplug the monitor. Describe the problem:

_____

7. After a minute, plug the monitor in. Did the system boot correctly?

_____

8. Experiment with your BIOS and record other changes you can make that affect the BOOT process:

_____

11

9. Now cause one problem from the preceding steps and switch places with another team. Do not tell the other team what problem you caused.

10. Detect, diagnose, and remedy the problem on the other team's PC.

REVIEW QUESTIONS

1. Of all the problems you studied during the lab, which one halts the boot process earliest in the process?

_____

2. Which problem results in messages about the operating system not being displayed?

_____

3. Why do you think being familiar with all steps in the boot process is useful?

_____

4. Which device was detected first during the boot process? Why is it important that this device be detected early?

_____

_____

_____

5. Did any of the other changes you made cause the computer not to boot? What were they?

_____

_____

_____

LAB 11.8 CRITICAL THINKING: TROUBLESHOOT A STARTUP PROBLEM

OBJECTIVES

The goal of this lab is to help you learn how to troubleshoot a problem that occurs during Windows Vista or XP startup. After completing this lab, you will be able to:

◢ Solve startup problems with Windows Vista or XP

◢ Use Windows tools to recover data when Windows will not boot

MATERIALS REQUIRED

This lab requires the following:

◢ A Windows Vista/XP computer designated for this lab

◢ Files on the Windows setup CD/DVD

◢ Backup media such as a blank floppy disk or USB drive

◢ Internet access

LAB PREPARATION

Before the lab begins, the instructor or lab assistant needs to do the following:

◢ Verify a Windows Vista/XP computer is working for each student or workgroup.

◢ Make available the Windows setup CD/DVD or setup files stored on the network or other location.

◢ Verify that Internet access is available.

ACTIVITY BACKGROUND

As stable as Windows is, problems can still occur. A PC support technician needs to know how to investigate these problems and solve them. This lab gives you a variety of experiences to help build your troubleshooting skills.

ESTIMATED COMPLETION TIME: 90 Minutes

 Activity

Imagine the following scenario:

Karen calls you in a desperate voice and says, "Please come over to my desk right away. My Windows Vista PC has crashed and I have an important Word document on it that isn't backed up. I have to have it for a closing tomorrow morning." As the only PC support technician in a small real estate firm, you find yourself responding far too often to desperate cries for help, and you've learned that protecting user data is actually the most important part of your job. For that reason, you have just installed a file backup server for the company. However, it's up to each user to decide to use the server. Therefore, you're a bit frustrated when you arrive at Karen's desk. Why didn't she back up like everyone else in her group is now doing?

Karen steps aside for you to take over the problem. On the black screen, you see a simple text message, "Invalid boot disk." You try not to alarm Karen as you suck in your breath with a soft whistle.

Use your knowledge of computers and the Internet to answer these questions:

1. The first thing you do is power down the system and turn it back on. You get the same message. If the computer booted normally this time, would your task be complete? Why or why not?

_____

_____

_____

2. Next, you try booting from the Windows Vista setup DVD. You get the same message. Why do you think the computer did not automatically boot to the DVD?

_____

_____

3. On the next boot, you are able to launch the System Recovery Options from the DVD, as shown in Figure 11-4, and get to the command prompt. Karen says the Word document is in her Documents folder and is named MichaelSmithClosing.doc. What is the exact path to the document? (Karen's user account is Karen Moore.)

_____

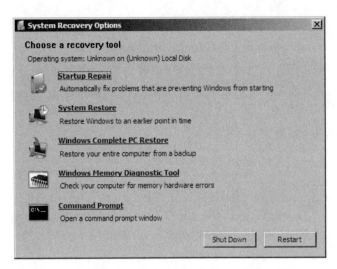

Figure 11-4   Vista's System Recovery Options window
Courtesy: Course Technology/Cengage Learning

4. Create an account named Karen Moore on your lab PC and put a file named MichaelSmithClosing.doc in the Documents folder (My Documents in XP) for this account.

5. List the commands to copy the document to a floppy disk in drive A or a USB drive, and test these commands at your lab PC using the Command Prompt (Recovery Console in XP).

_____

_____

_____

_____

_____

6. When you try to access drive C on Karen's PC, you receive an error message, "The path or file specified is not valid." You suspect a damaged master boot record. (More accurately, you hope the problem is this simple to solve!) What steps can you use to fix the MBR?

_____

7. What command can you use to check the hard drive for errors and possibly recover lost data?

_____

If this last command works, then you can most likely recover Karen's file. You should not trust this hard drive again. In a work environment, you should copy all data to another media, replace the drive, and reinstall Windows.

1. If you were not able to recover Karen's file, what can you tactfully say to Karen about the lost file and the need to make backups in the future?

_____

_____

2. Assume you were able to recover the file. After the file is safely in Karen's hands, what can you say to her to encourage her to use backups in the future?

_____

_____

Sometimes problems are not the result of failed hardware, but are caused by corrupted device drivers. If an error message appears during the boot that names the device or driver causing the problem, you can try to disable the device. If the error message goes away, reinstall the device or update the device drivers. Sometimes the error message doesn't contain enough information or there is no error message at all—the boot just hangs. Complete the following steps to learn how to handle these situations:

1. Boot to the Advanced Boot Options Menu and enable boot logging. What is the path and name of the boot log file?

_____

2. Now reboot with boot logging enabled. The system hangs, but hopefully the log contains enough information to help you solve the problem.

3. Boot into Safe Mode and view the log file. How do you display the log file on-screen?

_____

If you have a copy of a boot log file created when the system was healthy, you can compare the problem log file to the healthy one to help locate the source of the problem. Do the following:

1. On your lab PC, enable boot logging and reboot the system.

2. Open a command prompt window. List the commands to copy the log file to a floppy disk or USB drive.

_____

_____

Tools and utilities that can help you solve Windows problems are listed below:

◢ Last Known Good Configuration on the Advanced Boot Options Menu

◢ Safe Mode on the Advanced Boot Options Menu

◢ Boot logging on the Advanced Boot Options Menu

◢ Antivirus software

◢ Device Manager

◢ System Configuration Utility (Msconfig)

◢ System Restore

◢ Task Manager

◢ Services console

◢ Programs applet in Control Panel (Add or Remove Programs in XP)

◢ The hard drive's Properties window

11

Using the preceding list and other resources, answer the following questions:

1. What tool can be used to view all services loaded at startup or loaded as needed?

_____

2. What tool can be used to view all installed devices and their drivers?

_____

3. What tool can be used to view write errors to the hard drive?

_____

4. What tool can be used to view running processes?

_____

5. If you cannot boot to the normal Windows desktop, but you can boot into Safe Mode, which tool can you use to systematically identify the service or driver causing the problem?

_____

6. What function key is used to access the Advanced Boot Options Menu?

_____

7. What function key is used to boot directly into Safe Mode?

_____

REVIEW QUESTIONS

1. You have just installed new software and restarted the system, which now hangs before reaching the Windows desktop. What do you try first?

_____

2. The system hangs while your version of Windows is loading, but no error message is displayed. How can you determine which driver, program, or service is the source of the error?

_____

_____

3. After you have logged into your version of Windows, a strange error message appears about a service that failed to load. How can you find out from where this service is launched?

_____

_____

4. Users complain that data files are getting corrupted and you suspect the hard drive might be failing. What are at least two possible causes for this problem?

_____

_____

5. Numerous error messages appear as you load Windows, and you suspect the system is infected with a virus. No antivirus software is installed, but when you try to install the software from CD, you get error messages. What can you do to scan the hard drive for viruses without first booting to Windows?

_____

_____

LAB 11.9 CRITICAL THINKING: SABOTAGE AND REPAIR A SYSTEM

OBJECTIVES

The goal of this lab is to learn to troubleshoot a system by recovering from a sabotaged system.

MATERIALS REQUIRED

This lab requires the following:

◢ A PC (containing no important data) that has been designated for sabotage

◢ A workgroup of 2 to 4 students

LAB PREPARATION

Before the lab begins, the instructor or lab assistant needs to do the following:

◢ Verify that Windows starts with no errors.

◢ Verify that students' PCs contain no important data and can be sabotaged.

ACTIVITY BACKGROUND

You have learned about several tools and methods you can use to troubleshoot and repair a failed system or failed hardware devices. This lab gives you the opportunity to use these skills in a simulated troubleshooting situation. Your group will work with another group to sabotage a system and then repair another failed system.

ESTIMATED COMPLETION TIME: 60-90 Minutes

 Activity

1. If the hard drive contains important data, back it up to another medium. Back up anything else you would like to save before another group sabotages the system and note it here:

_____

2. Trade systems with another group and sabotage the other group's system while that group sabotages your system. Do something that will cause the system to fail to work or give errors after booting.

3. You can use any of the problems listed in earlier Labs such as 8.7, 11.4, 11.6, or 11.7. You can search the internet or your imagination to introduce a new non-destructive problem such as turning down the brightness on the monitor or removing

the CPU. Be creative and have fun. If you want to create something even more challenging, try combining more than one problem. What did you do to sabotage the other team's system?

_____

_____

4. Return to your system and troubleshoot it.

5. Describe the problem as a user would describe it to you if you were working at a help desk:

_____

_____

6. What is your first guess as to the source of the problem?

_____

7. List the steps you took in the troubleshooting process:

_____

_____

_____

_____

_____

8. What did you do that finally solved the problem and returned the system to good working order?

_____

_____

9. Repeat Steps 2–8 so that each member of your group has an opportunity to create and solve several problems.

REVIEW QUESTIONS

1. Thinking back on this troubleshooting experience to the problem that caused you the most difficulty, what would you do differently the next time you encounter the same symptoms?

_____

_____

2. Did you use any third-party software utilities or hardware devices to solve any of your problems? If so, what were they?

_____

3. Think of a computer problem you've experienced in the past. How did you handle the problem?

_____

_____

_____

4. Is there anything you could have done differently to diagnose the solution earlier or avoid the problem all together?

_____

11

CHAPTER 12

Installing Windows

Labs included in this chapter:

- **Lab 12.1:** Install or Upgrade to Windows 2000
- **Lab 12.2:** Determine Hardware Compatibility with Windows XP
- **Lab 12.3:** Install or Upgrade to Windows XP
- **Lab 12.4:** Install or Upgrade to Windows Vista
- **Lab 12.5:** Critical Thinking: Virtual PC
- **Lab 12.6:** Critical Thinking: Unattended Installation

LAB 12.1 INSTALL OR UPGRADE TO WINDOWS 2000

OBJECTIVES

The goal of this lab is to help you install or upgrade to Windows 2000 Professional. After completing this lab, you will be able to:

▲ Plan an upgrade or installation

▲ Identify the benefits of an upgrade or a new installation

▲ Install or upgrade to Windows 2000 Professional

MATERIALS REQUIRED

This lab requires the following:

▲ Windows 98 operating system

▲ Access to drivers or Internet access for downloading drivers

▲ Windows 2000 Professional installation files or installation CD

▲ Key from installation CD

LAB PREPARATION

Before the lab begins, the instructor or lab assistant needs to do the following:

▲ Verify that Windows starts with no errors.

▲ Provide each student with access to the Windows 2000 installation files or CD and key.

▲ Verify that any necessary Windows 2000 drivers are available.

ACTIVITY BACKGROUND

Many people are intimidated at the thought of installing or upgrading an operating system. The process doesn't need to be difficult. In fact, if you plan your installation carefully and are prepared to supply required information and device drivers, your main complaint might be that the process is time consuming. Even that annoyance can be minimized, using techniques designed to reduce the total installation time. In this lab, you plan and prepare for an installation or an upgrade to Windows 2000 Professional, and then perform the upgrade or installation.

ESTIMATED COMPLETION TIME: 120 Minutes

 Activity

Follow these steps to plan and prepare for a Windows 2000 Professional installation on your computer:

1. Obtain a list of devices in the system and detailed system specifications, such as processor speed and drive capacity. If no list currently exists, you can use Device Manager or SiSoftware Sandra Lite (installed in Lab 1.3) to compile one.

2. Make another list of important applications, and check to see whether they are compatible with Windows 2000. If you find any that aren't, check to see whether any patches or upgrades are available to make them compatible.

3. Check each system specification and device against the system requirements list for Windows 2000 on the Microsoft Support site (*http://support.microsoft.com/kb/304297*). Your system will probably be compatible with Windows 2000. However, when working on other systems,

you might discover significant incompatibilities. In that case, you would have to decide whether upgrading to Windows 2000 is really an option. If you decide to go ahead with the upgrade, you would have to decide which applications or hardware you need to upgrade before upgrading the operating system. The Windows 2000 installation CD offers a Check Upgrade Only mode that you can use to check for incompatibility issues in your system before you actually install the OS; however, the information on the Microsoft Web site, which you're using in this step, is often more current and easier to access. Answer the following:

◢ Does your system qualify for Windows 2000?

_____

◢ If not, what hardware or application doesn't qualify?

_____

◢ Will you install using FAT32 or NTFS? Explain your decision:

_____

_____

_____

4. Download or otherwise obtain all necessary drivers, service packs, and application patches from the manufacturer's or Microsoft Web site for installed applications and hardware. Record a summary of the components you were required to install to make your system compatible with Windows 2000:

_____

_____

_____

_____

5. Gather any network-specific information in preparation for the installation. If you're connected to a network, answer the following:

◢ If you're using a TCP/IP network, how is your IP address configured?

_____

◢ For a static IP address, what is the IP address?

_____

◢ What is the workgroup name or domain name of the network?

_____

◢ What is your computer name?

_____

6. Make sure you have the correct CD key for your installation CD. The CD key, provided with the Windows 2000 installation CD, usually consists of a set of alphanumeric characters. You must enter the CD key to complete the installation—even if you're installing the operating system from setup files located somewhere other than on the installation CD.

7. Review the information you have collected so far, and then decide whether to do a fresh installation or an upgrade. For instance, if all the important applications on your system are compatible with Windows 2000, an upgrade will probably save time because it leaves compatible applications in working condition. On the other hand, if you know you'll have to install new applications anyway because of incompatibilities, you might choose to perform a fresh installation. In many ways, a fresh installation is preferable because it ensures that no misconfigured system settings are carried over to the new operating system.

◢ Will you perform a clean install or an upgrade?

_____

◢ Give a brief explanation of why you chose that option:

_____

_____

8. Back up any critical data files (that is, any work you or others have stored on your computer that you can't afford to lose during the installation process).

◢ If you have critical data files on the PC, where did you back them up to?

_____

You're ready to begin installing Windows 2000 Professional. This lab assumes that you have another version of Windows installed and running such as Windows 98. This is not the only situation in which you would install or even upgrade to Windows 2000, but it's common. Installing the operating system is possible using files on the installation CD, a network drive, or a local hard disk. To speed up the installation process, consider copying the setup files from the installation CD (or from a network drive) to a local hard disk. This method takes extra time at first but is faster overall.

◢ Are you performing the installation from the Windows 2000 CD, files stored on your hard drive, or a network drive?

_____

The following steps are representative of a typical installation. Your installation will probably vary in minor ways, depending on the installation options you choose, your system's hardware configuration, and other factors. The following steps are a general guide to let you know what to expect during the process. Don't become alarmed if your experience differs slightly. Use your knowledge to solve any problems on your own, and ask your instructor for help if you get stuck. You might want to record any differences between these steps and your own experience. Also, record any decisions you make and any information you enter during the installation process.

1. Before you insert the installation CD or run the setup files from a location on your hard drive or network, use antivirus software to scan the computer's memory and hard drive for viruses. After the scan is finished, make sure to disable any automatic scans and close the antivirus program before beginning installation.

2. The Setup program starts after the setup CD has been inserted. This program guides you through the actual installation. If it doesn't begin automatically, click **Start, Run**, and run WINNT32.exe from the \I386 folder.

◢ Did Setup start automatically for you, or did you have to use the Run command?

_____

3. Setup informs you that you're running an older version of Windows and asks whether you want to upgrade to Windows 2000. Click **Yes** to continue and follow the instructions in the Setup program. Note that although Setup initially uses the word "upgrade," you're then given the option of doing an upgrade or a fresh installation of Windows 2000.

4. Accept the end user license agreement (EULA) and click **Next**.

5. When prompted, enter the CD key and click **Next**.

6. Setup examines your system and reports any situations that could cause problems during installation. You're given the opportunity to print the report and exit Setup to correct the problems. Even if some problems are reported, you have done your homework during planning and probably have the solution, so continue the installation.

7. You're given the opportunity to review the Hardware Compatibility List. If you want to review it again, do so and click **Next** to continue.

8. Specify your file system as NTFS and click **Next**. The system begins to copy files for the installation. Then the text portion of the installation, which has a command-line interface rather than a Windows GUI, begins. The text portion includes the following:

   ◢ Examining hardware

   ◢ Deleting old Windows files, if applicable

   ◢ Copying Windows 2000 operating system files

   ◢ Rebooting your computer automatically

> **Notes** Windows 98 doesn't support NTFS, so if you were setting up a dual-boot system that used that operating system, you should choose FAT32 as the file system.

After your computer reboots, the Windows 2000 Setup portion begins, which includes the following:

   ◢ Verifying the file system

   ◢ Checking the file structure

   ◢ Converting the file system to NTFS

   ◢ Rebooting automatically

1. Select **Windows 2000 Professional** in the startup menu. Because you converted your file system to NTFS, you should see a message indicating that the conversion was successful.

2. The system installs software for detected devices. When prompted, enter the requested network information. After you have specified how your network is configured, Setup performs some final setup tasks, including the following:

   ◢ Configuring the startup menu

   ◢ Registering components

   ◢ Upgrading programs and system settings

   ◢ Saving settings

   ◢ Removing temporary files

3. The computer reboots one more time. Now you can log on as an administrator and install any new applications or devices.

4. Verify that the system is working correctly.

On the following lines, record any differences you noted between these installation steps and your own experience. Also, record any decisions you made and any information you entered during the installation process:

_____

_____

_____

_____

_____

_____

REVIEW QUESTIONS

1. List five things you should do before starting the installation process:

_____

_____

_____

_____

_____

2. How can you find out whether your video card will work with Windows 2000?

_____

3. What type of installation can save time because it usually retains system settings and leaves applications in working condition?

_____

_____

4. What step is critical to ensure that you don't lose important data during installation?

_____

5. What step can you take to speed up the actual installation process?

_____

CHALLENGE ACTIVITY (ADDITIONAL 15 MINUTES)

Another alternative for upgrading the operating systems on an older Windows 98 machine is Microsoft Windows Fundamentals for Legacy PCs (FLP), which is optimized for older computers. Use the Internet to find answers to the following questions:

1. What are the minimum and recommended requirements for installing FLP?

_____

2. Will FLP support most Windows XP applications? Is there anything it doesn't support?

_____

_____

3. What would be some advantages and disadvantages of upgrading a Windows 98 machine to FLP?

_____

_____

_____

LAB 12.2 DETERMINE HARDWARE COMPATIBILITY WITH WINDOWS XP

OBJECTIVES

The goal of this lab is to help you determine whether your hardware is compatible with Windows XP. After completing this lab, you will be able to:

◢ Use Windows to identify system components

◢ Find and use the Microsoft Hardware Compatibility List (HCL)

MATERIALS REQUIRED

This lab requires the following:

◢ Windows 9x or Windows 2000 operating system

◢ Internet access

LAB PREPARATION

Before the lab begins, the instructor or lab assistant needs to do the following:

◢ Verify that Windows starts with no errors.

◢ Verify that Internet access is available.

ACTIVITY BACKGROUND

You can't assume that an operating system will support your hardware, especially with older devices, because software developers focus on supporting the most capable and popular devices. To verify that Microsoft operating systems support your hardware, you can check the Windows Logo'd Product List, formerly called the Microsoft Hardware Compatibility List (HCL), at _http://winqual.microsoft.com/HCL/Default.aspx?m=x_. The HCL includes devices that have drivers written by Microsoft or devices that have drivers tested and approved by Microsoft. In this lab, you use Device Manager to inventory devices in a system. Then you check the HCL to see whether Windows XP Professional supports the system's devices.

ESTIMATED COMPLETION TIME: 30 Minutes

 Activity

To use Device Manager to inventory your system, follow these steps:

1. Open Control Panel and double-click the **System** icon.

2. In Windows 2000, click the **Hardware** tab, and then click the **Device Manager** button. In Windows 9x, click the **Device Manager** tab. The Device Manager window opens.

3. In Device Manager, devices are arranged by category. To see what kind of video adapter is installed on your system, click the + (plus sign) to the left of Display Adapters.

4. Click your video adapter and click the **Properties** button. Record the information about the model and manufacturer that's displayed:

_____

_____

_____

5. Use Device Manager to find similar information for your network adapter, modem card, or sound card, and record that information here:

_____

_____

_____

Now that you have a list of devices installed on your system, check the Windows Logo'd Product List to see whether Windows XP supports these devices. Web sites change often, so the following steps might have to be adjusted to accommodate changes. If you have difficulty following these steps because of Web site changes, see your instructor for help.

1. Open your browser and go to **www.microsoft.com/whdc/hcl/default.mspx**. Click the **Windows XP Hardware Compatibility List** link.

2. At the left under **Devices**, point to **Components** and then click **Video Cards**. Using the information about your video adapter you recorded previously in Step 4, find your video card by scrolling the list or using the drop-down lists across the top.

3. Confirm that you have found your device by verifying that the correct manufacturer and model are listed.

4. Add a note to your list of devices indicating whether the device is compatible with Windows XP Professional.

5. Check the other devices in your list, and note whether they are compatible with Windows XP Professional.

6. If a device isn't listed in the HCL, what are your options when installing Windows XP? List at least two possibilities:

_____

_____

7. Does the hardware in your system qualify for Windows XP? If it doesn't, explain why:

_____

_____

REVIEW QUESTIONS

1. Explain how to compile a list of devices installed on your system:

_____

_____

_____

2. How are devices grouped in Device Manager?

_____

3. Where can you find the HCL?

_____

4. If a device isn't listed in the HCL, is there still a chance it will work in your machine?

_____

_____

5. Why might it be a bad idea to use a device that's not listed in the HCL?

_____

_____

LAB 12.3 INSTALL OR UPGRADE TO WINDOWS XP

12

OBJECTIVES

The goal of this lab is to help you install or upgrade to Windows XP Professional. After completing this lab, you will be able to:

◢ Plan an upgrade or installation

◢ Identify the benefits of an upgrade or new installation

◢ Install or upgrade to Windows XP Professional

MATERIALS REQUIRED

This lab requires the following:

◢ Windows 9x or Windows 2000 operating system

◢ Access to drivers or Internet access for downloading drivers

◢ Windows XP Professional installation CD or installation files

◢ Product Key from installation CD

◢ A storage medium for updated device drivers

LAB PREPARATION

Before the lab begins, the instructor or lab assistant needs to do the following:

◢ Verify that Windows starts with no errors.

◢ Provide each student with access to the Windows XP installation files and key.

◢ Verify that any necessary Windows XP drivers are available.

ACTIVITY BACKGROUND

Windows XP is designed to be reliable and has a different user interface from Windows 9x to give you a more personalized computing experience. The operating system's updated look uses more graphics to simplify the user interface. It has a task-oriented design, which gives you options specifically associated with the task or file you're working on. You can upgrade your computer's operating system to Windows XP Professional from Windows 98/98SE, Windows Me, Windows NT Workstation 4.0, Windows 2000, or Windows XP Home Edition. Installing or upgrading an operating system isn't difficult. Careful planning can minimize or eliminate many of the headaches some users have experienced when upgrading to Windows XP.

ESTIMATED COMPLETION TIME: 90–120 Minutes

 Activity

Your lab system will likely be compatible with Windows XP. However, when working on other systems, you might discover significant incompatibilities. In that case, you have to decide whether upgrading to Windows XP Professional is really an option. Many users have problems with device drivers when upgrading to a new version of Windows. For this reason, it's essential to do your research and download device drivers that are compatible with Windows XP Professional before you install the upgrade. You might need to visit the manufacturer Web sites for all your devices, such as scanners, printers, modems, keyboards, mouse, camera, and so on, to see whether they are compatible with Windows XP Professional. If the manufacturer provides an updated device driver to support Windows XP Professional, you need to download the files to a storage medium. Also, when planning an upgrade, recording information in a table, such as Table 12-1, is helpful. Follow these steps to create a plan and prepare for a Windows XP Professional upgrade on your computer:

1. Use Device Manager or SiSoftware Sandra (installed in Lab 1.3) to compile the information and fill in Table 12-1 as you complete the following steps.

Things to Do	Further Information
Does the PC meet the minimum or recommended hardware requirements?	**CPU:** **RAM:** **Hard drive size:** **Free space on the hard drive:**
Have you checked all your applications to verify that they qualify for Windows XP or if they need patches to qualify?	**Applications that need to be upgraded:**
Have you checked the Microsoft Web site to verify that all your hardware qualifies? (See lab 12.2.)	**Hardware that needs to be upgraded:**
Have you decided how you will join a network?	**Workgroup name:** **Domain name:** **Computer name:**
Can you find the product key?	**Product key:**
Have you backed up critical data?	**Location of backup files:**
Is your hard drive ready?	**Size of the hard drive partition:** **Free space on the partition:** **File system you plan to use:**

Table 12-1 Things to do and information to collect when planning a Windows upgrade

2. Compare your information to the Windows XP requirements in Table 12-2.

   ◢ Does your system meet the minimum requirements?

   _____

   ◢ Does your system meet the recommended requirements?

   _____

Component or Device	Minimum Requirement	Recommended Requirement
One or two CPUs	Pentium II 233 MHz or better	Pentium II 300 MHz or better
RAM	64 MB	128 MB up to 4 GB
Hard drive partition	2 GB	2 GB or more
Free space on the hard drive partition	640 MB (bare bones)	2 GB or more
CD-ROM drive	12×	12× or faster
Accessories	Keyboard and mouse or other pointing device	Keyboard and mouse or other pointing device

Table 12-2 Minimum and recommended requirements for Windows XP Professional

3. Make a list of important applications on your system and verify whether they are compatible with Windows XP Professional. If you find any that aren't, check to see whether patches or upgrades are available to make them compatible. List in Table 12-1 any applications that don't qualify or that need patches to qualify. List any software upgrades or patches you downloaded to prepare your applications for Windows XP:

   _____

   _____

   _____

   _____

4. Install any application upgrades or patches you have downloaded.
5. Start with the list compiled in Lab 12.2 and list in Table 12-1 any hardware devices that need updated drivers.
6. Download or otherwise obtain all necessary drivers from the manufacturers' Web sites or the Microsoft site for your hardware. List any drivers you were required to install to make your hardware compatible with Windows XP Professional:

   _____

   _____

   _____

12

7. Gather any network-specific information in preparation for the installation. If you're connected to a network, answer the following:

◢ If you're using a TCP/IP network, how is your IP address configured?

_____

◢ For a static IP address, what is the IP address?

_____

◢ What is the workgroup name or domain name of the network?

_____

◢ What is your computer name?

_____

Record the workgroup or domain name and the computer name in Table 12-1.

8. Make sure you have the correct CD key for your installation CD and record it in Table 12-1. The CD key, provided with the Windows XP Professional installation CD, usually consists of a set of alphanumeric characters. You must enter the CD key to complete the installation, even if you're installing the operating system from setup files located somewhere other than the installation CD.

9. Review the information you've collected so far, and answer the following:

◢ Does your system qualify for Windows XP Professional?

_____

◢ If not, what hardware or application doesn't qualify?

_____

10. Now decide whether to do a fresh installation or an upgrade. For instance, if all the important applications on your system are compatible with Windows XP Professional, an upgrade will probably save time because it leaves compatible applications in working condition. On the other hand, if you know you have to install new applications because of incompatibilities, you might choose to perform a fresh installation. In many ways, a fresh installation is preferable because it ensures that no misconfigured system settings are carried over to the new operating system.

11. Back up critical data files (that is, any work you or others have stored on your computer that you can't afford to lose during the installation process).

12. If you have critical files on the PC, to what location did you back them up? Record that information in Table 12-1.

13. The hard drive partition that is to be the active partition for Windows XP must be at least 2 GB and have at least 2 GB free. Record the size of the hard drive partition and the amount of free space on that partition in Table 12-1. Answer these questions:

◢ What Windows utilities or commands did you use to determine the size of the active partition?

_____

_____

◢ What Windows utilities or commands did you use to determine how much free space is on that partition?

_____

_____

14. When installing Windows XP, you have a choice of using the FAT or NTFS file system. For this installation, use the NTFS file system. Record that information in Table 12-1.

You're ready to begin installing Windows XP Professional. This lab assumes that you have another version of Windows installed and running. This is not the only situation in which you would install or upgrade to Windows XP Professional, but it's common. Installing Windows XP is possible using setup files stored on the installation CD, a network drive, or a local hard disk.

The following steps are representative of a typical upgrade. Your installation will probably vary in minor ways, depending on the installation options you choose, your system's hardware configuration, and other factors. The following steps are a general guide to let you know what to expect during the process. Don't become alarmed if your experience differs slightly. Use your knowledge to solve any problems on your own, and ask your instructor for help if you get stuck. You might want to record any differences between these steps and your own experience. Also, record any decisions you make and any information you enter during the installation process.

1. Before you insert the installation CD or run the installation files from a location on your hard drive or network, use antivirus software to scan the computer's memory and hard drive for viruses. After the scan is finished, make sure you disable any automatic scans and close the antivirus program before beginning the installation.

2. Insert the Windows XP Professional CD. The Setup program starts. This program guides you through the actual installation. If it doesn't begin automatically, click **Start, Run** and browse for the Setup.exe file to begin the installation.

3. The Welcome to Microsoft Windows XP window opens with some options. What options do you see?

_____

_____

_____

_____

_____

4. Click **Install Windows XP**. The Setup program begins collecting information, and the Welcome to Windows Setup window opens with Installation Type: Upgrade (Recommended) in the text box. Click **Next**.

5. Accept the EULA, and then click **Next**.

6. When prompted, enter the CD key, and then click **Next**.

7. If the Windows Setup Upgrade Report window opens, click the **Show me hardware issues and a limited set of software issues (Recommended)** option, and then click **Next**.

8. The Windows Setup Get Updated Setup Files window opens. Because you can check for updates later and are focusing on upgrading for now, click **No, skip this step and continue installing Windows,** and click **Next**.

9. Windows is now preparing the installation of Windows XP Professional by analyzing your computer. This setup takes approximately 60 minutes. Read the informational screens as they're displayed. You can gain a lot of knowledge of Windows XP through this minitutorial. Your computer restarts several times during the installation and setup process.

10. When the installation is finished and Windows XP has restarted for the last time, the Welcome to Microsoft Windows window opens. Click **Next** to continue.

11. If you see a Help Protect your PC screen, select **Help protect my PC by turning on Automatic Updates now** and click **Next**.

    In the Ready to activate windows screen, click **No, remind me every few days** and then click **Next**.

12. Now you may have an option to enter your user information. You can type the name of each person who will use this computer. Windows creates a separate user account for each person, so you can personalize the way you want Windows to organize and display information, protect your files and computer settings, and customize the desktop. The user names you enter appear in the Welcome window in alphabetical order. When you start Windows, you simply click your name in the Welcome window to begin working in Windows XP Professional. For now, enter only your first name, and then click **Next**.

13. When you see a Thank you! message, click **Finish** to continue.

14. You may also have the option to set a password for all Windows XP accounts. Enter a password to be used for all the listed accounts. If you want to change the passwords later, go to the User Accounts applet in Control Panel.

15. To begin using Windows XP, click your user name and enter your password. A Welcome window appears. Wait while Windows XP loads your personal settings. The first time you start Windows XP, the Start menu is displayed until you click something else. Thereafter, you open the Start menu by clicking the Start button at the left of the taskbar.

16. Remove the installation CD from the drive and return it to your instructor.

17. The basic installation is complete. The next steps would be to install a virus checker, check the operating system for updates, and upgrade any necessary drivers and applications.

18. Was the Windows XP upgrade a success? If so, what did you find to be most challenging about the upgrade process?

    _____

    _____

19. Describe the Windows XP desktop:

    _____

    _____

    _____

REVIEW QUESTIONS

1. By default, which icon appears on the Windows XP desktop?

   _____

2. Where did you find the Windows product key?

   _____

3. Why will an upgrade save time over a fresh installation?

_____

4. What possible locations can be used to store the setup files?

_____

5. Which should you do first, install a virus checker or check for updates to the operating system? Why?

_____

_____

LAB 12.4 INSTALL OR UPGRADE TO WINDOWS VISTA

OBJECTIVES

The goal of this lab is to help you install or upgrade to Windows Vista. After completing this lab, you will be able to:

◢ Plan an upgrade or installation

◢ Identify the benefits of an upgrade or new installation

◢ Install or upgrade to Windows Vista

MATERIALS REQUIRED

This lab requires the following:

◢ Windows 2000/XP operating system

◢ Access to drivers or Internet access for downloading drivers

◢ Windows Vista installation DVD or installation files

◢ Key from installation DVD

◢ A storage medium for updated device drivers

LAB PREPARATION

Before the lab begins, the instructor or lab assistant needs to do the following:

◢ Verify that Windows starts with no errors.

◢ Provide each student with access to the Windows Vista installation files and key.

◢ Verify that any necessary Windows Vista drivers are available.

ACTIVITY BACKGROUND

Windows Vista was designed to replace XP with a new line of operating systems that offer improved reliability, security, and ease of use. Some of the key new features in Vista include:

◢ A new 3D look known as the Aero glass interface

◢ A new version of Internet Explorer

◢ A sidebar full of small applications called gadgets

◢ Faster startup and shutdown

◢ A new spyware monitor called Windows Defender

Activity

The most common problem people have when installing Windows Vista is with incompatible hardware drivers. Therefore, it is important to research and download device drivers that are compatible with Windows Vista before you begin the install. Sometimes manufacturers of older products provide drivers for new operating systems, but usually they don't. Follow these steps to install Windows Vista:

1. Go online and research the minimum and recommended requirements for the version of Windows Vista that you will be using and enter them in the space below:

   _____

   _____

   _____

   _____

   _____

   _____

2. Gather the necessary information about your computer to answer the following questions (see Lab 12.3):

   ◢ Does your system meet the minimum requirements?

   _____

   ◢ Does your system meet the recommended requirements?

   _____

3. Make a list of important applications on your system and verify whether they are compatible with Windows Vista. If you find any that aren't, check to see whether patches or upgrades are available to make them compatible. List any software upgrades or patches you downloaded to prepare your applications for Windows Vista:

   _____

   _____

   _____

   _____

4. Install any application upgrades or patches you have downloaded.

5. Download or otherwise obtain all necessary drivers from the manufacturers' Web sites or the Microsoft site for your hardware. List any drivers you were required to install to make your hardware compatible with Windows Vista:

   _____

   _____

   _____

6. Gather any network-specific information in preparation for the installation. If you're connected to a network, answer the following:

   ◢ If you're using a TCP/IP network, how is your IP address configured?

   _____

   ◢ For a static IP address, what is the IP address?

   _____

   ◢ What is the workgroup name or domain name of the network?

   _____

   ◢ What is your computer name?

   _____

7. The product key, provided with the Windows Vista installation DVD, usually consists of a set of alphanumeric characters and determines the edition of Vista being installed. You must enter the key to complete the installation, even if you're installing the operating system from setup files located somewhere other than the installation DVD. Make sure you have the correct product key for your installation DVD and record it below:

   _____

8. Review the information you've collected so far, and then decide whether to do a fresh installation or an upgrade. For instance, if all the important applications on your system are compatible with Windows Vista, an upgrade will probably save time because it leaves compatible applications in working condition. On the other hand, if you know you have to install new applications because of incompatibilities, you might choose to perform a fresh installation. In many ways, a fresh installation is preferable because it ensures that no misconfigured system settings are carried over to the new operating system.

9. Back up critical data files (that is, any work you or others have stored on your computer that you can't afford to lose during the installation process).

The following steps are representative of a typical installation. Steps for both an upgrade and a clean installation are included. Your installation will probably vary in minor ways, depending on the installation options you choose, your system's hardware configuration, and other factors. The following steps are a general guide to let you know what to expect during the process. Don't become alarmed if your experience differs slightly. Use your knowledge to solve any problems on your own, and ask your instructor for help if you get stuck. You might want to record any differences between these steps and your own experience. Also, record any decisions you make and any information you enter during the installation process.

If you are performing an in-place upgrade to Vista, follow these steps:

1. Close any open applications that might interfere with the installation such as antivirus or boot management software.

2. From the Windows desktop, launch the Vista DVD. When the Setup program starts, click **Install now**. This program guides you through the actual installation. If it doesn't begin automatically, click **Start, Run** and browse for the Setup.exe file to begin the installation.

3. On the next screen, choose to allow the setup program to download updates. Click **Go online to get the latest updates for installation (recommended)**.

4. Enter the product key and click **Next**.

5. Accept the EULA, and then click **Next**.

12

6. Click **Upgrade**.

7. As the installation continues, the computer may reboot several times and you may be asked to enter some information about your location and hardware setup or whether you want to Help protect Windows automatically.

8. Next, you may be asked to enter a username, password, computer name, date, and time. Record all of your answers below:

_____

_____

_____

_____

9. At the end of the setup process, a logon screen appears.

If you are performing a clean install of Vista, follow these steps:

1. Insert the Windows Vista installation DVD and reboot your computer. If you receive a "Press any key to boot from CD/DVD" message, press a key. If your system is not configured to boot from the DVD drive, you will need to change the boot order in the BIOS (see Lab 5.1).

2. When the Install Windows window appears, you may have to select some configuration information such as your preferred language and keyboard type. When you're finished, click **Next**.

3. When the opening menu appears, click **Install now**.

4. Enter the product key and click **Next**.

5. Accept the EULA and click **Next**.

6. Click **Custom (advanced)**.

7. The next screen shows the list of partitions where you can install Vista. Copy this list below:

_____

_____

_____

8. Since this is a clean install, you want to replace the old operating system by installing Vista on top of the old Windows partition. Make your selection and click **Next**.

9. As the installation continues, the computer may reboot several times and you may be asked to enter some information about your location and hardware setup.

10. Next, you will be asked to enter a username, password, computer name, date, and time. Record all of your answers below:

_____

_____

_____

_____

11. At the end of the setup process, a logon screen appears.

12. At this point, you would log on and start installing the application, starting with your antivirus program followed by Windows updates.

13. Remove the installation DVD from the drive and return it to your instructor.

14. Was the Windows Vista installation a success? If so, what did you find to be most challenging about the installation process?

_____

_____

15. Describe the Windows Vista desktop:

_____

_____

_____

REVIEW QUESTIONS

1. How does the Windows Vista user interface differ from Windows XP?

_____

_____

_____

2. When would a clean install be preferable to an in-place upgrade?

_____

_____

3. When would an in-place upgrade be preferable to a clean install?

_____

_____

4. Why do you need to close applications before performing an in-place upgrade to Vista?

_____

_____

5. Where did you go to find the computer name while you were gathering information?

_____

_____

12

LAB 12.5 CRITICAL THINKING: VIRTUAL PC

OBJECTIVES

The goal of this lab is to help you do an installation of Windows in a virtual environment. After completing this lab, you will be able to:

⊿ Download and install Virtual PC

⊿ Perform an installation of Windows XP on a virtual machine

MATERIALS REQUIRED

This lab requires the following:

⊿ Windows Vista/XP operating system

⊿ Internet access or access to the Virtual PC executable file

⊿ Windows XP installation files or installation CD

⊿ Key from installation CD

LAB PREPARATION

Before the lab begins, the instructor or lab assistant needs to do the following:

⊿ Verify that Windows starts with no errors.

⊿ Provide each student with access to the Windows installation files or CD and key.

⊿ Verify that any necessary Windows drivers are available.

⊿ For labs that don't have Internet access, provide the Virtual PC executable file from *www.microsoft.com/downloads*.

ACTIVITY BACKGROUND

A virtual computer or virtual machine is software that simulates the hardware of a physical computer. Using this software, you can install and run multiple operating systems on a single PC. The two most popular virtual machine programs are Virtual PC by Microsoft and VMware by VMware, Inc. In this lab, you will install Windows on a virtual machine that you set up using Virtual PC.

ESTIMATED COMPLETION TIME: 90 Minutes

 Activity

Follow these steps to download and use Microsoft Virtual PC 2007 onto your computer:

1. Open your browser, go to **www.microsoft.com/downloads,** and search for Virtual PC 2007.

2. Click the **download** link and download the latest version of the Virtual PC installer for your machine.

3. Run the setup program by double-clicking the executable file. Accept the License Agreement and install the program.

4. Once the installation is complete, run the program. When the **New Virtual Machine Wizard** appears, click **Next**.

5. Select **Create a virtual machine** and click **Next**.

6. Enter a name and location for your virtual machine and record this information below:

_____

_____

7. Click **Next** to continue. The next screen allows you to choose which operating system will be installed and then allocates the appropriate resources. Choose **Windows XP** and then click **Next**.

8. The Memory screen allows you to choose how much RAM is reserved for the virtual machine. Generally, no more than half of your system's memory should be used for all of the virtual machines you plan to run at once. Stick with the recommended amount and click **Next**.

9. In the **Virtual Hard Disk Options** screen, select **A new virtual hard disk** and click **Next**.

10. Pick a location and size for the virtual hard drive and click **Next**.

11. Finally, click **Finish** to close the wizard.

12. In the **Virtual PC Console** window, select your virtual machine and click **Start**.

13. As the virtual machine attempts to boot (see Figure 12-1), note which version of BIOS it uses:

_____

14. Examine the **Settings** under the **Edit** drop-down menu and confirm how much memory is running on your virtual machine.

_____

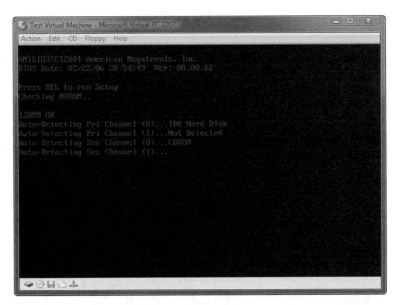

Figure 12-1   Virtual machine during boot up
Courtesy: Course Technology/Cengage Learning

15. To install an operating system, add the installation CD to the virtual machine by selecting **Use Physical Drive D:** from the **CD** drop-down menu. (*Note:* the letter assigned to your CD drive may vary depending on your system's configuration.)

16. Insert the Windows XP installation CD and restart the virtual machine to install Windows (see Lab 12.3).

REVIEW QUESTIONS

1. Why might an operating system on a virtual drive run slower than one installed directly on a PC?

   _____

   _____

2. Describe a situation where you might want to install several different virtual machines on a system.

   _____

   _____

   _____

3. Why can't you use all of your system memory to run a virtual machine?

   _____

   _____

4. Why do you think you can't change the amount of RAM on your virtual machine while it's running?

   _____

   _____

5. Why might it be important to set up a shared folder between the virtual machine and the physical computer?

   _____

   _____

LAB 12.6 CRITICAL THINKING: UNATTENDED INSTALLATION

OBJECTIVES

The goal of this lab is to help you do an unattended installation of Windows. After completing this lab, you will be able to:

◢ Use nLite to create an answer file for an unattended installation of Windows

◢ Identify the benefits of an unattended installation

◢ Perform an unattended installation of Windows XP

MATERIALS REQUIRED

This lab requires the following:

◢ Windows Vista/XP operating system with a burnable CD-ROM

◢ Internet access (optional)

◢ Windows XP installation files or installation CD

◢ Key from installation CD

LAB PREPARATION

Before the lab begins, the instructor or lab assistant needs to do the following:

◢ Verify that Windows starts with no errors.

◢ Provide each student with access to the Windows installation files or CD and key.

◢ Verify that any necessary Windows drivers are available.

◢ For labs that don't have Internet access, provide the nLite executable file from *www.nliteos.com*.

ACTIVITY BACKGROUND

System administrators may not have time to install Windows on dozens or even hundreds of machines. Instead, they can choose to perform an unattended installation where all the questions about the installation are answered ahead of time and stored in an answer file. Unattended installations work for both upgrades and clean installs. In this lab, an unattended installation will be performed with the help of a Freeware preinstallation tool called nLite.

ESTIMATED COMPLETION TIME: 90 Minutes

 Activity

Follow these steps to download nLite onto your computer:

1. Open your browser and go to **www.nliteos.com**.

2. Click the **download** link and download the latest version of the nLite installer.

3. Run the setup program by double-clicking the executable file and accept the License Agreement.

4. Accept all the defaults to finish the installation. Once the installation is complete, run nLite. The screen in Figure 12-2 should appear.

12

Figure 12-2 The nLite custom Windows installation wizard
Courtesy: Course Technology/Cengage Learning

5. Select your preferred language and click **Next**.

6. Select the location of your installation files or CD and click **Next**.

7. Choose a location where you want to save the installation files and wait while nLite copies the files. Click **Next** to continue.

8. The **Presets** screen allows you to load previous settings. Click **Next** to continue.

9. In the **Task Selection** screen, users can decide which features they would like to include in their installation, such as service packs or additional drivers. Take a moment to explore each of these options shown in Figure 12-3 and then select **Unattended** and **Bootable ISO** and click **Next** to continue.

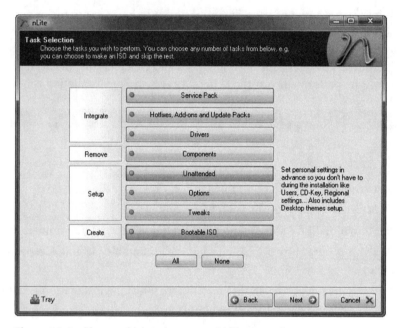

Figure 12-3 Choose which tasks you would like to perform
Courtesy: Course Technology/Cengage Learning

10. The **Unattended** screen presents all of the configuration questions that are usually resolved during the installation, such as the product key or the user name (see Figure 12-4). Take some time to review these options and then fill out the form with the same information that you used to install Windows XP (see Lab 12.3). When you are finished, click **Next** to continue.

11. Click **Yes** to begin the process and click **Next**.

12. At the **Bootable ISO** screen, in the **Mode** section, select **Direct Burn** and choose the device that will be used to burn the installation CD. Click **Burn**, then **Next**, and then **Finish**.

13. Once the new installation CD has been created, use it to perform an unattended installation of Windows XP.

14. Describe the installation process from the unattended installation CD you created.

_____

_____

_____

Figure 12-4 Unattended allows you to configure settings in advance
Courtesy: Course Technology/Cengage Learning

REVIEW QUESTIONS

1. Could the same unattended installation file be used on two different computers? Why or why not?

2. Describe a situation where you might want to remove a windows component before the installation:

3. Why does nLite also allow you to save the installation image as an .ISO file?

4. When might an unattended installation not save any time?

5. When might you choose to use nLite even if you're only doing a single installation?

12

Maintaining Windows

Labs included in this chapter:

- **Lab 13.1:** Perform Hard Drive Routine Maintenance
- **Lab 13.2:** Schedule Maintenance Tasks
- **Lab 13.3:** Back Up and Restore Files in Windows XP
- **Lab 13.4:** Manage User Accounts in Windows Vista/XP
- **Lab 13.5:** Set Disk Quotas
- **Lab 13.6:** Manage Virtual Memory
- **Lab 13.7:** Learn to Work from the Command Line
- **Lab 13.8:** Use the Xcopy and Robocopy Commands

LAB 13.1 PERFORM HARD DRIVE ROUTINE MAINTENANCE

OBJECTIVES

The goal of this lab is to help you perform routine maintenance on a hard drive. After completing this lab, you will be able to:

◢ Delete unneeded files on a hard drive

◢ Defragment a hard drive

◢ Scan a hard drive for errors

MATERIALS REQUIRED

This lab requires the following:

◢ Windows Vista/XP operating system

LAB PREPARATION

Before the lab begins, the instructor or lab assistant needs to do the following:

◢ Verify that Windows starts with no errors.

ACTIVITY BACKGROUND

To ensure that your hard drive operates in peak condition, you should perform some routine maintenance tasks regularly. For starters, you need to ensure that your hard drive includes enough unused space (which it requires to operate efficiently). In other words, you should remove unnecessary files from the drive.

In addition, files on a hard drive sometimes become fragmented over time; defragmenting the drive can improve performance because files can be read sequentially without jumping around on the drive. Other routine maintenance tasks include scanning the hard drive for errors and repairing them. In this lab, you learn about three tools you can use for important disk maintenance tasks. You should use these tools on a scheduled basis to keep your hard drive error free and performing well.

ESTIMATED COMPLETION TIME: 30-45 Minutes

 Activity

Follow these steps to delete unnecessary files on your hard drive:

1. Close all open applications.

2. Click **Start**, click **All Programs**, click **Accessories**, click **System Tools**, and then click **Disk Cleanup**. If Windows asks you to choose which files to clean up, select **Files from all users on this computer**. If Vista opens a UAC box, click **Continue**.

3. If the Disk Cleanup Drive Selection (Select Drive in XP) dialog box opens, select the drive you want to clean up in the drop-down list, and click **OK** to close the Disk Cleanup Drive Selection dialog box.

4. The Disk Cleanup dialog box opens. You need to select the types of files you want Disk Cleanup to delete. Select all possible options. Depending on your system, these options might include Downloaded Program Files, Recycle Bin, Temporary files, and Temporary Internet files.

◢ How much disk space does each group of files take up?

_____

_____

_____

_____

◢ Based on information in the Disk Cleanup dialog box, what is the purpose of each group of files?

_____

_____

_____

_____

◢ What is the total amount of disk space you would gain by deleting these files?

_____

◢ What types of files might you not want to delete during disk cleanup? Why?

_____

_____

5. Click **OK** to delete the selected groups of files.

6. When asked to confirm the deletion, click **Delete Files** (or **Yes** in XP). The Disk Cleanup dialog box closes, and a progress indicator appears while the cleanup is under way. The progress indicator closes when the cleanup is finished, returning you to the desktop.

The next step in routine maintenance is to use Windows Chkdsk to examine the hard drive and repair errors.

Follow these steps:

1. Close any open applications so they aren't trying to write to the hard drive while it's being repaired.

2. Click **Start** and type **cmd** in the Start Search box (in XP, click **Start, Run** and type **cmd** in the Run dialog box) and press **Enter**. The command prompt window opens.

3. Several switches (options) are associated with the Chkdsk utility. To show all available switches, type **chkdsk /?** at the command prompt and press **Enter**. Answer the following:

◢ What are two switches used to fix errors that Chkdsk finds?

_____

◢ Why do the /I and /C switches in Chkdsk reduce the amount of time needed to run the defragmentation?

_____

4. To use the Chkdsk utility to scan the C: hard drive for errors and repair them, type **chkdsk C: /R** and press **Enter**. (_Note:_ You may have to substitute a different drive letter depending on your computer's configuration.)

5. When Chkdsk is finished, close the command prompt window.

13

The last step in routine hard drive maintenance is to use the Disk Defragmenter tool to locate fragmented files and rewrite them to the hard drive in contiguous segments. You should do the defragmentation last because other actions, like cleaning up files, will further fragment the files on the disk. Follow these steps:

1. Close all open applications.

2. Click **Start**, click **All Programs**, click **Accessories**, click **System Tools**, and then click **Disk Defragmenter**. If Vista opens a UAC box, click **Continue**. The Disk Defragmenter window opens.

3. In Windows Vista, click **Defragment now...** (click **Defragment** in Windows XP). If prompted, select the drive you want to defragment. Disk Defragmenter begins defragmenting the drive, displaying a progress indicator of estimated fragmentation before and after it works.

> **Notes** Fully defragmenting your hard drive can take a few hours, depending on how fragmented it is. If you don't have time to wait, you can stop the process by clicking **Cancel defragmentation** (click **Stop** in Windows XP).

4. In Windows XP, you can observe a graphical representation of the defragmentation process.

5. To see what happens in XP when you open an application while the hard drive is defragmenting, open Microsoft Word or another program. Use the program for a moment and then close it. Answer the following:

   ◢ What happened to Disk Defragmenter when you opened another application?

   _____

6. When defragmentation is completed, close the Disk Defragmenter window.

REVIEW QUESTIONS

1. Why should you run Disk Cleanup before running Disk Defragmenter?

   _____

   _____

2. How does defragmentation improve performance?

   _____

   _____

3. Why shouldn't you attempt to use other programs while chkdsk is running?

   _____

   _____

4. Which type of files removed by disk cleanup took up the most space? Do you think this will usually be the case?

   _____

   _____

LAB 13.2 SCHEDULE MAINTENANCE TASKS

OBJECTIVES

The goal of this lab is to help you schedule automatic maintenance on your computer. After completing this lab, you will be able to:

⊿ Open the Windows Task Scheduler and view scheduled tasks

⊿ Use the Windows Task Scheduler to schedule weekly hard drive defragmentation

MATERIALS REQUIRED

This lab requires the following:

⊿ Windows Vista/XP operating system

LAB PREPARATION

Before the lab begins, the instructor or lab assistant needs to do the following:

⊿ Verify that Windows starts with no errors.

ACTIVITY BACKGROUND

Windows includes a tool called the Task Scheduler that can be used to automate some of the routine maintenance on your PC. Tasks like file defragmentation, virus scanning, or checking your hard drive for errors can be set to run automatically at times that do not interfere with your day-to-day activities, like weekends or evenings. In Vista, many of these tasks are already scheduled to run when needed.

ESTIMATED COMPLETION TIME: 30 Minutes

13

 Activity

Follow these steps to open the Task Scheduler and schedule a weekly defragmentation of your hard drive:

1. Log in as an administrator and close all open applications. (*Note:* Some tasks may require that the administrator account have a password.)

2. Click **Start** and open the Control Panel.

3. Click **System and Maintenance (Performance and Maintenance** in XP).

4. Scroll down to **Administrative Tools** and click **Schedule tasks** (in XP, click **Scheduled Tasks**). If Windows needs your permission to continue, click **Continue**.

In Windows XP, follow these steps:

1. Double-click **Add Scheduled Task**. When The Scheduled Task Wizard opens, click **Next**.

2. Click **Browse**, locate defrag.exe in the windows\system32 folder, and then click **Open**.

3. Name the task WeeklyDefrag and click the **Weekly** radio button. Click **Next** to continue.

4. Choose to schedule the task for every Wednesday at 1:00AM and click **Next**.

5. If prompted, enter your password and click **Next**.

6. Select **Open advanced properties for this task when I click Finish** and click **Finish**.

7. Add the volume letter of the hard drive you want to defrag (i.e., defrag C:) in the Run box after the existing command and click **OK**.

8. Again, enter your password and click **OK**.

9. Finally, close the Scheduled Tasks window.

Windows Vista already schedules most of the routine maintenance your computer will need. To view the tasks that have already been scheduled, follow these steps:

1. In the Task Status section of the Task Scheduler window, determine how many tasks have been started in the past 24 hours.

   _____

2. Scroll down to a group of tasks called ManualDefrag and click the + to expand the category.

3. Select the most recent ManualDefrag task and determine when it was last run.

   _____

4. The automatically scheduled defragmentation is labeled ScheduledDefrag in the Vista Task Scheduler. You can determine more information about the ScheduledDefrag task in the Task Scheduler Library (shown in the left column of Figure 13-1). Use the Task Scheduler Library to answer the following questions:

   ◢ Which user account is used to run this task?

   _____

   ◢ When does this task run?

   _____

   ◢ Will the task scheduler wake the computer to start this task?

   _____

5. When you're finished, close the Scheduled Tasks window.

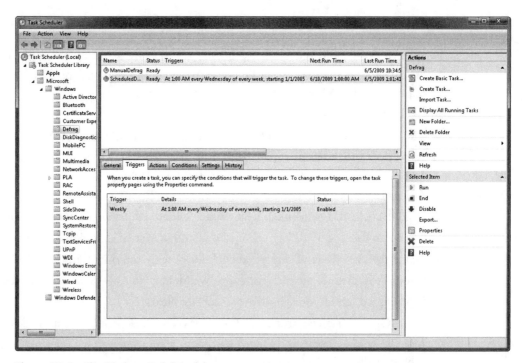

Figure 13-1 The Windows Task Scheduler
Courtesy: Course Technology/Cengage Learning

6. Next, use the Task Scheduler Library to determine when Windows Defender runs an MP Scheduled Scan.

7. When you are finished, close the task scheduler.

REVIEW QUESTIONS

1. Why are some tasks scheduled in the middle of the night?

2. Besides defragmentation, what are some other tasks you might choose to automate?

3. Why are some tasks set to run whether the user is logged in or not?

4. Why might you want to disable some of the automatic tasks set up in Vista?

5. Why do you think some tasks are set to only run if a network connection is available?

13

LAB 13.3 BACK UP AND RESTORE FILES IN WINDOWS XP

OBJECTIVES

The goal of this lab is to help you use the Windows XP Backup and Recovery Tools to back up and recover lost files. After completing this lab, you will be able to:

◢ Back up files

◢ Delete files

◢ Recover deleted files

MATERIALS REQUIRED

This lab requires the following:

◢ Windows XP operating system

LAB PREPARATION

Before the lab begins, the instructor or lab assistant needs to do the following:

◢ Verify that Windows starts with no errors.

◢ Ensure access to an Administrator and User account

ACTIVITY BACKGROUND

Windows provides the Backup and Recovery Tools to help you safeguard data in Windows system files. Using these tools, you can back up a single file or even an entire drive from the local or remote computer. Backups, compressed into a single file, can be saved to a location of your choice, without the need for a dedicated backup device, such as a tape drive. In this lab, you back up, delete, and restore data files using the Backup and Recovery Tools.

ESTIMATED COMPLETION TIME: 45 Minutes

 Activity

Follow these steps to select the files or folders you want to back up:

1. Log on as an Administrator.

2. Create folders called **C:\Backups** and **C:\BackMeUp**.

3. Create a text file on the root of the C: drive called singlefile.txt. Also create several text files in the C:\BackMeUp folder called file1.txt, file2.txt, and file3.txt.

4. Click **Start**, point to **All Programs**, point to **Accessories**, point to **System Tools**, and then click **Backup**. Click **Advanced Mode**. The Windows Backup and Recovery Tools utility opens. What three options are available on the Welcome tab?

   _____

   _____

   _____

5. Click the **Backup** tab. In the left pane, click the + (plus sign) next to drive C and then select the drive itself. The right pane displays all the items you can back up.

6. First, you back up an entire folder. Click the check box next to the **BackMeUp** folder in the right pane; doing so indicates that you want to back up the entire contents of that folder.

7. Also, instruct the system to back up the entire contents of the Documents and Settings folder. Explain how you performed this task:

   _____

   _____

   _____

8. In addition to the folders you just selected for backup, you'll select a single file, single-file.txt, for backup.

9. Click the **singlefile.txt** check box to specify that you want to back up this file.

10. In the Backup media or file name text box, type **C:\Backups\Lab13.bkf,** which specifies the name and location of the backup file you're creating.

Follow these steps to start the backup process:

1. In the Backup tab, click **Start Backup**. The Backup Job Information dialog box opens. The Backup description text box displays date and time information about this backup. This information is displayed later to help you identify the backup during a recovery process. If you need to perform many backup operations (and, therefore, have to keep track of multiple backup sets), you should always use this text box to describe the files in this set. Alternatively, you might want to keep a backup log book and refer to an entry number that describes in detail what's in this backup set. Because this is your initial backup, you can ignore the other sections of the dialog box and click **Start Backup**.

2. The Backup Job Information dialog box opens. Click **Start Backup** in this dialog box.

3. The Backup begins and displays information about its progress. Answer these questions:

   ◢ What three items give you an idea of how the backup is progressing?

   _____

   _____

   _____

   ◢ Can you tell how many files must be backed up?

   _____

   ◢ Can you tell which files have already been completed or are currently being processed?

   _____

   ◢ What information continues to change even when the backup process is paused?

   _____

4. When the backup is finished, click **Report** in the Backup Progress dialog box to open the Backup log in Notepad.

5. Print and examine the report. What errors and causes are reported?

   _____

   _____

   _____

6. When you're finished, close Notepad and click **Close** in the Backup Progress dialog box.

Follow these steps to delete files and observe the effects:

1. Log off and log on as a different user. Ensure the Recycle Bin is empty. Right-click **Recycle Bin** on the desktop, and click **Empty Recycle Bin** in the shortcut menu. Click **Yes** to confirm that you want to empty the Recycle Bin.

2. Open a command prompt window. At the command prompt, type **DEL C:\BackMeUp*.*** and press **Enter** to delete all files in the C:\BackMeUp directory. Confirm the deletion when prompted. Close the command prompt window.

3. In Windows Explorer, delete C:\singlefile.txt.

13

4. Double-click **Recycle Bin** and note which files are displayed:

_____

_____

_____

5. Empty the Recycle Bin again and then, in Windows Explorer, look for your text files in C:\ and C:\BackMeUp to confirm that they are gone.

Follow these steps to restore the deleted files:

1. Log off and log on as an administrator.

2. Click **Start**, point to **All Programs**, point to **Accessories**, point to **System Tools**, and then click **Backup**. The Backup window opens.

3. Click **Advanced Mode** and click the **Restore and Manage Media** tab. In the left pane, click the + (plus sign) to expand the File symbol, and then click to expand **Lab13.bkf** created _Date at Time_.

4. Select **Lab13.bkf** in the C:\Backups folder. Your backup is displayed in the left pane of the Restore and Manage Media tab.

5. To restore files and folders, click the necessary check boxes, and then click **Start Restore**. Do you think you could choose to restore only part of the information? If so, how?

_____

_____

6. The Confirm Restore dialog box opens. Click **OK** to continue.

7. The Restore Progress dialog box opens. When the restore operation is finished, click **Close** to close the Restore Progress dialog box and then close the Backup utility.

8. To confirm that the restore is complete, look for your text files using Explorer.

REVIEW QUESTIONS

1. Is it more important to back up Windows system files or data files? Why?

_____

_____

2. What is the Start menu path for launching Windows Backup and Restore Tools?

_____

3. What features of Windows Backup and Restore Tools can you use if you're unfamiliar with the backup and restore process?

_____

_____

4. What does the Backup Job Information dialog box allow you to define? Why is this function useful?

_____

_____

_____

5. If you forgot the name of your backup file, how else might you identify it?

_____

_____

LAB 13.4 MANAGE USER ACCOUNTS IN WINDOWS VISTA/XP

OBJECTIVES

The goal of this lab is to give you experience adding and modifying user accounts by using Computer Management. After completing this lab, you will be able to:

⬧ Add users

⬧ Reset passwords

⬧ Control password policies

MATERIALS REQUIRED

This lab requires the following:

⬧ Windows Vista/XP Professional operating system

⬧ An administrator account and password

LAB PREPARATION

Before the lab begins, the instructor or lab assistant needs to do the following:

⬧ Verify that Windows starts with no errors.

ACTIVITY BACKGROUND

Maintaining Windows involves more than just managing physical resources like hard drives; you also sometimes need to manage users and their access to these resources. Windows needs just a few pieces of information to set up a user account: a unique user name, the user's full name, a description of the user (typically title and department), and a password. Managing users can take quite a bit of administrative time, however. Much of this time is spent helping users who have forgotten their passwords or entered their passwords incorrectly multiple times, causing Windows to lock their accounts. In this lab, you practice managing user accounts and passwords in Computer Management.

ESTIMATED COMPLETION TIME: 30 Minutes

 Activity

To examine the user account information available via Computer Management, follow these steps:

1. Log on as an administrator.

13

2. Click **Start, Control Panel**, and then click **System and Maintenance** (**Performance** and **Maintenance** in XP).

3. Click **Administrative Tools** and double-click **Computer Management**. If you are presented with a UAC dialog box, click **Continue**. The Computer Management window opens, similar to the one in Figure 13-2.

Figure 13-2   The Computer Management console
Courtesy: Course Technology/Cengage Learning

4. Click the arrow (+ sign in XP) next to Local Users and Groups to expand the category and select the **Users** folder. Examine the Computer Management window and answer the following questions:

◢ Based on your knowledge of Windows, what two user accounts are included on a Windows system by default?

_____

◢ Does your system contain any personal user accounts? If so, list them here:

_____

_____

◢ What user groups are included on your Windows system?

_____

In Computer Management, you can add and configure users on a local computer by following these steps:

1. In the left pane under Local Users and Groups, if necessary, click the **Users** folder to display a list of current user names.

2. Right-click **Users** and click **New User** in the shortcut menu. The New User dialog box opens.

3. In the User name text box, type **James**.

4. In the Full name text box, type **James Clark**.

5. In the Description text box, type **Supervisor**.

6. In the Password text box, type **newuser**.

7. Confirm the password, make sure the **User must change password at next logon** and **Account is disabled** check boxes are cleared.

◢ What other check box could you select?

_____

_____

8. Click **Create** and close all open windows.

When Windows creates a new user, that user is added only to the Users group, which means the account can't create, delete, or change other accounts; make system wide changes; or install software. To give the account administrative privileges, do the following:

1. Open Computer Management and select the **James Clark** account.

2. Double-click the **James Clark** account to open the test Properties window, and then click the **Member Of** tab.

3. To what group(s) does James Clark currently belong?

_____

4. Click **Add** to open the Select Groups window.

5. Click **Advanced** and click **Find Now**.

6. Select the **Administrators** group and click **OK** and **OK** again to close the Select Groups window. To what groups does the James Clark account now belong?

_____

7. Log off your computer and log on as James Clark. List the steps you took to accomplish that task:

_____

_____

_____

Occasionally, administrators have to reset user passwords. To reset a user's password, do the following:

1. Log on with the original administrator account.

2. Open Computer Management and select the **James Clark** account.

3. Right-click the **James Clark** account and select **Set Password**. If a user knows his or her password and wants to change it, what can he or she do?

_____

_____

4. Click **Proceed** and enter a password called **newpass**.

5. Confirm the password and click **OK**.

6. Click **OK** again to acknowledge that the password has been changed.

7. Try to log on with the James Clark account using the old password. What error do you get?

_____

_____

8. Now test the new password by logging on successfully.

9. Finally, log back on as the administrator and delete the James Clark account. List the steps that you used:

_____

_____

_____

_____

REVIEW QUESTIONS

1. Besides adding and deleting users, what other tasks can you perform with Computer Management in the Local Users and Groups category?

_____

2. List three of the differences between User and Administrator accounts:

_____

_____

_____

3. List the steps to change the group to which an account belongs:

_____

_____

_____

_____

4. Why do you think new users are not automatically members of the Administrators group?

_____

_____

_____

5. Why is it a good idea to have users change their passwords the first time they log on?

_____

_____

_____

LAB 13.5 SET DISK QUOTAS

OBJECTIVES

The goal of this lab is to show you how to set and monitor disk quotas. After completing this lab, you will be able to:

- Convert a logical drive from FAT to NTFS
- Set disk quotas for new users
- Monitor quota logs
- Identify when quotas have been exceeded

MATERIALS REQUIRED

This lab requires the following:

- Windows Vista/XP Professional operating system
- A computer containing a partition (which can be the partition where Windows is installed) that has no important information

LAB PREPARATION

Before the lab begins, the instructor or lab assistant needs to do the following:

- Verify that Windows starts with no errors.

ACTIVITY BACKGROUND

When a system is used by more than one account or when server storage space is limited, setting storage limits for each user is often a good idea. No one account should monopolize storage space by filling up the server and preventing other users from storing data. Note, however, that you can impose disk quotas only on drives formatted with NTFS. In this lab, you use disk quotas to limit user storage space.

13

ESTIMATED COMPLETION TIME: 30 Minutes

 Activity

In the following steps, you set very small disk quotas for all users. That way, you can easily exceed the disk quota limit later and observe the results. Do the following to verify that you're using the NTFS file system:

1. Log on as an administrator.
2. Open Windows Explorer, right-click drive C (or another logical drive designated by your instructor), and click **Properties** in the shortcut menu. The Local Disk (C:) Properties dialog box opens. (If you selected another drive letter, the dialog box name will be different.) On the General tab, verify that the drive is using the NTFS file system.

If you currently have the FAT32 file system and need to convert to NTFS, use the following steps, and then open the Local Disk (C:) Properties dialog box again. If you already have NTFS, skip the next three steps.

1. Open a command prompt window.
2. At the command prompt, type **convert C: /fs:ntfs** and press **Enter**. (If necessary, substitute the drive letter for another logical drive in the command, as specified by your instructor.)
3. After the command runs, reboot your computer to complete the conversion to NTFS.

To enable disk quotas, do the following:

1. In the Local Disk (C:) Properties dialog box, click the **Quota** tab.

2. Click **Show Quota Settings** and click the **Enable quota management** check box. If Windows presents you with a UAC box, click **Continue**. This option allows you to set and change quotas.

3. Click the **Deny disk space to users exceeding quota limit** check box. This option prevents users from using more disk space after reaching their quota.

4. Verify that the **Limit disk space to** option button is selected and that **1** appears in the text box to the right. Then click **MB** in the drop-down list to set the disk quota to 1 MB of storage space.

5. In the Set warning level to text box, type **500**, and then verify that **KB** is displayed in the text box to the right. This setting ensures that users receive warnings after they have used 500 KB of disk space.

6. Click **Log event when a user exceeds their quota limit**. This option ensures that a record is made when a user exceeds the quota limit.

7. Click **Log event when a user exceeds their warning level**. This option ensures that a record is made when users reach their warning limit. (You can view these records in the Local Disk (C:) Properties dialog box.)

8. Click **OK** to apply the new settings, and click **OK** to close the Local Disk (C:) Properties dialog box.

Follow these steps to exceed the quota limits you have just set:

1. Using what you learned in Lab 13.4, create a new restricted user called **Quota Test**.

2. Create a directory called **Quota** in the root of the NTFS drive.

3. Log off as an administrator, and log on as **Quota Test**.

4. In Windows Explorer, open the Windows or WINNT folder, and click the **Show the contents of this folder** link. One at a time, copy (*do not cut*) all .gif and .bmp files in the Windows or WINNT folder, and paste them into the Quota folder.

   ◢ What happens when you exceed the warning level and then the storage quota?

   _____

   _____

5. Log off as the Quota Test user.

Because of the options you selected when you created the disk quota, logs were created when you exceeded the warning level and the storage quota. To view these quota logs, follow these steps:

1. Log on as an administrator.

2. Open the Local Disk (C:) Properties dialog box, and then click the **Quota** tab. Click the **Show Quota Settings** button, and then click the **Quota Entries** button. The Quota Entries window opens, displaying the log of quota entries for certain events.

   ◢ What types of information are displayed for each entry?

   _____

   _____

3. Double-click an entry for Quota Test. The Quota Settings dialog box for that user opens. Note that you can raise or lower the user's disk quotas.

4. Check the quota settings for each entry, and record any entry for which you were unable to adjust settings:

_____

_____

Because disk quotas may interfere with future labs, it is important to remove the quotas. To disable disk quotas, do the following:

1. In the Local Disk (C:) Properties dialog box, click the **Quota** tab.

2. Click **Show Quota Settings** and deselect the **Enable quota management** check box.

3. Click **OK** and close any open windows.

REVIEW QUESTIONS

1. How would you set up disk quotas on a drive formatted with FAT32?

_____

_____

2. Why might you want to impose disk quotas?

_____

3. What option must be selected to specify a warning level?

_____

_____

4. What options must be selected to prevent users from exceeding their quotas?

_____

_____

5. Explain how to monitor and change disk quotas:

_____

_____

LAB 13.6 MANAGE VIRTUAL MEMORY

OBJECTIVES

The goal of this lab is to learn to manage virtual memory. After completing this lab, you will be able to:

⊿ Locate the Windows tool for adjusting virtual memory settings

⊿ Change the size of the paging file

MATERIALS REQUIRED

This lab requires the following:

◢ Windows Vista/XP Professional operating system

◢ Internet access

◢ A printer

LAB PREPARATION

Before the lab begins, the instructor or lab assistant needs to do the following:

◢ Verify that Windows starts with no errors.

◢ Verify that Internet access is available.

ACTIVITY BACKGROUND

Virtual memory allows the OS to make use of an HDD (hard drive) to simulate RAM. This option can be useful when, for instance, the OS is running a number of applications, and each requires an allocation of RAM reserved for its use. Ideally, the Virtual Memory Manager protects actual RAM for the most active applications by moving the data other applications use to a swap file on the hard drive. In Windows Vista/XP, the swap file is called a "paging file." The virtual memory default settings allow Windows to manage the paging file, increasing or decreasing the size as needed.

In most situations, allowing Windows to manage virtual memory with default settings works fine, but this practice can cause pauses in application response time when the OS switches to an application with data stored in the paging file. This delay is caused by longer access time when reading from a drive instead of reading from RAM. The access time increases especially if the file is on the boot partition or any other partition subject to heavy use. If performance has become a problem, you might want to specify virtual memory settings manually.

ESTIMATED COMPLETION TIME: 30 Minutes

 Activity

Log on to your computer using an account with administrative privileges. Complete the following steps to gather information about your system:

1. Click **Start, Control Panel**. The Control Panel window opens.

2. Click **System and Maintenance** (**Performance and Maintenance** in XP). The Control Panel window changes to System and Maintenance.

3. Click **System** and the System window opens (System Properties in XP).

4. Note how much RAM is installed (in the General tab in XP) and then click **Back** in the System window (**Close** in the System Properties window in XP).

5. Click **Administrative Tools** and double-click the **Computer Management** shortcut. The Computer Management console opens.

6. In the left pane, click **Disk Management**, and review the information in the right pane. List the required information on the following lines, and then close the Computer Management console and Administrative Tools window.

◢ Disks installed:

◢ Partitions and letters assigned:

_____

◢ Partition designated as the system partition:

_____

◢ Disk with unallocated space:

_____

7. Close any open windows.

It's unlikely that you would ever have to make changes to the paging file in Vista. You won't be making the changes because Vista does a much better job managing memory than earlier versions of Windows did with the same task. Visit the Microsoft Web site at *http://support.microsoft.com* and search the Knowledge Base for the following articles on managing the XP paging file:

◢ Article 314482: How to Configure Paging Files for Optimization and Recovery in Windows XP

◢ Article 307886: How to Move the Paging File in Windows XP

Print and read these articles, and then answer the following questions:

1. What is the paging file's default or recommended size?

_____

2. What is a disadvantage of totally removing the paging file from the boot partition?

_____

_____

3. What performance-degrading issue is the paging file subject to if it's moved to a partition containing data?

_____

_____

4. What additional benefit is there to setting up a paging file on multiple hard drives?

_____

_____

5. According to Article 307886, how do you select the partition on which you want to modify paging file settings?

_____

_____

Next, you work with the Virtual Memory dialog box to view and record paging file settings. The information about the paging file's recommended maximum size might not be clear. As you record your settings, notice that the maximum size is the same as the recommended size.

Follow these steps:

1. Click **Start, Control Panel**. The Control Panel window opens.

2. Click **System and Maintenance**. Control Panel changes to the System and Maintenance window.

13

3. Click the **System** icon in System and Maintenance (Performance and Maintenance in XP).

4. Click **Advanced system settings** (the **Advanced** tab in XP). If a UAC box opens, click **Continue**.

5. In the Performance section of the Advanced tab, click **Settings**. The Performance Options dialog box opens.

6. In the Performance Options dialog box, click the **Advanced** tab, shown in Figure 13-3.

Figure 13-3   Use the Performance Options dialog box to access information on your computer's paging file
Courtesy: Course Technology/Cengage Learning

7. In the Virtual memory section, click the **Change** button. The Virtual Memory dialog box opens (see Figure 13-4). List the current settings on the following lines.

◢ Does your computer have multiple paging files?

_____

◢ Drive(s) where a paging file is located:

_____

◢ Current size of the paging file:

_____

◢ Recommended size:

_____

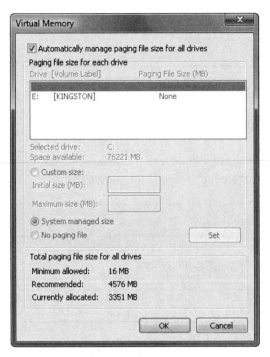

Figure 13-4 The Virtual Memory dialog box
Courtesy: Course Technology/Cengage Learning

Based on information in the Knowledge Base articles and the data you have collected about your computer, answer the following questions:

1. Given your computer's current physical configuration, is the paging file set for optimal performance? Explain:

   _____

   _____

2. What actions and paging file settings do you recommend to maximize performance? Explain:

   _____

   _____

3. Consider a 32-bit Windows computer with the following configuration:

   ◢ 512 MB RAM

   ◢ HDD0 C: (system) 17 GB NTFS with 2.8 GB unallocated disk space

   ◢ HDD1 D: (general storage) 20 GB NTFS with no unallocated disk space

   ◢ Paging file on the C drive with a custom size of 384 MB initial and 786 MB maximum

Based on what you've learned so far, what is your recommendation to maximize virtual memory performance while allowing the use of debugging information?

   _____

   _____

   _____

REVIEW QUESTIONS

1. What is meant by the term "virtual memory"?

   _____

   _____

2. What is the swap file called in Windows Vista/XP?

   _____

3. Why would you want to move the paging file off the boot partition?

   _____

   _____

4. When could fragmentation of the paging file occur?

   _____

   _____

5. What is the main reason for slight pauses in an application when retrieving information from the paging file?

   _____

   _____

6. *Bonus*: Because Microsoft acknowledges a performance advantage in locating the paging file off the boot partition, what's the main reason the boot partition is its default location?

   _____

   _____

LAB 13.7 LEARN TO WORK FROM THE COMMAND LINE

OBJECTIVES

The goal of this lab is to introduce you to some commands used when working from the command line. You change and examine directories and drives, and then perform a copy operation. You also learn to use the command-line Help feature and how to read Help information. After completing this lab, you will be able to:

◢ Create a file and folder with Notepad and Computer (My Computer in XP)

◢ Examine directories

◢ Switch drives and directories

◢ Use various commands at the command prompt

MATERIALS REQUIRED

This lab requires the following:

◢ Windows Vista/XP operating system

◢ A blank formatted floppy disk (optional)

LAB PREPARATION

Before the lab begins, the instructor or lab assistant needs to do the following:

⊿ Verify that Windows starts with no errors.

ACTIVITY BACKGROUND

In Lab 2.1, you used the DIR command to explore file structure. Experienced technicians can use the command line for tasks that just can't be done in a graphical interface, especially when troubleshooting a system. For most tasks, however, you'll rely on a graphical interface, such as Windows Explorer. In this lab, you use Windows Explorer (Computer) to create a new folder and a new file. Then you use the command line to delete that file. In this lab, it's assumed that Windows is installed on the C drive. If your installation is on a different drive, substitute that drive letter in the following steps.

ESTIMATED COMPLETION TIME: 30 Minutes

 Activity

To create a new folder and text file in My Computer, follow these steps:

1. Click **Start,** and then click **Computer** (**My Computer** in XP).

2. Right-click anywhere in the blank area of the drive C window, point to **New** on the shortcut menu, and then click **Folder.** A new folder icon appears with "New Folder" highlighted as the default name, ready for you to rename it.

3. To rename the folder Tools, type **Tools** and press **Enter.**

4. To create a file in the Tools folder, double-click the **Tools** folder icon, and then right-click anywhere in the blank area of the Tools window. Point to **New,** and then click **Text Document.** A new file icon appears in the Tools window with "New Text Document.txt" highlighted to indicate it's ready for renaming.

5. Double-click the **New Text Document.txt** icon to open the file in Notepad.

6. On the Notepad menu, click **File, Save As.**

7. In the Save As dialog box, name the file **Deleteme,** and make sure the selection in the Save as type drop-down list is **Text Documents.** Click the **Save** button.

8. Close Notepad.

9. In Computer, right-click **New Text Document.txt** and click **Delete** in the shortcut menu. Click **Yes** to confirm the deletion.

10. Close all open windows.

To practice using the command-line environment, follow these steps:

1. To open a command prompt window, click **Start, Run,** type **cmd,** and press **Enter.** The command prompt window opens, and the cursor is flashing at the command prompt.

2. The title bar of the command prompt window varies with different versions of Windows and depends on the user name of the person currently logged in, for example:

C:\Documents and Settings\James Clark>

The command prompt indicates the working drive (drive C) and working directory (the \Windows directory, the root directory indicated by the backslash, or the current user's Documents and Settings directory). Commands issued from this prompt apply to this folder unless you indicate otherwise.

3. Type **DIR** and press **Enter**. Remember that DIR is the command used to list a directory's contents. If the list of files and directories DIR displays is too large to fit on one screen, you see only the last few entries. Entries with the <DIR> label indicate that they are directories (folders), which can contain files or other directories. Also listed for each entry are the time and date it was created and the number of bytes it contains. (This information is displayed differently depending on which version of Windows you're using.) The last two lines in the list summarize the number of files and directories in the current directory, the space they consume, and the free space available on the drive.

As you'll see in the next set of steps, there are two ways to view any files that aren't displayed because of the length of the list and the window size. To learn more about displaying lists of files in the command-line environment, perform the following steps:

1. Type **DIR /?** and press **Enter** to display Help information for the directory command. You can view Help information for any command by entering the command followed by the /? parameter (also called a "switch").

2. Type **DIR /W** and press **Enter**. What happened?

_____

_____

3. Type **DIR /P** and press **Enter**. What happened?

_____

_____

4. Type **DIR /OS** and press **Enter**. What happened?

_____

_____

5. Type **DIR /O-S** and press **Enter**. What happened? What do you think the hyphen between O and S accomplishes?

_____

_____

6. Insert a blank disk in the floppy drive (if available). Type **A:** and press **Enter**. The resulting prompt should look like this: A:\>. What does the A: indicate?

_____

_____

7. What do you think you would see if you issued the DIR command at this prompt?

_____

_____

8. Type **DIR** and press **Enter**. Did you see what you were expecting?

_____

_____

9. Change back to the C: drive by typing **C:** and pressing **Enter**.

10. Type **DIR C:\Tools** and press **Enter**. This command tells the computer to list the contents of a specific directory without actually changing to that directory. In the resulting file list, you should see the file you created earlier, Deleteme.txt.

File attributes are managed by using the Attrib command. Follow these steps to learn how to view and manage file attributes:

1. To make C:\Tools the default directory, type **CD C:\Tools** and press **Enter**.

2. To view the attributes of the Deleteme.txt file, type **Attrib Deleteme.txt** and press **Enter**.

3. To change the file to a hidden file, type **Attrib +H Deleteme.txt** and press **Enter**.

4. View the attributes of the Deleteme.txt file again.

   ◢ What command did you use?

   _____

   ◢ How have the attributes changed?

   _____

5. To view the contents of the C:\Tools directory, type **DIR** and press **Enter**. Why doesn't the Deleteme.txt file show in the directory list?

   _____

6. To change the attributes so that the file is a system file, type **Attrib +S Deleteme.txt** and press **Enter**. What error message did you get?

   _____

7. Because you can't change the attributes of a hidden file, first remove the hidden attribute by typing **Attrib -H Deleteme.txt** and pressing **Enter**.

8. Now try to make the file a system file. What command did you use?

   _____

9. Use the DIR command to list the contents of the C:\Tools directory. Are system files listed?

10. To remove the file's system attribute, type **Attrib -S Deleteme.txt** and press **Enter**.

11. Move to the root directory, type **CD C:** and press **Enter**.

To learn how to delete a file from the command prompt, follow these steps:

1. Type **DEL Deleteme.txt** and press **Enter** to instruct the computer to delete that file. You'll see a message stating that the file couldn't be found because the system assumes that commands refer to the working directory unless a specific path is given. What command could you use to delete the file without changing to that directory?

   _____

2. The current prompt should be C:\>. The \ in the command you typed indicates the root directory.

3. Type **CD Tools** and press **Enter**. The prompt now ends with "Tools>" (indicating that Tools is the current working directory).

13

4. Now type **DEL Deleteme.txt /p** and press **Enter**. You're prompted to type **Y** for Yes or **N** for No to confirm the deletion. If you don't enter the /p switch (which means "prompt for verification"), the file is deleted automatically without a confirmation message. It's a good practice to use this /p switch, especially when deleting multiple files with wildcard characters. Also, when you delete a file from the command line, the file doesn't go to the Recycle Bin, as it would if you deleted it in Windows Explorer or Computer (My Computer in XP). Because deletion from the command line bypasses the Recycle Bin, recovering accidentally deleted files is more difficult.

5. Type **Y** and press **Enter** to delete the Deleteme.txt file. You're returned to the Tools directory.

To display certain files in a directory, you can use an asterisk (*) or a question mark (?) as wildcard characters. Wildcard characters are placeholders that represent other unspecified characters. The asterisk can represent one or more characters, and the question mark represents any single character. The asterisk is the most useful wildcard, so it's the one you'll encounter most often. To learn more, follow these steps:

1. Return to the root directory. What command did you use?

_____

2. Type **DIR *.*** and press **Enter**. How many files are displayed?

_____

3. Type **DIR C*.*** and press **Enter**. How many files are displayed?

_____

4. Explain why the results differed in the previous two commands:

_____

_____

CRITICAL THINKING (ADDITIONAL 30 MINUTES)

Follow these steps to practice using additional commands at the command prompt:

1. Copy the program file Notepad.exe from the \Windows to the \Tools directory. What command did you use?

_____

2. Rename the file in the \Tools directory as **Newfile.exe**. What command did you use?

_____

3. Change the attributes of Newfile.exe to make it a hidden file. What command did you use?

_____

4. Type **DIR** and press **Enter**. Is the Newfile.exe file displayed?

_____

5. Unhide **Newfile.exe**. What command did you use?

_____

6. List all files in the \Windows directory that have an .exe file extension. What command did you use?

_____

_____

7. Create a new directory named **\New** in \Windows and then copy **Newfile.exe** to the \New directory. What commands did you use?

_____

_____

8. Using the /p switch to prompt for verification, delete the **\New** directory. What commands did you use?

_____

_____

9. Open the Help and Support Center. Use the Search text box or the Internet to answer the following questions:

◢ What is the purpose of the Recover command?

_____

_____

◢ What is the purpose of the Assoc command?

_____

_____

REVIEW QUESTIONS

1. What command/switch do you use to view Help information for the DIR command?

_____

2. What do you add to the DIR command to list the contents of a directory that's not the current working directory?

_____

3. What command do you use to change directories?

_____

4. What command do you use to delete a file?

_____

5. What command do you use to switch from drive A to drive C?

_____

13

LAB 13.8 USE THE XCOPY AND ROBOCOPY COMMANDS

OBJECTIVES

The goal of this lab is to help you observe differences in the Xcopy and Robocopy commands. After completing this lab, you will be able to:

▲ Copy files and folders with the Xcopy or Robocopy command

MATERIALS REQUIRED

This lab requires the following:

▲ Windows Vista/XP operating system

▲ Floppy drive and formatted floppy disk or another form of removable media such as a USB drive

LAB PREPARATION

Before the lab begins, the instructor or lab assistant needs to do the following:

▲ Verify that Windows starts with no errors.

ACTIVITY BACKGROUND

The Copy command allows you to copy files from one folder to another folder. Using a single Xcopy command, you can copy files from multiple folders, duplicating an entire file structure in another location. The Robocopy command (Vista only) is basically a new version of Xcopy with a few more features, such as the ability to schedule copying to run automatically or delete the source files when the copying is finished. In this lab, you learn to copy files using either of these commands.

ESTIMATED COMPLETION TIME: 30 Minutes

 Activity

Before you begin using the Xcopy and Robocopy commands, you need to create a test directory to use when copying files. Follow these steps:

1. Open a command prompt window, and make the root of drive C the current directory. The quickest way to change to the root of a drive is to type **X:** (where *X* is the drive letter) and press **Enter**.

2. Make a directory in the drive C root called **copytest**.

Now you can begin experimenting with the Xcopy command. Follow these steps:

1. Type **Xcopy /?** and press **Enter**. Xcopy Help information is displayed. Notice all the switches you can use to modify the Xcopy command. In particular, you can use the /e switch to instruct Xcopy to copy all files and subdirectories in a directory, including any empty subdirectories, to a new location.

2. If you are using a Windows Vista machine, type **Robocopy /?** and press **Enter**. What are some new features unique to Robocopy?

_____

_____

_____

_____

3. Type **Xcopy C:\"program files"\"internet explorer" C:\copytest /e** and press **Enter**. (You must use quotation marks in the command line to surround a folder name containing spaces.) You'll see a list of files scroll by as they are copied from the C:\program files\internet explorer folder to the C:\copytest folder.

4. When the copy operation is finished, check the copytest folder to see that the files have been copied and the subdirectories created.

5. Insert a blank floppy disk into drive A or attach an equivalent removable device, type **md A:\copytest**, and then press **Enter**. This command creates a directory named copytest on the A drive. (*Note:* You may have to substitute A: with the drive letter associated with your storage device.)

6. To copy all files in the copytest directory on the hard drive to the copytest directory on drive A, type **Xcopy C:\"program files"\ "internet explorer" A:\copytest** and press **Enter**.

7. The system begins copying files, but the floppy disk lacks the capacity to hold the entire \internet explorer directory. As a result, the system displays a message stating that the disk is out of space and asking you to insert another disk. What is the exact error message?

_____

_____

13

8. In this case, you don't want to copy the entire directory to the floppy disk, so you need to stop the copying process. To do that, press **Ctrl+Pause/Break**. You're returned to the command prompt.

CRITICAL THINKING (ADDITIONAL 15 MINUTES)

Do the following to create and use a Windows Vista/XP bootable floppy disk:

1. Using Windows Explorer on a Windows Vista/XP computer, format a floppy disk.

2. Copy **Ntldr, Ntdetect.com,** and **Boot.ini** from the root of drive C to the root of the floppy disk.

3. Use the bootable floppy disk to boot the system. What appears on your screen after the boot?

_____

_____

4. How might this bootable floppy disk be useful in troubleshooting?

_____

_____

REVIEW QUESTIONS

1. Can a single Copy command copy files from more than one directory?

   _____

2. What switch do you use with Xcopy or Robocopy to copy subdirectories?

   _____

3. Why might you want to schedule a Robocopy command to occur at a later time?

   _____

   _____

4. Which Xcopy switch suppresses overwrite confirmation?

   _____

Optimizing Windows

Labs included in this chapter:

- **Lab 14.1:** Customize Windows Vista

- **Lab 14.2:** Use the Microsoft Management Console

- **Lab 14.3:** Analyze a System with Event Viewer

- **Lab 14.4:** Use Task Manager

- **Lab 14.5:** Edit the Registry with Regedit

- **Lab 14.6:** Critical Thinking: Use Windows Utilities to
  Speed up a System

LAB 14.1 CUSTOMIZE WINDOWS VISTA

OBJECTIVES

The goal of this lab is to help you become familiar with customizing the Windows Vista user interface. After completing this lab, you will be able to:

◢ Customize the taskbar

◢ Work with a program shortcut

◢ Customize the Start menu

◢ Clean up the Windows desktop

◢ Locate essential system information

MATERIALS REQUIRED

This lab requires the following:

◢ Windows Vista operating system

LAB PREPARATION

Before the lab begins, the instructor or lab assistant needs to do the following:

◢ Verify that Windows starts with no errors.

ACTIVITY BACKGROUND

Becoming proficient at navigating a new operating system can require some time and effort. Upgrading from Windows XP to Windows Vista is a big step, especially after you look at the differences in the user interface. From the redesigned Start menu to the new Windows Sidebar, just about everything looks a bit different in Windows Vista, and locating previously used utilities might prove a challenge. In this lab, you explore how Windows Vista handles some routine tasks.

> **ESTIMATED COMPLETION TIME: 30 Minutes**

 Activity

To work with the taskbar, follow these steps:

1. Place the mouse pointer over an empty part of the taskbar, and drag the taskbar to the right side of the screen.

   ◢ Were you able to move the taskbar? If not, what do you think the problem might be?

   _____

   _____

2. Right-click an empty area of the taskbar. Click **Lock the Taskbar** to deselect this option. Now try to move the taskbar to the right side of the screen. Return the taskbar to its default position.

   ◢ Were you able to move the taskbar?

   _____

   _____

You can create shortcuts and place them on the desktop to provide quick access to programs. You can also rename and delete a shortcut on your desktop. To create, rename, and delete a desktop shortcut, follow these steps:

1. Click **Start**, click **All Programs**, and click **Accessories**.

2. Right-click **Calculator**. In the menu that opens, point to **Send To**, and then click **Desktop (create shortcut)**. Windows adds the shortcut to your desktop. (You might need to close the Start menu by clicking the desktop to see it.)

3. Right-click the shortcut, and click **Rename** in the shortcut menu.

4. Type a new name for the shortcut, and press **Enter**.

5. To delete a shortcut icon from the desktop, right-click it, and click **Delete** in the shortcut menu. In the Confirm Delete File dialog box that opens, click **Yes**. The shortcut is deleted from the desktop.

The Start menu has been reorganized in Windows Vista to give you easy access to programs. When you install most programs, they are added automatically to the Start menu. If a program isn't added during installation, you can add it yourself. Windows Vista enables you to "pin" a program to your Start menu. To customize the Start menu, follow these steps:

1. First, you need to find a program to pin to the Start menu. In this case, you'll pin the calculator applet to the Start menu. Click **Start**, point to **All Programs**, and click **Accessories**.

2. Right-click **Calculator**, and click **Pin to Start Menu** in the shortcut menu. The program is added to your Start menu. Write the steps you would take to unpin the Calculator from the Start menu:

_____

_____

_____

If you're accustomed to the older Windows Start menu style, now called the Classic menu, you might find that changes to the Start menu take some getting used to. Giving the new Start menu a try is recommended, however, because it was designed to increase efficiency. If you're unable to adjust, you can revert to the Classic version of the Start menu by following these steps:

1. Right-click **Start** and click **Properties** in the shortcut menu. If necessary, click the **Start Menu** tab.

2. Click the **Classic Start menu** option button, and then click **Apply**. Click **OK** and take some time to explore the Classic start menu.

3. Which Start menu version do you prefer, and why?

_____

_____

4. Return to the new Start menu. List the steps you performed to do this:

_____

_____

In the next steps, you locate essential system information using Computer and Control Panel. Remember, however, with the new interface, locating some items might not be as easy.

1. Click **Start,** and then click **Computer.**

   ◢ Click the **Views** pull-down menu. List all the views that are available:

   _____

   _____

   ◢ What additional information is displayed with the Details view that isn't shown with the List view?

   _____

   _____

   ◢ What happens at the bottom of the Computer window when you click the drive C: icon?

   _____

   _____

2. Double-click the drive C icon.

   ◢ Describe how Windows Vista displays information about your hard drive:

   _____

   _____

   ◢ What happens when you click the **Date modified** column header?

   _____

   _____

3. Click the **Back** button and close the Computer window.

4. Click **Start,** and click **Control Panel.** Make sure **Control Panel Home** is selected.

   ◢ What categories of information are displayed in Control Panel?

   _____

   _____

   _____

   ◢ List the steps you would take to view information or make changes to your mouse settings:

   _____

   _____

   _____

◢ Do you prefer the categories listed in the Classic view? Why or why not?

_____

_____

_____

5. Close Control Panel and return to the Windows desktop.

REVIEW QUESTIONS

1. What steps must you take to locate Computer?

_____

2. Why might it be important to view files sorted by the date they were modified?

_____

_____

_____

3. What Windows control panel category would you use to change your mouse settings?

_____

4. Why does Windows allow you to change to a Classic Start menu?

_____

5. Why does Windows allow you to lock your taskbar?

_____

_____

LAB 14.2 USE THE MICROSOFT MANAGEMENT CONSOLE

OBJECTIVES

The goal of this lab is to help you add snap-ins and save settings using the Microsoft Management Console (MMC) to create a customized console. After completing this lab, you will be able to:

◢ Use the MMC to add snap-ins

◢ Save a customized console

◢ Identify how to launch a console from the Start menu

MATERIALS REQUIRED

This lab requires the following:

◢ Windows Vista/XP Professional operating system

LAB PREPARATION

Before the lab begins, the instructor or lab assistant needs to do the following:

◢ Verify that Windows starts with no errors.

ACTIVITY BACKGROUND

The Microsoft Management Console (MMC) is a standard management tool you can use to create a customized console by adding administrative tools called snap-ins. You can use snap-ins provided by Microsoft or other vendors. Many of the administrative tools you have already used (such as Device Manager) can be added to a console as a snap-in. The console itself serves as a convenient interface that helps you organize and manage the administrative tools you use most often. In this lab, you use the MMC to create a customized console.

ESTIMATED COMPLETION TIME: 30 Minutes

 Activity

Follow these steps to build a customized console:

1. If necessary, log on as an administrator.

2. Click **Start**.

3. In the Start Search box, type **mmc** and then press **Enter**. If Windows needs your permission to continue, click **Continue**. (In XP, click **Run**, type **mmc**, and then click **OK**.) An MMC window named Console1 opens, and within it is another window named Console Root, which is used to display the console's contents.

4. From the Console1 menu, click **File, Add/Remove Snap-in . . . .** The Add or Remove Snap-ins dialog box opens. Console1 is currently empty—that is, it doesn't contain any snap-ins yet. As you can see in the Selected snap-ins list box, any new snap-ins are added to the Console Root folder.

5. The Selected snap-ins list box opens, displaying a list of available snap-ins, as pictured in Figure 14-1. Note that this list includes some administrative tools you have already used, such as Device Manager and Event Viewer.

6. Click **Device Manager**, and then click **Add**.

7. The Device Manager dialog box opens, where you specify which computer you want this Device Manager snap-in to manage. You want it to manage the computer you're currently working on, so verify that the **Local computer** option button is selected, and then click **Finish**.

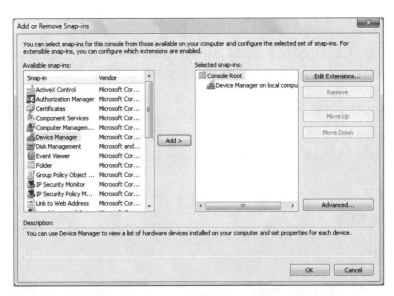

Figure 14-1 Adding Snap-ins to the Microsoft Management Console
Courtesy: Course Technology/Cengage Learning

8. Next, you add Event Viewer as a snap-in. Click **Event Viewer** in the Available Snap-ins list, and then click **Add**. The Select Computer dialog box opens.

9. Verify that the **Local computer** option button is selected, and then click **OK**.

10. Click **OK** to close the Add or Remove Snap-ins dialog box.

You have finished adding snap-ins for the local computer to your console. Next, you add another Event Viewer snap-in to be used on a network computer. If your computer isn't connected to a network, you can read the following set of steps, but don't attempt to perform them. If your computer is connected to a network, follow these steps:

1. Add another Event Viewer snap-in, and then click the **Another computer** option button in the Select Computer dialog box. Now you need to specify the name of the computer to which you want this Event Viewer snap-in to apply. You could type the name of the computer, but it's easier to select the computer by using the Browse button.

2. Click the **Browse** button. A different Select Computer dialog box opens. Click **Advanced** and click **Find Now** to begin searching the network for eligible computers. Eventually, it displays a list of eligible computers.

3. Click the name of the computer to which you want to apply this Event Viewer snap-in, and then click **OK**. The second Select Computer dialog box closes, and you return to the first Select Computer dialog box.

4. Click **OK** to close all three Select Computer dialog boxes, and a second Event Viewer snap-in is added below the first. The new Event Viewer listing is followed by the name of the remote computer in parentheses.

At this point, regardless of whether your computer is connected to a network, the Add or Remove Snap-ins dialog box should be open. You're finished adding snap-ins and are ready to return to the Console1 window and save your new, customized console so that you can use it whenever you need it. Follow these steps:

1. Click **OK**. The Add or Remove Snap-ins dialog box closes, and you return to the Console1 window. The left pane of the Console Root window (within the Console1 window) now contains the following items: Device Manager on local computer, Event Viewer (Local), and Event Viewer (*remote computer name*).

2. In the Console1 window, click **File, Save As** from the menu. The Save As dialog box opens with the default location set to the Administrative Tools folder. If you save your customized console in this location, Administrative Tools is also added to the Start menu. Instead, use the Save in drop-down list box to choose the Programs folder for the save location.

3. Name the console **Custom.msc**, and then click **Save**. The Save As dialog box closes.

4. Close the Custom window.

Follow these steps to open and use your customized console:

1. Click **Start**, point to **All Programs**, and click **Custom**. If a UAC dialog box opens, click **Continue**. Your customized console opens in a window named Custom - [Console Root].

2. Maximize the console window, if necessary.

3. In the left pane, click **Device Manager on local computer** and observe the options in the middle pane.

4. In the left pane, click the arrow next to Event Viewer (Local). Subcategories are displayed below Event Viewer (Local). List the subcategories you see:

_____

_____

_____

14

5. Click **Event Viewer** (*remote computer name*), and observe that the events displayed are events occurring on the remote computer.

6. From the Custom - [Console Root] menu, click **File, Exit**. A message box opens, asking if you want to save the current settings.

7. Click **Yes**. The console closes.

8. Launch the customized console from the Start menu again, and record the type of information displayed in the middle pane when the console opens:

_____

_____

REVIEW QUESTIONS

1. What term is used to refer to the specialized tools you can add to a console with the MMC? What are they used for?

_____

_____

_____

2. Suppose you haven't created a customized MMC yet. How would you start MMC?

_____

_____

_____

3. How can a customized console be used to manage many computers from a single machine?

_____

_____

_____

4. Why might you want the ability to manage a remote computer through a network?

_____

_____

_____

5. How do you add a customized console to the Start menu?

_____

_____

_____

LAB 14.3 ANALYZE A SYSTEM WITH EVENT VIEWER

OBJECTIVES

The goal of this lab is to help you learn to work with Windows Vista/XP Event Viewer. After completing this lab, you will be able to use Event Viewer to:

◢ View Windows events

◢ Save events

◢ View events logs

◢ Compare recent events to logged events

MATERIALS REQUIRED

This lab requires the following:

⊿ Windows Vista/XP Professional operating system

⊿ Network access using the TCP/IP protocol suite

⊿ An administrator account and password

LAB PREPARATION

Before the lab begins, the instructor or lab assistant needs to do the following:

⊿ Verify that Windows starts with no errors.

ACTIVITY BACKGROUND

Most of the things that happen to your computer while running Windows Vista/XP are recorded in a log. In this lab, you will take another look at a tool called Event Viewer, an application that provides information on various operations and tasks (known as events) in Windows. Event Viewer notes the occurrence of various events, lists them chronologically, and gives you the option of saving the list so that you can compare it to a future list. You can use Event Viewer to find out how healthy your system is and to diagnose nonfatal startup problems. Fatal startup problems don't allow you into Windows far enough to use Event Viewer.

ESTIMATED COMPLETION TIME: 30 Minutes

 Activity

Follow these steps to begin using Event Viewer:

1. If necessary, boot the system and log on as an administrator.

2. Click **Start, Control Panel** to open the Control Panel window.

3. Click **System and Maintenance** (**Performance and Maintenance** in XP), and then click **Administrative Tools**. The Administrative Tools applet opens.

4. Double-click **Event Viewer** to open the Event Viewer window. If Windows opens a UAC dialog box, click **Continue**. The latest events of each type are displayed in chronological order from most recent to oldest (see Figure 14-2).

5. Locate the listings for the four most recent events on your system by double-clicking **Windows Log** and then choosing **System** (choose **System** in XP). The symbols to the left of each event indicate important information about the event. For example, a lowercase "i" in a circle indicates an event providing information about the system, and an exclamation mark in a triangle indicates a warning, such as a disk being near its capacity. The listing for each event includes a brief description and the time and date it occurred.

For each event, list the source (what triggered the event), time, and date:

_____

_____

_____

_____

14

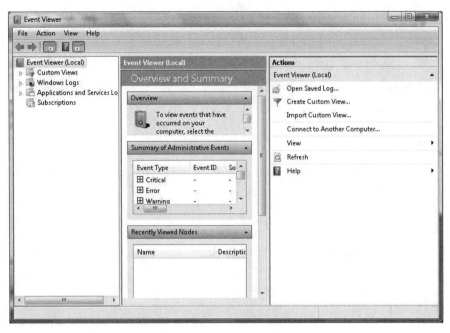

Figure 14-2 Event Viewer tracks failed and successful events
Courtesy: Course Technology/Cengage Learning

6. Double-click the top (most recent) event. The Event Properties dialog box opens. What additional information does this dialog box provide? Note that you can also see an event's properties by clicking an event to select it, and then clicking **Action, Event Properties** from the menu.

_____

_____

_____

7. Close the Event Properties dialog box.

You can save the list of events shown in Event Viewer as a special file called a log file. When naming a log file, it's helpful to use the following format: EV*mm-dd-yy*.evt (*mm* = month, *dd* = day, and *yy* = year). For example, you would name a log file saved on January 13, 2009 as EV01-13-09.evtx. After you create a log file, you can delete the current list of events from Event Viewer, allowing the utility to begin creating an entirely new list of events. Follow these steps to save the currently displayed events as a log file, and then clear the current events:

1. Open Windows Explorer, and create a folder called **Logs** in the root directory of drive C.

2. Leaving Windows Explorer open, return to Event Viewer and click somewhere on the Event Viewer window so that no event is selected. Then click **Action, Save Event As** from the menu.

3. Navigate to the **Logs** folder created in Step 1, name the file **EV*mm-dd-yy*.evtx**, and then click **Save** and click **OK**. Now you're ready to clear the current list of events from Event Viewer.

4. Click **Action, Clear Log** from the menu.

5. When asked if you want to save the System log, click **Clear**. The Event Viewer window no longer displays any events.

6. Close Event Viewer.

Next, you try to create an intentional problem by attempting to remove a system file. Recall that the Windows Resource Protection (Windows File Protection in XP) feature doesn't allow you to delete or rename a system file. If you try to do that, the event is recorded in Event Viewer. To attempt to delete a system file, do the following:

1. Return to Windows Explorer, and locate the Tcpip.sys file in the \windows\system32\drivers folder.

2. Click **tcpip.sys** and press **Delete**. When you're asked to confirm sending this file to the Recycle Bin, click **Yes**. Would Windows allow you to delete this file? How do you know?

   _____

   _____

3. The file makes it possible for the computer to communicate over the network and is a protected system file, so Windows protects the file. (You learn more about TCP/IP in Chapter 18.)

4. Close Windows Explorer and open Event Viewer. Open **Windows Logs**, click **Security**, and find the event you just caused. Answer these questions:

   ◢ What is the description of the event?

   _____

   _____

   _____

   ◢ What is the type assigned to this event?

   _____

5. Close the Event Properties dialog box.

6. Open Windows Explorer. Is Tcpip.sys in the \WINNT\system32\drivers folder?

   _____

Next, you create an intentional problem by disconnecting the network cable from your PC, and then see how the resulting errors are recorded in Event Viewer. Do the following:

1. Carefully disconnect the network cable from the network port on the back of your PC.

2. Restart the computer and log on as an administrator. Record the messages you receive, if any:

   _____

   _____

3. Open Network (My Network Places in XP). Are you able to browse the network?

   _____

4. Close Network, and then open Event Viewer. How many new events are displayed?

   _____

5. List the source, date, and time for any error events (indicated by a red icon) you see:

   _____

   _____

   _____

   _____

   _____

14

6. Click each error or warning event, and read the details. How does Event Viewer describe what happened when you unplugged the network port?

_____

_____

_____

_____

_____

_____

When troubleshooting a system, comparing current events with a list of events you previously stored in a log file is often helpful because you can spot the time when a particular problem occurred. Follow these steps to compare the current list of events to the log you saved earlier:

1. Open another instance of Event Viewer (that is, open a second Event Viewer window without closing the first one).

2. In the new Event Viewer window, click a blank area of the window so that no event is selected. Then click **Action, Open Saved Log** from the menu.

3. If necessary, open the **Logs** folder, click the log file you created earlier, and click **OK**.

4. To position the two instances of Event Viewer on your desktop so that you can compare them, right-click a blank spot on the taskbar. A shortcut menu opens, giving you options for how to arrange all open windows. Click **Show Windows Side by Side** to position the two open windows side by side.

5. You might notice that the current list of events contains one more successful event than the log of previous events. One of these successful events might be the cause of a failed event. For instance, a service starting and allocating resources that another component was previously using would be listed as a successful event. However, allocating resources currently in use would cause the component that had been using the resources to fail, thereby resulting in a failed event. Judging by the log file you created earlier, how many events occur in a normal startup?

_____

To restore the network connection and verify that the connection is working, follow these steps:

1. Reconnect the network cable to the network port on the back of your computer, restart your computer, and log on. Did you receive any messages after you started Windows this time?

_____

2. Open Event Viewer and verify that no errors occurred during startup.

3. Open another instance of Event Viewer, open the log you saved earlier (in the Logs folder), and verify that the same events occurred in both windows.

4. Close both Event Viewer windows.

CRITICAL THINKING (ADDITIONAL 30 MINUTES)

Using the Internet for research, find answers to the following questions. Be sure to list the URLs that support your answers.

1. Which version of Windows introduced Windows Resource Protection? Explain what Windows File Resource does:

   _____

   _____

2. How could Windows event viewer be used to determine the health of your system?

   _____

   _____

3. How might Event Viewer be used to diagnose a Windows Startup problem?

   _____

   _____

4. What are the key differences between Windows File Protection used in XP and Windows Resource Protection used in Vista?

   _____

   _____

REVIEW QUESTIONS

1. Judging by the path to Event Viewer using the Start menu, what type of tool is Event Viewer?

   _____

2. Based on what you learned in this lab, what might be your first indication that a problem occurred after startup?

   _____

3. How can you examine events after you have cleared them from Event Viewer?

   _____

   _____

4. Explain how to compare a log file with the current set of listed events:

   _____

   _____

14

5. Why might you like to keep a log file of events that was made when your computer started correctly? List the steps to create this log of a successful startup:

_____

_____

_____

_____

_____

LAB 14.4 USE TASK MANAGER

OBJECTIVES

The goal of this lab is to help you use Task Manager to examine your system. After completing this lab, you will be able to:

◢ Identify applications that are currently running

◢ Launch an application

◢ Display general system performance and process information in Task Manager

MATERIALS REQUIRED

This lab requires the following:

◢ Windows Vista/XP Professional operating system

◢ Installed CD/DVD drive, installed/on-board sound card, and an audio CD

LAB PREPARATION

Before the lab begins, the instructor or lab assistant needs to do the following:

◢ Verify that Windows starts with no errors.

◢ Verify that a CD drive and sound card have been installed on student computers.

ACTIVITY BACKGROUND

Task Manager is a useful tool that allows you to switch between tasks, end tasks, and observe system use and performance. In this lab, you use Task Manager to manage applications and observe system performance.

ESTIMATED COMPLETION TIME: 30 Minutes

 Activity

Follow these steps to use Task Manager:

1. If necessary, log on as an administrator.

2. Press **Ctrl+Alt+Del** and click **Start Task Manager**, or right-click any blank area on the taskbar and click **Task Manager** in the shortcut menu. The Task Manager

dialog box opens, with tabs you can use to find information about applications, processes, and programs running on the computer and information on system performance.

3. If necessary, click the **Applications** tab. What information is currently listed in the Task list box?

_____

_____

_____

4. Use the Start menu to open Windows Help and Support and then observe the change to the Task list in the Applications tab. What change occurred in the Task list?

_____

5. Right-click the new task and click **Go To Process**. What process is associated with this task?

_____

6. On the Applications tab, click the **New Task** button. The Create New Task dialog box opens, which is almost identical to the Run dialog box you open from the Start menu in Windows XP.

7. In the Open text box, type **command.com**, and then click **OK**. A command prompt window opens. Examine the Application tab in Task Manager, and note that \windows\system32\command.com now appears in the Task list.

8. Click the title bar of the command prompt window. It's now the active window, but notice that Task Manager remains on top of all other open windows. This ensures that you can keep track of changes in the system while opening and closing applications.

You can customize Task Manager to suit your preferences. Among other things, you can change the setting that keeps Task Manager on top of all other open windows and change the way information is displayed. To learn more about changing Task Manager settings, make sure the command prompt window is still open, and follow these steps:

1. In Task Manager, click **Options** on the menu bar. A menu with a list of options opens. Note that the check marks indicate which options are currently applied. The Always On Top option is currently selected, which keeps the Task Manager window on top of all other open windows. List the available menu options here:

_____

_____

_____

2. Click **Always On Top** to clear the check mark, and then click the command prompt window. What happens?

_____

_____

_____

14

3. Click **Options** on the Task Manager menu bar, and then click **Always On Top** to select it again.

4. On the Task Manager menu bar, click **View**. You can use the options on this menu to change how quickly the information is updated. List the available and current settings:

_____

_____

_____

Follow these steps in Task Manager to end a task and observe system use information:

1. On the Applications tab, notice that three types of information are listed in the bar at the bottom of Task Manager. What three types of information do you see, and what are their values?

_____

_____

_____

2. While observing these three values, move your mouse around the screen for several seconds and then stop. Did any of the values change?

_____

3. Next, move your mouse to drag an open window around the screen for several seconds and then stop. How did this affect the values?

_____

4. In the Task list, click **Windows Help and Support** and then click the **End Task** button.

5. Compare the number of processes, CPU usage, and commit charge (memory usage) to the information recorded in Step 1. How much memory was Windows Help and Support using?

_____

Follow these steps in Task Manager to observe process and performance information:

1. In Task Manager, click the **Processes** tab. This tab lists current processes in the Image Name column and displays information about each process, such as the percent age used by the CPU (CPU) or the memory usage (Memory).

2. Scroll down and examine each process. What process is currently using the highest CPU and Memory resources?

_____

3. Click the **View** tab and click **Select Columns**. Which column would you select to appear on the Process page if you wanted to know the process identifier for each process?

_____

4. Use the Start menu to start Windows Help and Support.

5. Drag the Help and Support window to position it so that it is visible to the left of the Task Manager window.

6. Verify that the Help window is the active window, and then observe the process information in Task Manager as you select various topics in the Help and Support window. Which process or processes begin to use more CPU resources as the mouse moves from topic to topic?

7. In the Processes tab of Task Manager, click **HelpPane.exe** (**HelpSvc.exe** in Windows XP), and then click **End Process**. What message is displayed?

8. In addition to processes for optional user applications, the Processes tab displays and allows you to end core Windows processes. *Caution*: Be careful about ending tasks; ending a potentially essential task (one that other processes depend on) could have serious consequences. Because Windows Help and Support is not critical to core Windows functions, it's safe to end this task. Click **End process** to end.

9. Click the **Performance** tab, which displays CPU usage and memory usage in bar graphs. This tab also shows a running history graph for both CPU usage and Memory usage. What other categories of information are displayed in the Performance tab?

10. Insert an audio CD. Configure it to begin playing, if necessary. Observe the CPU and page file or memory usage values, and record them here:

11. Stop the CD from playing, and again observe the CPU usage and page file or memory usage. Compare these values to the values from Step 9. Which value changed the most?

12. When you're finished, close all open windows.

REVIEW QUESTIONS

1. Explain one way to launch Task Manager:

2. Which Task Manager tab do you use to switch between applications and end a task?

3. Why could it be dangerous to end a process with Task Manager?

14

4. How could you tell whether the processor had recently completed a period of intensive use but is now idle?

_____

_____

5. Did the playback of an audio CD use more system resources than moving the mouse? Explain:

_____

_____

_____

LAB 14.5 EDIT THE REGISTRY WITH REGEDIT

OBJECTIVES

The goal of this lab is to learn how to save, modify, and restore the Windows registry. After completing this lab, you will be able to:

▲ Back up and modify the registry

▲ Observe the effects of a damaged registry

▲ Restore the registry

MATERIALS REQUIRED

This lab requires the following:

▲ Windows Vista/XP operating system

LAB PREPARATION

Before the lab begins, the instructor or lab assistant needs to do the following:

▲ Verify that Windows starts with no errors.

ACTIVITY BACKGROUND

The registry is a database of configuration information stored in files called hives. Each time Windows boots, it rebuilds the registry from the configuration files and stores it in RAM. When you need to modify the behavior of Windows, you should consider editing the registry as a last resort. Errors in the registry can make your system inoperable, and there's no way for Windows to inform you that you have made a mistake. For this reason, many people are afraid to work with the registry. If you follow the rule of backing up the system before you make any change, however, you can feel confident that even if you make a mistake, you can restore the system to its original condition. In this lab, you back up, change, and restore the registry.

ESTIMATED COMPLETION TIME: 45 Minutes

 Activity

Windows allows you to create a restore point so that you can restore Windows to a time before any changes were made. Follow these directions to back up the system (including the registry):

1. Open the **System Properties** dialog box by clicking **Start, Control Panel, System and Maintenance, System,** and the **System protection** task. If Windows presents a UAC dialog box, click **Continue.**

2. Click **Create** and add a name for your restore point. The current time and date will be added automatically. Click **Create** again to create the restore point.

3. When the backup is completed, click **OK** to close the System Protection dialog box and **OK** again to close the System Properties dialog box. By default, Windows stores restore points automatically.

4. Open System Properties again and click **System Restore** on the System protection tab. Select **Choose a different restore point** and click **Next**. Determine the name and description of the backup you just created by checking the date and time the file was created. Record the name, date, and time of this file:

_____

5. Click **Cancel** to close the System Restore wizard and **Cancel** again to exit from System Properties.

6. Close any open windows.

As you know, you can use Windows tools such as Control Panel to modify many features from the color of the background to the power-saving features. Sometimes, however, the only way to make a modification is to edit the registry. These modifications are sometimes referred to as registry tweaks or hacks. In these steps, you will make a relatively small change to the registry by editing the name of the Recycle Bin. Follow these steps:

1. Click **Start,** type **regedit,** and press **Enter.** (In XP, Click **Start,** type **Run,** type **regedit,** and then click **OK.**) If Windows presents a UAC dialog box, click **Continue.** The Registry Editor opens, displaying the system's registry hierarchy in the left pane and any entries for the selected registry item in the right pane.

The registry is large, and searching through it manually (by scrolling through all the entries) can be tedious even if you have a good idea of where to look. To save time, use the Registry Editor's search feature to find the section governing the Recycle Bin:

1. To make sure you're searching the entire registry, select **Computer** and then click **Edit, Find** from the menu.

2. Make sure **Match whole string only** is checked and type **Recycle Bin** in the Find what text box. You can narrow your search by limiting which items to search. What other three ways can you further refine your search?

_____

_____

3. Click the **Find Next** button and then double-click the **(Default)** entry. The Edit String dialog box opens.

4. In the Value data text box, replace "Recycle Bin" with **Trash,** and then click **OK.**

5. Notice that "Trash" has replaced "Recycle Bin" in the right pane.

6. Close the Registry Editor, and then click **File, Exit** from the menu. You weren't prompted to save your changes to the registry because they were saved the instant you made them. This is why editing the registry is so unforgiving: There are no safeguards. You can't undo your work by choosing to exit without saving changes, as you can, for instance, in Microsoft Word.

7. Right-click the desktop, and then click **Refresh** in the shortcut menu. Note that the Recycle Bin icon is now named Trash.

Finally, you need to undo your changes to the Recycle Bin. Follow these steps to use the System Restore to restore the registry's previous version:

1. Open System Properties again and click **System Restore** on the System Protection tab. Select **Choose a different restore point** and click **Next.**

14

2. Choose the restore point you created earlier and click **Next.**

3. When you're asked to confirm your restore point, click **Finish.** Click **Yes** when the system warns you that a system restore cannot be undone.

4. After the system restore, the computer will have to reboot.

5. After the boot is completed, notice that the name of the Recycle bin has been restored.

Use Windows Help and Support or the Internet to answer the following questions about the registry:

◢ How often does Windows save the registry automatically?

_____

◢ Where are registry backups usually stored?

_____

◢ What files constitute the Vista and XP registry? What type of file are they saved as during backup?

_____

_____

REVIEW QUESTIONS

1. Why does Windows automatically save the registry?

_____

_____

2. Where is the registry stored while Windows is running?

_____

3. What type of safeguards does the Registry Editor have to keep you from making mistakes?

_____

4. How many files make up the registry on your system?

_____

5. In this lab, how did you check to make sure your Registry was restored?

_____

LAB 14.6 CRITICAL THINKING: USE WINDOWS UTILITIES TO SPEED UP A SYSTEM

OBJECTIVES

The goal of this lab is to help you learn how to clean up processes that might slow Windows. After completing this lab, you will be able to:

◢ Use Windows tools to clean up startup

◢ Investigate processes that are slowing down Windows

◢ Configure the system to keep it clean and free of malware

MATERIALS REQUIRED

This lab requires the following:

⊿ A Windows Vista/XP computer designated for this lab

⊿ Internet access

LAB PREPARATION

Before the lab begins, the instructor or lab assistant needs to do the following:

⊿ Make available a Windows Vista/XP computer. For the best student experience, try to use systems that are not optimized and need the benefits of this lab.

⊿ Verify that Internet access is available.

ACTIVITY BACKGROUND

A troubleshooting problem you'll often face as a PC support technician is a sluggish Windows system. Customers might tell you that when their Windows computer was new, it ran smoothly and fast with no errors, but now it hangs occasionally, is slow to start up or shut down, and is slow when working. There is no one particular problem that stands out above the rest, but a customer just says, "Please make my system work faster." When solving these types of general problems, it helps to have a game plan. This activity will give you just that. You'll learn how to speed up Windows, ridding it of unneeded and unwanted processes that are slowing it down.

ESTIMATED COMPLETION TIME: 60 Minutes

 Activity

Before you make any changes to the system, first get a benchmark of how long it takes for Windows to start up. Do the following:

1. Power down the computer and turn it on. Using a watch with a second hand, note how many minutes are needed for the system to start. Startup is completed after you have logged onto Windows, the hard drive activity light has stopped, and the mouse pointer looks like an arrow. How long does startup take?

   _____

2. Describe any problems you observed during startup:

   _____

   _____

   This lab assumes that Windows might be slow starting, but does start up without errors. If you see error messages on-screen or the system refuses to boot, you need to solve these problems before you continue with a general cleanup. Troubleshooting startup problems will be covered in Chapter 16.

You're now ready to begin a general cleanup. Do the following:

1. If valuable data is on the hard drive that is not backed up, back up that data now.

2. Run antivirus (AV) software. Here are your options:

   ⊿ If AV software is not installed and you have the AV software setup CD, install it. If it fails to install (some viruses block software installations), boot into Safe Mode and install and run it from there.

14

◢ If you don't have access to the AV software setup CD, you can download software from the Internet. If your PC cannot connect to the Internet (such as when Internet access is blocked by an active virus), you can download the software on another PC and burn a CD with the downloaded file. But before you do that, first try to connect to the Internet using the Safe Mode with Networking option on the Advanced Boot Options menu. (This option might not load a virus that prevents Internet access.)

◢ If you don't have AV software installed and don't have access to an AV software setup CD, but you can connect the computer to the Internet, you can run an online virus scan from an AV Web site. For example, Trend Micro (*www.trendmicro.com*) offers a free online virus scan. (This free online scan has been known to find viruses that other scans do not.)

◢ List the steps you took to run the AV software:

_____

_____

_____

◢ List any malware the AV software found:

_____

_____

_____

3. Reboot the system. Is there a performance increase? How long does startup take?

_____

_____

4. If the system is still running so slowly you find it difficult to work, you can temporarily use MSconfig to control startup processes hogging system resources. Click **Start** and type **msconfig** in the Start Search box (in XP, enter **msconfig** in the Run dialog box) and press **Enter**. If Windows presents a UAC dialog box, click **Continue**. The System Configuration utility window opens. Click the **Startup** tab, as shown in Figure 14-3.

5. You can keep services from starting by unchecking them in this window. List all of the services that are run at startup and use the Internet to determine the purpose of each of them:

_____

_____

_____

_____

_____

_____

_____

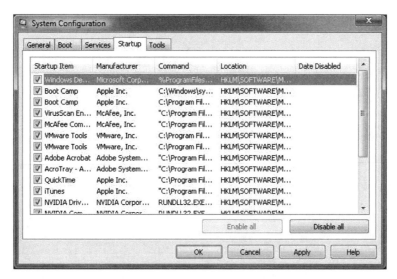

Figure 14-3 Use the System Configuration utility window to control startup processes until you can further clean up a slow Windows system
Courtesy: Course Technology/Cengage Learning

6. Uncheck all the services except the ones associated with your antivirus program. Reboot the system to cause these changes to take effect.

7. Is there a performance increase? How long does startup take?

_____

8. Clean up the hard drive. Delete temporary files, defrag the hard drive, and check for errors. If the system is slow while doing these tasks, do them from Safe Mode. Note that you need about 15 percent free hard drive space to defragment the drive. If you don't have that much free space, find some folders and files you can move to a different media. Windows requires this much free space to run well.

9. Reboot the system. Is there a performance increase? How long does startup take?

_____

10. Check Device Manager for hardware devices that are installed but not working or devices that are no longer needed and should be uninstalled. Did you find any devices that need fixing or uninstalling? How did you handle the situation?

_____

_____

CHALLENGE ACTIVITY (ADDITIONAL 15 MINUTES)

MSconfig doesn't necessarily show all the processes that run at startup. So, to get a more thorough list, you need to use a more powerful startup manager such as Autoruns from Sysinternals.

1. Go to http://technet.microsoft.com/en-us/sysinternals/default.aspx and download and install the latest version of Autoruns.

2. Run Autoruns and select the Logon tab, as shown in Figure 14-4.

14

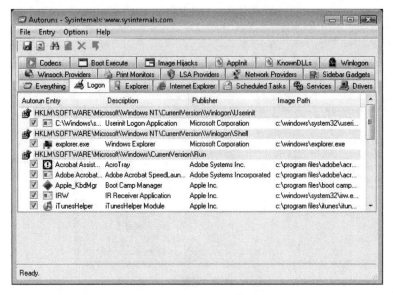

Figure 14-4 Autoruns startup manager by Sysinternals
Courtesy: Course Technology/Cengage Learning

3. How does the list of startup processes differ from the list generated by msconfig? List any additional processes identified:

_____

_____

_____

_____

REVIEW QUESTIONS

1. If AV software is not installed and you don't have access to the Internet, how can you install it?

_____

2. Which window is used to defrag a hard drive and check it for errors?

_____

3. What two folders can contain programs to be launched when a specific user logs onto the system?

_____

4. When cleaning up startup, why should you not delete a program file you find in a startup folder?

_____

5. What utility lists all currently running processes?

_____

Tools for Solving Windows Problems

Labs included in this chapter:

- **Lab 15.1:** Use Windows Help and Troubleshooters
- **Lab 15.2:** Restore the System State
- **Lab 15.3:** Update Drivers with Device Manager
- **Lab 15.4:** Install the XP Recovery Console as an Option on the Startup Menu
- **Lab 15.5:** Use the XP Recovery Console to Copy Files
- **Lab 15.6:** Use the Vista Recovery Environment (Windows RE) to Repair Windows

LAB 15.1 USE WINDOWS HELP AND TROUBLESHOOTERS

OBJECTIVES

The goal of this lab is to demonstrate how to use Windows Help tools to find information and how to use Windows Troubleshooters to correct common problems. After completing this lab, you will be able to:

◢ Find information on various topics in Windows Help

◢ Use a Windows Troubleshooter

MATERIALS REQUIRED

This lab requires the following:

◢ Windows Vista/XP Professional operating system

LAB PREPARATION

Before the lab begins, the instructor or lab assistant needs to do the following:

◢ Verify that Windows starts with no errors.

ACTIVITY BACKGROUND

You can use Windows Help to look up information on topics related to the operating system. To access Windows Help, use the Start menu or, with the desktop active, press F1. Windows Help is useful when you just need information. If you want help actually solving a problem, however, you should use the Windows Troubleshooters, which are interactive utilities that walk you through the problem of repairing a misconfigured system. Windows Troubleshooters are often launched automatically when Windows detects a problem. You can also start them manually from Windows Help.

ESTIMATED COMPLETION TIME: 30 Minutes

 Activity

In the following steps, you learn to use the main features of Windows Help. Note that pressing F1 starts Help for whatever application happens to be active at that time. To start Windows Help, you need to close or minimize any open applications, thereby making the desktop active, and then you can press F1 to start Windows Help. To learn more, follow the procedure for your operating system.

In Windows Vista/XP, follow these steps:

1. Log on to your computer as an administrator.

2. Close or minimize any applications that start automatically so that the desktop is active.

3. Press F1. (Instead of activating the desktop and pressing F1, you could simply click **Start, Help and Support.**) Windows Help opens. As you can see, the Windows Help interface is similar to a Web browser. Answer the following questions:

   ◢ What general categories are available in Windows Help?

   _____

   _____

◢ What steps would you follow to find information on how to locate lost files?

_____

_____

4. Move the pointer over **What's new?** (in XP, move the pointer over the **What's new in Windows XP** topic in the left pane), and note that the pointer becomes a hand, as it does in a Web browser when you move it over a link. When you point to a topic, it becomes underlined, like a hyperlink.

In Windows XP:

1. Click **What's new in Windows XP** in the left pane. This topic expands in the left pane, displaying subtopics. Click **What's new**. Subtopics are displayed in the right pane.

2. Scroll the right pane to get a sense of what information is available, and then click **What's new with files and folders** in the right pane. The topic expands to show a description of the contents as well as links to more information.

3. Click **New ways of viewing files and pictures**. The topic expands to add a brief overview and additional subcategories. Click **Viewing files and folders overview**. The right pane displays a list of ways to arrange and identify your files. Record the possible view options here:

_____

_____

_____

4. The Windows Help toolbar has buttons similar to those in a Web browser, including a Back button (a left-facing arrow) you can use to display a previous topic. Click the **Back** button in Windows Help. The What's new with files and folders screen is displayed again in the right pane.

In Windows Vista:

1. Click the **What's new?** icon and a list of subtopics appears on the left. Click **Tips for finding files** in the **Searching and organizing** section.

2. What three search methods are recommended for finding files?

_____

_____

_____

You can also look for topics in Windows Help by using the Search Help box, where you type keywords to locate the information you need. This feature is useful when you're familiar with Windows Help but don't know where to look for a specific topic in the Table of Contents. Follow these steps to use the Search feature:

1. Type **automatic updates** in the Search Help box and press **Enter**. The list of topics should now include one on how to turn on automatic updates in Windows. Follow the link to learn how to turn on automatic updates. How does Windows suggest you turn on automatic updates?

_____

_____

_____

15

With the Add to Favorites button in XP, you can record a list of topics you want to refer to again without having to search for them. Follow these steps:

1. Click the **Add to Favorites** button and click **OK**.

2. A pop-up window is displayed, stating that the page has been added to your favorites list.

Windows Help enables you to search for information on topics related to using Windows. Windows Troubleshooters provide information on how to fix problems with Windows and its applications. You can access Troubleshooters from Windows Help. In the following steps, you use a Troubleshooter to repair a nonfunctioning sound card:

1. Search for **sound troubleshooter** in the Search Help box and click **Troubleshoot sound problems** (click **Sound Troubleshooter** in XP).

2. The Windows Troubleshooter for sound asks you for details about the problem you're troubleshooting so that it can provide a solution tailored to that problem. For this portion of the lab, assume the following:

    ⊿ A sound appears to play, but you don't hear anything.

    ⊿ Your speakers can't play system sounds.

    ⊿ Your volume is not set too low, and audio is not muted.

3. To troubleshoot the problem, select the option for the specified scenario. In XP, click **Next** to advance through the Troubleshooter windows. What Windows utility is suggested for making sure your computer has an enabled sound card?

    _____

4. Now go back and troubleshoot a slightly different problem. This time, assume the following:

    ⊿ The sound is distorted or scratchy.

    ⊿ You aren't using an excessively high volume level.

    ⊿ You don't have a hardware device conflict.

5. Answer the following questions:

    ⊿ What options are offered to correct the problem?

    _____

    _____

    ⊿ Where does Windows suggest you look for further information?

    _____

    _____

REVIEW QUESTIONS

1. Windows Help is similar in appearance to what type of program?

    _____

2. What can you do if you're not sure where to look for a specific topic?

    _____

3. What are two ways to launch Windows Help?

    _____

4. What tool accessible from Windows Help takes you step by step through the process of diagnosing and perhaps repairing common problems?

_____

5. Are Troubleshooters ever launched automatically? Explain:

_____

_____

LAB 15.2 RESTORE THE SYSTEM STATE

OBJECTIVES

The goal of this lab is to help you restore the system state on a Windows Vista/XP computer. After completing this lab, you will be able to:

◢ Create a restore point by using System Restore

◢ Change system settings

◢ Restore the system state with the restore point you created

MATERIALS REQUIRED

This lab requires the following:

◢ Windows Vista/XP Professional operating system

LAB PREPARATION

Before the lab begins, the instructor or lab assistant needs to do the following:

◢ Verify that Windows starts with no errors.

ACTIVITY BACKGROUND

15

The System Restore tool in Windows Vista/XP enables you to restore the system to the state it was in when a snapshot, called a "restore point," was taken of the system state. The settings recorded in a restore point include system settings and configurations and files needed for a successful boot. When the system state is restored to a restore point, user data on the hard drive isn't affected, but software and hardware might be. Restore points are useful if, for example, something goes wrong with a software or hardware installation. In this lab, you create a restore point, make changes to system settings, and then use the restore point to restore the system state.

ESTIMATED COMPLETION TIME: 30 Minutes

 Activity

To use the System Restore tool to create a restore point, follow these steps:

1. Click **Start**, click **All Programs**, click **Accessories**, click **System Tools**, and then click **System Restore**. If Windows opens a UAC box, click **Continue**.

In Windows XP:

1. The System Restore window opens with two choices: **Restore my computer to an earlier time** and **Create a restore point**. The first option restores your computer to an existing restore point. Read the information at the left and answer these questions:

   ◢ Can changes made by System Restore be undone? What type of data does System Restore leave unaffected?

   _____

   ◢ What is the term for the restore points the system creates automatically?

   _____

   ◢ As you've read, it's helpful to create a restore point before you install software or hardware. In what other situations might you want to create a restore point?

   _____

   _____

2. Click the **Create a restore point** option button, and then click **Next**.

3. In the next window, type a description of the restore point. The description should make it easy to identify the restore point later, such as "Restore *today's date*."

4. Click the **Create** button.

5. A message is displayed stating that the restore point was created and showing the date, time, and name of the restore point. Click the **Close** button.

In Windows Vista:

1. If there are already several restore points on your system, the System Restore window opens with two choices: **Recommended restore** and **Choose a different restore point**. Click **How does System Restore work?** and read through this section. Then click **System Restore: frequently asked questions** and answer these questions:

   ◢ Can changes made by System Restore be undone? What type of data does System Restore leave unaffected?

   _____

   ◢ What feature regularly creates and saves restore points on your computer?

   _____

2. Close Windows Help and Support and click **open System Protection** to create a restore point.

3. Click the **Create . . .** button and assign your restore point a name.

4. Click the **Create** button and a restore point is created.

5. Click **OK** and then close any open windows.

Next, you make a change to the system by changing the display settings:

1. In Control Panel, click **Appearance and Personalization** (**Appearance and Themes** in XP), and then click **Personalization** (**Display** in XP).

2. Click **Desktop Background** (or the **Desktop** tab in XP), select a different background, and then click **OK**.

3. Close the Control Panel window. Notice that the desktop background has changed to the one you selected.

Follow these steps to use the restore point you created to restore the system state:

1. Open the System Restore tool as explained earlier in this lab.

2. Click **Choose a different restore point** (**Restore my computer to an earlier time** in XP) option button, and then click **Next**.

3. A window opens showing all dates on which restore points were made.

   ◢ How many restore points were created in the current month?

   _____

   ◢ List the reasons the restore points were made:

   _____

   _____

   _____

4. Click the name of the restore point you created earlier in the lab, and then click **Next**. (In Windows XP, first select the current date.)

5. When a confirmation window is displayed, click **Finish** to continue (click **Next** in XP). If necessary, click **Yes** to proceed.

   Describe what happens when you proceed with a restore:

   _____

   _____

6. After the system restarts, logon to the Windows desktop. In Windows XP, a message is displayed stating that the restoration is complete. Click **OK**.

   ◢ Did the display settings change back to their original settings?

   _____

REVIEW QUESTIONS

1. List three situations in which you might want to create a restore point:

   _____

   _____

   _____

2. What types of restore points are created by the system, and what types are created by users?

   _____

   _____

3. How often does the system create restore points automatically?

   _____

4. Can more than one restore point be made on a specific date?

   _____

15

5. Does Windows track more than one restore point? Why?

_____

_____

_____

LAB 15.3 UPDATE DRIVERS WITH DEVICE MANAGER

OBJECTIVES

The goal of this lab is to explore the functions of Device Manager. After completing this lab, you will be able to:

◢ Select your display adapter in Device Manager

◢ Update the driver for your display adapter from Device Manager

MATERIALS REQUIRED

This lab requires the following:

◢ Windows Vista/XP Professional operating system

◢ Updated driver files for the display adapter

LAB PREPARATION

Before the lab begins, the instructor or lab assistant needs to do the following:

◢ Verify that Windows starts with no errors.

◢ Locate or download updated driver files for the display adapter (video card).

ACTIVITY BACKGROUND

With Device Manager, you can update device drivers as well as monitor resource use. If you find a new driver for a device, you can use Device Manager to select the device and update the driver. In this lab, you use Device Manager to update the driver for your display adapter.

ESTIMATED COMPLETION TIME: 30 Minutes

Activity

1. Open Control Panel and click **System and Maintenance**. Select **Device Manager**, and click **Continue** if Windows needs your permission to continue. In XP, click **Performance and Maintenance**, click **System**, select the **Hardware** Tab, and click **Device Manager**.

2. Click the + sign next to **Display adapters** to expand this category, and click your display adapter to select it.

3. Open the Properties dialog box for your display adapter by right-clicking the adapter and selecting **Properties**. Then click the **Driver** tab.

4. Click the **Driver Details** button. Which folders contain the drivers used by your display adapter?

   _____

   _____

5. Return to the Driver tab in the display adapter's Properties dialog box by clicking **OK**, and then click **Update Driver**.

6. Click **Browse my computer for driver software**.

7. In Windows XP, click **No, not at this time** to keep from connecting to Windows Update and then click **Next**. Click **Install from a list or specific location (Advanced)** and then click **Next**. Click the **Include this location in the search** check box.

8. Type the location of the driver installation file, or click the **Browse** button to select a location your instructor has designated. After you have specified a location, click **Next**. Windows searches the location and reports its findings.

9. If the wizard indicates it has found a file for the device you selected in Step 2 (the display adapter), click **Next** to continue. If the wizard reports that it can't find the file, verify that you have entered the installation file's location correctly.

10. After Windows locates the drivers, it copies the driver files. If a file being copied is older than the file the system is currently using, you're prompted to confirm that you want to use the older file. Usually, newer drivers are better than older drivers. However, you might want to use an older one if you've had problems after updating drivers recently. In this case, you might want to reinstall the old driver that wasn't causing problems.

11. When the files have been copied, click **Finish** to complete the installation.

12. Close all open windows and restart the computer if prompted to do so.

CRITICAL THINKING (ADDITIONAL 30 MINUTES)

Use Device Manager to identify the installed display adapter. Next, search the device manufacturer's Web sites for new video, network card, sound card, and motherboard drivers. If you find drivers newer than the one in use, install the updated drivers.

REVIEW QUESTIONS

1. Describe the steps to access Device Manager:

   _____

   _____

2. How can you access a device's properties in Device Manager?

   _____

   _____

3. What tab in the Properties dialog box do you use to update a driver?

   _____

4. Besides typing the path, what other option do you have to specify a driver's location?

   _____

   _____

15

5. Why might you want to use an older driver?

_____

_____

LAB 15.4 INSTALL THE XP RECOVERY CONSOLE AS AN OPTION ON THE STARTUP MENU

OBJECTIVES

The goal of this lab is to help you install the Recovery Console as a startup option. After completing this lab, you will be able to:

⊿ Install the Recovery Console

⊿ Open the Recovery Console from the Startup menu

MATERIALS REQUIRED

This lab requires the following:

⊿ Windows XP operating system

⊿ Windows XP installation CD or installation files

LAB PREPARATION

Before the lab begins, the instructor or lab assistant needs to do the following:

⊿ Verify that Windows starts with no errors.

⊿ Provide each student with access to the Windows XP installation files, if needed.

ACTIVITY BACKGROUND

The Recovery Console tool in Windows XP allows you to start the computer when other startup and recovery options, such as System Restore, Safe Mode, and the Automated System Recovery (ASR) process, don't work. In the Recovery Console, you can use a limited group of DOS-like commands to format a hard drive, copy files from a floppy disk or CD to the hard drive, start and stop certain system processes, and perform other administrative tasks and troubleshooting tasks. If the Recovery Console isn't installed on your computer, you have to run it from the Windows XP installation CD. This lab shows you how to install the Recovery Console on your Windows XP computer so that it appears as an option when the computer starts.

ESTIMATED COMPLETION TIME: 30 Minutes

 Activity

Follow these steps to install the Recovery Console as a startup option:

1. Insert the Windows XP installation CD into your CD-ROM drive. If the Autorun feature launches, close it. If your instructor has given you another location for the installation files, what drive letter do you use to access them?

_____

2. Click **Start, Run.** The Run dialog box opens. Type **cmd** and then click **OK.** A command prompt window opens.

3. To switch to your CD-ROM drive (or other drive with the installation files), type the drive letter followed by a colon, and then press **Enter.**

4. Next, you run the Windows XP setup program stored on this drive. The path to the program might vary, depending on the release of Windows XP you're using. Try the following possibilities until you locate the command that runs the program:

    ◢ Type **\i386\winnt32.exe /cmdcons** and press **Enter.**

    ◢ Type **\english\winxp\pro\i386\winnt32.exe /cmdcons** and press **Enter.**

    ◢ Type **\english\winxp\home\i386\winnt32.exe /cmdcons** and press **Enter.**

    ◢ Which command launched the setup program?

    _____

> **Notes** If you've upgraded XP to a later service pack than the one bundled with the installation CD, you might need to boot from the CD to start setup.

5. A message box is displayed, asking if you want to install the Recovery Console. Click **Yes** to continue.

6. The Windows Setup window opens and shows that Setup is checking for updates. When the update check is finished, a progress indicator appears. When the installation is finished, a message box is displayed stating that the Recovery Console was installed successfully. Click **OK** to continue.

7. Restart your computer.

8. When the Startup menu is displayed, select **Microsoft Windows Recovery Console** and press **Enter.** What do you see when the Recovery Console opens?

    _____

    _____

    _____

    _____

9. Type **1** (to log on to your Windows installation) and press **Enter.**

10. When prompted, type the administrator password for your computer and press **Enter.**

11. Type **help** and press **Enter** to see a list of commands available in the Recovery Console. You may have to continue pressing **Enter** to scroll through the list. Answer the following questions:

    ◢ What command deletes a directory?

    _____

    ◢ What command can you use to list services that are running?

    _____

    ◢ Name at least two tasks you might not be able to perform in the Recovery Console:

    _____

    _____

15

12. Type **exit** and press **Enter** to close the Recovery Console and restart the computer to Windows.

REVIEW QUESTIONS

1. What is the advantage of being able to access the Recovery Console from your hard drive instead of the CD-ROM drive?

   _____

   _____

2. Describe a situation where recovery console would not be the best tool for solving a Windows problem:

   _____

   _____

3. Why is an administrator password needed for access to the Recovery Console?

   _____

   _____

4. Why do you think Recovery Console only supports command-line utilities?

   _____

   _____

LAB 15.5 USE THE XP RECOVERY CONSOLE TO COPY FILES

OBJECTIVES

The goal of this lab is to help you learn how to copy files using the Recovery Console. After completing this lab, you will be able to:

◢ Copy files from a storage medium to your hard drive using the Recovery Console

MATERIALS REQUIRED

This lab requires the following:

◢ Windows XP operating system

◢ A floppy disk or other storage medium such as a USB flash drive

◢ Completion of Lab 15.4

LAB PREPARATION

Before the lab begins, the instructor or lab assistant needs to do the following:

◢ Verify that Windows starts with no errors.

ACTIVITY BACKGROUND

The Windows XP Recovery Console is useful when you need to restore system files after they have been corrupted (perhaps by a virus) or accidentally deleted from the hard drive.

In this lab, you use the Recovery Console (which you installed in Lab 15.4) to restore a system file, System.ini, from a floppy disk or other storage medium such as a USB flash drive. (Windows XP doesn't need this file to boot; it's included in Windows XP for backward compatibility with older Windows software.)

ESTIMATED COMPLETION TIME: 30 Minutes

 Activity

Follow these steps to copy the file System.ini to a floppy disk and then copy it from the floppy to the hard drive using the Recovery Console:

1. Insert the floppy disk in the floppy drive.

2. Open Windows Explorer, and then locate and click the **System.ini** file (which is usually in the C:\Windows folder).

> **Notes** In these steps, a floppy disk is used as the storage medium, but you can adapt the steps to whatever storage medium you're using.

3. Copy the **System.ini** file to the floppy disk, and then eject the floppy disk from the drive.

4. Locate System.ini on your hard drive again and rename it as **System.old**. When prompted, click **Yes** to confirm that you want to rename the file.

5. Restart the computer and select the **Microsoft Windows Recovery Console** option and press **Enter**.

6. Insert the floppy disk in the floppy disk drive. In the Recovery Console, log on with the administrator password. Type **copy a:\ system.ini c:\windows\system.ini** and press **Enter**. This command copies System.ini from the floppy disk to its original location (C:\Windows). What message does Recovery Console display?

   _____

7. If C:\Windows is not the active directory, change to that directory and then use the **dir** command to view its contents. Verify that System.ini was copied to this directory. You might have to use the Spacebar to scroll down.

8. Exit the Recovery Console and restart the computer.

REVIEW QUESTIONS

1. You could have used the Recovery Console to rename the System.old file instead of copying the original version from the floppy disk. What command do you use to perform this task?

   _____

2. Assume you moved the System.ini file to the My Documents folder. What command do you use in the Recovery Console to move it back to the C:\Windows folder?

   _____

3. When might it be useful to be able to copy files from a CD to the hard drive by using the Recovery Console?

   _____

4. Why does Windows XP include the System.ini file?

   _____

15

5. When might you want to use the Recovery Console to copy files from the hard drive to a floppy disk?

_____

_____

LAB 15.6 USE THE VISTA RECOVERY ENVIRONMENT (WINDOWS RE) TO REPAIR WINDOWS

OBJECTIVES

The goal of this lab is to help you learn how to use the Windows Vista Recovery Environment (Windows RE). After completing this lab, you will be able to:

⊿ Boot to Windows RE

⊿ Repair a Windows installation using Windows RE

MATERIALS REQUIRED

This lab requires the following:

⊿ Windows Vista operating system

⊿ Vista installation DVD

LAB PREPARATION

Before the lab begins, the instructor or lab assistant needs to do the following:

⊿ Verify that Windows starts with no errors.

ACTIVITY BACKGROUND

The Windows Vista Recovery Environment (RecEnv.exe), also known as Windows RE, is an operating system launched from the Vista DVD that provides a graphical and command-line interface. In this lab, you will become familiar with Windows RE and use it to solve some simple startup problems.

ESTIMATED COMPLETION TIME: 30 Minutes

 Activity

Follow these steps to start up and explore Windows RE:

1. Using a computer that has Windows Vista installed, boot from the Vista setup DVD. (To boot from a DVD, you might have to change the boot sequence in CMOS setup to put the optical drive first above the hard drive.) The screen in Figure 15-1 appears. Select your language preference and click **Next**.

2. The Install Windows screen appears, as shown in Figure 15-2. Click **Repair your computer**. The recovery environment (RecEnv.exe) launches and displays the System Recovery Options dialog box (see Figure 15-3).

3. Select the Vista installation to repair and click **Next**.

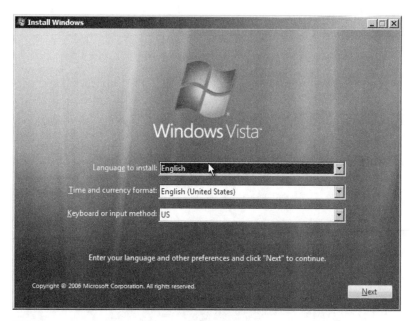

Figure 15-1 Select your language preference
Courtesy: Course Technology/Cengage Learning

Figure 15-2 Launch Windows RE after booting from the Vista DVD
Courtesy: Course Technology/Cengage Learning

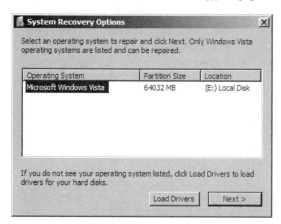

Figure 15-3 Select an installation of Vista to repair
Courtesy: Course Technology/Cengage Learning

4. The System Recovery Options window in Figure 15-4 appears, listing recovery options.

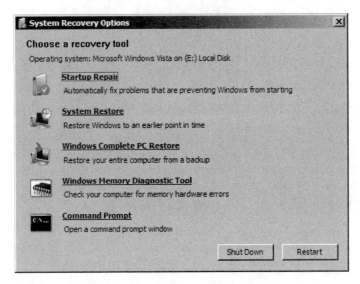

Figure 15-4   Recovery tools in Windows RE
Courtesy: Course Technology/Cengage Learning

5. The first tool, Startup Repair, can automatically fix many Windows problems, including those caused by a corrupted BCD file and missing system files. You can't cause any additional problems by using it and it's easy to use. Therefore, it should be your first recovery option when Vista refuses to load. Click **Startup Repair** and the tool will examine the system for errors (see Figure 15-5).

Based on what Startup Repair finds, it will suggest various solutions. For example, it might suggest you use System Restore or suggest you immediately reboot the system to see if the problem has been fixed (see Figure 15-6). Did Startup Repair find any errors on your system?

_____

_____

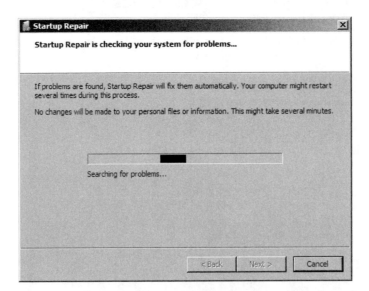

Figure 15-5   Startup Repair searches the system for problems it can fix
Courtesy: Course Technology/Cengage Learning

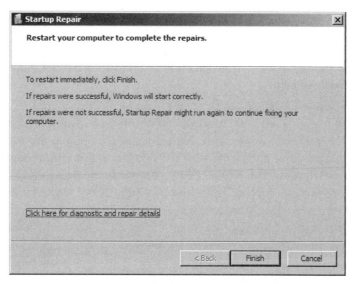

Figure 15-6   Startup Repair has attempted to fix the problem
Courtesy: Course Technology/Cengage Learning

6. To see a list of items examined and actions taken by Startup Repair, click **Click here for diagnostic and repair details**. If no problems were detected on your system, you can click **View diagnostic and repair details**. The dialog box showing the list of repairs appears, as shown in Figure 15-7. A log file can also be found at C:\Windows\System32\LogFiles\SRT\SRTTrail.txt.

What steps would you take to print this log file?

_____

_____

7. Click **Close** to close the dialog box and then click **Finish** in the Startup Repair window to get back to the System Recovery Options window.

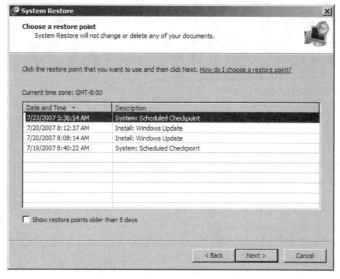

Figure 15-7   Choose from a list of restore points
Courtesy: Course Technology/Cengage Learning

15

8. System Restore in the System Recovery Options window works the same as Windows Vista System Restore from the desktop to return the system to its state when a restore point was made (see Lab 15.2). Click **System Restore** and click **Next**. A list of restore points appears (see Figure 15-7). Get back to the System Recovery Options windows by canceling the System Restore.

   Windows Complete PC Restore can be used to completely restore drive C and possibly other drives to their state when the last backup of the drives was made. When you use Complete PC Restore, everything on the hard drive is lost because the restore process completely erases the drive and writes to it the OS, user information, applications, and data as they were captured at the time the last Complete PC Backup was made. Therefore, before using Complete PC Restore, consider how old the backup is. Perhaps you can use it to restore drive C and then boot into Windows, reinstall applications installed since the last backup, and use other backups of data more recent than the last Complete PC Backup was made to restore the data.

9. Use the Windows Memory Diagnostic Tool to test memory. Did the diagnostic tool find any memory errors?

   _____

   _____

10. After the computer reboots, get back to the Systems recovery Options window and click **Command Prompt** to open a command prompt window. You can use this window to repair a corrupted Vista system or recover data (see Figure 15-8).

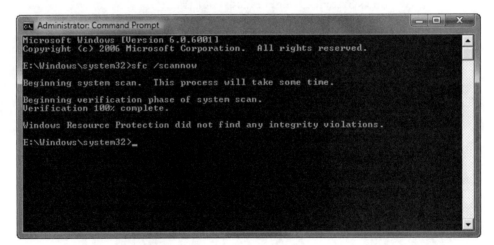

Figure 15-8   The command prompt window
Courtesy: Course Technology/Cengage Learning

11. Several of the commands in the Vista Recovery environment have been changed from the command used in the Windows XP Recovery Console. Use the help command and the Internet to answer the following questions:

   ◢ What Recovery Console command has been replaced with the command **BootRec /ScanOS**?

   _____

   ◢ What Recovery Console command has been replaced with the command **BootRec /FixBoot**?

   _____

▲ What Recovery Console command has been replaced with the command **BootRec /FixMbr**?

_____

12. Exit from the command prompt.

13. As you use a tool in the System Recovery Options window, be sure to reboot after each attempt to fix the problem to make sure the problem has not been resolved before you try another tool. To exit the Recovery Environment, click **Shut Down** or **Restart**.

CRITICAL THINKING (ADDITIONAL 15 MINUTES)

1. Using Windows Explorer, rename the BootMgr file in the root directory of drive C. Reboot the system. What error message do you see?

_____

_____

2. Use Windows RE to restore the BootMgr file. List the steps taken to complete the repair:

_____

_____

_____

_____

REVIEW QUESTIONS

1. If your computer would not boot, which Windows RE recovery tool would you try first? Why?

_____

_____

2. Why does Windows RE need to boot from the DVD?

_____

3. Why do you think Windows RE has still included an option for a command-line interface?

_____

4. What must be done before you can do a complete PC restore?

_____

5. Why is it important to reboot after each attempt to fix a problem with Windows RE?

_____

_____

15

Fixing Windows Problems

Labs included in this chapter:

- **Lab 16.1:** Troubleshoot Failed Windows Installations
- **Lab 16.2:** Recover Data from a Computer That Will Not Boot
- **Lab 16.3:** Finding a Driver for an Unknown Device
- **Lab 16.4:** Fixing Internet Explorer
- **Lab 16.5:** Critical Thinking: Sabotage and Repair Windows XP
- **Lab 16.6:** Critical Thinking: Sabotage and Repair Windows Vista

LAB 16.1 TROUBLESHOOT FAILED WINDOWS INSTALLATIONS

OBJECTIVES

The goal of this lab is to help you learn how to troubleshoot problems with various Windows installations. After completing this lab, you will be able to:

- Research problems with Windows installations
- Transfer user data and preferences
- Modify an answer file
- Share an external drive between a PC and a MAC

MATERIALS REQUIRED

This lab requires the following:

- A Windows Vista/XP computer designated for this lab
- Internet access

LAB PREPARATION

Before the lab begins, the instructor or lab assistant needs to do the following:

- Verify that Internet access is available.

ACTIVITY BACKGROUND

PC support technicians are often called on to upgrade Windows or install Windows on a new hard drive. Installations don't always go smoothly, so you need to know what to do when problems arise. When researching a problem, the Microsoft support site (support.microsoft.com) is an excellent resource. You also need to know about transferring user settings and data from one computer to another. These skills are covered in this lab.

ESTIMATED COMPLETION TIME: 45 Minutes

 Activity

Imagine the following scenario. As a PC support technician in a large organization, you work with a team of technicians supporting the users and equipment on a large enterprise network including personal computers, laptops, printers, and scanners. Corporations are sometimes slow to upgrade operating systems and equipment, and several users in the organization use Mac computers, so you find yourself researching many problems as they arise. Use the Internet to research the following problems:

A group of PCs are being converted from Windows 2000 to Windows XP, and your coworker, Larry, has already set up these unattended installations of Windows XP using the System Preparation (Sysprep) utility (see Lab 12.6). Larry is not available and your boss has asked you to make a change to a particular desktop computer being upgraded. He gives you the change he wants you to make but assumes you know how to implement it. Answer the following questions:

1. Can an answer file be edited after it has been created? If so, how?

2. What is the name of the answer file for the unattended Windows installation?

_____

3. You know that Windows will be installed in the C:\Windows folder. What is the path to the answer file?

_____

You are asked to enable disk quotas on a Windows XP computer that serves double duty as a user's PC and a file server running IIS. When you begin to make the change, you notice that the Properties window for the drive used as the file server (drive D) does not have the Quota tab. Answer the following questions:

1. What would cause the Quota tab to be missing?

_____

2. What command can you use from a command prompt window to convert the FAT32 drive D to a NTFS drive?

_____

3. Is there a risk any data will be lost during the conversion? What can you do to guard against this risk?

_____

_____

Linda has just received a new desktop computer on which Windows Vista has been newly installed. Her old Windows XP computer and her new computer are both connected to the network. After you finish moving her data and user preferences to the new computer, you intend to reformat the old computer's hard drive, reinstall Windows XP and applications, and assign the computer to another user. Answer the following questions:

1. What utility can be used to transfer Linda's documents and user preferences from her old Windows XP computer to this new Windows Vista computer?

_____

2. Can her applications also be transferred or do they have to be reinstalled?

_____

3. Your company policy is to keep the old computer in your storage room for one month before reformatting the hard drive. Why do you think this policy is needed?

_____

_____

Jennifer is a graphics artist who works a lot with Adobe Illustrator on her desktop PC, but occasionally works at a customer's location where she uses the same application on a Mac. She wants to use a FireWire external hard drive with her desktop PC at work that she can take with her to the off-site location and have the Mac read her large files on the external drive. Answer these questions:

1. If she uses the NTFS file system on the external drive, can files be read by the Mac using OS X?

_____

2. Can files be written to the drive by the Mac?

_____

16

3. Can the Mac execute software that has been installed by the PC on the external drive?

_____

REVIEW QUESTIONS

1. Besides the Microsoft support site, were there any Web sites that you found particularly useful in researching Windows problems? What were they?

_____

_____

2. What file system is required if you are using disk quotas in XP?

_____

3. What is the default file system for Mac OS X, and can it be read by a PC?

_____

4. Why is it a good idea to reformat and reinstall the operating system before reassigning a computer?

_____

_____

LAB 16.2 RECOVER DATA FROM A COMPUTER THAT WILL NOT BOOT

OBJECTIVES

The goal of this lab is to help you learn how to recover data from a computer that will not boot. After completing this lab, you will be able to:

◢ Copy data from a nonbooting computer

◢ Use data-recovery software

MATERIALS REQUIRED

This lab requires the following:

◢ Two Windows Vista/XP computers designated for this lab

◢ Internet access

LAB PREPARATION

Before the lab begins, the instructor or lab assistant needs to do the following:

◢ Verify that Internet access is available.

ACTIVITY BACKGROUND

If Windows is corrupted and the system will not boot, recovering your data might be your first priority. One way to get to the data is to remove your hard drive from your computer and install it as a second nonbooting hard drive in another working system. After you boot up the system, you should be able to use Windows Explorer to copy the data to another medium such as a USB flash drive. If the data is corrupted, you can try to use data-recovery software. In this lab, you will remove the hard drive from a computer and attempt to recover information.

ESTIMATED COMPLETION TIME: 45 Minutes

 Activity

First you need to create some data on the first computer that will need to be rescued:

1. Boot the first computer and log in as **Administrator**.

2. Create a new user called **User1** (see Lab 13.4).

3. Log on as **User1**.

4. You will now create some files to represent important information that might be saved in various locations on this computer. Use Notepad to create three text files named file1.txt, file2.txt, and file3.txt, and save one in each of the following locations:

   ◢ User1's Document's folder (My Document's in XP)

   ◢ The Public Documents folder (Shared Documents in XP)

   ◢ The root (probably C:\)

5. Open Internet Explorer and bookmark at least three locations on the Internet.

6. Log out and shut down this computer.

Now pretend that this computer is no longer able to boot. Since a backup or restore point has not been created recently, you have decided to remove the hard drive and attempt to recover some important files before attempting to determine why the computer won't boot.

1. Remove the main hard drive and install it as a second hard drive in another Windows machine (see Lab 8.3).

> **Notes** You can save time by purchasing an external IDE/SATA-to-USB converter kit for about $30 and use the kit to temporarily connect a hard drive to a USB port on a working computer.

2. Boot this computer and log on as **Administrator**.

3. Use Windows Explorer to locate the three text files on the hard drive you just installed.

4. List the path where each of these files can be found:

   ◢ file1.txt

   _____

   ◢ file2.txt

   _____

   ◢ file3.txt

   _____

5. Determine the name and location of the file containing your IE favorites:

   _____

16

6. Can you think of any other locations that could contain information a user might want to recover?

_____

_____

_____

_____

In some cases, the files might be corrupt or you may not be able to access the drive at all. In these cases, you can attempt to use file-recovery software.

1. Open **Computer** (**My Computer** in XP) and right-click the drive that contains the files you would like to recover.

2. Click **Properties** and select the **Tools** tab, as shown in Figure 16-1.

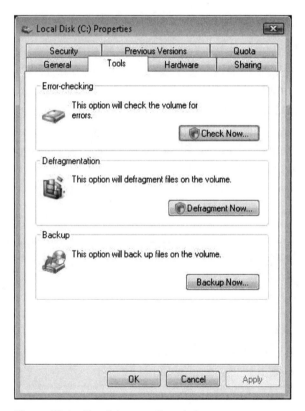

Figure 16-1 The disk properties window
Courtesy: Course Technology/Cengage Learning

3. Click **Check Now** . . . in the Error-checking section. If a UAC dialog box opens, click **Continue**.

4. Check **Scan for and attempt recovery of bad sectors** and click **Start**.

5. Did Error-checking find any errors?

6. If Error-checking did find errors but was unable to recover them, you can try using a utility designed for the brand of hard drive you're using (see Lab 8.4).

7. Shut down the system you're using and return the other hard drive to its computer.

8. Boot both computers back up and ensure that everything is working before shutting them both down.

REVIEW QUESTIONS

1. Why might you want to recover lost data before attempting to resolve a boot problem?

   _____

   _____

2. How could scheduled backups have saved you a lot of time?

   _____

   _____

3. What might have caused the first computer not to boot? List three possible causes:

   _____

   _____

   _____

4. If you suspect the first computer is not booting because it is infected with a virus, what should you ensure before installing its hard drive in your system?

   _____

   _____

LAB 16.3 FINDING A DRIVER FOR AN UNKNOWN DEVICE

16

OBJECTIVES

The goal of this lab is to help you learn how to find the drivers for an unknown device. After completing this lab, you will be able to:

◢ Use third-party software to determine brand and model information of an unknown device

◢ Use the Internet to find and download a driver

MATERIALS REQUIRED

This lab requires the following:

◢ A Windows Vista/XP computer designated for this lab

◢ Internet access

◢ A burnable CD and a marker for labeling

LAB PREPARATION

Before the lab begins, the instructor or lab assistant needs to do the following:

◢ Verify that Internet access is available.

ACTIVITY BACKGROUND

Someone has come to you for help with her computer. She is unable to connect to the Internet and is not sure why. After some investigation, you realize that she has just replaced the network adapter, but has lost the driver CD for the adapter and its documentation. Windows does not recognize the device type and there is no model information on the device itself. To find the correct drivers on the Internet, you need to know the exact brand and model of the device.

ESTIMATED COMPLETION TIME: 30 Minutes

 Activity

Use the following steps to retrieve this information. By following these steps, you'll learn to use the Ultimate Boot CD, which can be a valuable utility to add to your PC repair kit.

1. Go to the Ultimate Boot CD download page at *www.ultimatebootcd.com/download. html* and read the directions about creating the Ultimate Boot CD. The CD is created using an ISO image. An ISO image is a file that contains all the files that were burned to an original CD or DVD. This ISO image is then used to create copies of the original CD or DVD. The process has three steps: (1) Download the ISO image as a compressed, self-extracting .exe file; (2) decompress the compressed file to extract the ISO file having an .iso file extension; (3) use CD-burning software to burn the CD from the ISO image.

2. Follow the directions to download to your hard drive a self-extracting executable (.exe) file containing the ISO image. What is the most recent non-beta version of the software?

   _____

3. Read through the section called Frequently Asked Questions and answer the following questions:

   ◢ What utilities are included for partitioning hard drives?

   _____

   _____

   ◢ How could you load the Ultimate Boot Disk on a USB flash drive?

   _____

   _____

   ◢ Name several programs that you can use to burn an ISO image under Windows:

   _____

   _____

4. Double-click the downloaded file to execute it and extract the ISO image. (For Version 4.1.1, the new file will be named ubcd411.iso.)

5. You'll need software to burn the ISO image to the CD. (Do not just burn the .iso file to the CD. The software extracts the files inside the ISO image and burns these files to the CD to create a bootable CD holding many files.) The Ultimate Boot CD Web site suggests some free CD-burning software that supports ISO images. Download and execute one of these products to burn the ISO image to the CD. Using a permanent marker, label the CD "Ultimate Boot CD," and include the version number that you downloaded.

6. Boot the computer from the CD and find a tool that will retrieve the brand and model number of the NIC (network adapter). What software on the CD did you decide to use?

   _____

7. Use the program to find the make and model number of the NIC installed in your system and write down this information:

   _____

   _____

8. Using the acquired information, search the Internet for the correct driver. What is the name of this driver and where did you find it on the Internet?

   _____

   _____

9. Does this driver match the driver currently installed on your system?

   _____

10. When you're finished, remove the CD and reboot your system.

REVIEW QUESTIONS

1. Name some advantages to using a boot CD over just running diagnostic programs in Windows:

   _____

   _____

2. What are ISO images and can Windows use them without additional software?

   _____

   _____

3. Describe two other situations where the Ultimate Boot CD would be useful:

   _____

   _____

   _____

4. How much does the Ultimate Boot CD cost?

   _____

16

LAB 16.4 FIXING INTERNET EXPLORER

OBJECTIVES

The goal of this lab is to help you fix problems that can occur with Internet Explorer. After completing this lab, you will be able to:

◢ Repair Internet Explorer

◢ Disable IE add-ons

◢ Clean the browser history

◢ Reset Internet Explorer settings

◢ Repair a Corrupted Cache Index

MATERIALS REQUIRED

This lab requires the following:

◢ A Windows Vista/XP computer designated for this lab

◢ Internet access

LAB PREPARATION

Before the lab begins, the instructor or lab assistant needs to do the following:

◢ Verify that Internet access is available.

ACTIVITY BACKGROUND

When application problems occur, our first instinct is to restart the system. However, before you do the restart, make sure you understand the problem that is currently displayed on the screen so that you know how to reproduce it after the restart. If you are concerned that the source of the problem might be a failing OS or hard drive, save any important data to another media before you begin. The system might not boot after you restart and saving the data then will be more complicated. After you restart the system, log on as an administrator and verify whether the problem still exists.

This lab supposes that you have problems with Internet Explorer 8.0. The steps may vary slightly if you are using a different version of the program.

ESTIMATED COMPLETION TIME: 90 Minutes

 Activity

Begin troubleshooting by following these steps:

1. Log on as an administrator.

2. *Verify that you have Internet access.* Before you assume the problem is with Internet Explorer, verify that the local network is working and you have Internet access. Don't just assume you have Internet access if your home page opens. It might be a cache file stored locally on your computer. Try opening a new Web page such as *www.microsoft.com*. Can you access the Internet?

If the Web page won't open, try to use an application other than IE that requires Internet access. Open a command prompt window and try to ping the Web site by typing **ping www.microsoft.com**. If the ping command does not work, then treat the problem as a network problem. Network troubleshooting will be covered in Chapter 17.

3. *Verify that all Vista updates are current.* Windows Vista considers Internet Explorer and Windows Mail (formerly Outlook Express) program files to be part of the full set of Windows system files. Therefore, updates to Windows Vista include updates to these apps, and these updates might solve the problem. Does Windows have the latest updates?

4. *Using updated antivirus software, scan the system for viruses.* If your AV software finds malware, scan again to make sure the system is infection free. Is your system virus free?

5. *Use the Error Reporting feature of Vista to search for solutions.* Click **Start,** click **All Programs,** click **Maintenance,** and click **Problem Reports and Solutions** to open the Problem Reports and Solution window, as shown in Figure 16-2. Do you see any problems that pertain to Internet Explorer?

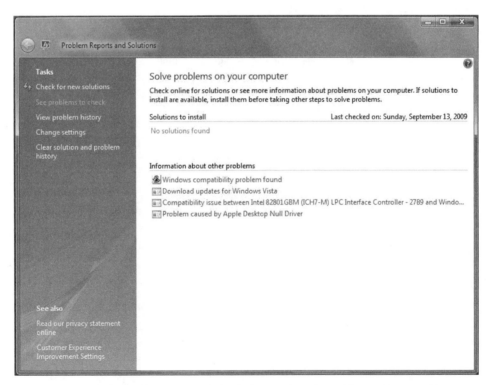

Figure 16-2 Use the Problem Reports and Solutions tool to view a history of past problems
Courtesy: Course Technology/Cengage Learning

6. *Verify that other applications are not causing the problem.* Other applications might be in conflict with IE. Close all other open applications and check Task Manager to make sure all are closed.

7. If the problem still persists, then follow the instructions given next where you'll learn to eliminate add-ons, IE history, IE settings, the cache index, and corrupted OS files as sources of the problem.

Most Internet Explorer problems are caused by add-ons. You can temporarily disable all add-ons so they can be eliminated as the source of a problem. Follow these steps:

1. Click **Start, All Programs, Accessories, System Tools,** and **Internet Explorer (No Add-ons).** (Alternately, you can enter **iexplore.exe –extoff** in the Start Search box.) Internet Explorer opens, showing the Information bar message in Figure 16-3.

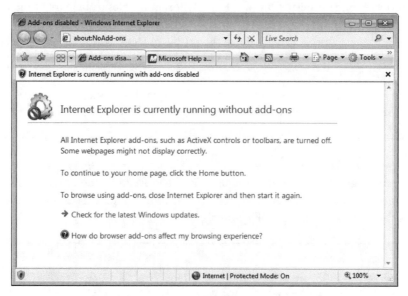

Figure 16-3   Internet Explorer is running with no add-ons
Courtesy: Course Technology/Cengage Learning

2. If the problem has disappeared, then you can assume the source of the problem is an add-on. Click the yellow information bar and click **Manage Add-ons.** What types of add-ons are listed?

_____

_____

3. To return Internet Explorer to run with add-ons, close the IE window and then open IE as usual.

The IE problem might be caused by a corrupted browser history, which might prevent access to particular Web sites. Also, deleting the browser history is a good best practice to protect your privacy when you are finished using Internet Explorer on a public computer. To clean the history, follow these steps:

1. In Internet Explorer, click **Tools** and **Internet Options.** The Internet Options dialog box appears, as shown on the left in Figure 16-4.

2. Under Browsing history, click **Delete.** The Delete Browsing History dialog box appears, as shown in the right of Figure 16-4. You can select particular items to delete or select all to clean out the entire browsing history. When using a public computer, definitely click all of the check boxes to completely delete history files. List the types of data that can be deleted:

_____

_____

_____

_____

3. When you're finished, click **OK** to close the Internet Options window.

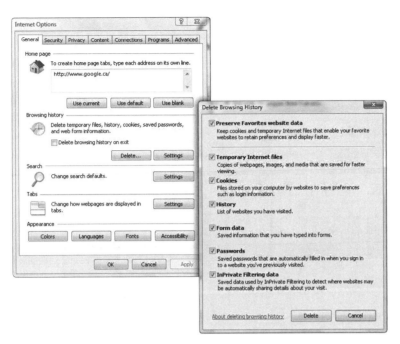

Figure 16-4 Internet Options dialog box
Courtesy: Course Technology/Cengage Learning

After you have eliminated add-ons and the browser history as the source of the problem, the next step is to eliminate IE settings. There are two approaches to doing that: resetting IE to default settings (all customized settings are lost and all add-ons are deleted), or the less drastic approach of manually changing one setting at a time, searching for the one that might be causing the problem.

If Internet Explorer does not use many customized settings, resetting IE is the quickest way to eliminate settings as the problem. Follow these steps to reset Internet Explorer:

1. If necessary, open Internet Explorer and click **Tools**. From the Tools menu, select **Internet Options**. The Internet Options box appears, as shown earlier in Figure 16-4. (Alternately, you can enter **inetcpl.cpl** in the Start Search box.)

2. Click the **Advanced** tab and then click **Reset** (see Figure 16-5). Note in the box on the right that Vista warns that all cookies, passwords, toolbars, and add-ons will be deleted. Therefore, use this method with caution and consider exporting cookies before you reset. Click **Reset** to complete the task. What personal settings are not affected by the default resetting Internet Explorer?

_____

_____

Sometimes IE problems are caused by a corrupted index file in the cache folder. To solve the problem, you need to delete the hidden file index.dat. The easiest way to delete the file is to delete the entire IE cache folder for the user account that has the problem. The next time the user logs on, the folder will be rebuilt. To delete the folder, follow these steps:

1. Log onto the system using a different account that has administrative privileges.

2. Use Windows explorer to delete C:\Users_username_\AppData\Local\Microsoft\ Windows\Temporary Internet Files. You will not be able to delete the folder if this user is logged on.

3. Log out and log back in as your original user and open Internet Explorer. Did Internet Explorer rebuild the folder?

16

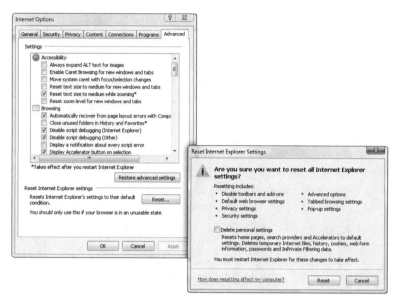

Figure 16-5   Reset Internet Explorer customized settings and add-ons
Courtesy: Course Technology/Cengage Learning

If you still have a problem with IE and you are certain the problem is not with the network or with Internet access, follow the steps listed below to repair Internet Explorer. However, know that each step is progressively more drastic than the next and you might find that, in using the method described, you change other Windows configuration settings and components. Therefore, after you try a step, check to see if your problem is fixed. Don't move on to the next step unless your problem is still present.

1. Use the Windows Vista System File Checker (sfc.exe) to check Windows system files and replace corrupted ones. Close all open applications and open a command prompt. Type **sfc /scannow**, as shown in Figure 16-6. Did your system find any corrupted files?

2. *Upgrade Internet Explorer*. At the time of this writing, Internet Explorer 8 was the most recent version. However, by the time you are reading this, a new version of Internet Explorer may be available. What is the most recent version of Internet Explorer available?

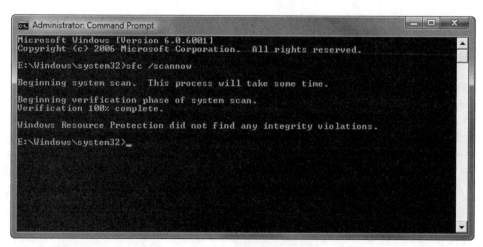

Figure 16-6   Use System File Checker to verify Vista system files
Courtesy: Course Technology/Cengage Learning

3. *Run Internet Explorer in Safe Mode with Networking.* Press **F8** at startup to display the Advanced Boot Options menu and select Safe Mode with Networking from the menu. If Internet Explorer works in Safe Mode, then you can assume the problem is not with IE but with the operating system, device drivers, or other applications that load at startup which are conflicting with IE. In this situation, approach the problem as a Windows problem rather than an Internet Explorer problem.

4. *Repair a corrupted Windows Vista installation.* If Internet Explorer refuses to work, even in Safe Mode with Networking, you can assume that the Vista installation is corrupted.

REVIEW QUESTIONS

1. What troubleshooting techniques from this lab might work to fix any Windows application?

   _____

   _____

   _____

   _____

2. Why can't you assume Internet Explorer is working if you can open your home page?

   _____

   _____

3. Why is deleting the browser history a good idea?

   _____

   _____

4. What should you do before restarting the system if an application is not working properly?

   _____

   _____

LAB 16.5 CRITICAL THINKING: SABOTAGE AND REPAIR WINDOWS XP

OBJECTIVES

The goal of this lab is to learn to troubleshoot Windows XP by repairing a sabotaged system. After completing this lab, you will be able to:

◢ Troubleshoot and repair a system that isn't working correctly

MATERIALS REQUIRED

This lab requires the following:

◢ Windows XP Professional installed on a PC designated for sabotage

◢ Windows XP Professional installation CD or installation files

◢ A workgroup of 2 to 4 students

LAB PREPARATION

Before the lab begins, the instructor or lab assistant needs to do the following:

◢ Verify that Windows starts with no errors.

◢ Provide each workgroup with access to the Windows XP installation files, if needed.

ACTIVITY BACKGROUND

You have learned about several tools and methods you can use to recover Windows XP when it fails. This lab gives you the opportunity to use these skills in a troubleshooting situation. Your group will sabotage another group's system while that group sabotages your system. Then your group will repair its own system.

ESTIMATED COMPLETION TIME: 45 Minutes

Activity

1. If your system's hard drive contains important data, back it up to another medium. Is there anything else you would like to back up before another group sabotages the system? Record the name of that item here, and then back it up:

   _____

2. Trade systems with another group, and sabotage the other group's system while they sabotage your system. Do one thing that will cause the system to fail to boot, display errors after the boot, or prevent a device or application from working. The following list offers some sabotage suggestions. Do something in the following list, or think of another option. Be inventive and have fun, but do *not* alter the hardware since this was already done in Lab 11.9.

   Notes Windows XP has several features designed to prevent sabotage, so you might find it a little challenging to actually prevent the system from booting by deleting or renaming system files.

   ◢ Find a system file in the root directory that's required to boot the computer, and rename it or move it to a different directory. (Don't delete the file.)

   ◢ Using the Registry Editor (Regedit.exe), delete several important keys or values in the Registry.

   ◢ Locate important system files in the \Windows directory, and rename them or move them to another directory.

   ◢ Put a corrupted program file in the folder that will cause the program to launch automatically at startup. Record the name of that program file and folder here:

   _____

   ◢ Use display settings that aren't readable, such as black text on a black background.

   ◢ Disable a critical device driver.

3. Reboot the system and verify that a problem exists.

4. How did you sabotage the other team's system?

_____

_____

_____

5. Return to your system and troubleshoot it.

6. Describe the problem as a user would describe it to you if you were working at a help desk:

_____

_____

7. What is your first guess as to the source of the problem?

_____

8. List the steps you took in the troubleshooting process:

_____

_____

_____

9. How did you finally solve the problem and return the system to good working order?

_____

_____

_____

REVIEW QUESTIONS

1. What would you do differently the next time you encountered the same symptoms?

_____

_____

2. What Windows utilities did you use or could you have used to solve the problem?

_____

_____

3. In a real-life situation, what might cause this problem to happen? List three possible causes:

_____

_____

_____

16

4. If you were the PC support technician responsible for this computer in an office environment, what could you do to prevent this problem from happening in the future or limit its impact on users if it did happen?

_____

_____

LAB 16.6 CRITICAL THINKING: SABOTAGE AND REPAIR WINDOWS VISTA

OBJECTIVES

The goal of this lab is to learn to troubleshoot Windows Vista by repairing a sabotaged system. After completing this lab, you will be able to:

▲ Troubleshoot and repair a system that isn't working correctly

MATERIALS REQUIRED

This lab requires the following:

▲ Windows Vista installed on a PC designated for sabotage

▲ Windows Vista Professional installation DVD or installation files

▲ A workgroup of 2 to 4 students

LAB PREPARATION

Before the lab begins, the instructor or lab assistant needs to do the following:

▲ Verify that Windows starts with no errors.

▲ Provide each workgroup with access to the Windows Vista installation files, if needed.

ACTIVITY BACKGROUND

You have learned about several tools and methods you can use to recover Windows Vista when it fails. This lab gives you the opportunity to use these skills in a troubleshooting situation. Your group sabotages another group's system while that group sabotages your system. Then your group repairs its own system.

ESTIMATED COMPLETION TIME: 45 Minutes

 Activity

1. If your system's hard drive contains important data, back it up to another medium. Is there anything else you would like to back up before another group sabotages the system? Record the name of that item here, and then back it up:

_____

2. Trade systems with another group, and sabotage the other group's system while it sabotages your system. Do one thing that will cause the system to fail to boot, display errors after the boot, or prevent a device or application from working. The following list offers

some sabotage suggestions. Do something in the following list, or think of another option. (Do *not* alter the hardware.)

◢ Find a system file in the root directory that's required to boot the computer, and rename it or move it to a different directory. (Don't delete the file.)

◢ Using the Registry Editor (Regedit.exe), delete several important keys or values in the Registry.

◢ Locate important system files in the \Windows directory, and rename them or move them to another directory.

◢ Put a corrupted program file in the folder that will cause the program to launch automatically at startup. Record the name of that program file and folder here:

_____

◢ Use display settings that aren't readable, such as black text on a black background.

◢ Disable a critical device driver.

3. Reboot the system and verify that a problem exists.

4. How did you sabotage the other team's system?

_____

_____

_____

5. Return to your system and troubleshoot it.

6. Describe the problem as a user would describe it to you if you were working at a help desk:

_____

_____

7. What is your first guess as to the source of the problem?

_____

8. List the steps you took in the troubleshooting process:

_____

_____

_____

9. How did you finally solve the problem and return the system to good working order?

_____

_____

_____

16

REVIEW QUESTIONS

1. What would you do differently the next time you encountered the same symptoms?

   _____

   _____

2. What Windows utilities did you use or could you have used to solve the problem?

   _____

   _____

3. In a real-life situation, what might cause this problem to happen? List three possible causes:

   _____

   _____

   _____

4. If you were the PC support technician responsible for this computer in an office environment, what could you do to prevent this problem from happening in the future or limit its impact on users if it did happen?

   _____

   _____

CHAPTER 17

Networking Essentials

Labs included in this chapter:

- **Lab 17.1:** Connect Two Computers
- **Lab 17.2:** Inspect Cables
- **Lab 17.3:** Compare Options for a Home LAN
- **Lab 17.4:** Understand the OSI Model
- **Lab 17.5:** Share Resources on a Network
- **Lab 17.6:** Simulate Modem Problems
- **Lab 17.7:** Critical Thinking: Use NetBEUI Instead of TCP/IP

LAB 17.1 CONNECT TWO COMPUTERS

OBJECTIVES

The goal of this lab is to install and configure an Ethernet network interface card (NIC). After completing this lab, you will be able to:

▲ Remove a NIC (and network protocols, if necessary)

▲ Install a NIC (and network protocols, if necessary)

▲ Perform a loopback test

MATERIALS REQUIRED

This lab requires the following:

▲ Windows Vista/XP operating system

▲ A NIC and drivers

▲ Windows installation CD/DVD or installation files

▲ A PC toolkit with antistatic ground strap

▲ A crossover cable or two patch cables and a small repeater (hub)

▲ A workgroup partner

LAB PREPARATION

Before the lab begins, the instructor or lab assistant needs to do the following:

▲ Verify that Windows starts with no errors.

▲ Provide each student with access to the Windows installation files, if needed.

ACTIVITY BACKGROUND

A computer connects to a wired network through a network interface card (NIC). In this lab, you install a NIC, configure necessary network settings, and verify that the NIC is functioning correctly. Working with a partner, you create a simple network of two PCs. By default, Windows Vista/XP has the protocols already installed for two computers to communicate.

ESTIMATED COMPLETION TIME: 30 Minutes

 Activity

Follow these steps to install and configure your NIC:

1. Physically install your NIC as you would other expansion cards. If you need a refresher on the process, review Lab 4.2.

2. Boot the system. The Found New Hardware Wizard detects the NIC and begins the driver installation process. In some cases, Windows doesn't allow using non-Microsoft drivers. If this option is available, however, click **Locate and install driver software (recommended)** (**Have Disk** in XP) and provide the manufacturer's drivers for the NIC. Reboot if prompted to do so. If you need help in installing the driver, see Lab 15.3.

Next, you give the computer an IP address, a computer name, and a workgroup name, as shown in the following chart. Write your name and your partner's name in the chart, and then follow these steps to assign an IP address to the computer:

> **Notes** If you want to force Windows to use manufacturers' drivers, run the setup program on the CD or floppy disk that comes bundled with the NIC *before* you physically install the NIC. After you boot with the new card installed, Windows then finds the already installed manufacturers' drivers and uses them.

To configure the IP address in Windows Vista:

1. Click **Start**, right-click **Network**, and click **Properties**. The Network and Sharing Center window appears.

2. Click **Manage network connections**, right-click **Local Area Connection**, and click **Properties** in the shortcut menu. If Windows needs your permission to continue, click **Continue**. The Local Area Connection Properties dialog box opens, as shown in Figure 17-1.

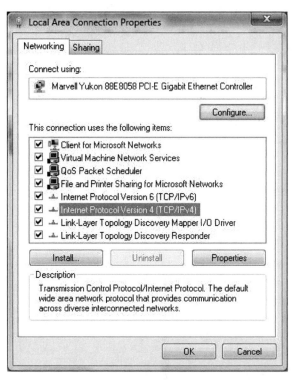

Figure 17-1   The Local Area Connection Properties dialog box
Courtesy: Course Technology/Cengage Learning

17

3. In the list of connection items, click **Internet Protocol Version 4 (TCP/IPv4)**, and then click the **Properties** button. The Internet Protocol (TCP/IP) Properties dialog box opens. Click **Use the following IP address** and enter your IP address (192.168.1.1 or 192.168.1.2) and subnet mask (255.255.255.0). Click **OK** and **Close** and then close all open windows.

Your names:		
IP address:	192.168.1.1	192.168.1.2
Computer name:	Lab1	Lab2
Workgroup name:	NIC LAB	NIC LAB

To configure the IP address in Windows XP:

1. Click **Start**, right-click **My Network Places**, and click **Properties** in the shortcut menu. The Network Connections window appears.

2. Right-click **Local Area Connection** and click **Properties** in the shortcut menu. The Local Area Connection Properties dialog box opens.

3. In the list of connection items, click **Internet Protocol (TCP/IP)**, and then click the **Properties** button. The Internet Protocol (TCP/IP) Properties dialog box opens. Click **Use the following IP address** and enter your IP address (192.168.1.1 or 192.168.1.2) and subnet mask (255.255.255.0). Click **OK** in the Internet Protocol (TCP/IP) Properties dialog box, and then close all open windows.

Next, you assign a computer name and workgroup name to your computer.

In Windows Vista, follow these steps:

1. Click **Start**, right-click **Computer**, and click **Properties**. The System window opens.

2. Click **Change settings** and click **Continue** if Windows needs your permission to continue. Click the **Change. . .** button and the Computer Name/Domain Changes dialog box opens (see Figure 17-2).

Figure 17-2 Computer Name/Domain Changes dialog box
Courtesy: Course Technology/Cengage Learning

3. Enter the computer name (**Lab1** in the example shown in Figure 17-2). Each computer name must be unique within a workgroup or domain.

4. Click **Workgroup** and enter the name of the workgroup (**NIC LAB** in this example).

5. Click **OK** and close any open windows. Restart your computer when prompted for changes to take effect.

In Windows XP, follow these steps:

1. Click **Start**, right-click **My Computer**, and click **Properties** in the shortcut menu. The System Properties dialog box opens.

2. In Windows XP, click the **Computer Name** tab, and then click the **Change** button. The Computer Name Changes dialog box opens.

3. Enter the computer name (**Lab1** or **Lab2**). Each computer name must be unique within a workgroup or domain.

4. Click **Workgroup** and enter the name of the workgroup (**NIC LAB** in this example).

5. Click **OK** and close any open windows. Restart your computer when prompted for changes to take effect.

Now follow these steps to test your NIC:

1. Open a command prompt window.

2. Type **ping 127.0.0.1** and press **Enter**. Ping is a TCP/IP utility used to test whether an address can be reached and is able to respond. Any 127.*x.x.x* address is a loopback address, which is essentially a stand-in for your computer's own address. When you use a loopback address in a ping test, the Ping utility sends packets to your local computer's NIC, thereby allowing you to verify that your computer's NIC has a functioning TCP/IP connection.

3. Examine the results of the loopback test and answer these questions:

   ◢ How many bytes were sent in each packet?

   _____

   ◢ How many packets were sent with one Ping command?

   _____

   ◢ How many responses were received from one Ping command?

   _____

   ◢ Were any packets lost?

   _____

Next, use the Ipconfig utility to verify your IP configuration. Do the following to check your NIC's configuration:

1. At the command prompt, type **ipconfig /all |more** and press **Enter**. An IP configuration report is displayed one screen at a time. If necessary, press **Enter** to see each new line. Answer the following questions:

   ◢ Is the configuration the same information you configured originally?

   _____

   ◢ What is the physical address (MAC address) of your NIC?

   _____

In Windows, another way to test a NIC is to use its assigned IP address in a ping test, as follows:

1. Use the ping command with the IP address you assigned to your computer. The results should be similar or identical to the loopback test results, except for the address listed in the Ping results. Was the ping successful?

   _____

17

2. Now, before attaching any network cables, ping your partner's IP address. Describe what happened to the request:

_____

_____

_____

Now you will create a small network and then test it:

1. Close the command prompt window, and shut down both computers.
2. Connect the two PCs with the crossover cable or attach both PCs to the hub with a patch cable.
3. Reboot the computers, and open a command prompt window.
4. Ping your partner's IP address. How do these results differ from your earlier attempt to ping your partner's IP address?

_____

_____

CHALLENGE ACTIVITY (ADDITIONAL 15 MINUTES)

For an additional challenge, try connecting two computers with different operating systems, one with Windows Vista and one with Windows XP.

REVIEW QUESTIONS

1. Where do you configure network adapters and protocols?

_____

2. What two text boxes are used to identify a computer on a workgroup?

_____

_____

3. Other than the IP address, what information is required for TCP/IP communication?

_____

4. What are two ways to use the Ping utility to test a local computer's NIC?

_____

_____

5. What conclusion should you draw from a loopback test that reports dropped packets or an unreachable host?

_____

_____

LAB 17.2 INSPECT CABLES

OBJECTIVES

The goal of this lab is to help you visually inspect a set of cables and use a multimeter to test them. After completing this lab, you will be able to:

- Identify two Cat 5e wiring systems
- Test cables with a multimeter
- Draw pin-outs for cable connectors
- Determine whether a cable is a patch cable (also known as a straight-through cable) or a crossover cable
- Visually inspect cables and connectors

MATERIALS REQUIRED

This lab requires the following:

- A variety of cables, including a patch cable and a crossover cable
- A multimeter
- Internet access

LAB PREPARATION

Before the lab begins, the instructor or lab assistant needs to do the following:

- Verify that Internet access is available.

ACTIVITY BACKGROUND

For a network connection to function properly, the cables must be connected correctly and be without any defects. In this lab, you physically inspect cables and the connector, and then test the cable for continuity and pin-outs using a multimeter.

ESTIMATED COMPLETION TIME: 45 Minutes

 Activity

1. Open your browser, and go to **http://www.lanshack.com/**. You can also search the Internet for information about a patch cable diagram, a crossover cable diagram, and a Cat 5e wiring diagram. List the two standards for unshielded twisted pair (UTP) wiring schemes. What Web site did you use?

2. For both wiring schemes, print a wiring diagram for a patch cable and a crossover cable.

Follow these steps to visually inspect cables:

1. Examine the length of the cable for obvious damage, such as a cut or abrasion in the outer sleeve with further damage to the twisted pairs inside. A completely cut strand is an obvious problem, but the conductor inside the cable might be broken even if the insulator is intact. Any visible copper is an indication you need a new cable.

2. Inspect the RJ-45 connectors. In particular, look for exposed twisted pairs between the clear plastic connector and the cable sleeve. This indicates that the cable was assembled

17

improperly or excessive force was used when pulling on the cable. The cable sleeve should be crimped inside the RJ-45 connector. Sometimes you can identify a nonconforming wiring scheme by noting the color of the insulation through the clear connector, but you should check the cable with a multimeter to verify its condition.

3. Next, verify that the retaining clip on the connector is present. When an assembled cable is pulled, this clip often snags on carpet or other cables and breaks off. This results in a connector that's likely to become loose or fall out of the jack. Worse still, this connection might be intermittent. Some cables have hooded guards to prevent the clip from snagging when pulled, but these guards can cause problems when seating the connector in the jack if the guard has slid too far toward the end of the cable.

4. Test your cables with a multimeter, and fill in Table 17-1.

		End A			End B		Questions About the Cable
	Pin #	Insulator color	Pin tied to pin at End B	Insulator color	Pin tied to pin at End A		Is the cable good or bad?
Cable 1	1						
	2						Wired with what scheme?
	3						
	4						
	5						Is the cable a crossover or patch cable?
	6						
	7						
	8						
	Pin #	Insulator color	Pin tied to pin at End B	Insulator color	Pin tied to pin at End A		Is the cable good or bad?
Cable 2	1						
	2						Wired with what scheme?
	3						
	4						
	5						Is the cable a crossover or patch cable?
	6						
	7						
	8						
	Pin #	Insulator color	Pin tied to pin at End B	Insulator color	Pin tied to pin at End A		Is the cable good or bad?
Cable 3	1						
	2						Wired with what scheme?
	3						
	4						
	5						Is the cable a crossover or patch cable?
	6						
	7						
	8						

Table 17-1 Pin connections for selected cables

REVIEW QUESTIONS

1. If you can see a copper conductor in a cable, what should you do with the cable?

   _____

2. What type of connector is used with Cat 5e cable?

   _____

3. Based on your research, which cabling scheme is more common, straight-through or crossover?

   _____

4. On a patch cable, pin 3 on one end connects to pin _____ on the opposite end of the cable.

5. On a crossover cable, pin 2 on one end connects to pin _____ on the other end of the cable.

LAB 17.3 COMPARE OPTIONS FOR A HOME LAN

OBJECTIVES

The goal of this lab is to help you research the costs and capabilities of wired and wireless home LANs. After completing this lab, you will be able to:

◢ Research wired and wireless Ethernet

◢ Research 802.11 standards

◢ Identify the strengths and weaknesses of each option

MATERIALS REQUIRED

This lab requires the following:

◢ Internet access

LAB PREPARATION

Before the lab begins, the instructor or lab assistant needs to do the following:

◢ Verify that Internet access is available.

ACTIVITY BACKGROUND

As the price of equipment and computers falls, installing a home LAN has become increasingly popular. In this lab, you research wired and wireless Ethernet and determine which option is best in certain situations.

ESTIMATED COMPLETION TIME: 30 Minutes

17

 Activity

Use your favorite search site to investigate and answer the following questions about wireless LAN standards:

1. List the 802.*x* standards for specifying wireless networks:

   _____

   _____

2. What industry name is associated with 802.11g?

_____

3. What is the simplest form of a wireless network? What devices are needed to create this type of network, and what mode does this type of network use?

_____

_____

_____

4. What device connects wireless users to a wired network?

_____

5. What standard speeds are supported by 802.11x?

_____

_____

_____

6. What kind of encryption is used with 802.11n?

_____

7. Give four examples of devices (besides PCs) that will probably eventually run on wireless LANs:

_____

_____

_____

_____

8. What does the acronym Wi-Fi stand for?

_____

9. What is the approximate maximum range for 802.11b, 802.11g, and 802.11n technologies?

_____

_____

_____

10. What inherent feature of 802.11b, seen as a major problem by businesses, might affect your decision to use Wi-Fi at home?

_____

_____

11. In the context of how they physically interface with a computer, what are the three basic types of wireless adapters?

   _____

   _____

   _____

12. What mode requires a wireless access point?

   _____

13. How many 802.11x devices can be used at one time with a single access point?

   _____

14. What radio band and speed does 802.11a use?

   _____

15. Which standard offers a faster transfer rate: 802.11a, 802.11b, 802.11g, or 802.11n? List their transfer rates:

   _____

   _____

   _____

   _____

16. List the components required to connect four PCs in ad hoc mode and include their prices. List the device and extra expense needed to connect the same four PCs to a cable modem:

   _____

   _____

   _____

   _____

   Use the Internet to research and answer these questions on an Ethernet home LAN:

   1. What is the maximum cable length for a 100BaseT Ethernet LAN?

   _____

   2. Must you use a hub to connect three PCs? Two PCs? Explain:

   _____

   _____

   _____

17

3. What type of cabling is typically used for 100BaseT?

_____

4. Are special tools required when working with Cat 5e cabling to create patch or crossover cables?

_____

5. What feature of Windows Vista or Windows XP allows more than one computer to share a connection to the Internet?

_____

6. What type of cable connector is used for fast Ethernet?

_____

7. What standard supports a speed of 100 Mbps using two sets of Cat 3 cable?

_____

8. What is the name for a cable that connects a computer to a hub?

_____

9. Suppose you have a LAN consisting of a 100BaseT hub, two computers with 10BaseT NICs, and a computer with a 10/100BaseT NIC. At what speed would this LAN operate? Why?

_____

_____

10. Given a budget of $200 to connect five computers, would you choose a wired system or wireless? Explain your choice:

_____

_____

_____

11. What is the name for a cable that connects a hub to a hub?

_____

12. In theory, if a file is transferred in 4.5 seconds on a fast Ethernet LAN, how long would the same file transfer take on a 10BaseT LAN?

_____

13. Give three examples of ways to physically interface a NIC to a computer:

_____

_____

_____

14. What device can you use to connect two or more PCs to a single cable modem?

_____

15. List the components, including cables, required to connect four PCs. Include the price of each component. List the changes and additional devices required to connect all four PCs to a cable modem and provide a hardware firewall:

_____

_____

_____

_____

_____

REVIEW QUESTIONS

1. Based on your research, does wireless or 100BaseT offer the best performance for the money?

_____

_____

2. Is wireless or 100BaseT easier to configure in a home? Why?

_____

_____

3. What factors dictate the transmission range of 802.11*x*?

_____

_____

_____

4. What determines the speed of a LAN that consists of both 10 Mbps and 100 Mbps devices?

_____

_____

5. Could you combine a wireless and wired LAN in the same home? Why would you?

_____

_____

_____

17

LAB 17.4 UNDERSTAND THE OSI MODEL

OBJECTIVES

The goal of this lab is to help you understand some of the concepts and principles of networking technology. After completing this lab, you will be able to:

⊿ Describe the OSI layers

⊿ Apply the OSI layer principles to networking

MATERIALS REQUIRED

This lab requires the following:

⊿ Windows Vista/XP operating system

⊿ A DHCP server

⊿ Internet access

LAB PREPARATION

Before the lab begins, the instructor or lab assistant needs to do the following:

⊿ Verify that Windows starts with no errors.

⊿ Verify that Internet access is available.

ACTIVITY BACKGROUND

Network architects use a variety of principles and concepts for communication when designing and implementing networks. Collectively, this architectural model is called the OSI (Open Systems Interconnection) model. The OSI model consists of seven layers. As a PC support technician, you do not need to understand network architecture. However, you might find it interesting to know a little about these fundamental concepts, which can help you better understand how the TCP/IP protocols work.

ESTIMATED COMPLETION TIME: 30 Minutes

 Activity

Using the Internet for your research, answer the following questions:

1. What are the seven OSI layers? Enter their names in the empty boxes on the left side of Table 17-2.

2. TCP/IP is a suite of protocols that follow the concepts of the OSI model. The four TCP/IP layers are shown on the right side of Table 17-2. E-mail is one example of a TCP/IP application that works in the Application layer. What are two more examples of applications that work in this layer?

_____

_____

OSI Layer		TCP/IP Protocol Stack Layer
7		Application Layer (E-mail using SMTP and IMAP protocols)
6		
5		
4		Transport Layer (TCP protocol)
3		Internet Layer (IP protocol)
2		Network Interface Layer (Network card using Ethernet protocol)
1		

Table 17-2 Describing the OSI model

3. The TCP protocol works at the Transport layer of TCP/IP. Briefly describe the function of the TCP protocol as used in Internet communications:

_____

_____

4. The IP protocol, working at the Internet layer, is responsible for locating the network and host for a data packet being transmitted by TCP. What is the name of each address on the Internet that identifies a unique network and host?

_____

5. Other than a network card (NIC), what is one more example of a device that works at the Network layer of the TCP/IP stack?

_____

6. Other than IP, what is another example of a protocol that works at the Internet layer of TCP/IP?

_____

7. At what TCP/IP layer does a MAC address function?

_____

8. At what TCP/IP layer does the TLS protocol work?

_____

9. At what TCP/IP layer does the HTTPS protocol work?

_____

17

10. Why do you think TCP/IP is often called a protocol stack rather than a protocol suite?

_____

_____

REVIEW QUESTIONS

1. List the four layers of the protocol stack used when an e-mail client requests e-mail over the Internet:

   _____

   _____

2. What protocol does a Web browser normally use?

   _____

3. At what TCP/IP layer does a Web browser work?

   _____

4. When more than one application is running on a server, how does IP know which service should be presented a data packet?

   _____

5. When configuring a network connection to the Internet, you might need to enter the IP address of the computer, the DNS server, the subnet mask, and the default gateway. Of these four items, which is used to determine whether a remote computer is on the same network or a remote network?

   _____

6. Of the four items in Question 5, which is used to relate a domain name to an IP address?

   _____

LAB 17.5 SHARE RESOURCES ON A NETWORK

OBJECTIVES

The goal of this lab is to understand the process of sharing resources and using these shared resources on a remote computer on the network. After completing this lab, you will be able to:

- Share resources
- Control access to shared resources
- Connect to shared resources

MATERIALS REQUIRED

This lab requires the following:

- Two or more Windows Vista/XP computers on a network
- Windows installation CD/DVD or installation files

⬤ Local printer attached to computer (optional)

⬤ A workgroup of 2 to 4 students

LAB PREPARATION

Before the lab begins, the instructor or lab assistant needs to do the following:

⬤ Verify that Windows starts with no errors.

⬤ Provide each student with access to the Windows installation files, if needed.

ACTIVITY BACKGROUND

The primary reason to network computers is to make it possible to share files, printers, Internet connections, and other resources. To share resources in a Windows workgroup, you need to make sure each computer has two Windows components installed: Client for Microsoft Networks and File and Print Sharing. Those components are installed by default in Windows XP/Vista. In this lab, you will share resources and connect to these shared resources on another computer.

ESTIMATED COMPLETION TIME: 30 Minutes

 Activity

To share resources on a Windows peer-to-peer network, computers must belong to the same workgroup. Do the following to verify that all computers in your group belong to the same Windows workgroup:

1. Determine the workgroup name (see Lab 17.1). What is the workgroup name for this computer?

   _____

2. Change the workgroup name, if necessary, so that all computers in your group belong to the same workgroup. If you're asked to reboot the PC, wait to do that until after you have installed the components in the next set of steps.

For each computer, follow these steps to see whether Client for Microsoft Networks and File and Print Sharing are installed, and if necessary, install those components:

In Windows Vista:

1. Click **Start**, right-click the **Network**, and click **Properties** in the shortcut menu. The Network and Sharing Center window opens.

2. Under Sharing and Discovery, ensure that File sharing and Printer sharing are both set to on and that Password protected sharing is set to off.

3. Close all open Windows and reboot.

In Windows XP:

1. Click **Start**, right-click **My Network Places**, and click **Properties** in the shortcut menu. The Network Connections dialog box opens. Click your active connection and click **Change settings of this connection**.

2. If Client for Microsoft Networks is not listed as an installed component, you need to install it. To do that, click **Install**. The Select Network Component Type dialog box opens.

3. Click **Client**, and then click **Add**. The Select Network Client dialog box opens.

4. In the Select Network Client dialog box, click **Microsoft**, and then click **Client for Microsoft Networks** in the right pane. Click **OK** to continue. You return to the Local Area Connection Properties dialog box.

17

5. If File and Print Sharing for Microsoft Networks isn't listed as an installed component in the Network Properties dialog box, you need to install it. To do that, click **Install**. The Select Network Component Type dialog box opens again.

6. Click **Service**, and then click **Add**. The Select Network Service dialog box opens.

7. Click **File and Printer Sharing for Microsoft Networks**, and then click **OK**. If necessary, insert the Windows installation CD or point to the location of the installation files, as instructed in the dialog box that opens. When the service is installed, you return to the Local Area Connection Properties dialog box.

8. Click **OK** to close the Local Area Connection Properties dialog box and save your new settings. The Systems Settings Change message box opens and notifies you that before the settings take effect, the system must be restarted. Click **Yes** to reboot.

Now that you have installed file and printer sharing, you're ready to set up folders or printers on your PC to be shared by others on the network. Follow these steps to share folders and control access to their contents:

In Windows Vista:

1. Open Windows Explorer, and create three folders at the root of drive C named **Reader**, **Contributor**, and **Co-owner**. Create a text file called **readtest.txt** in the Reader folder, a text file called **contest.txt** in the Contributor folder, and a text file called **cotest.txt** in the Co-owner folder. Type a short sentence in each text file, save your changes, and close the files.

2. In the right pane of Windows Explorer, right-click the **Reader** folder and click **Share. . .** in the shortcut menu. From the drop-down menu, select **Everyone** and click **Add**.

3. Make sure the permission level is set to **Reader** and click **Share**. If Windows opens a UAC, click **Next**. This setting gives users read-only access to all files in the Read folder.

4. Click **Done** to close the Window.

5. Repeat Steps 2 through 4 for the other two folders you just created, selecting the access types associated with their names.

In Windows XP:

1. Open Windows Explorer, and create three folders at the root of drive C named **Read**, **Full**, and **Change**. Create a text file called **readtest.txt** in the Read folder, a text file called **fulltest.txt** in the Full folder, and a text file called **changetest.txt** in the Change folder. Type a short sentence in each text file, save your changes, and close the files.

2. In the right pane of Windows Explorer, right-click the **Read** folder and click **Sharing and Security** in the shortcut menu. The Read Properties dialog box opens, with the Sharing tab selected.

3. Select **Share this folder** and click the **Permissions** button.

4. When the Permissions for Read window opens, select read in the allow column and click **OK**. This gives everyone permission to read the contents of this folder.

5. Repeat Steps 2 through 4 for the other two folders you just created, selecting the permissions associated with their names. For the Full folder, allow Full Control. For the Change folder, allow Change.

So far, you have verified that all computers sharing resources are in the same workgroup, have installed Windows components to share resources, and have set up the folders to be shared. Now you're ready to use shared resources over the network. Follow these steps to access shared folders:

1. Click **Start** and then click **Network**. The Network window displays a list of computers on the network.

2. Double-click your partner's computer icon to display the shared resources available on that computer.

3. Double-click the **Reader** (**Read** in XP) folder.

4. The contents of the Reader (Read in XP) folder are displayed in Windows Explorer.

5. Double-click **readtest.txt**. The file opens in Notepad. Attempt to save the file, and record your results:

_____

_____

6. Now attempt to save the file in the Documents folder (My Documents in XP) on your computer. Record the results on the following lines. Why did your results in Step 5 differ from your results here?

_____

_____

_____

7. Close Notepad, click the **Network** icon (**My Network Places** in XP) in the left pane of Windows Explorer, and double-click the icon for your partner's computer in the right pane.

8. Open the other two files and attempt to save them in the Documents folder (My Documents in XP) on your computer, and record the results on the following lines. Did you note any difference between the results of Step 5 and 6? If so, explain the difference:

_____

_____

9. Close Notepad, return to the desktop, and open your **Documents** (**My Documents** in XP) folder.

10. Rename the cotest.txt (fulltest.txt in XP) file with a new name of your choice. Attempt to copy, or drag and drop, this file into the Co-owner folder (Full folder in XP) on your partner's PC. Were you successful? Why or why not?

_____

_____

You have just seen how you can use Network to access shared folders on the network. You can make these shared folders appear to be a local drive on your PC, thereby making it more convenient to access these folders. When a shared folder on the network appears to be a local drive on your PC, the folder is called a network drive. Follow these steps to map a network drive and configure it to connect at logon:

1. Click **Start** and click **Network**. A list of computers on your network is listed in the right pane.

2. Double-click the icon for your partner's computer. A list of shared resources is displayed.

3. Right-click the **Co-owner** folder and click **Map Network Drive. . .** in the shortcut menu. In XP, click the **Full** folder and click **Map Network Drive** off the Tools menu. The Map Network Drive dialog box opens.

4. In the Drive drop-down list box, click the drive letter you want to assign to this folder.

5. Click the **Reconnect at logon** check box, and then click **Finish**.

6. The drive is connected, and a window opens displaying the contents of the Full folder. The title bar includes the drive letter you assigned.

17

7. Check Windows Explorer and verify that the drive letter is now listed under Computer (My Computer in XP).

8. Log off and then log back on to test that the drive reconnects. What did you have to do to reconnect when you logged back on?

_____

_____

REVIEW QUESTIONS

1. What is the main advantage of connecting computers into networks?

_____

_____

2. What term refers to the process of allowing others to use resources on your computer?

_____

3. What two Windows network components must be installed before you can grant others access to resources on your computer and use their resources?

_____

4. How can you provide full access to some of your files while giving read-only access to other files shared on the network?

_____

_____

5. Explain how to allow some people to make changes to files in shared folders while allowing others to just view and read the contents of the same folder:

_____

_____

_____

_____

LAB 17.6 SIMULATE MODEM PROBLEMS

OBJECTIVES

The goal of this lab is to help you simulate, diagnose, and remedy common modem problems. After completing this lab, you will be able to:

◢ Diagnose problems with a modem

◢ Remedy problems with a modem

MATERIALS REQUIRED

This lab requires the following:

◢ Windows XP operating system

◢ A modem installed in a PC and connected to a phone line

◢ A PC toolkit with antistatic ground strap

◢ Modem installation drivers

◢ Windows installation CD/DVD or installation files

◢ A standard phone

◢ A lab partner with whom you can swap PCs

LAB PREPARATION

Before the lab begins, the instructor or lab assistant needs to do the following:

◢ Verify that Windows starts with no errors.

◢ Provide each student with access to the Windows installation files, if needed.

ACTIVITY BACKGROUND

Although high-speed connections are quickly growing in popularity, dial-up are still common in many rural areas where high-speed Internet is not available. Dial-up connections are notoriously unreliable. One of the challenges of troubleshooting these connections is determining whether a dial-up failure is related to a problem with the modem or the phone line. In this lab, you diagnose and remedy common modem problems. Mastering these skills makes it easier for you to determine when the modem is the source of trouble in a dial-up connection.

ESTIMATED COMPLETION TIME: 90 Minutes

 Activity

1. To verify that your modem is working, start HyperTerminal, dial any reliable phone number, and listen for the sound of the modem dialing and attempting to connect. (The actual connection isn't necessary at this point.) Disconnect the call and close HyperTerminal.

2. Sabotage your modem by introducing one of these problems:

    ◢ If your modem has jumpers or DIP switches, record the original settings on the following lines, and then change the settings:

    _____

    _____

    ◢ In BIOS or Device Manager, disable the modem's COM port.

    ◢ Loosen the modem card in the expansion slot so that it doesn't make good contact.

    ◢ Unplug the phone cord from the wall.

    ◢ Change the port to which the phone line connects on the back of the modem.

    ◢ Uninstall the modem in Device Manager.

    ◢ Change or disable the IRQ for the modem.

    ◢ Using Device Manager, disable the modem in the current hardware configuration.

17

3. Swap PCs with your partner, and then troubleshoot and repair your partner's PC.

4. Answer these questions:

◢ What is the initial symptom of a problem as a user would describe it?

_____

_____

◢ How did you discover the source of the problem?

_____

_____

_____

_____

◢ What did you do to solve the problem?

_____

_____

_____

_____

5. Introduce another problem from the list in Step 2, and swap again. Continue this process until you have introduced and remedied all the problems listed in Step 2.

6. Suppose a user says, "I can't dial out using my modem." List the first three things you would check in the order you would check them:

_____

_____

_____

REVIEW QUESTIONS

1. What was the easiest problem to diagnose and why?

_____

_____

2. Which problems aren't apparent in Device Manager but would result in no dial tone when dialing?

_____

_____

3. Did all the problems listed in Step 2 actually prevent the modem from working? Which (if any) did not?

_____

_____

4. What was the simplest way to determine whether there was definitely a dial tone?

_____

_____

5. Why are modems much less common in computers today?

_____

_____

LAB 17.7 CRITICAL THINKING: USE NETBEUI INSTEAD OF TCP/IP

OBJECTIVES

Most networks use the TCP/IP network protocol suite. The goal of this lab is to demonstrate how to replace TCP/IP with NetBEUI. After completing this lab, you will be able to:

◢ Install NetBEUI

◢ Remove TCP/IP

◢ Observe the results of using NetBEUI

MATERIALS REQUIRED

This lab requires the following:

◢ Windows XP operating system

◢ A NIC configured to use only TCP/IP

◢ IP address information or a DHCP server on the network

◢ Internet access

◢ Windows XP Professional installation CD or installation files

◢ A network workgroup consisting of two computers

◢ A workgroup of 2 to 4 students

LAB PREPARATION

Before the lab begins, the instructor or lab assistant needs to do the following:

◢ Verify that Windows starts with no errors.

◢ Provide each student with access to the Windows installation files, if needed.

◢ Verify that Internet access is available.

17

ACTIVITY BACKGROUND

TCP/IP is probably the network protocol you're most familiar with, but it's not the only network protocol, nor is it the best for all situations. IBM originally developed NetBIOS Enhanced User Interface (NetBEUI) to make it possible to use NetBIOS names as official network addresses. NetBEUI is faster than TCP/IP and much easier to configure. Its main disadvantage is that it's nonroutable (meaning it can communicate only with computers on its network). In this lab, you configure one computer in your workgroup to use NetBEUI, and then observe the effect of this change on both computers in the workgroup. Then you use NetBEUI as the only network protocol in your workgroup.

ESTIMATED COMPLETION TIME: 30 Minutes

 Activity

First, you need to determine what the network looks like before you install NetBEUI and remove TCP/IP. Follow these steps:

1. On one of the two computers in the workgroup, open My Network Places via Windows Explorer. Click **View workgroup computers**. A list of computers on your network is displayed. Take and print a screen shot of this list.

> **Notes** To take a screen shot, press **Alt+Print Screen**, which copies the window into the Clipboard. Open Windows Paint, and click **Edit, Paste** from the menu. To print the screen shot, click **File, Print** from the menu. Close Windows Paint without saving your work.

2. Repeat Step 1 for the other computer on your network.

Now follow these steps to install NetBEUI as the network protocol on one of the computers in your workgroup:

1. Insert the Windows XP installation CD and locate the Valueadd\MSFT\Net\NetBEUI folder.

2. Copy the Nbf.sys file to the C:\System32\Drivers folder and copy the Netnbf.inf file to the C:\Windows\Inf folder. (*Note:* The Inf folder is hidden by default.)

3. In Windows Explorer, right-click **My Network Places** and click **Properties** in the short-cut menu. The Network Connections window opens.

4. Right-click the **Local Area Connection** icon and click **Properties** in the shortcut menu. The Local Area Connection Properties dialog box opens.

5. Click **Install**. The Select Network Component Type dialog box opens.

6. Click **Protocol**, and then click **Add**. The Select Network Protocol dialog box opens.

7. Click **NetBEUI Protocol**, and then click **OK**. The Select Network Protocol and Select Network Component Type dialog boxes close.

Your next job is to uninstall TCP/IP on the computer where you installed NetBEUI. You begin by recording the TCP/IP configuration information for that computer, and then uninstall TCP/IP. (You need this configuration information when you reinstall TCP/IP at the end of this lab.) Follow these steps:

1. Right-click **My Network Places** and click **Properties** in the shortcut menu. The Network Connections or Network and Dial-Up Connections window opens.

2. Right-click the **Local Area Connection** icon and click **Properties** in the shortcut menu. The Local Area Connection Properties dialog box opens.

3. Click **Internet Protocol (TCP/IP)** in the list of components, and then click **Properties**. The TCP/IP Properties dialog box opens.

4. Record the configuration information available in this window:

_____

_____

_____

_____

5. Click **Cancel** to close the TCP/IP Properties dialog box.

6. In the Local Area Connection Properties dialog box, click **Internet Protocol (TCP/IP)**, and then click **Uninstall**. A message appears informing you that you're about to remove the protocol from all connections.

7. Click **Yes** to continue. Internet Protocol (TCP/IP) is removed from the Local Area Connection Properties dialog box.

8. The Local Network dialog box opens and informs you that you must restart the computer before the changes can take effect.

9. Click **Yes** to restart the computer.

Follow these steps to observe the effects of using NetBEUI:

1. Go to the computer that you didn't alter (the computer still running TCP/IP).

2. If it's not already open, open the **My Network Places** window. Click **View workgroup computers** and answer these questions:

   ◢ What computers are displayed?

   _____

   _____

   _____

   _____

   ◢ Compare the current screen to the screen shot you created earlier. What computers are missing?

   _____

   _____

   ◢ Why are they missing?

   _____

   _____

3. Go to the computer where you installed NetBEUI.

17

4. Open My Network Places, and then click **View workgroup computers** (Windows XP). Answer the following questions:

◢ What computers are displayed?

_____

_____

_____

_____

◢ Compare the current screen to the screen shot you created earlier. What computers are missing?

_____

_____

◢ Why are they missing?

_____

_____

5. Press **F5** to refresh the list of computers on the network. Did any new ones appear? Why or why not?

_____

_____

_____

_____

6. On the computer where you installed NetBEUI, attempt to connect to the Internet, and then answer these questions:

◢ What message did you receive?

_____

_____

_____

_____

◢ Why do you think you were unable to connect to the Internet?

_____

_____

Next, you use some network utilities to test your network connections. You start by running a loopback ping test, as you did in Lab 17.1. Follow these steps:

1. On the computer running TCP/IP (the one you didn't change), open a command prompt window, type **ping 127.0.0.1**, and press **Enter**. Record the results of the loopback test:

   _____

   _____

   _____

2. Next, you use the Ipconfig utility to test network configuration and connectivity. Type **ipconfig /all** and press **Enter**. Record the results of the command:

   _____

   _____

   _____

3. On the computer where you installed NetBEUI, open a command prompt window, and then repeat Steps 1 and 2. Record the results. Why did you get these results?

   _____

   _____

   _____

   _____

Follow these steps to reinstall TCP/IP:

1. On the computer where you installed NetBEUI, right-click **My Network Places** and click **Properties** in the shortcut menu. The Network Connections or Network and Dial-up Connections window opens.

2. Right-click the **Local Area Connection** icon and click **Properties** in the shortcut menu. The Local Area Connection Properties dialog box opens.

3. Click **Install**. The Select Network Component Type dialog box opens.

4. Click **Protocol**, and then click **Add**. The Select Network Protocol dialog box opens.

5. Click **TCP/IP Protocol**, and then click **OK**. The Select Network Protocol and Select Network Component Type dialog boxes close.

6. The Local Network dialog box opens and informs you that you must restart the computer before the changes can take effect. Click **Yes** to restart the computer.

You've finished reinstalling TCP/IP. Now you need to reconfigure the necessary TCP/IP settings. Follow these steps:

1. Right-click **My Network Places** and click **Properties** in the shortcut menu. The Network Connections or Network and Dial-Up Connections window opens.

2. Right-click the **Local Area Connection** icon and click **Properties** in the shortcut menu. The Local Area Connection Properties dialog box opens.

3. Click **Internet Protocol (TCP/IP)**, and then click **Properties**. The Internet Protocol (TCP/IP) Properties dialog box opens.

17

4. Reconfigure the settings to match the ones you recorded earlier in this lab.

5. Click **OK** twice to close the Internet Protocol (TCP/IP) Properties and Local Area Connection Properties dialog boxes and save your settings.

6. Test your settings by connecting to another computer or the Internet.

CHALLENGE ACTIVITY (ADDITIONAL 20 MINUTES)

1. Install NetBEUI and remove TCP/IP on one more computer in your workgroup so that NetBEUI is the only network protocol installed on two computers.

2. Using NetBEUI, transfer files from one computer to the other.

3. Install TCP/IP and configure it, and then remove NetBEUI as an installed networking protocol.

REVIEW QUESTIONS

1. Is it possible to have more than one network protocol installed on the same network? Explain how you arrived at your answer:

_____

_____

_____

2. If you had to access the Internet from your computer, which protocol would you use?

_____

3. What features of NetBEUI make it appealing for a small network that doesn't need Internet access?

_____

_____

4. Of the two network protocols covered in this lab, which is better suited for trouble-shooting problems? Why?

_____

_____

5. What type of computer name is used on a NetBEUI network?

_____

CHAPTER 18

Networking Practices

Labs included in this chapter:

- **Lab 18.1:** Install Software to Delete Cookies
- **Lab 18.2:** Use FTP to Download a Browser
- **Lab 18.3:** Configure and Use Remote Access Service
- **Lab 18.4:** Use Remote Desktop
- **Lab 18.5:** Share an Internet Connection
- **Lab 18.6:** Set Up a Wireless Router
- **Lab 18.7:** Troubleshoot with TCP/IP Utilities
- **Lab 18.8:** Solve Network Connectivity Problems

LAB 18.1 INSTALL SOFTWARE TO DELETE COOKIES

OBJECTIVES

The goal of this lab is to help you install software that deletes cookies each time you boot your computer. After completing this lab, you will be able to:

▲ Locate, download, and install the software

▲ Delete cookies using the software you downloaded

MATERIALS REQUIRED

This lab requires the following:

▲ Internet access

▲ Windows Vista/XP operating system

LAB PREPARATION

Before the lab begins, the instructor or lab assistant needs to do the following:

▲ Verify that Windows starts with no errors.

▲ Verify that Internet access is available.

ACTIVITY BACKGROUND

When you visit certain Web sites, cookies are placed on your system to collect information about you, including what Web sites you visit. Although cookies can be useful by storing your preferences for when you revisit sites, they can also be a security risk, passing on information you don't want to make accessible to others. For example, this information could be passed on to companies that then sell it to a mailing list or use it for advertising purposes. Several utilities on the market can clean cookies from your computer. One is Webroot's Window Washer, which is available for trial download. In this lab, you install Window Washer and use it to delete cookies.

ESTIMATED COMPLETION TIME: 45 Minutes

 Activity

Follow these steps to download Webroot's Window Washer software. As you know, Web sites change often, so your steps might differ slightly from the following:

1. Open your browser, and go to **www.webroot.com**.
2. Find the Free Downloads section.
3. Scroll down and click the link to download a free trial of Window Washer.
4. The File Download – Security Warning dialog box opens, indicating that you have chosen to download the installation file for Window Washer. Click the **Run** button.

5. A dialog box opens indicating the progress of the installation. Depending on your connection speed, it could take a few minutes. While you're waiting, look on the Webroot site for information about Window Washer and record a short description of what it does:

_____

_____

_____

_____

6. When the download is finished, an Internet Explorer - Security Warning dialog box opens. Click **Run** to verify that you want to install and run the trial version of Window Washer.

7. If a UAC dialog box opens, click **Continue**.

8. The Window Washer installation program launches. In the first window, click **I Agree** to accept the license agreement.

9. Select the **Typical Installation** option if necessary, and then click **Next**. The Installation Status window shows the progress of the installation. When a completion message is displayed, click **Next**.

10. In the Custom Wash Item Detection window, leave the defaults selected, and then click **Next**. Leave the e-mail check box and text box blank, and then click **Next**.

11. In the Successful Installation window, click to clear **Run Window Washer**, and then click **Finished**.

Follow these steps to use Window Washer to delete cookies:

1. Open Internet Explorer, if necessary, and browse the Web for a couple of minutes, visiting a variety of sites, such as news sites and commercial sites. Click a few links and ads on those sites. Close Internet Explorer.

2. Open Windows Explorer, and then open the **Cookies** folder, which is usually located under C:\Users*username*\AppData\Roaming\Microsoft\Windows\Cookies (C:\Documents and Settings*username* in Windows XP). If the Cookies folder is hidden, open the Folder Options dialog box, select the **View** tab, and clear the **Hide protected operating system files** check box. Cookies are stored as text files.

   ◢ How many cookies are listed?

   _____

   ◢ What sites appear to have stored cookies on your computer?

   _____

   _____

   _____

3. Click **Start**, point to **All Programs**, and then click **Webroot**. If the Webroot folder does not open automatically, click **Window Washer**.

4. On the right side of the window, notice that no data is listed under Wash Statistics for the Last wash item. Click the **Wash My Computer Now** button.

5. If a Ready to Wash window opens, click **Start**.

6. The Wash screen opens. When the Washing completed screen appears, click **Finished**.

18

7. In Windows Explorer, open the **Cookies** folder again to verify that the cookies are gone.

8. When you're finished, close any open windows.

If you still see cookies in the Cookies folder after you run Window Washer, you might need to verify that you selected all the options indicating which files you want to delete before running Window Washer again.

REVIEW QUESTIONS

1. What other items can Window Washer clean besides cookies?

   _____

   _____

2. List some reasons you might not want cookies on your system:

   _____

   _____

   _____

3. What information did the Webroot site provide about how Window Washer works?

   _____

   _____

4. Can you specify your own wash items—that is, items that aren't already listed in Window Washer? Explain:

   _____

   _____

5. How might cookies be useful?

   _____

   _____

LAB 18.2 USE FTP TO DOWNLOAD A BROWSER

OBJECTIVES

The goal of this lab is to help you use FTP from the command prompt to download a browser. After completing this lab, you will be able to:

◢ Use common FTP commands from a command prompt

◢ Download a browser via FTP

MATERIALS REQUIRED

This lab requires the following:

◢ Windows Vista/XP operating system

◢ Internet acccss

LAB PREPARATION

Before the lab begins, the instructor or lab assistant needs to do the following:

◢ Verify that Windows starts with no errors.

◢ Verify that Internet access is available.

ACTIVITY BACKGROUND

File Transfer Protocol (FTP) is a quick and easy way to transfer files over the Internet without converting them to ASCII text first. You might use FTP when transmitting files too large to be sent as e-mail attachments, for example. For this lab, imagine that your Web browser has been rendered inoperable by a virus or because you accidentally deleted some vital files, but you can still connect to the Internet. How can you get your browser back? If you're using a network, it might be possible for you to go to another computer on the network, use that computer's browser to download a new browser, and then transfer the downloaded browser file to your computer. Another option is to reinstall Windows on your computer, a process that installs Internet Explorer. However, if these options aren't available or practical, you can use FTP to download a browser. If you have no user-friendly GUI FTP software installed on your computer, you can use FTP from the command prompt. In this lab, you use FTP commands from the command prompt to locate and download the latest version of Netscape.

ESTIMATED COMPLETION TIME: 45 Minutes

 Activity

Follow these steps to connect to the Netscape FTP site from a command prompt and download the latest version of the Netscape browser:

1. When you download the browser, you should store the file in a location on your hard drive that's easy to find. In Windows Explorer, create a folder on your C drive called **Downloads**.

2. Leave Windows Explorer open, and open a command prompt window.

3. When the command prompt window opens, the C:\Users*username* directory (C:\Documents and Settings*username* in Windows XP) is probably the active directory. When you use FTP, the files you download are stored in whatever directory was active when you began the session. To change to the Downloads directory, type **cd c:\downloads** and press **Enter**.

4. When the Downloads directory is active, type **ftp** and press **Enter**. How did the command prompt change?

_____

5. To enter the Netscape FTP site, type **open ftp.netscape.com** and press **Enter**.

6. A message is displayed, stating that you're connected to the Netscape site and the server is ready, followed by a user prompt. Many sites, including this one, allow limited access to the site via an anonymous logon. Type **anonymous** at the user prompt and press **Enter**.

7. A message asks you to specify your password. Type **anonymous** and press **Enter**. What message do you see?

_____

18

8. You now have access to certain files on the Netscape FTP site. Browse to the location of the latest version of the Netscape browser. Note which options such as operating systems, versions, and languages are available. Use the **dir** command to list the contents of various directories and the **cd** command to change directories as necessary. If necessary, unblock the Windows Firewall and respond to the UAC to continue. At the time of this writing, Netscape 9.0 was located in the path *ftp.netscape.com/pub/netscape9/ en-US/9.0/windows/win32/netscape-navigator-9.0.exe*. The names and locations of downloadable files can change as versions and site structure change, so you might find the file stored in a different directory. The exact filename might be different as well, depending on what the most current browser version is. If the location or name of the latest version of the browser setup file differs from the one mentioned earlier in this step, record the correct information here:

_____

9. After you have located the file, type **bin** and press **Enter**. This command sets the download mode to specify that you want the file downloaded as a binary (not ASCII) file.

10. To download the file, type **get netscape-navigator-9.0.exe** (substituting the correct filename if you noted a different one in Step 8). Remember that FTP commands are case sensitive.

11. Press **Enter**. What messages are displayed?

_____

_____

_____

12. Return to Windows Explorer (in XP click **View, Refresh** from the menu), open the **Downloads** folder, and verify that the file was downloaded successfully.

13. To verify that the browser setup program you downloaded works, double-click the file you downloaded. The setup program opens.

14. At this point, you can follow the instructions to install the browser or simply close the setup program.

15. Return to the command prompt window. Type **bye** and press **Enter** to close the FTP session and close any open windows.

REVIEW QUESTIONS

1. List all the FTP commands you used in this lab, with a short description of each:

_____

_____

_____

_____

_____

_____

2. In what mode did you download the browser setup file? Why is using this mode necessary?

_____

_____

_____

_____

3. For what other operating systems and languages is Netscape available for download?

_____

_____

4. If you were using FTP to upload a text file created in Notepad, which mode (ASCII or binary) should you choose to upload it and why?

_____

_____

5. You're downloading FileABC.txt from the FTP site of CompanyXYZ.com. The file is located in the /pub/documentation/ folder of that site and uses *guest* as both the username and password. Your FTP client defaults to binary mode for download. List in order all the commands you would use to open the FTP connection, download the file, and close the connection:

_____

_____

_____

_____

_____

LAB 18.3 CONFIGURE AND USE REMOTE ACCESS SERVICE

OBJECTIVES

The goal of this lab is to give you practice using Remote Access Service to allow dial-up access to a computer. After completing this lab, you will be able to:

- Set up Remote Access Service
- Configure Remote Access Service
- Connect to a network through a dial-up connection

MATERIALS REQUIRED

This lab requires the following:

- Two Windows XP computers
- A modem and telephone line for each computer
- A workgroup of 2 to 4 students

18

LAB PREPARATION

Before the lab begins, the instructor or lab assistant needs to do the following:

◢ Verify that Windows starts with no errors.

◢ Provide students with the phone numbers of both machines.

ACTIVITY BACKGROUND

You can set up your Windows computer to receive dial-up connections from other computers. You might want to do this if you travel and want to be able to transfer files to and from your home computer while away. You can allow incoming calls by default by using Remote Access Service (RAS). In this lab, you connect two Windows XP machines through a dial-up connection.

ESTIMATED COMPLETION TIME: 45 Minutes

 Activity

Follow these steps to configure one machine to accept a remote connection:

1. Click **Start**, right-click **My Network Places**, and click **Properties**. The Network Connections window opens.

2. Click **Create a new connection**, and then click **Next**.

3. Click **Set up an advanced connection**, and then click **Next**.

4. Click **Accept incoming connections**, and then click **Next** again.

5. Click to select the modem installed in your machine, and then click **Next**.

6. Click **Do not allow virtual private connections**, and then click **Next**.

7. Select the user that you want to use this connection and click **Add**. Enter the information and record it here:

_____

8. Click **Next** to advance to the next screen.

9. Click **Next** in the Networking Software screen to accept the default settings.

10. Finally, click **Finish**.

Follow these steps to connect remotely to your first machine:

1. Click **Start**, right-click **My Network Places**, and click **Properties**. The Network Connections window opens.

2. Click **Create a new connection**, and then click **Next**.

3. Click **Connect to the network at my workplace**, and then click **Next**.

4. Click **Dial-up connection**, and then click **Next**.

5. Enter a name for this connection, and then click **Next**.

6. Next, enter the phone number of the machine accepting the remote connection.

7. If prompted, click **Anyone's use** to specify how this connection can be used, and then click **Next**.

8. Click **Finish** to complete the wizard. A window for the new connection should open automatically.

9. Enter the name and password of the new user account you created while configuring the first machine.

10. Finally, click **Dial** to connect to the remote machine. How long did it take to connect?

_____

11. When you're finished, disconnect from the remote machine and close any open windows.

CRITICAL THINKING (ADDITIONAL 15 MINUTES)

Change the workgroup identity on one of the computers so that the two computers no longer belong to the same workgroup. Attempt to connect and transfer files. At what point did the process fail?

_____

_____

REVIEW QUESTIONS

1. Which Windows XP component handles dial-up connections?

_____

2. Why doesn't remote access work if both computers aren't on the same workgroup?

_____

3. Why might you need to have more than one object in the Dial-up section of the Network Connections window?

_____

_____

4. How does each computer disconnect from a Dial-Up Server session?

_____

_____

5. Can you think of any disadvantage of connecting through RAS?

_____

_____

LAB 18.4 USE REMOTE DESKTOP

18

OBJECTIVES

The goal of this lab is to learn how to log on to another computer remotely by using Windows Remote Desktop. After completing this lab, you will be able to:

◢ Configure Remote Desktop

◢ Use Remote Desktop to log on to another computer remotely

MATERIALS REQUIRED

This lab requires the following:

◢ Windows Vista/XP Professional operating system

◢ A network workgroup consisting of two computers

◢ A workgroup of 2 to 4 students

LAB PREPARATION

Before the lab begins, the instructor or lab assistant needs to do the following:

◢ Verify that Windows starts with no errors.

◢ Verify that a network connection is available.

ACTIVITY BACKGROUND

Windows allows users to connect remotely from other Windows machines. With a remote connection, you can control a computer from another location, such as work or home. This feature might be useful if you need to access files or programs from another location, for example. In this lab, you configure one computer to accept a remote connection, and then connect to it from another machine.

ESTIMATED COMPLETION TIME: 30 Minutes

 Activity

To configure a computer to accept a remote connection, follow these steps:

1. Log on to an account with administrative privileges. Write down the account name and password:

   _____

2. To determine the computer name, open Control Panel, click **System and Maintenance** (**Performance and Maintenance** in XP), and click **System**. In XP, click the **Computer Name** tab. Write down the computer name:

   _____

3. In Vista, click **Remote settings** in the System window and click **Continue** if a UAC dialog box opens. If necessary, click the **Remote** tab, and then click **Allow connections from computers running any version of Remote Desktop (less secure)**. Note that you would click **Allow users to connect remotely to this computer** in XP. See Figure 18-1.

   > **Notes** The administrator already has access. You could grant access to other users with the Select Users (Select Remote Users in XP) button.

4. Click **OK** in the System Properties dialog box and log off the system. You must be logged off before you can remotely log on.

To establish a remote connection, follow these steps:

1. Move to another computer on the same network, and log on.

2. Click **Start**, click **All Programs**, click **Accessories** (in XP SP1 or earlier, click **Communications**), and click **Remote Desktop Connection**.

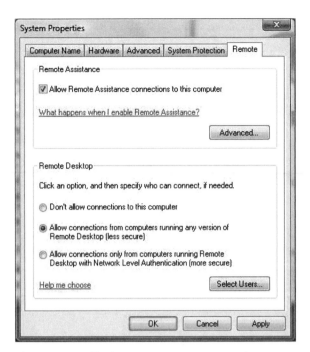

Figure 18-1 Allowing users to connect remotely to a computer
Courtesy: Course Technology/Cengage Learning

> **Notes** Windows Firewall in XP SP2 or later blocks the port used by remote access if the Don't allow exceptions check box is selected when configuring firewall settings.

3. Enter the computer name (of the remote computer) or its IP address (which you learned how to determine in Lab 17.1), and then click **Connect**.

4. Log on to the other computer remotely with the account information you wrote down earlier.

5. When you're finished, log off to close the connection.

REVIEW QUESTIONS

1. Describe two situations when you might want to use Remote Desktop Connection:

_____

_____

_____

_____

2. How can you tell if you are connected remotely to another computer?

_____

3. How can you determine the name of the remote computer before connecting?

_____

_____

18

4. How might other programs, such as firewalls, interfere with a remote connection?

_____

_____

_____

LAB 18.5 SHARE AN INTERNET CONNECTION

OBJECTIVES

The goal of this lab is to share an Internet connection between two computers using Windows ICS. After completing this lab, you will be able to:

◢ Configure two computers to use ICS

MATERIALS REQUIRED

This lab requires the following:

◢ Two computers running the Windows Vista operating system

◢ Internet access

LAB PREPARATION

Before the lab begins, the instructor or lab assistant needs to do the following:

◢ Verify that Windows starts with no errors.

◢ Verify that Internet access is available.

ACTIVITY BACKGROUND

In Lab 17.1, you learned how to connect two computers with a single crossover cable or a pair of patch cables and a hub. Now let's look at how to connect two or more computers in a small network so they can share this one Internet connection. The computer with the direct connection to the Internet will act as the host and share its connection.

Windows Internet Connection Sharing (ICS) is designed to manage these types of connections. Using ICS, the host computer stands as a gateway between the network and the Internet and ICS manages the gateway. These types of connections, which don't use a router as a gateway, were popular when routers were quite expensive. Now that routers are relatively inexpensive, one computer serving as a gateway to the Internet for other computers is not as popular as it once was.

ESTIMATED COMPLETION TIME: 20 Minutes

 Activity

Follow these steps to configure Windows on two computers so that they can share the Internet connection:

1. Depending how you connect to the Internet, your gateway computer (the one connected directly to the Internet) will probably require two network cards: one to connect to the Internet and the other to the other computer. If necessary, add a second network card to this computer (see Lab 4.2).

2. Log on as Administrator on your gateway computer, open the Network and Sharing Center, and click **Manage network connections**. The Network Connections window opens.

3. Right-click the connection that you want to share, select **Properties** from the shortcut menu, and respond to the UAC box. In the Properties box, click the **Sharing** tab (see the left side of Figure 18-2).

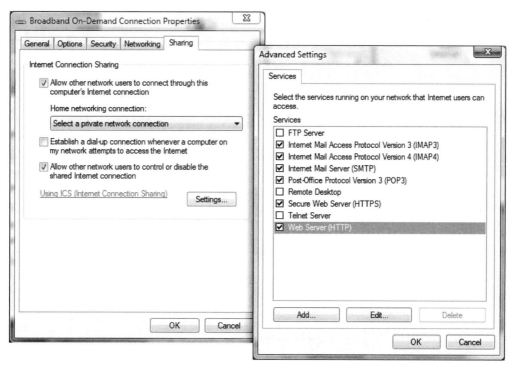

Figure 18-2 Allow others on your network to use this Internet connection
Courtesy: Course Technology/Cengage Learning

4. Check **Allow other network users to connect through this computer's Internet connection**. You can check the second box if you want to allow users on the network to be able to control the shared connection.

5. Click **Settings** to open the Advanced Settings window shown on the right side of Figure 18-2. Select the services that you want to allow Internet users to access on your network. A dialog box appears; click **OK** to close the box. Do this for each service you want to share.

6. Click **OK** twice to close both boxes.

The disadvantage of this type of shared connection is that the host computer must always be running for another computer on the network to reach the Internet. Another disadvantage is this network is not as secure as it would be if we had a hardware firewall installed. Both these problems can be solved by using a router in our network. How to set up a router on a network is covered in Lab 18.6.

1. Log on to the other computer and test the Internet connection by opening your browser and going on the Internet.

2. Can both computers access the Internet at the same time?

3. What happens to the Internet connection when no one is logged on the gateway computer?

18

4. What happens to the Internet connection when the gateway computer is shut down altogether?

_____

5. When you're finished, shut down both systems and remove the second network card from the gateway computer.

REVIEW QUESTIONS

1. What are two disadvantages of using ICS?

_____

_____

2. What device has mostly eliminated the need for ICS?

_____

3. If you had two computers, a desktop and a laptop, which would be the better choice to act as the gateway? Why?

_____

_____

4. Why are two network cards required on the gateway computer?

_____

_____

LAB 18.6 SET UP A WIRELESS ROUTER

OBJECTIVES

The goal of this lab is to install and configure a wireless router. After completing this lab, you will be able to:

◢ Install and configure a wireless router

◢ Configure PCs to connect to a wireless router

MATERIALS REQUIRED

This lab requires the following:

◢ Windows Vista/XP computer designated for this lab

◢ A wireless router with setup CD or user's manual

◢ A wireless NIC

LAB PREPARATION

Before the lab begins, the instructor or lab assistant needs to do the following:

◢ Verify that Windows starts with no errors.

◢ Verify that a network connection is available.

ACTIVITY BACKGROUND

In Lab 18.5, you learned how to share an Internet connection using ICS. A more popular way to share a connection is to use a router. Routers offer several advantages over ICS, including:

◢ A gateway computer will not be a bottleneck to slow down performance for other computers using the Internet.

◢ Access to the Internet does not depend on a gateway computer being turned on.

◢ The router can add additional security by providing a hardware firewall and limiting access to the Internet.

◢ The router can provide additional features such as functioning as a DHCP server.

In this lab, you will set up and configure a wireless router and then connect to it from a remote system.

ESTIMATED COMPLETION TIME: 30 Minutes

 Activity

Follow these steps to set up your router:

1. If your router comes with a setup CD (see Figure 18-3), run the setup program on one of your computers on the network (it doesn't matter which one). Follow the instructions on the setup screen or in the accompanying user's manual to disconnect the Internet connection from your host computer and connect it to the router.

Figure 18-3 A typical wireless router with setup CD and instruction manual
Courtesy: Course Technology/Cengage Learning

18

2. Connect the computers on your network to the router. A computer can connect directly to a network port on the router (see Figure 18-4), or you can connect through a switch or hub to the router. Plug in the router and turn it on.

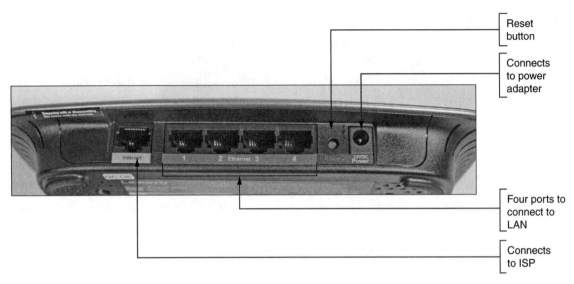

Figure 18-4 Connectors and ports on the back of a Linksys router
Courtesy: Course Technology/Cengage Learning

3. Firmware on the router (which can be flashed for updates) contains a configuration program that you access using a Web browser from anywhere on the network. In your browser address box, enter the IP address of the router (for our router, it's 192.168.1.1) and press **Enter**. What is the name and IP address for your router?

_____

4. You'll probably be required to sign in to the utility using a default password. The first thing you want to do is reset this password so that others cannot change your router setup. What is your new router password?

_____

5. The main Setup window appears, as shown in Figure 18-5. For most situations, the default settings on this and other screens should work without any changes. The setup program will take you through the process of configuring the router. After you've configured the router, you might have to turn your cable or DSL modem off and back on so that it correctly syncs up with the router. What basic steps did the setup program have you follow to configure the router?

_____

_____

_____

_____

6. Spend some time examining the various features of your router. What security features does it appear to have?

_____

_____

_____

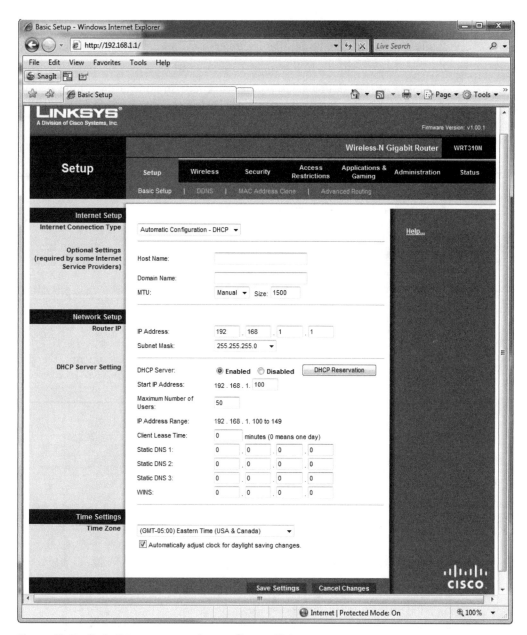

Figure 18-5 Basic Setup screen used to configure a Linksys router
Courtesy: Course Technology/Cengage Learning

7. What is the IP address of the router on the ISP network?

_____

8. Why is it necessary for the router to have two IP addresses?

_____

_____

18

Notes It is important to use the security features available on your router. Securing a wireless network will be covered in Chapter 20.

Follow these steps to connect to your wireless router from another PC.

1. On your computer, attach your wireless NIC and install the necessary drivers.

2. Boot the computer and log on as Administrator.

3. Mouse over or double-click the network icon in your notification area. Vista reports when wireless networks are available (see Figure 18-6).

Figure 18-6 Windows reports when wireless networks are available
Courtesy: Course Technology/Cengage Learning

4. Click **Connect to a network**. A list of available networks appears (see Figure 18-7). List all the networks that are available:

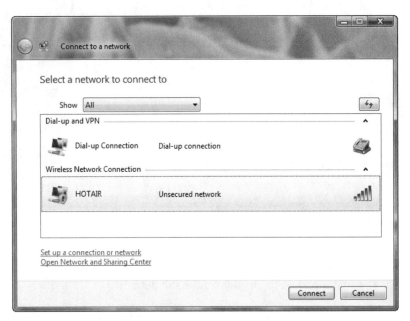

Figure 18-7 List of available networks
Courtesy: Course Technology/Cengage Learning

5. If you select an unsecured network, Vista warns you about sending information over it. Click **Connect Anyway**.

6. Vista reports the connection is made using the window in Figure 18-8. If you are comfortable with Vista automatically connecting to this network in the future, check **Save this network**. Close the window. If you mouse over the network icon in the notification area or double-click it, you can see the network to which you are connected.

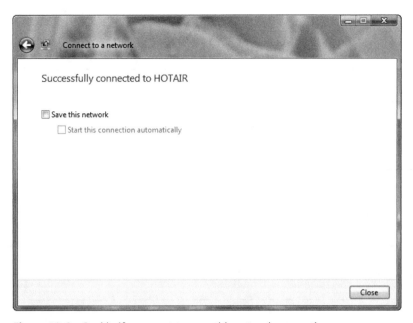

Figure 18-8 Decide if you want to save this network connection
Courtesy: Course Technology/Cengage Learning

7. To verify firewall settings and check for errors, open the Network and Sharing Center window (see Figure 18-9). Verify that Vista has configured the network as a public network and that Sharing and Discovery settings are all turned off. In the figure, you can see there is a problem with the Internet connection from the HOTAIR network to the Internet.

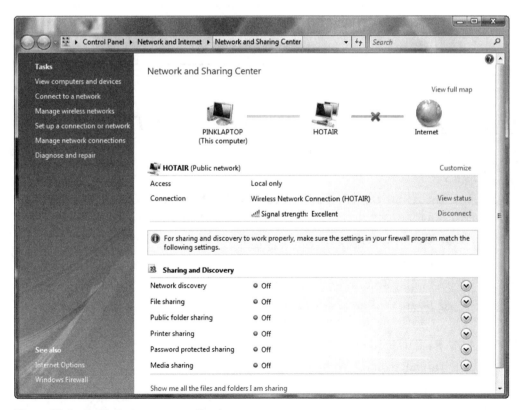

Figure 18-9 Verify that your connection is secure
Courtesy: Course Technology/Cengage Learning

8. Open your browser to test the connection.

9. What speed is your Wireless connection? How does this compare with your wired network?

_____

_____

10. When you're finished, reset and uninstall the wireless router and NIC.

REVIEW QUESTIONS

1. What are some of the additional features available on your router?

_____

_____

2. Name two ways your router can limit Internet access:

_____

_____

3. Name one advantage and one disadvantage of a wireless connection compared to a wired network:

_____

_____

4. Most wireless routers have a reset switch. Give an example of when this might be useful:

_____

_____

LAB 18.7 TROUBLESHOOT WITH TCP/IP UTILITIES

OBJECTIVES

The goal of this lab is to help you use Windows Vista/XP TCP/IP utilities to troubleshoot connectivity problems. After completing this lab, you will be able to:

◢ Use the Ipconfig utility

◢ Use the Ping utility

◢ Use the Tracert utility

◢ Identify the point at which your packets will no longer travel

MATERIALS REQUIRED

This lab requires the following:

◢ Windows Vista/XP operating system

◢ A DHCP server

◢ Internet access

LAB PREPARATION

Before the lab begins, the instructor or lab assistant needs to do the following:

◢ Verify that Windows starts with no errors.

◢ Verify that Internet access is available.

ACTIVITY BACKGROUND

Perhaps nothing frustrates users more than a suddenly unavailable network connection. As a PC technician, you might be asked to restore these connections, and sometimes you even have to deal with several failed connections at one time. When troubleshooting network connections, it helps to know whether many users in one area of a network are having the same connection problem. That information can help you narrow down the source of the problem. After you have an idea of what machine is causing the problem, you can use a few TCP/IP utilities to test your theory without physically checking the system. In this lab, you learn to use TCP/IP utilities to isolate connection problems.

ESTIMATED COMPLETION TIME: 30 Minutes

Activity

Follow these steps to display IP settings in Windows:

1. Click **Start**, right-click **Network** (**My Network Places** in XP) and click **Properties** in the shortcut menu. In Windows Vista, the Network and Sharing Center opens; in Windows XP, the Network Connections window opens.

2. In Vista, click **Manage network connections**. Right-click **Local Area Connection** and click **Properties** in the shortcut menu. If Windows opens a UAC, click **Continue**. The Local Area Connection Properties dialog box opens.

3. Click **Internet Protocol Version 4 (TCP/IPv4)**, (**Internet Protocol (TCP/IP)** in XP) and then click the **Properties** button. When the Internet Protocol Version 4 (TCP/IPv4) dialog box opens, notice the different options. What two ways can you set up the IP configuration?

_____

_____

4. Verify that **Obtain an IP address automatically** is selected.

5. Click **OK** to close the Internet Protocol Version 4 (TCP/IPv4) dialog box, and then close the Local Area Connection Properties dialog box. Close any open Windows.

Follow these steps to adjust the command prompt so that you can view more information at a time:

1. Open a command prompt window.

2. Right-click the title bar of the command prompt window and click **Properties** in the shortcut menu. The Command Prompt Properties dialog box opens.

3. Click the **Layout** tab, if necessary. In the Screen Buffer Size section, type **150** for width and **300** for height. These settings enable you to scroll in the command prompt window and view the last 300 lines of 150 characters. If you want, you can adjust settings in the Window Size section, but generally, it's best to adjust a command prompt window after it opens so that you don't make the window too large for your monitor's display settings. Click **OK** to save the settings.

18

4. The Apply Properties dialog box opens. To specify that you want to apply the properties every time you open a command prompt window, click **Save properties for future windows with same title**, and then click **OK**.

Follow these steps to learn how to display IP information from the command line:

1. At the command prompt, type **ipconfig** and press **Enter**. What is the IP address and subnet mask?

_____

_____

_____

2. To get more information about your IP settings, type **ipconfig /all** and press **Enter**. Answer these questions:

◢ What is the purpose of DHCP?

_____

_____

◢ What is the address of the DHCP server?

_____

◢ What is the address of the DNS server?

_____

◢ What is the address of the Default Gateway?

_____

◢ What is the physical address (MAC)?

_____

◢ What is the address of the DHCP server?

_____

3. Because your system is using DHCP to obtain an IP address, type **ipconfig /renew** and press **Enter**. The command prompt window again displays IP information.

4. Again, type **ipconfig /all** and press **Enter**. Compare the current IP address lease information to the information in the screen shot. What information changed?

_____

_____

5. Next, type **ipconfig /release** and press **Enter**. What message is displayed? What implications do you predict this command will have on connectivity?

_____

_____

6. Using your screen shot as a reference, attempt to ping the DHCP server and the DNS server. What are the results?

_____

_____

7. Type **ipconfig** and press **Enter**. Note that your adapter has no IP address and no subnet mask. These two parameters are necessary to communicate with TCP/IP.

8. To get an IP address lease again, type **ipconfig /renew** and press **Enter**. New IP information, which might be the same address as before, is assigned.

9. Find your new IP address lease information. List the command you used to find this information and the lease information:

_____

_____

_____

In Windows, you can use the Network and Sharing Center (Network Connections in XP) window to release and renew the IP address.

1. Click **Start** and right-click **Network** (**My Network Places** in XP) and click **Properties** in the shortcut menu. In Vista, click **Diagnose and repair**.

2. In XP, the Network Connections window opens. Click the network connection you want to repair, and then click **Repair this connection**. You can also right-click the network connection you want to repair and click **Repair** in the shortcut menu.

If you're connected to the Internet, follow these steps to determine what route your packets take to reach an Internet address:

1. If necessary, open a command prompt window.

2. Type **tracert** followed by a single space and then a domain name on the Internet (for example, **tracert www.yahoo.com**). Press **Enter**.

3. The DNS server resolves the domain name to an IP address, and that address is listed, indicating you can reach at least one DNS server. This information tells you that your packets are traveling at least that far. Next, each hop (or router your packet passed through) is listed with the time in milliseconds the packet took to reach its destination. How many hops did the packet take to reach the domain you specified?

_____

4. Now use the Tracert command with an illegal name, such as **www.mydomain.c**. What are the results of this command?

_____

18

5. When you're finished, close any open windows.

When troubleshooting connectivity problems, always consider the number of users experiencing the problem. If many users have similar difficulties, it's unlikely the problem lies with any one user's computer. Therefore, you can probably eliminate the need to run extensive local tests on each computer. Instead, you can examine a device that all computers commonly use.

As a general rule, when troubleshooting, you should start by examining devices close to the computer exhibiting problems and then move farther away. The following steps show you how to apply this principle by examining the local computer first, and then moving outward to other devices on the network.

1. Verify that the computer is physically connected (that both ends of the cable are connected).

2. Verify that the NIC is installed and TCP/IP is bound to the NIC.

3. Perform a loopback test to verify that the NIC is functioning correctly.

4. Check the IP settings with the **ipconfig /all** command. Verify that an IP address is assigned.

5. Ping other computers on the local network. If you get no response, begin by examining a hub or punchdown panel (a panel where cables convene before connecting to a hub).

6. If you can ping other computers on the local network, ping the default gateway, which is the first stop for transmissions being sent to addresses that aren't on the local network.

7. Continue troubleshooting connections, beginning with nearby devices and working outward until you discover an IP address that returns no response. That device will be the source of the trouble.

8. If the device is under your supervision, take the necessary steps to repair it. If the device is out of your control, contact the appropriate administrator.

REVIEW QUESTIONS

1. Name four additional pieces of information that the Ipconfig command with the /all switch provides that the Ipconfig command alone does not:

_____

_____

_____

_____

2. What type of server resolves a domain name to an IP address?

_____

3. In Windows Vista/XP, what command discards the IP address?

_____

4. What command do you use to determine whether you can reach another computer on the local network? Would this command work if the default gateway were down?

_____

_____

5. If many users suddenly encountered connection problems, would you suspect problems with their local computers or problems with other devices on the network? Explain:

_____

_____

_____

LAB 18.8 SOLVE NETWORK CONNECTIVITY PROBLEMS

OBJECTIVES

The goal of this lab is to troubleshoot and remedy common network connectivity problems. After completing this lab, you will be able to:

◢ Diagnose and solve connectivity problems

◢ Document the process

MATERIALS REQUIRED

This lab requires the following:

◢ Windows Vista/XP operating system

◢ A PC connected to a network and to the Internet

◢ Windows installation CD/DVD or installation files

◢ A PC toolkit with antistatic wrist strap

◢ A workgroup partner

LAB PREPARATION

Before the lab begins, the instructor or lab assistant needs to do the following:

◢ Verify that Windows starts with no errors.

◢ Provide each student with access to the Windows installation files, if needed.

ACTIVITY BACKGROUND

To a casual user, Internet and network connections can be confusing. When users have a connectivity problem, they usually have no idea how to remedy the situation. In this lab, you introduce and solve common connectivity problems.

ESTIMATED COMPLETION TIME: 60 Minutes

Activity

1. Verify that your network is working correctly by browsing the network and connecting to a Web site.
2. Do one of the following:
   - ◢ Change your PC's IP address.
   - ◢ Change your PC's subnet mask.
   - ◢ Remove your PC's network cable.
   - ◢ Remove TCP/IP from your PC.
   - ◢ Remove your PC's adapter in the Local Area Connection Properties dialog box.
   - ◢ Unseat or remove your PC's NIC, but leave it installed in the Local Area Connection Properties dialog box.
   - ◢ Disable your PC's NIC in Device Manager.
   - ◢ Release your PC's IP address (if DHCP is enabled).

18

3. Swap PCs with your partner and troubleshoot your partner's PC.

4. On a separate sheet of paper, answer these questions about the problem you solved:

◢ What is the initial symptom of the problem as a user might describe it?

_____

_____

◢ What steps did you take to discover the source of the problem?

_____

_____

_____

_____

◢ What steps did you take to solve the problem?

_____

_____

_____

_____

5. Repeat Steps 1 through 4 until you and your partner have used all the options listed in Step 2. Be sure to answer the questions in Step 4 for each troubleshooting situation.

REVIEW QUESTIONS

1. What problem could you solve by issuing only one command? What was the command you used?

_____

_____

2. Which problem (or problems) forced you to reboot the computer after repairing it?

_____

_____

_____

_____

3. What two pieces of information are necessary for TCP/IP communication on the local network?

_____

4. What TCP/IP utility was the most useful, in your opinion, for troubleshooting these problems? Why?

_____

_____

5. Why should you always check for physical problems like unplugged network cables before considering logical problems like missing drivers?

_____

_____

18

Security Essentials

Labs included in this chapter:

- **Lab 19.1:** Audit Computer and Network Activity in XP

- **Lab 19.2:** Monitor Security Events in Vista

- **Lab 19.3:** Research PC Security

- **Lab 19.4:** Secure a Private Folder

- **Lab 19.5:** Work with Offline Files

- **Lab 19.6:** Challenge Activity: Set Up a VPN

LAB 19.1 AUDIT COMPUTER AND NETWORK ACTIVITY IN WINDOWS XP

OBJECTIVES

The goal of this lab is to help you learn how to use event logging in Windows XP and CMOS setup so that you can audit events as needed to help secure a computer or network. After completing this lab, you will be able to:

- Use Windows tools for event logging
- Use CMOS setup for event logging

MATERIALS REQUIRED

This lab requires the following:

- Two Windows XP computers connected to a network

LAB PREPARATION

Before the lab begins, the instructor or lab assistant needs to do the following:

- Make a networked Windows XP computer available for each student or workgroup.
- The computer should not belong to a Windows domain.

ACTIVITY BACKGROUND

It is often necessary to monitor or audit computer or network events, such as logon events, failed hardware events, data access events, and other event activity. Auditing is necessary when you are looking for security breaches or troubleshooting hardware or software problems. This lab covers event logging for both of these situations.

ESTIMATED COMPLETION TIME: 90 Minutes

 Activity

Samuel works as a PC support technician in a patent attorney's office. The attorneys are especially interested in a high level of security because their clients often trust them with information they are expected to protect. The attorneys know that, in the past, hackers have tried to steal inventions by penetrating the office's computers and networks. Therefore, Samuel wants to implement all available techniques to audit the Windows XP computers that contain client records on the local wired and wireless network.

Samuel has decided he wants to audit events in four areas: network activity, Windows logon, access to private folders, and errors that occur when a computer is booted. All four areas are covered in this lab. Follow these steps to configure your computer for the lab:

1. Log on as Administrator and create a user account named **Attorney Miller**.

2. In Miller's My Documents folder, create a folder named Miller_Client_Inventions.

   If you are using the NTFS file system, any folder that is part of your user profile in the Documents and Settings folder can be made private using the folder Properties window. For example, to make the folder shown in Figure 19-1 private, check **Make this folder private**.

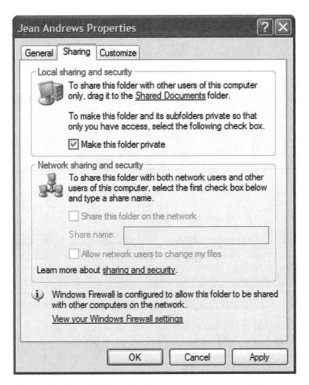

Figure 19-1 A folder that belongs to a user profile can be made private
Courtesy: Course Technology/Cengage Learning

3. Make Attorney Miller's My Documents folder private so that other users who are logged on to the computer or the network cannot see this folder. (See Lab 17.5.) Is the Miller_Client_Inventions folder also private? How do you know?

_____

_____

4. Create a folder named **C:\Client_Inventions**. Share the folder so that all users have full access to it.

5. Create two document files in the folder. Name the files Smith_Invention and Williams_Invention. Encrypt the contents of the Client_Inventions folder. To encrypt a folder, click the **Advanced** button on the **General** tab of the folder Properties window (see Figure 19-2), check the **Encrypt contents to secure data** check box, and click **OK**.

6. From another computer on the network, verify that you can see the two files in the Client_Inventions folder. Can you open either file from the remote computer? Why or why not?

_____

Follow these steps to audit network activity:

1. Using Windows Firewall, enable security logging. In the Windows Firewall window, under Security Logging, click the **Settings** button on the **Advanced** tab. Under Logging options, configure the Log Settings dialog box, as shown in Figure 19-3.

2. From another computer on the network, try to access the Client_Inventions folder. Examine the log file that shows this event. What is the name and path to the log file?

_____

19

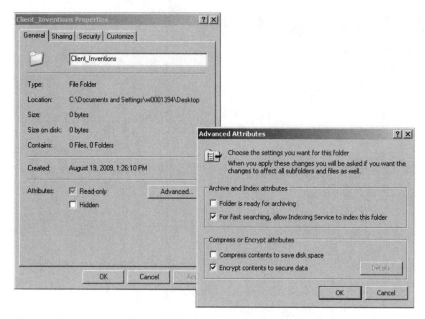

Figure 19-2   Encrypt a file or folder using the Properties window
Courtesy: Course Technology/Cengage Learning

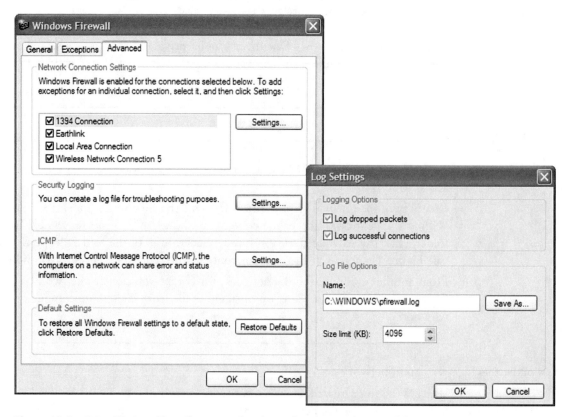

Figure 19-3   Using Windows Firewall, you can log dropped packets and successful connections
Courtesy: Course Technology/Cengage Learning

3. In the log file, how is a user or computer identified?

4. What is one good reason to use static IP addressing in this office rather than dynamic IP addressing?

Using Windows XP Professional, you can use Group Policy and Event Viewer to monitor Windows logon events. (Windows XP Home Edition does not support this feature.) Do the following:

1. Log on to the system as an administrator.

2. Click **Start, Control Panel,** double-click **Administrative Tools,** and double-click **Local Security Policy.** Select **Audit Policy** in the **Local Policy** folder and double-click **Audit account logon events,** as shown in Figure 19-4.

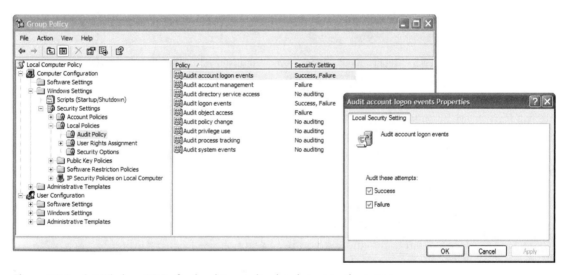

Figure 19-4 Set Windows XP Professional to monitor logging on to the system
Courtesy: Course Technology/Cengage Learning

3. Configure Windows to log all logon events, regardless of whether they are successes or failures. Do the same for the policy named **Audit logon events.**

4. Log off your computer and then log back on.

5. From another computer on the network, attempt to view the contents of the Client_Inventions folder.

6. Click **Start, Control Panel,** double-click **Administrative Tools,** and open **Event Viewer.** Look at the Security events log. How many logged events have occurred since you started this lab?

7. How are remote computers identified in the event log?

8. Double-click an event to see detailed information about the event, as shown in Figure 19-5.

19

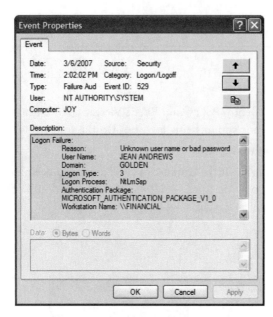

Figure 19-5 Details about a logged event are displayrd in the Event Properties
dialog box for that event
Courtesy: Course Technology/Cengage Learning

9. In Event Viewer, right-click **Security** to open the Security Properties window. Set the
Security events log so that events will not be overwritten. (See Figure 19-6.) Close Event
Viewer.

10. Using the Registry Editor, export the HKLM\SYSTEM\CurrentControlSet\Control\Lsa
key. Then change the DWORD value of the key to 1, which causes the system to halt if
the Security event log fills up. Answer these questions:

◢ What command did you use to launch the Registry Editor?

Figure 19-6 Control the Security log file settings
Courtesy: Course Technology/Cengage Learning

◢ What menu in the editor did you use to export the Registry key?

_____

◢ What did you name the exported key?

_____

11. How often do you think you need to clear the Security events log?

_____

12. Describe what you must do if you forget to clear the log, which will cause the system to halt:

_____

_____

_____

Do the following to monitor access to private folders:

1. Click **Start, My Computer,** and **Folder Options** from the **Tools** menu. Click the **View** tab and turn off simple file sharing by unchecking **Use simple file sharing (recommended).**

2. Click **Start, Control Panel,** double-click **Administrative Tools,** and double-click **Local Security Policy.** Use the Local Security Policy to set the Audit object access policy so that both successes and failures are monitored.

3. Right-click the **Client_Inventions** folder, click **Properties,** and click **Advanced.** Using the **Auditing** tab of the Advanced Security Settings window for the Client_Inventions folder, configure Windows to monitor the folder for all successful and failed accesses by all users (Everyone).

4. Using Windows Explorer, open the Client_Inventions folder and then open a file inside the folder.

5. Open Event Viewer. How many logged events are recorded for this folder?

_____

6. When you're finished, close any open windows.

In Windows, failed hardware events are recorded in Event Viewer in the System log. However, some computer BIOSs can log failed hardware events during or after startup. Do the following to find out if your BIOS has this ability:

1. Reboot your system and enter CMOS setup.

2. Look on all menus for the ability to record errors during or after startup. Did you find this option? If so, describe exactly what type of error is recorded and how to enable the option:

_____

_____

19

Notes To refresh a window in Windows Explorer or Event Viewer, press the **F5** key. To lock a workstation without waiting for the screen saver to activate, press Win+L.

To return event logging to the way it was before you started this lab, do the following:

1. Turn off network monitoring.
2. Restore the Group Policy settings so that logon events and object access events are not logged.
3. Restore the Registry key you changed by double-clicking the exported key file. Then delete the exported file.
4. Remove all auditing from the Client_Inventions folder.
5. Turn on simple file sharing.

Answer the following questions. You might find it interesting to discuss your answers with others in this lab.

1. Sometimes, too much information keeps you from effectively monitoring a system. In this lab, you have monitored many types of failed and successful events, which all generate a lot of data to plow through. How do you think Samuel could improve the monitoring methods and options used in this lab?

    _____

    _____

    _____

2. The current network is configured as a Windows workgroup. Give two reasons Samuel should recommend that the attorneys convert the network to a Windows domain:

    _____

    _____

    _____

    _____

REVIEW QUESTIONS

1. What is the name of the Windows XP Firewall log file that monitors network activity?

    _____

2. What happens when the allowable size of the log file that monitors network activity has been exceeded?

    _____

3. Which applet in Control Panel is used to turn simple file sharing on and off?

    _____

4. What is the name of the Group Policy console program file?

    _____

5. What are the two main categories of policies in the Group Policy console?

    _____

LAB 19.2 MONITOR SECURITY EVENTS IN VISTA

OBJECTIVES

The goal of this lab is to use Event Viewer to monitor security events such as failed attempts to log into the system or changes to files and folders. After completing this lab, you will be able to:

◢ Set Event Viewer to track failed login attempts

◢ Set Event Viewer to monitor changes to files and folders

MATERIALS REQUIRED

This lab requires the following:

◢ Windows Vista operating system installed on an NTFS partition

LAB PREPARATION

Before the lab begins, the instructor or lab assistant needs to do the following:

◢ Verify that Windows starts with no errors.

ACTIVITY BACKGROUND

As part of managing the security of a computer or network, your organization might ask you to report incidents of suspicious events such as attempts to log on or change certain files. You can track either of these events with the Windows Event Viewer. In this lab, you will configure Windows to monitor these events.

ESTIMATED COMPLETION TIME: 30 Minutes

 Activity

Follow these steps to set Event Viewer to track failures when people are attempting to log on to the system:

1. Log on as an administrator and create a new standard user account called **Newuser.**
2. Click **Start, Control Panel, System and Maintenance,** and **Administrative Tools.**
3. Double-click **Local Security Policy.** If a UAC box opens, click **Continue.** The Local Security Policy window opens. (Windows Vista Home Editions do not support this feature.)
4. Double-click **Local Policies** and select **Audit Policy,** as shown in Figure 19-7.
5. Double-click **Audit account logon events.** The Audit logon events Properties dialog box opens. Check **Failure** and click **OK.** Do the same for **Audit logon events** and then close the Local Security Policy window.
6. Examine the other local security policies and determine which would be used to monitor when a password is changed:

   _____

7. To see the events that are logged, open **Event Viewer** and select **Security** in Windows Logs in the left pane (see Figure 19-8). Does Event Viewer currently list any logon failures?
8. Log out and attempt to log back in to an account with the wrong password.
9. Now successfully log back in as Administrator.

19

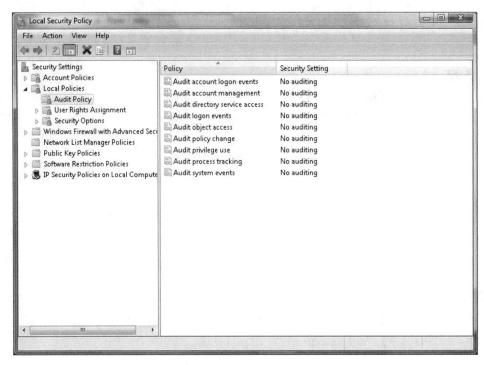

Figure 19-7   Event tracking can be enabled using the Local Security Policy window
Courtesy: Course Technology/Cengage Learning

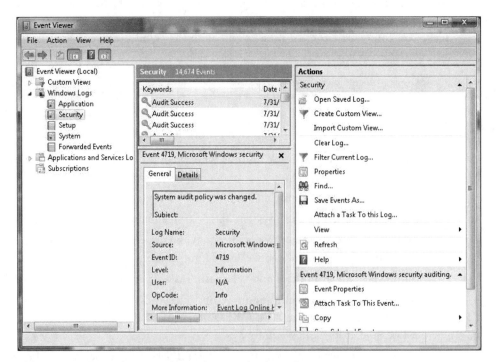

Figure 19-8   Event Viewer can be used to examine logs of past events
Courtesy: Course Technology/Cengage Learning

10. Open Event Viewer and select Security again. What information did Event Viewer record about the failed login attempt?

11. When you're finished, close any open windows.

Follow these steps to monitor changes to files and folders:

1. Open the Local Security Policy window as you did previously in Steps 2-4 and double-click **Audit object access**. Check **Failure** and click **OK**.

2. Close the Local Security Policy Window.

3. Open the **Properties** window of the C:\Users\Public folder and click the **Security** tab, as shown in Figure 19-9.

Figure 19-9 Security policies can be set in the Properties window
Courtesy: Course Technology/Cengage Learning

4. Click **Advanced**, select the **Auditing** tab, and click **Continue**. If a UAC box opens, click **Continue**.

5. The Advanced Security Settings window opens, as shown in Figure 19-10. You can now add users or groups that you want to monitor.

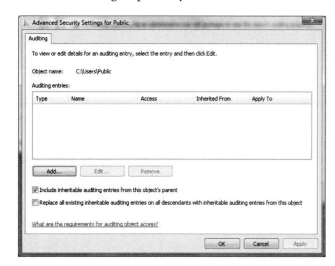

Figure 19-10 In the Advanced Security Settings window, you can add groups or users you want to monitor
Courtesy: Course Technology/Cengage Learning

19

6. Click **Add**, click **Advanced**, click **Find Now**, select **Newuser**, and click **OK**.

7. Click **OK** to close the Select User or Group window.

8. Check the **Full control** boxes for **Successful** and **Failed** attempts, as shown in Figure 19-11, and click **OK** to close the Auditing Entry window.

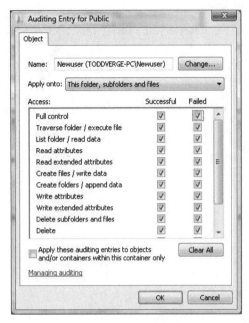

Figure 19-11   The Auditing Entry window allows you to select which events will be tracked
Courtesy: Course Technology/Cengage Learning

9. Close all windows to exit and log out as Administrator.

10. Log in as Newuser and open the C:\Users\Public folder. While you're there, use Notepad to create a short text file. What did you name your text file?

11. Log out as Newuser and log back in as Administrator.

12. Open **Event Viewer**, select **Event Viewer (local)**, and double-click **Audit Success** in the Summary of Administrative Events section.

13. Explore the recent events in this section until you find the ones that are associated with Newuser's attempt to access the C:\Users\Public folder. How many separate events were created?

14. Which one of the events recorded the creation of the new text file?

REVIEW QUESTIONS

1. How could you use the Local Security Policy to determine if someone was trying to hack into a user account?

2. Why is it important to also record failed attempts to access files?

_____

3. Besides failed logon attempts, name two other events that would seem suspicious:

_____

_____

4. What would be a more efficient way to monitor the activities of a collection of users?

_____

_____

5. Why would accessing one file create several separate events?

_____

_____

LAB 19.3 RESEARCH PC SECURITY

OBJECTIVES

The goal of this lab is to research various ways to secure a computer. During this lab, you will research how to:

◢ Enable and manage Windows Firewall

◢ Enable Windows Defender

◢ Unhide file extensions

MATERIALS REQUIRED

This lab requires the following:

◢ Windows Vista/XP Professional operating system

◢ Internet access

LAB PREPARATION

Before the lab begins, the instructor or lab assistant needs to do the following:

◢ Verify that Windows starts with no errors.

◢ Verify that Internet access is available.

19

ACTIVITY BACKGROUND

There is no single solution for protecting your PC from the wide variety of security threats that you face every day. Running a personal firewall as well as a selection of third-party software and monitoring tools can provide some protection from malware. You can also avoid a lot of problems by following a handful of basic rules like not opening unknown e-mail attachments and always limiting the use of administrative accounts. It's important to keep in mind, however, that no defense will ever substitute for keeping good backups. Data loss isn't a matter of *if* but *when*. In this lab, you will use the Internet as well as any built-in Windows help files to research several popular methods of protecting your computer.

Activity

A firewall is hardware or software that keeps worms or hackers from getting into your system. It works by examining the information coming in and out of the PC and blocking any unwanted data. Windows already has a built-in software firewall. Answer the following questions about the Windows Firewall:

1. Vista automatically configures Windows Firewall based on the type of network it believes you are connected to. What are the three types of network profiles, and which one offers the most protection through the firewall?

   _____

   _____

   _____

2. List the steps required to open the Network and Sharing Center in Vista:

   _____

   _____

   _____

   _____

3. What are the main differences between the Public and Private network settings?

   _____

   _____

4. Why might you need to grant a firewall exception for File and Print Sharing on a public network?

   _____

   _____

5. List the steps necessary to make this change:

   _____

   _____

   _____

   _____

Windows Defender is an antiadware and antispyware program integrated into Windows Vista. By default it downloads updates and scans your system every day at 2:00AM. It also monitors your system and reports suspicious activity using a bubble that appears in the lower-right corner of the screen. Use Windows help and the Internet to answer these questions:

1. How would you determine if Windows Defender had been turned off?

2. What steps would you follow to turn on Windows Defender?

3. How would you use Windows Defender to perform a quick scan of the system right away?

4. Is Windows Defender also available for Windows XP?

5. A Trojan is malware such as a virus that disguises itself as a harmless file like a picture and when you double-click to open it, it installs itself on your system. The key to avoiding a Trojan is to always examine the extension to make sure it is consistent with the file type you are expecting. However, sometimes Windows hides file extensions, making this more difficult. How would you change your folder options to show hidden files and folders and not hide the extensions for known file types?

REVIEW QUESTIONS

1. How could opening an unknown e-mail attachment be a security risk?

2. Why would the firewall for a public network be more restrictive?

3. What would you suspect if you saw a file named coolpic.exe?

4. Can a firewall be configured to grant an exception for one program rather than be turned off altogether?

19

LAB 19.4 SECURE A PRIVATE FOLDER

OBJECTIVES

The goal of this lab is to help you learn how to apply Windows tools to secure a private folder. After completing this lab, you will be able to:

▲ Share a folder on the network.

▲ Control which users can read or modify the folder

MATERIALS REQUIRED

This lab requires the following:

▲ Two Windows Vista/XP computers connected on a network for each workgroup of two or more students

▲ Microsoft Excel or an equivalent open source spreadsheet application (optional)

▲ Access to a printer (optional)

LAB PREPARATION

Before the lab begins, the instructor or lab assistant needs to do the following:

▲ Make a networked Windows Vista/XP computer available for each student or student workgroup.

ACTIVITY BACKGROUND

In an office environment, employees often share files and folders as they work together on a common project. Sensitive information in these shared files and folders often needs to be kept private from others in the organization. A PC support technician will probably be asked to solve these types of security issues for the office. In this lab, you learn how to apply Windows security tools and features to solve these security problems.

ESTIMATED COMPLETION TIME: 60 Minutes

 Activity

Michael is team leader of the payroll department of Peaceful Arbor, Inc., a corporation that manages assisted living facilities. He and his two other team members, Sharon and Jason, share payroll files that others in the accounting department are not allowed to view. The payroll data is stored on the file server in the C:\Payroll folder, and everyone in the accounting department who is not on the payroll team knows not to open the folder. Recently, Michael suspects that others have been poking around where they don't belong, so he has turned to Linden, the PC support technician, for help.

Working with a team member, re-create the problem on your two networked lab computers by doing the following:

1. On Computer 1, which will be your file server, create a user account named Linden and assign administrative privileges to the account. Be sure to assign a password to this account. What is the password?

2. On Computer 1, create the folder C:\Payroll. Create three spreadsheet files named MasterPayroll.xls, October2009.xls, and November2009.xls. Put some sample data in each file, and store all three files in the C:\Payroll folder. If you don't have access to a spreadsheet program, substitute three text files.

3. On Computer 1, create the folder C:\Budget. Create two spreadsheet files named Budget2009.xls and Budget2010.xls. Put some sample data in each file, and store the files in the C:\Budget folder.

4. Configure Computer 2 so that passwords of at least six characters are required for all user accounts. To do this, use the policy Minimum password length, shown in Figure 19-12.

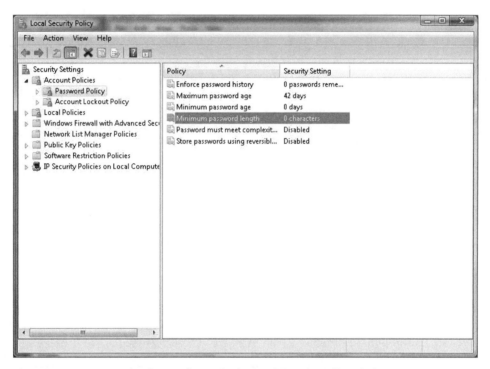

Figure 19-12 Password policy can be set in the Local Security Policy window
Courtesy: Course Technology/Cengage Learning

5. On Computer 2, create a limited user account named Michael. Michael belongs to the payroll team and needs full access to the Payroll folder. He also needs access to the Budget folder. What is the password to the Michael account?

_____

6. On Computer 2, create a limited user account named Sharon. Sharon belongs to the payroll team and needs full access to the Payroll folder. She does not need any access to the Budget folder. What is the password to the Sharon account?

_____

7. Create a limited user account named Jason on Computer 2. Jason belongs to the accounting department and needs full access to the Budget folder, but should not have any access to the Payroll folder. What is the password to the Jason account?

_____

19

8. Using Windows tools, set the permissions and access controls so that Michael, Sharon, and Jason can read and write to the folder they need, but cannot view the contents of the folder they are not allowed to see. List the steps you took to do the job:

_____

_____

_____

_____

_____

_____

_____

_____

9. Test your security measures by doing the following:
   ◢ Log on to Computer 2 as Michael. Edit a file in the Budget folder and a file in the Payroll folder.
   ◢ Log on to Computer 2 as Sharon. Edit a file in the Payroll folder.
   ◢ Verify that Sharon cannot view the contents of the Budget folder.
   ◢ Log on to Computer 2 as Jason. Edit a file in the Budget folder.
   ◢ Verify that Jason cannot view the contents of the Payroll folder.

10. When you are convinced you have solved the problem, do the following to further test your system:
    ◢ Ask someone on another team to try to hack through your security measures using Computer 2. Was this person able to break through? If so, how?

    _____

    _____

    ◢ Ask the same person to attempt to hack through your security measures using Computer 1. Was this person able to break through? If so, how?

    _____

    _____

11. Correct any security problems that have come to light by your testing. What, if anything, did you need to do?

    _____

    _____

    _____

    _____

12. Set up event logging so that you can view a log of unauthorized attempts to view a folder. How did you do it?

_____

_____

_____

_____

13. Test your auditing method by logging on to Computer 2 as Jason and attempting to view the Payroll folder. If possible, print the screen that shows the logged event.

14. When you're finished, remove the new accounts and undo any changes.

REVIEW QUESTIONS

1. Did your system use simple file sharing?

_____

2. Would this setup be sufficient for securing the payroll information at a large company? Why or why not?

_____

_____

3. What utility is used to require that each user account have a password?

_____

4. Why is it important for people besides your own team to test a security system that your team has put in place?

_____

5. Why is auditing an important component of file security?

_____

LAB 19.5 WORK WITH OFFLINE FILES

19

OBJECTIVES

The goal of this lab is to help you learn to work with offline files. After completing this lab, you will be able to:

◢ Enable offline files in Windows

◢ Make network files available offline

◢ Sync offline files with the network

MATERIALS REQUIRED

This lab requires the following:

▲ At least two systems running the Windows Vista operating system

▲ The ability to network both computers

▲ Internet access

LAB PREPARATION

Before the lab begins, the instructor or lab assistant needs to do the following:

▲ Verify that Windows starts with no errors.

▲ Verify that Internet access is available.

▲ Set up a simple network with two computers.

ACTIVITY BACKGROUND

Sometimes, you need access to network files when the network is not available. Maybe you're traveling and you can't find a wireless connection or maybe the server is being updated and it's temporarily unavailable. Windows allows you to work with offline files and then sync up the changes with the network files later. In this lab, you will set up some network files so they can be changed offline.

> **ESTIMATED COMPLETION TIME: 45 Minutes**

 Activity

1. Begin with two networked Windows computers and use one of the methods from Lab 18.7 to test your network connection. What method or utility did you use?

   _____

2. On Computer 1, which will be your server, create a shared folder that contains a small text file. (See Lab 17.5.) What is the name and path of your shared folder and file?

   _____

   _____

3. On Computer 2, create a drive mapping to the shared folder and open the text file to test your connection.

4. Click **Start, Control Panel, Network and Internet,** and **Offline Files** to open the Offline Files configuration window pictured in Figure 19-13. If necessary, select the **General** tab and check to see if Offline Files are enabled and then click **OK**.

You can work with offline files by following these steps:

1. On Computer 2, open Windows Explorer, right-click the drive mapping to the shared folder, and select **Always Available Offline**.

2. Windows will then make a copy of the network files on your local machine.

3. Temporarily remove Computer 2 from the network by unplugging the network cable or disabling the wireless connection. Windows will automatically enable offline files whenever the network is not available.

4. Open Windows Explorer and open the offline version of the shared text file.

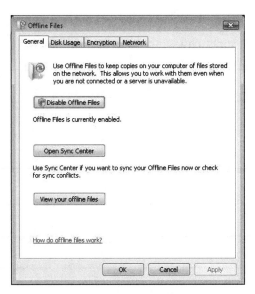

Figure 19-13 Check to see if Offline Files are enabled
Courtesy: Course Technology/Cengage Learning

5. Make a small change to this file. What change did you make?

_____

6. Open the Offline Files configuration window and answer the following questions:
   ◢ What objects are listed when you click **View your offline files**?

   _____

   _____

   ◢ How would you change the amount of space available for storing offline files on your computer?

   _____

   _____

   ◢ What other options or features are available for working offline?

   _____

   _____

7. Now reconnect Computer 2 with the network.

8. Windows updates offline files automatically but not continuously. To make sure the file is updated, open Windows Explorer, select the shared folder, and click **Sync** from the toolbar.

9. Log on to Computer 1, if necessary, and open the shared file. Did the file update with offline changes made from Computer 2?

   _____

10. Will the Sync button also update the offline content with changes made on the network?

   _____

REVIEW QUESTIONS

1. What are some reasons why you might choose to set up offline files?

   _____

   _____

2. How is working with offline files different from simply making a second copy of the files you need to access?

   _____

   _____

   _____

   _____

3. Why might encrypting your offline files be necessary?

   _____

   _____

4. Why might you choose to work with offline files even if the network is available?

   _____

   _____

LAB 19.6 CHALLENGE ACTIVITY: SET UP A VPN

OBJECTIVES

The goal of this lab is to help you set up a secure VPN. After completing this lab, you will be able to:

◢ Set up a VPN in Windows

◢ Use third-party software to securely access the Internet from a public network

MATERIALS REQUIRED

This lab requires the following:

◢ Windows Vista operating system

◢ Internet access

◢ VPN server (optional)

LAB PREPARATION

Before the lab begins, the instructor or lab assistant needs to do the following:

◢ Verify that Windows starts with no errors.

◢ Verify that Internet access is available.

⊿ Set up a VPN server and record the server's IP address (optional).

⊿ Set up a user account on the VPN server and record the username and password (optional).

ACTIVITY BACKGROUND

A Virtual Private Network (VPN) offers a very secure connection between two computers. It uses a process called tunneling to form a private connection that encrypts communications independently of the type of network being used. VPNs are often used when a user has to connect to a network over a nonsecure public network such as a wireless hotspot. In this lab, you will learn how to set up a VPN connection in Windows as well as a third-party utility.

ESTIMATED COMPLETION TIME: 45 Minutes

 Activity

To connect to a VPN server in Windows, follow these steps:

1. Log on as Administrator.
2. Click **Start**, click **Connect To**, and click **Set up a connection or network**.
3. Select **Connect to a workplace**, as shown in Figure 19-14, and click **Next**.

Figure 19-14 Select Connect to a workplace to set up a VPN connection in Windows
Courtesy: Course Technology/Cengage Learning

19

4. Click **Use my Internet connection** (VPN).
5. Enter the Internet address and Destination name provided by your instructor (optional) to connect to a real VPN, or just enter the IP address of another computer on your network. What name and address did you use?

_____

_____

6. To connect to an actual VPN server, enter the User name and Password provided by your instructor. Otherwise, click **Cancel** to close the window. What name and password did you use?

_____

_____

Several companies offer programs to secure Internet access from public wireless connections using VPNs. One such program is Hotspot Shield from AnchorFree. To set up a secure connection, follow these steps:

1. Log on as an administrator.

2. Open your browser and go to **www.hotspotshield.com**.

3. Click the **Download** button and follow the on-screen instructions to download and install Hotspot Shield. During the installation process:

   ◢ Deselect the Include the Hotspot Shield Community Toolbar checkbox.

   ◢ Accept the default configuration.

   ◢ Click **Install** if any Windows Security windows open.

4. When the installation is complete, launch Hotspot Shield and wait for an automatic connection to a VPN server.

5. Look at several Web sites. How do you know that Hotspot Shield is running?

_____

6. When you're finished, uninstall Hotspot Shield and close any open windows.

REVIEW QUESTIONS

1. Will VPNs work on both wired and wireless networks?

_____

_____

2. What process do VPNs use to form a private connection between computers?

_____

3. Why would it be dangerous to do online banking transactions through a public Internet hotspot without a VPN?

_____

_____

4. How does a VPN connection differ from using Remote Desktop?

_____

_____

5. Why is a VPN more secure than other forms of wireless encryption such as WEP?

_____

_____

_____

_____

19

CHAPTER 20

Security Practices

Labs included in this chapter:

- **Lab 20.1:** Protect Your Computer from Viruses and Adware
- **Lab 20.2:** Use Encryption
- **Lab 20.3:** Secure a Wireless LAN
- **Lab 20.4:** Investigate Startup Processes
- **Lab 20.5:** Deal with a Rootkit

LAB 20.1 PROTECT YOUR COMPUTER FROM VIRUSES AND ADWARE

OBJECTIVES

The goal of this lab is to help you use antivirus and antiadware software to protect your computer. After completing this lab, you will be able to:

◢ Install antivirus software

◢ Scan your system for viruses and adware

MATERIALS REQUIRED

This lab requires the following:

◢ Windows Vista/XP operating system

◢ Internet access

◢ *Optional:* An installed antivirus program

LAB PREPARATION

Before the lab begins, the instructor or lab assistant needs to do the following:

◢ Verify that Windows starts with no errors.

◢ Verify that Internet access is available.

ACTIVITY BACKGROUND

One of the best ways to protect your computer against malicious software is to always run current antivirus and antispyware software. Many excellent antivirus programs, such as Norton AntiVirus or McAfee VirusScan, are available commercially. As well, many Web-based programs are available to scan and disinfect your system. In this lab, you "infect" your computer with a fake virus, and then use a Web-based antivirus program to disinfect your system.

> **ESTIMATED COMPLETION TIME: 60 Minutes**

Activity

1. Open your browser, and go to **www.eicar.org**. Attempt to download the **eicar.com** malware test file. If you're already running an antivirus program, you'll probably be alerted that the file is infected and the download will be blocked or isolated.

2. What alert or warning does your antivirus program display when you try to download this file?

   _____

3. Next, go to **http://housecall.trendmicro.com** and click **Launch HouseCall**. On the next page, accept the terms of use and click the **Launch HouseCall** button.

4. Follow the on-screen instructions, and then click the appropriate button to do a complete scan of the computer. Depending on your system, this process might take some time.

5. When the scan is finished, you can choose to delete any infected files. How many infections did HouseCall find?

   _____

6. Exit the program and close your browser.

Occasionally, some infected files, particularly adware, manage to avoid detection by one program or another. For this reason, running several antiadware programs on your computer is often useful. Follow these steps to download and run two antiadware programs:

1. Open your Web browser, if necessary, and go to **www.lavasoft.com**. Click to download **Ad-Aware Free**, and install it on your system. Leave your Web browser open.

2. Use this program to perform a system scan of your computer, which could take several minutes. How many critical objects were recognized?

   _____

3. Next, go to **www.spybot.info**. Click **English,** click to download **Spybot Search and Destroy,** and install it on your system.

4. Use the program to check your computer for problems. Did Spybot find any adware that the first program missed?

   _____

5. Exit the program.

REVIEW QUESTIONS

1. List some ways your computer might become infected with a virus:

   _____

2. Why is it important to allow your antivirus program to update its virus definition files automatically?

   _____

3. Why do some companies bundle adware with their programs?

   _____

4. Why does scanning your hard drive for viruses take so long?

   _____

5. What can you do if you aren't running antivirus software and suspect your computer is infected?

   _____

LAB 20.2 USE ENCRYPTION

OBJECTIVES

The goal of this lab is to help you work with encryption and observe the effects of trying to use an encrypted file without permission. After completing this lab, you will be able to:

▲ Encrypt a directory

▲ Save files to the encrypted directory

▲ Access the encrypted files as a different user

20

MATERIALS REQUIRED

This lab requires the following:

◢ Windows Vista/XP Professional operating system installed on an NTFS partition

◢ A blank floppy disk or USB flash drive

LAB PREPARATION

Before the lab begins, the instructor or lab assistant needs to do the following:

◢ Verify that Windows starts with no errors.

ACTIVITY BACKGROUND

Despite your best efforts, unauthorized users might gain access to sensitive files. To protect these files from this type of security breach, you can use file encryption, which prevents unauthorized users from being able to view files, even if they do manage to gain access to them. You can encrypt individual files or entire directories. As with disk quotas, you can use file encryption only on NTFS drives. FAT file systems don't support file encryption. In this lab, you create and encrypt an entire directory, and then create a test file in that encrypted directory.

ESTIMATED COMPLETION TIME: 30 Minutes

 Activity

Follow these steps to create an encrypted directory and a test file in that directory:

1. Log on as an administrator.

2. In Windows Explorer, create two new directories in the NTFS root. Name the directories **Encrypt** and **Normal**.

3. Right-click the **Encrypt** folder, and then click **Properties**. The Encrypt Properties dialog box opens.

4. Click the **Advanced** button to open the Advanced Attributes dialog box.

5. Click the **Encrypt contents to secure data** check box to encrypt the contents of the Encrypt folder.

6. Click **OK** to apply the settings and close the Advanced Attributes dialog box. You return to the Encrypt Properties dialog box.

7. Click **OK** to apply encryption.

8. In Windows Explorer, double-click the **Encrypt** folder to open it.

9. From the Windows Explorer menu, click **File**, point to **New**, and click **Text Document**. Double-click **New Text Document** and type **This file is encrypted**. Close the file, saving it as **Secure.txt**.

Follow these steps to see the effects of encrypting a file in Windows:

1. Double-click **Secure.txt** in the Encrypt folder and record what happens:

_____

2. Log off as an administrator, and log on again as a different user.

3. Double-click **Secure.txt** in the Encrypt folder and record the results:

_____

4. Copy **Secure.txt** to the Normal folder and record the results:

_____

5. Log off, and then log on again as an administrator.
6. Copy **Secure.txt** to the Normal folder and record the results:

_____

7. Copy **Secure.txt** to some form of removable media that is not formatted with NTFS, such as a USB flash drive or a blank, formatted floppy disk, and record the results:

_____

8. Log off, and then log on again as the previous user.
9. Double-click **Secure.txt** in the Normal folder and record the results:

_____

10. Double-click **Secure.txt** in the removable drive and record the results:

_____

_____

11. Right-click the **Secure.txt** file in the removable drive, and then click **Properties**. The file's Properties dialog box opens. Is there an Advanced button?

_____

12. Right-click the **Secure.txt** file in the Normal folder, and then click **Properties**. The file's Properties dialog box opens.
13. Click the **Advanced** button, click to clear the **Encrypt contents to secure data** check box, and then click **OK**. Record the results:

_____

_____

REVIEW QUESTIONS

1. Which file system must be used to enable encryption?

_____

2. How do you encrypt a single file?

_____

3. What happens when an unauthorized user tries to open an encrypted file?

_____

_____

4. What happens when an unauthorized user tries to unencrypt a file?

_____

_____

20

5. What happens to an encrypted file that's removed from an NTFS partition?

_____

_____

LAB 20.3 SECURE A WIRELESS LAN

OBJECTIVES

The goal of this lab is to learn how to set up and configure security options on your wireless router. After completing this lab, you will be able to:

◢ Download a manual for a wireless router

◢ Explain how to improve wireless security

◢ Describe some methods of securing a wireless LAN

MATERIALS REQUIRED

This lab requires the following:

◢ Windows Vista/XP Professional operating system

◢ Internet access

◢ Adobe Acrobat Reader installed for viewing .pdf files

◢ Wireless router (optional)

◢ Laptop or desktop with compatible wireless access (optional)

LAB PREPARATION

Before the lab begins, the instructor or lab assistant needs to do the following:

◢ Verify that Windows starts with no errors.

◢ Verify that Internet access is available.

ACTIVITY BACKGROUND

Wireless networks have become common in recent years and are a simple way to include a laptop in your home network. Without adequate security, however, you can open up your network to a wide range of threats. In this lab, you learn how to enable and configure some security features of your wireless router.

ESTIMATED COMPLETION TIME: 45 Minutes

 Activity

1. Open your Web browser, and go to **www.linksys.com**.

2. Click **Downloads**.

3. In the drop-down list of products, click **Routers,** and then click **WRT54G2.**

Notes Your instructor might choose to substitute the manual for another wireless router instead of having you download the Linksys user guide.

4. Click the **User Guide** link. The manual opens in a separate window in .pdf format. Use it to answer the following questions:

◢ Most wireless routers can be configured with a Web-based utility by entering the router's IP address in the browser's Address text box. What's the default IP address of this router?

_____

◢ Describe how you would log in to the router for the first time:

_____

_____

_____

Most routers are easily configured with a setup utility that asks a series of questions about your network and Internet service provider. The default settings, however, might not enable all your router's security features. These are the six most important steps in securing your LAN:

◢ Updating the router's firmware from the manufacturer's Web site so any known security flaws have been fixed

◢ Setting a password on the router itself so that other people can't change its configuration

◢ Disabling remote configuration of the router

◢ Changing the network's name (called a service set identifier—SSID) and turning off the SSID broadcast to anyone who's listening

◢ Using some kind of encryption (WEP is good, WPA is better, WPA2 is better still.)

◢ Enabling MAC filtering so that you can limit access to only your computers

Now continue to use the manual to answer the following additional questions:

◢ Which window in the router's Web-based utility do you use to change the user name and password?

_____

◢ List the steps for changing the router's SSID:

_____

_____

_____

_____

◢ How many hexadecimal characters must be used for 64-bit Wired Equivalent Privacy (WEP) encryption?

_____

20

◢ Describe the steps to limit access to everything but your laptop through MAC filtering:

_____

_____

_____

_____

CHALLENGE ACTIVITY (ADDITIONAL 30 MINUTES)

Set up an actual secure wireless connection by following these steps:

1. Set up a nonsecure wireless connection with the router, as covered in Lab 18.6.

2. Go to the router manufacturer's Web site and update the router's firmware (if necessary) to the latest version. Did your router require an update? What version of the firmware is it now running?

_____

3. Set a strong password for the router. What password did you use?

_____

4. Disable remote configuration for the router so the router cannot be configured wirelessly. List the steps you went through to complete this task:

_____

_____

_____

_____

5. Change the router's name (SSID). What was the router's default name and what did you change it to?

_____

6. Disable the broadcast of the new SSID.

7. Set up some kind of encryption on the router. What form of encryption did you use?

_____

8. Enable MAC filtering so that only your wireless PC or laptop can connect. How did you determine the MAC address of your wireless computer?

_____

_____

9. Connect to the network with your wireless computer, as covered in Lab 18.6, and test your wireless connection by opening your browser.

10. When you're finished, undo the changes you made on the wireless client and reset the router.

REVIEW QUESTIONS

1. How are most wireless routers automatically configured?

   _____

2. Why should you update your router's firmware before making any other security changes?

   _____

   _____

3. How could not changing your router's password compromise all of your other security changes?

   _____

   _____

4. Why wouldn't "password" or "linksys" make a good password for your router?

   _____

5. How can you configure your router once you've disabled remote configuration?

   _____

   _____

LAB 20.4 INVESTIGATE STARTUP PROCESSES

OBJECTIVES

The goal of this lab is to help you identify malicious software running on your computer by examining all running processes. After completing this lab, you will be able to:

◢ Identify all processes running on your computer at startup

◢ Use the Internet to determine the function of each process

MATERIALS REQUIRED

This lab requires the following:

◢ Windows Vista/XP Professional operating system

◢ Internet access

LAB PREPARATION

Before the lab begins, the instructor or lab assistant needs to do the following:

◢ Verify that Windows starts with no errors.

◢ Verify that Internet access is available.

ACTIVITY BACKGROUND

There's an old saying that a rose is a weed in the vegetable garden. Malicious software, for the same reason, is any software you don't want using up valuable resources on your computer.

20

The amount of malicious software on your computer tends to grow over time and eventually slows your computer down. It gets in your system by associating itself with software that you do want, such as updated drivers or applications. The first step in removing it is realizing it's there. In this lab, you learn to investigate all the startup processes on your computer and identify any you want to remove.

ESTIMATED COMPLETION TIME: 45 Minutes

Activity

1. Use Task Manager to list all the running processes on your machine. (You might want to refer to Lab 14.4 for a review of this process.)

2. On a separate piece of paper, make a list of each process running on the computer. How many processes are running?

   _____

3. Now reboot the computer in Safe Mode, and use Task Manager to list the running processes again. How many processes are running now?

   _____

4. Which processes didn't load when the system was running in Safe Mode?

   _____

   _____

   _____

   _____

5. Use the Internet to research each process identified in Step 4, and write a one-sentence explanation of each process on a separate piece of paper.

6. Did you find any malicious processes running? If so, list them:

   _____

   _____

   _____

7. Suppose one of the processes running on your computer is named whAgent.exe. What program is associated with this process?

   _____

8. Why isn't disabling the Lsass.exe process a good idea?

   _____

9. How could you use msconfig to temporarily disable a process?

   _____

   _____

10. List the steps you could take to remove this program from your computer:

_____

_____

_____

_____

REVIEW QUESTIONS

1. Why might antivirus and antispyware software not detect malicious software?

_____

_____

2. Why would you expect fewer processes to be running in Safe Mode?

_____

_____

3. How might a malicious process get onto your computer?

_____

_____

4. Why is it a good idea to temporarily disable a process before removing it altogether?

_____

_____

LAB 20.5 DEAL WITH A ROOTKIT

OBJECTIVES

The goal of this lab is to help you identify and remove a rootkit running on your system. After completing this lab, you will be able to:

◢ Download and install antirootkit software

◢ Use antirootkit software to scan your PC for rootkits

MATERIALS REQUIRED

This lab requires the following:

◢ Windows Vista/XP Professional operating system

◢ Internet access

◢ Ultimate Boot CD created in Lab 16.3 (optional)

20

LAB PREPARATION

Before the lab begins, the instructor or lab assistant needs to do the following:

◢ Verify that Windows starts with no errors.

◢ Verify that Internet access is available.

ACTIVITY BACKGROUND

A rootkit is a type of malware that uses sophisticated methods to hide itself on the system. They can prevent Windows components such as Windows Explorer, Task Manager, or the registry editor from displaying the rootkit processes. This stealthy behavior makes them difficult for your antivirus software to detect. If you have already tried other methods, such as antivirus software, to clean your system, and you still believe your system might be infected, you can try using antirootkit software. In this lab you will use a popular antirootkit program called Rootkit Revealer by Sysinternals.

ESTIMATED COMPLETION TIME: 60 Minutes

 Activity

1. Before running antirootkit software, it's best to double-check that your problem isn't a simple virus. For best results, run the antivirus software from another PC by temporarily moving the hard drive (see Lab 8.3) or run the antivirus software from a bootable CD. The Ultimate Boot CD created in Lab 16.3 contains several antivirus programs. Which antivirus program did you use?

_____

2. Log on as an administrator.

3. Open your browser and go to *http://technet.microsoft.com*. In the search box at the top, search for **Rootkit Revealer,** and follow the links to download the latest version. What is the latest version of Rootkit Revealer available?

_____

4. Read through the information on Rootkit Revealer and answer the following questions:

   ◢ What versions of Windows support the program?

   _____

   ◢ What are the four types of rootkits listed and how do they differ?

   _____

   _____

   _____

   _____

◢ In your own words, how does Rootkit Revealer find rootkits?

_____

_____

_____

_____

5. Download and install the program on your computer.

6. When the installation is complete, close any open applications, including your antivirus software, and launch the product. Figure 20-1 shows the Rootkit Revealer running on the Vista desktop.

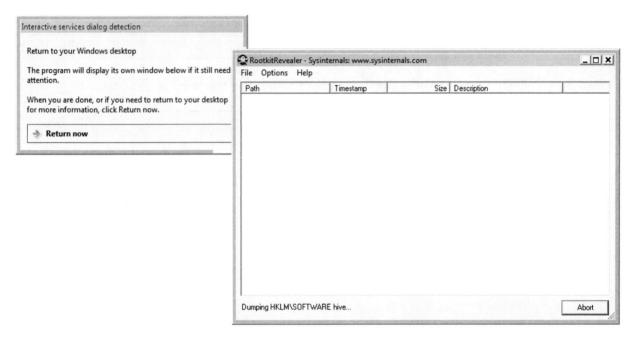

Figure 20-1   Rootkit Revealer scanning for rootkits
Courtesy: Course Technology/Cengage Learning

> **Note**   While Rootkit Revealer is running, it takes control of the system so that you cannot use your computer.

7. Did you find any discrepancies that might indicate a rootkit is running? If so, list them:

_____

_____

_____

8. When you're finished, close any open programs.

20

REVIEW QUESTIONS

1. How are rootkits different from other forms of malware?

_____

_____

2. Why does running antivirus software from another operating system do a better job?

_____

_____

3. Why are kernel-mode rootkits more dangerous than user-mode ones?

_____

_____

_____

4. Why should all other applications be closed before scanning for rootkits?

_____

_____

_____

CHAPTER 21

Supporting Notebooks

Labs included in this chapter:

- **Lab 21.1:** Examine Notebook Documentation
- **Lab 21.2:** Compare Notebooks and Desktops
- **Lab 21.3:** Manage Power-Saving Options
- **Lab 21.4:** Use Notebook Display Options
- **Lab 21.5:** Use Notebook Diagnostic Software
- **Lab 21.6:** Replace a Notebook Hard Drive
- **Lab 21.7:** Critical Thinking: Replace a Notebook LCD Panel

LAB 21.1 EXAMINE NOTEBOOK DOCUMENTATION

OBJECTIVES

The goal of this lab is to help you find documentation for a notebook on a manufacturer's Web site and become familiar with it. After completing this lab, you will be able to:

▲ Locate documentation for specific notebook computer models

▲ Download the documentation

▲ Use the documentation section to find critical information

MATERIALS REQUIRED

This lab requires the following:

▲ Internet access

LAB PREPARATION

Before the lab begins, the instructor or lab assistant needs to do the following:

▲ Verify that Internet access is available.

ACTIVITY BACKGROUND

Notebooks are designed for portability, compactness, and energy conservation, and their designs are often highly proprietary. Therefore, establishing general procedures for supporting notebooks is more difficult than for desktop computers. Often, consulting the documentation for a particular model is necessary to get information on technical specifications and support procedures. In this lab, you locate and download documentation for two different notebook computers, and then use that documentation to answer questions about each model.

ESTIMATED COMPLETION TIME: 30 Minutes

 Activity

Follow these steps to locate and download documentation:

1. Choose two notebook manufacturers listed in Table 21-1, go to their Web sites, and select one model from each to research. List your two choices here:

_____

_____

2. In the Support section of each Web site, search for documentation on the respective model and follow the directions to download the documentation. Were you able to find documentation for the two models? If not, try other models until you have located documentation for two and list them below:

_____

_____

Manufacturer	Web Site
Acer	http://global.acer.com
Apple	www.apple.com
ASUS	www.asus.com
Dell	www.dell.com
Gateway	www.gateway.com
Hewlett-Packard	www.hp.com
Lenovo	www.lenovo.com
Samsung	www.samsung.com
Sony	www.sonystyle.com/vaio
Toshiba	www.toshiba.com

Table 21-1   Notebook manufacturers

3. Using the documentation you found, answer the following questions for your first model. If you can't answer a question because the information isn't included in the documentation, write "information unavailable."

  ◢ What type of processor does the notebook use and how much RAM is installed?

  _____

  ◢ What operating system is currently installed on the notebook?

  _____

  ◢ Could you download or save the documentation locally, or did you have to view it on the company's Web site?

  _____

  ◢ Does the notebook offer Quick Launch keys for commonly used applications? If so, can you customize them? How? If they can't be customized, what buttons are offered, and which applications do they launch?

  _____

  _____

  _____

  ◢ List the functions assigned to keys F1 through F4:

  _____

  _____

  _____

  _____

21

◢ Does the notebook have a sleep or hibernation mode? If so, how do you activate it? How does activating this mode differ from shutting down the computer?

_____

_____

_____

◢ What other types of downloads are offered besides the manual?

_____

_____

◢ What type of optical storage (CD, CD-RW, DVD, and so forth) does the notebook offer?

_____

◢ What type of networking (modem, NIC, infrared port, wireless LAN port, and so forth) comes built in?

_____

_____

◢ What upgrades, such as RAM, hard drive, or battery, are available?

_____

_____

4. Using the documentation you found, answer the following questions for your second model. If you can't answer a question because the information isn't included in the documentation, write "information unavailable."

◢ What type of processor does the notebook use and how much RAM is installed?

_____

◢ What operating system is currently installed on the notebook?

_____

◢ Could you download or save the documentation locally, or did you have to view it on the company's Web site?

_____

◢ Does the notebook offer Quick Launch keys for commonly used applications? If so, can you customize them? How? If they can't be customized, what buttons are offered, and which applications do they launch?

_____

_____

_____

◢ List the functions assigned to keys F1 through F4:

_____

_____

_____

_____

◢ Does the notebook have a sleep or hibernation mode? If so, how do you activate it? How does activating this mode differ from shutting down the computer?

_____

_____

_____

◢ What other types of downloads are offered besides the manual?

_____

_____

◢ What type of optical storage (CD, CD-RW, DVD, and so forth) does the notebook offer?

_____

◢ What type of networking (modem, NIC, infrared port, wireless LAN port, and so forth) comes built in?

_____

_____

◢ What upgrades, such as RAM, hard drive, or battery are available?

_____

_____

Alternate Activity

If you have access to a notebook computer, do the following:

1. Go to the manufacturer's Web site for your notebook computer and download the user manual, if available. List other downloads that are available:

_____

_____

_____

21

2. From the list of available downloads, choose a device driver or system update for your notebook. Download and install it following the instructions on the site. List the driver or update and the steps you took to install it on your notebook:

_____

_____

_____

_____

_____

REVIEW QUESTIONS

1. On a manufacturer's Web site, where do you usually find support and documentation information?

_____

2. For which model was it easiest to find documentation? Which manufacturer site did you think was the most user friendly and, in general, offered the best support?

_____

_____

3. Besides the questions you researched in the lab, what other type of information is available in the manuals you reviewed?

_____

_____

4. Of the notebooks you researched, which one would you purchase? Explain your answer:

_____

_____

LAB 21.2 COMPARE NOTEBOOKS AND DESKTOPS

OBJECTIVES

The goal of this lab is to help you compare the specifications and costs for notebook and desktop computers. After completing this lab, you will be able to:

◢ Compile a list of specifications for a computer according to its purpose

◢ Locate a desktop computer and a notebook computer with similar specifications

◢ Compare the price of a desktop computer to a similar notebook computer and decide which you would purchase

MATERIALS REQUIRED

This lab requires the following:

◢ Internet access

◢ Access to a printer (optional)

LAB PREPARATION

Before the lab begins, the instructor or lab assistant needs to do the following:

◢ Verify that Internet access is available.

ACTIVITY BACKGROUND

When you shop for a computer, your purchasing decisions are generally driven by questions such as the following: For what will the computer be used? What features are required to accomplish your goals? What features would be nice to have but aren't essential? What features are you willing to compromise on to gain others? What future needs do you anticipate? If you understand your needs before you start shopping, you're less likely to regret your purchase.

One of the most basic decisions is whether to choose a notebook computer or a desktop. Unlike desktops, notebooks are portable; however, to make notebooks portable, manufacturers often sacrifice performance, storage space, or other features. In addition, you usually pay more for a notebook than for a desktop computer with comparable features. In this lab, you compile a list of requirements for a computer, locate a notebook and desktop computer with those features, and compare the two systems.

ESTIMATED COMPLETION TIME: 30 Minutes

Activity

1. Determine your requirements by answering the following questions:

   ◢ For what will the computer be used? (Possible uses include office applications, video playback, high-end gaming, and software development.)

   _____

   ◢ What features are required to make the computer usable for its intended purpose? Include in your list the amount of memory and hard drive space you want. (Some features you might consider include wireless support, display or screen type, software packages supported, PC card support, and external device support.)

   _____

   _____

   _____

   _____

   _____

21

◢ List any additional features you would like but don't require:

_____

_____

_____

_____

2. Use computer manufacturer Web sites (such as the ones listed in Table 21-1) or comparison Web sites (such as *www.cnet.com* or *www.pricewatch.com*) to find one notebook and one desktop computer that fulfill as many of your requirements as possible and are as similar to each other as possible. Summarize your findings by filling in Table 21-2. If possible, print the Web pages supporting your gathered information.

Features	Desktop Computer	Notebook Computer
Manufacturer and model		
Processor type and frequency		
Memory installed		
Hard drive space		
Operating system		
Video card		
Optical drive		
Display size		
External ports		
Preinstalled applications		
Cost		

Table 21-2 Desktop and notebook computer specifications

3. Which features are upgradable in a desktop system? Which ones are upgradable in a notebook?

_____

_____

4. Based on your research and the requirements you listed in Step 1, would you purchase a desktop computer or a notebook? Explain your answer:

_____

_____

_____

REVIEW QUESTIONS

1. In general, which computer was more expensive: the desktop or the notebook? Is the less expensive one always the better value?

   _____

   _____

2. What features varied the most between desktops and notebooks?

   _____

   _____

3. Did future upgradability influence your decision?

   _____

   _____

4. Did you change your requirements or expectations based on the available products? Explain your answer:

   _____

   _____

   _____

5. Was it easier to find a comparable desktop and notebook from the same manufacturer or from a different manufacturer? Why or why not?

   _____

   _____

   _____

LAB 21.3 MANAGE POWER-SAVING OPTIONS

OBJECTIVES

The goal of this lab is to demonstrate the effect that power-management features have on the running time of a notebook battery. After completing this lab, you will be able to:

▲ Manage notebook power-saving features

▲ Troubleshoot power problems

MATERIALS REQUIRED

This lab requires the following:

▲ A Windows Vista/XP notebook computer

▲ Internet access

21

LAB PREPARATION

Before the lab begins, the instructor or lab assistant needs to do the following:

◢ Verify that Windows starts with no errors.

◢ Verify that Internet access is available.

ACTIVITY BACKGROUND

Many factors affect the running time or battery life of a notebook PC. A typical lithium ion notebook battery might last anywhere between one and four hours of normal use. As you might expect, however, "normal use" is a subjective term. The way you use your notebook can affect battery life dramatically. For instance, editing text in a word processor doesn't require much power compared with playing a DVD. The word processor uses only a little processor time and occasionally reads or writes to the hard drive. Playing a DVD is processor intensive and requires powering the laser in the drive, thus requiring more power than the word processor.

What the notebook does when you stop using it for a time also affects battery life. For instance, if you don't use the notebook for 10 minutes, it might go into hibernation mode automatically to conserve power. Notebooks also have a few additional power-management features to extend battery life during inactivity and to protect data when the battery charge becomes low. Some of these features depend on the notebook being able to accurately judge how much life is left in the battery. In this lab, you explore how power management and battery life are related.

ESTIMATED COMPLETION TIME: 30–90 Minutes

 Activity

1. Examine your notebook computer's CMOS setup utility (see Lab 5.1) and the Power Options icon (Power Management in XP) in Control Panel. Usually, a computer's BIOS offers a wider range of options for defining a power-management profile than does Windows. Fill in the following chart to compare the power-management options offered in BIOS and Windows:

Power-Management Options and Settings	In BIOS	In Windows

Although the two power-management systems might work together, to avoid possible conflict, Microsoft recommends using BIOS power management as the preferred method if BIOS power management conforms to ACPI standards. These standards have been set by a group of manufacturers, including Microsoft, Intel, and Compaq.

In addition to the BIOS features you just explored, notebooks often have features or settings that allow the computer to shut down or suspend activity if the battery is about to run out of power. But how does the computer know when power is about to run out? Electronically programmable read-only memory (EPROM) is often included in the battery assembly to inform the computer about remaining battery life.

The following steps explain the basic procedure for calibrating a battery's EPROM. For specific steps for your notebook, consult its documentation or search the manufacturer's Web site.

1. Verify that your notebook has a fully charged battery attached to AC power.

2. Enter the CMOS setup utility and select the **Power Management** section.

3. In the Power Management section, disable the **Power Savings** option so that the computer doesn't attempt to save power during the calibration process.

4. In the Power Management section, disable any **Suspend on Low Battery** options to prevent interference with calibration.

5. In the Power Management section, select the **Battery Calibration** option. A warning message indicates that the calibration should be carried out only with a fully charged battery and prompts you to confirm that you want to continue.

6. Remove the AC power, and then immediately press **Y** or **Enter** to continue. A message displays the estimated remaining battery life. In a real-life situation, when you actually need to calibrate your notebook's battery, this information would likely be incorrect.

7. Wait for the battery to drain, which might take more than an hour.

8. The manufacturer might specify that the battery should be left to cool for a period after it is drained and the notebook switches off. When appropriate, reattach AC power, boot the laptop, and enter CMOS setup.

9. Select the **Power Management** section, and then select the **Battery Reset** option. This option tells the EPROM that the battery is at (or very near) zero charge and takes you back to the Power Management section of CMOS.

10. Reapply your preferred power management settings, and then save and exit CMOS setup. The battery is now calibrated so that the related power-management and suspend features will work correctly.

If you have access to a notebook and the permission of your instructor, do the following to calibrate the battery:

1. Locate documentation (in the user manual or on the Web) that explains how to calibrate the battery. Note how these steps differ from the ones listed previously:

   _____

   _____

   _____

   _____

   _____

2. Follow the specific steps for your notebook to calibrate the battery. (Do *not* attempt this procedure unless you have the specific steps; otherwise, you might do damage to the notebook or battery.)

Some factors can prevent power management from functioning as intended. For instance, word-processing programs often include an auto-save feature that continually saves changes to a document at specific intervals. This feature is intended to safeguard against lost work but tends to interfere with hard disk power-down

21

settings. Many screen savers cause similar effects and can prevent a computer from entering or exiting standby or suspend modes. Now, using a combination of Windows help and research on the Internet, answer the following questions:

1. When does your computer enter hibernation and how much disk space does this require?

   _____

2. When running off the battery, how long does the computer wait before turning off the display?

   _____

3. What effect does closing the lid have on your notebook?

   _____

4. Which power plan (or scheme) are you currently using?

   _____

5. What action(s) will bring your computer out of hibernation?

   _____

REVIEW QUESTIONS

1. What types of activity might decrease the battery life of a fully charged battery more quickly than reading a document or spreadsheet? Give three examples:

   _____

   _____

   _____

2. When wouldn't you want to use aggressive power management on a notebook computer?

   _____

   _____

   _____

3. Should BIOS power management always be used with Windows Power Management? Why or why not?

   _____

   _____

4. If you configure Windows on a notebook to hibernate after 30 minutes of inactivity, but the notebook remains functioning after that period of time, what might be the problem?

   _____

   _____

   _____

5. How do some programs, such as word processors, interfere with your computer's power-saving options?

_____

_____

_____

LAB 21.4 USE NOTEBOOK DISPLAY OPTIONS

OBJECTIVES

The goal of this lab is to help you learn how to support notebook video. Support technicians are often called on to support a variety of computers and peripherals; therefore, it's important to learn to use more than one type of notebook. If possible, perform this lab using more than one type of notebook and with more than one operating system. After completing this lab, you will be able to:

◢ Change the display settings

◢ Use an external monitor or video projector

◢ Communicate with difficult users

MATERIALS REQUIRED

This lab requires the following:

◢ Notebook computer running Windows XP or Vista

◢ Second notebook computer (optional)

◢ External monitor or projector

LAB PREPARATION

Before the lab begins, the instructor or lab assistant needs to do the following:

◢ Verify that the notebook computer and external video device are available and working.

ACTIVITY BACKGROUND

PC support technicians often find themselves needing to respond to emergencies created by the lack of preparation by others. As you respond to these types of technical challenges, experience helps! Good communication and professional behavior are also needed to help calm nervous users in desperate situations.

ESTIMATED COMPLETION TIME: 60 Minutes

Activity

1. Sharon has worked for two weeks to put together a PowerPoint presentation to support her important speech to the executives in her company. The presentation is scheduled for 9:00 this Friday morning. On Monday, she requests a projector in the conference room by Thursday afternoon, so that she'll have plenty of time to make sure all is working before people start to arrive around 8:45 on Friday morning. Late Thursday evening, she puts the

21

finishing touches on the presentation and prints 25 copies, more than enough for the expected 20 attendees. She arrives at work about 8:00 AM the next day and heads for the conference room to hook up her notebook to the video projector. So far, so good. But when she arrives in the conference room with printouts, notebook, and coffee in hand, she finds no projector! She calls technical support (that's you) to fix the problem. You, too, have just arrived at work and are busy making yourself a cup of coffee when you answer the phone to hear an angry, frantic user tell you in no uncertain terms you've screwed up and need to get down here immediately with a projector. You don't recall ever receiving her request. What do you say on the phone and what questions do you ask?

_____

_____

_____

_____

2. You find a projector and bring it to the conference room. Sharon has powered up her Windows notebook and opened the PowerPoint presentation. She turns her back to you as you set the projector down, making it clear to you that she is not in a friendly mood. You turn to leave the room. "Wait!" Sharon says, "Aren't you going to connect it?" In your organization, you know that users are expected to manage their own projectors and laptops for these presentations. Obviously, Sharon is not technically prepared. With only 15 minutes before the presentation starts, what do you say and do?

_____

_____

Listed below are the steps to connect the projector and set up the display so that PowerPoint is displayed on Sharon's notebook and also on the projector. (In a lab environment where you don't have a projector, use a monitor to practice these steps.)

1. Physically attach the second display to the notebook. What kind of connector does it use?

_____

2. On your particular notebook, what key do you use along with the Fn key to toggle the display between video devices?

_____

_____

3. For your notebook, list other keys that can be used along with the Fn key and the purpose of each keystroke combination:

_____

_____

Notes When connecting a notebook to a projector, know that the projector must support the screen resolution used by the notebook. If the projector shows a blank screen, try a different screen resolution setting on the notebook.

4. If Sharon pauses too long during the presentation, the screen saver might activate and cause the screen to go blank or the system might go into standby mode. How do you set the power options and display settings so that these interruptions to the presentation won't happen?

_____

_____

5. Sharon decides she needs her Windows desktop available on the notebook's screen at the same time the PowerPoint presentation is displayed on the projector, but she has no clue how to do this. List the steps to make this adjustment:

_____

_____

_____

_____

_____

6. Throughout this entire ordeal, Sharon has yet to say anything friendly or positive to you, not even one word of thanks. Your frustration is growing, but so far you've kept your cool. Executives begin to fill the room. Nervously, Sharon notices more than 20 people are present, and it's still only five minutes to nine. She turns to you and sheepishly asks, "Would you do me a favor? Please make me 10 more copies of this presentation." How do you respond?

_____

_____

_____

_____

7. If you're working with other groups, try working through this scenario while others take notes on your performance. Were you communicating well, being a good listener, and doing your best to calm the user and respond appropriately? Ask the other student to comment on your conversation with the user and record his or her comments below:

_____

_____

_____

_____

21

REVIEW QUESTIONS

1. Based on the other student's comments, how can you improve your communication skills?

   _____

   _____

2. Notebooks vary in the key combination used to toggle video. Without having a user manual available, describe how you would figure out which key combination to use on a notebook:

   _____

   _____

3. What steps are used to extend the Windows desktop onto an external projector or monitor?

   _____

   _____

4. When troubleshooting an LCD panel that is giving problems or is blank, how can using an external monitor help you?

   _____

   _____

LAB 21.5 USE NOTEBOOK DIAGNOSTIC SOFTWARE

OBJECTIVES

The goal of this lab is to help you learn to research and use diagnostic software to troubleshoot problems with notebook computers. After completing this lab, you will be able to:

◢ Research and use diagnostic software on a notebook computer

◢ Research replacing a part on a notebook

MATERIALS REQUIRED

This lab requires the following:

◢ A working notebook computer

◢ Internet access on this or another computer

LAB PREPARATION

Before the lab begins, the instructor or lab assistant needs to do the following:

◢ Verify that a working notebook is available for each student or workgroup.

◢ Verify that Internet access is available.

ACTIVITY BACKGROUND

Servicing notebooks is different from servicing desktop systems in many respects. One difference is that because notebooks are more proprietary in design, you are more dependent on tools and manuals provided by the notebook manufacturer than you are when working with desktops. Some manufacturers provide excellent service manuals that you can download from their Web sites. On video hosting sites such as *www.youtube.com*, you can also find good step-by-step tutorials.

Many notebook manufacturers store diagnostic software on the notebook's hard drive that can be accessed at startup. This software can be used to test key hardware components and can be useful when troubleshooting a notebook. In this lab, you learn about service manuals, diagnostic software, and other tools that are available and how to access and use them.

ESTIMATED COMPLETION TIME: 60 Minutes

 Activity

You run a small PC repair shop, and Janice comes in with a notebook computer that has been dropped. The notebook is an HP Pavilion ze4145 with model number F4893H that is not under warranty. She tells you that she thinks the entire computer is useless because it appeared "dead" when she turned it on. She's especially upset over data on the hard drive that she believes has been lost.

1. After you fill out the customer intake form, you are now ready to face the problem. List the first three things you should do to try to save the data and troubleshoot the problem:

   _____

   _____

   _____

2. After you plug in the AC adapter and turn on the laptop, you discover the lights on the notebook are lit and you hear the fan running, but the LCD panel is blank. When you connect an external monitor, you see the Windows XP logon screen. Janice breathes a sign of relief. What do you do now?

   _____

   _____

You suspect the LCD panel is broken, but you decide it would be a good idea to run hardware diagnostic software to check for other hardware problems. Diagnostic software is written specifically for a particular brand notebook and is often stored in a hidden utility partition on the hard drive or on the recovery CD that comes with the notebook. The software is accessed by pressing a key at startup or by booting from a recovery CD. Also know that, for some notebooks, the diagnostic software in the hidden partition is disabled by default and must be enabled in CMOS setup before you can use it.

Most notebook manufacturers provide diagnostic software hidden on the hard drive that can be accessed at startup by pressing a certain key. Do the following to find out about diagnostic software and how to use it:

1. Go to the Hewlett-Packard (HP) Web site (*www.hp.com*) and download the service manual for this notebook. What is the name of the downloaded PDF file?

   _____

2. What key do you press at startup to access the diagnostic software stored on this notebook?

   _____

21

3. What two types of tests can you run using the e-DiagTools software?

_____

_____

4. If the hard drive is broken, what other method can you use to run the e-DiagTools software?

_____

_____

5. After you repair this notebook, what three types of tests docs HP recommend you run to verify the repair?

_____

_____

_____

6. Based on the information in the service manual, what is the part number of the LCD panel?

_____

7. What is the price of the LCD panel if you buy it from the HP Web site?

_____

8. Research the service manual and list the high-level steps to replace the LCD panel:

_____

_____

_____

_____

_____

9. Before you commit to replacing a notebook's internal component, you need to be confident that you have enough information and directions to open the notebook, access the part, and reassemble the notebook. Do you think you have enough information to do the repair? Why or why not?

_____

_____

10. If you don't think you have enough information, what is your next step?

_____

HP offers excellent diagnostic software, but not all notebook manufacturers do that. Also, HP makes its notebook service manuals available on the Web, but many notebook manufacturers release their service manuals only to authorized service centers. For these manufacturers, you can sometimes use an Internet search engine to find alternative tutorials and advice. Using your lab notebook, available documentation for the notebook, and the Internet, answer these questions:

1. What is the brand and model of your notebook? What is the Web site of your notebook manufacturer?

   _____

   _____

2. Can you obtain the service manual for your notebook? If so, from where?

   _____

   _____

3. Does your notebook have diagnostic software? If so, how is it accessed? List all the methods:

   _____

   _____

   _____

   _____

4. If you have diagnostic software, how does this software compare to the HP e-DiagTools software?

   _____

   _____

5. If you have diagnostic software, run it using the most thorough test that the software offers. List the results of the test:

   _____

   _____

REVIEW QUESTIONS

1. What kinds of information can be found in a technical service manual?

   _____

   _____

2. Why would you want to run diagnostic software after you have repaired a notebook and verified the repaired component does work?

   _____

   _____

3. Before you purchase an internal notebook part to replace a broken one, what should you verify?

   _____

21

4. List three places where you might find diagnostic software designed specifically for a particular notebook:

_____

_____

_____

5. List three troubleshooting situations in which diagnostic software might be useful:

_____

_____

_____

LAB 21.6 REPLACE A NOTEBOOK HARD DRIVE

OBJECTIVES

The goal of this lab is to show you the process of replacing a hard drive in a notebook computer. After completing this lab, you will be able to:

◢ Locate the hard drive in a notebook computer

◢ Remove the hard drive from a notebook computer

◢ Replace the hard drive in a notebook computer

MATERIALS REQUIRED

This lab requires the following:

◢ A notebook computer or Internet access

◢ Printer access

◢ A PC toolkit with antistatic ground strap

◢ Additional smaller screwdrivers, if necessary

LAB PREPARATION

Before the lab begins, the instructor or lab assistant needs to do the following:

◢ Verify that Internet access is available.

ACTIVITY BACKGROUND

Hard disk drives are by nature delicate devices. Dropping one, even a few inches, can cause permanent damage to the read/write heads, platter surfaces, or both. Notebook systems are, of course, often moved and commonly subjected to forces that most other hard drives never encounter. Although drives intended for notebook systems are designed to be resistant to movement and shock, they are still more likely to fail than any other notebook component. In this lab, you remove a hard drive from a notebook computer, and then reinstall the same hard drive. If you don't have access to a notebook, skip to the alternate activity at the end of this lab.

Hard drives designed for notebook computers tend to be 50 percent to 75 percent more expensive than the standard 3.5-inch drives of comparable capacity for desktop computers. Also, the majority of newer notebooks support most 2.5-inch drives designed for notebooks, but sometimes a notebook computer requires a proprietary hard drive. For these reasons, researching your replacement options before you purchase a new drive is important. Read the documentation that came with your notebook to determine what drives it supports. If this information isn't available in the documentation, search the manufacturer's Web site. For the purpose of this lab, you remove the existing drive, and then reinstall the same drive. The steps for your notebook might be slightly different from the procedures in this lab, so make sure you study the documentation before you begin.

ESTIMATED COMPLETION TIME: 30 Minutes

Activity

1. What are the manufacturer and model of your notebook computer?

   _____

2. Based on the notebook's documentation or information on the manufacturer's Web site, what type of hard drive can be used to replace the existing hard drive? Be as specific as you can:

   _____

   _____

3. Search the Internet for a replacement hard drive that meets your notebook's requirements. Print the Web page showing the specifications and cost for the drive. How much space does the hard drive have?

   _____

4. Look for specific directions (in the documentation or on the Web site) for removing and replacing your notebook's hard drive. If you find any, summarize those directions here. (If you're using the Web site as your source of information, print any relevant Web pages.)

   _____

   _____

   _____

   _____

Follow these general steps to remove the hard drive from a notebook computer. Note that these directions might not list every step necessary for your model. Refer to specific directions in the documentation or the manufacturer's Web site, as needed.

1. Remove the main battery or batteries and, if necessary, unplug the computer from the AC adapter. Close the screen and turn the computer so that the bottom is facing up.
2. Locate and remove the access panel or component enclosing the drive bay. In many notebooks, the hard drive is located beneath a floppy drive or other removable device, as shown in Figure 21-1.

21

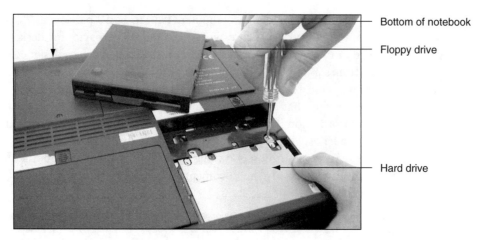

Figure 21-1   Remove the floppy or optical drive to reveal the hard drive cavity
Courtesy: Course Technology/Cengage Learning

3. After you have accessed the drive, determine how it's secured in the system. It's commonly attached to a frame or "cradle" with small screws, and the cradle is often attached directly to the system chassis. This cradle helps locate and support the drive inside the drive bay. Remove the screws securing the cradle.

4. In most notebooks, data cables don't connect the hard drive to the motherboard, as is the case with desktop computers. Instead, a hard drive connects to the notebook's motherboard by way of an edge connector, similar to those on expansion cards in desktop computers. This type of direct connection has two advantages. First, it improves reliability because it reduces the total number of connection points; fewer connection points mean fewer connections that could shake loose as the notebook is moved around in daily use. The second advantage is that the lack of data cables reduces the notebook's overall size and weight. To remove the drive-cradle assembly, slide the cradle away from the connector. Slide the assembly back until all pins are clear of the connector. When the pins are clear, lift the assembly straight up out of the drive bay.

5. Note the orientation of the drive in the cradle so that when you reinstall the drive, you can mount it in the same direction. Remove the screws securing the drive in the cradle, and then remove the drive.

Follow these general steps to reinstall the hard drive in the notebook computer. Note that these directions might not list every step necessary for your model. Refer to specific directions in the documentation or the manufacturer's Web site, as needed.

1. If necessary, configure the jumper settings to indicate master or slave. Place the drive in the cradle so that the pins are oriented correctly, and then secure it with screws.

2. Set the drive-cradle assembly straight down into the drive bay. Gently slide the assembly to the connector, and verify that the pins are aligned correctly with the connector. Slide the assembly until the drive is fully seated in the connector. The cradle should now align with the holes in the chassis. If the holes don't align, you should remove the assembly, loosen the drive-retaining screws, and adjust the drive's position in the cradle. Repeat this process until the drive is fully seated so that there's no room for it to move after the cradle is secured. When the assembly is seated, secure it with screws.

3. Replace any drives or access covers you removed to get at the hard drive.

4. Reinstall any batteries and reconnect to AC power, if necessary. As with any other hard drive, a notebook drive must be recognized by BIOS correctly, and then partitioned and formatted before it can be used. This process isn't necessary in this lab because you haven't installed a new hard drive.

Alternate Activity

If you don't have access to a notebook computer, follow these steps:

1. Using the documentation for one of the notebooks you selected in Lab 21.1 as your source, write in the space below the specific requirements for a replacement hard drive:

   _____

   _____

2. Search the Internet for information on replacement hard drives, and print the Web page showing the correct specifications for a replacement hard drive. What is the cost of the drive? How much space does the drive have?

   _____

3. Locate the steps for replacing the hard drive. To find this information, use the manuals you downloaded in Lab 21.1, the manufacturers' Web sites, and other Internet resources (such as Web sites for manufacturers of replacement notebook hard drives). How do the steps you found differ from the steps in this lab? Note the differences here:

   _____

   _____

   _____

   _____

   _____

   _____

   _____

   _____

REVIEW QUESTIONS

1. Why should you research hard drives thoroughly when replacing one in a notebook computer?

   _____

   _____

2. Why is cabling commonly not included in notebook systems?

   _____

   _____

3. How was the installation procedure for your computer different from the one in this lab?

   _____

   _____

21

4. Suppose you need to install a hard drive in a notebook that doesn't include an access panel for the hard drive. Where should you look for the hard drive inside the notebook?

_____

_____

5. What do you have to do in CMOS setup before a new hard drive can be used?

_____

_____

LAB 21.7 CRITICAL THINKING: REPLACE A NOTEBOOK LCD PANEL

OBJECTIVES

The goal of this lab is to help you troubleshoot hardware problems with a notebook's LCD panel. After completing this lab, you will be able to:

◢ Identify hardware problems with the LCD panel

◢ Replace LCD panel components

MATERIALS REQUIRED

This lab requires the following:

◢ A notebook computer that can be disassembled

◢ The notebook's technical reference manual that contains instructions for disassembly

◢ Internet access on this or another computer

LAB PREPARATION

Before the lab begins, the instructor or lab assistant needs to do the following:

◢ Provide each student or workgroup with a notebook computer that can be disassembled.

◢ Provide a technical reference manual that matches the notebook computer being disassembled.

◢ Verify Internet access is available.

ACTIVITY BACKGROUND

The A+ exams require that you know about replacing a few internal notebook components. Computer components that field technicians are expected to be able to replace are called field replaceable units (FRUs). The internal FRUs for a notebook computer might include the hard drive, RAM memory optical drive, floppy drive, LCD panel assembly, Mini PCI card, motherboard, CPU, keyboard, PC Card socket, sound card, and battery pack. Depending on the notebook, the LCD panel assembly FRU might be the entire LCD assembly or the individual parts, which are the LCD panel itself, the inverter, and the video card (if one is present). Notebook computers vary drastically in the way they are assembled and disassembled. As a PC support technician, you are not required to know how to disassemble every brand and model of notebook. However, if you have a technical reference manual that includes the steps to disassemble a notebook to replace a component, you should be able to do the job. This lab gives you that information and experience. This lab uses an older IBM ThinkPad X20. However, you will most likely use a different notebook with its own reference manual.

ESTIMATED COMPLETION TIME: 3 Hours

 Activity

Joseph brings you his notebook computer complaining that it is dead, and asks you to repair it. Before you service any notebook, always ask these questions:

1. Does it hold important data not backed up?

2. What recently happened?

3. What must I do to reproduce the problem?

4. Is the notebook under warranty?

In asking these four questions, you find out the notebook does hold important data and that it is not under warranty. You also find out that Joseph allowed a coworker to carry his notebook from one building to another along with a bunch of other computers and components. Joseph suspects the coworker was not careful when handling the notebook. The first time Joseph turned on the notebook after this move, he found it "dead."

You're now ready to investigate the problem. You plug in the notebook, turn it on, and make these observations: The LCD panel appears blank, but the notebook is not "dead." The keyboard lights are lit and you hear the sound of the fan when you first turn on the computer. You look very carefully at the LCD panel and notice a faint display that you cannot read. You next try to use the keys to increase the LCD panel brightness. Even when you have increased the brightness as far as possible, you still can't read what's on the screen. Next, you plug in an external monitor and use the appropriate keys to direct video output to this device. You can now read the display on the external monitor. What is the next very important thing you should do?

_____

_____

_____

You're now ready to discuss the repairs with Joseph. The notebook does not use a video card, so the two FRUs that apply to video are the LCD panel and the inverter. It is likely a damaged inverter is causing the dim display. The price of the inverter is minimal compared to the value of the notebook. However, you make sure that Joseph understands the entire LCD panel might need replacing. Because the notebook is several years old, you suspect that replacing the LCD panel will cost more than the notebook is worth.

Research and answer these questions:

1. What is the brand and model of your notebook?

_____

_____

2. What is the price of the video inverter?

_____

21

3. What is the price of the LCD panel? Print the Web page supporting your answer.

4. What is the value of this notebook? Determining the value of a notebook can be a little difficult and is usually a best guess. Try searching auction sites such as eBay.com for a match or near match.

5. What sources of information did you use to determine the value of the notebook?

After discussing the price of components and his options, Joseph decides to have you try replacing the inverter. If that doesn't solve the problem, then he plans to buy a new notebook. After purchasing the inverter, you're ready to replace this component. Listed below are the steps to replace the inverter in the ThinkPad X20. The steps for your notebook will vary.

1. Power down the notebook, unplug it, and remove the battery.

2. Following directions in the technical reference manual, the next step is to remove the keyboard. Remove four screws on the bottom of the notebook. These four screws are marked by two triangles imprinted beside each screw. Be sure to keep removed screws well organized and labeled so you will later be able to put the right screws in the right holes when you reassemble.

3. Push up on the keyboard from the bottom and carefully lift the keyboard out of the cavity, as shown in Figure 21-2.

> 📝 **Notes** Be careful as you work. Many parts are plastic and are fragile. If you force them, they might snap or break.

Figure 21-2   Lift up on the keyboard to remove it
Courtesy: Course Technology/Cengage Learning

4. Remove the keyboard ribbon cable from the notebook so you can lift the keyboard out and place it out of your way. See Figure 21-3. Don't stack components as you remove them.

Figure 21-3   Disconnect the keyboard cable and then remove the keyboard
Courtesy: Course Technology/Cengage Learning

5. You're now ready to remove the LCD assembly. Begin by removing two screws on the back of the notebook near the LCD panel hinges. Next, remove the hinge covers. You can then remove the two screws holding the LCD panel to the notebook. As shown in Figure 21-4, disconnect the video ribbon cable from the notebook and lift the LCD panel from the notebook.

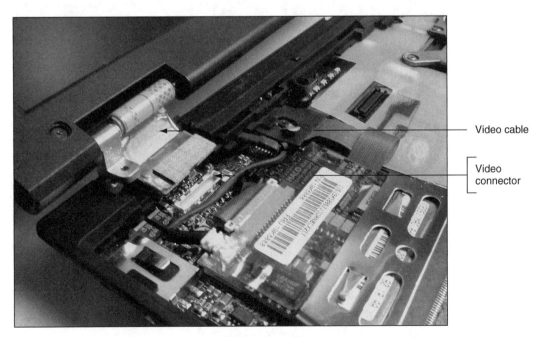

Figure 21-4   Disconnect the video cable and then remove the LCD panel
Courtesy: Course Technology/Cengage Learning

21

6. By removing the screws along the sides and bottom of the LCD panel assembly, you can carefully lift the LCD panel out of its enclosure to expose the inverter, as shown in Figure 21-5. Also shown in the figure is the new inverter. Before proceeding, make sure your new component will fit the space and the connectors match. This new inverter is not an exact match, but it does fit.

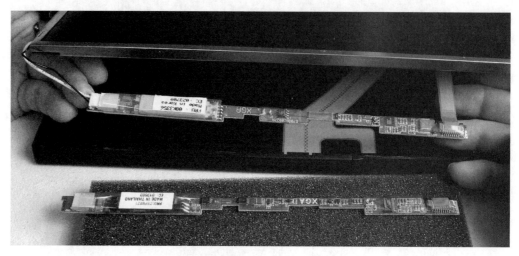

Figure 21-5 The inverter is exposed and is compared to the new one
Courtesy: Course Technology/Cengage Learning

7. Disconnect the old inverter and install the new one. When disconnecting the ribbon cable from the old inverter, notice you must first lift up on the lock holding the ZIF connector in place, as shown in Figure 21-6.

Figure 21-6 Lift up on the ZIF connector locking mechanism before removing the ribbon cable
Courtesy: Course Technology/Cengage Learning

8. Install the new inverter.
9. Reassemble the LCD panel assembly. Make sure the assembly is put together with a tight fit so that all screws line up well.
10. Reattach the LCD panel assembly to the notebook.

11. Replace the keyboard and replace the four screws on the bottom of the notebook holding the keyboard in place.

12. Plug in the AC adapter and power up the notebook.

REVIEW QUESTIONS

1. What are the three FRUs of the video subsystem?

2. Of the three video FRUs, which one is optional?

3. When replacing the LCD panel on any notebook, is it always necessary to first remove the hard drive?

4. To protect the user's investments in time and money, before disassembling a notebook, what two very important questions should a technician always ask the user?

5. Generally, if a notebook display has a broken inverter, is it worth replacing?

21

Supporting Printers

Labs included in this chapter:

LAB 22.1 INSTALL AND SHARE A LOCAL PRINTER

OBJECTIVES

The goal of this lab is to help you install and share a printer. After completing this lab, you will be able to:

◢ Install a local printer on a computer

◢ Share a local printer with other users on the network

◢ Using another computer on the network, install and use a shared network printer

MATERIALS REQUIRED

This lab requires the following:

◢ A printer and its printer drivers

◢ Two or more Windows Vista/XP computers connected to a network

◢ Windows installation CD/DVD or installation files

◢ A workgroup of 3 to 4 students

LAB PREPARATION

Before the lab begins, the instructor or lab assistant needs to do the following:

◢ Verify that Windows starts with no errors.

◢ Provide each student with access to the Windows installation files, if needed.

ACTIVITY BACKGROUND

A printer can be connected to and dedicated to one PC (called a local printer), or it can be shared with other PCs on the network (called a network printer). For a printer to be shared on a Windows operating system, it must be physically connected to and installed on one computer and then shared with others in the same Windows workgroup. The computer with the printer physically connected to it must have File and Printer Sharing for Microsoft Networks installed. In Windows XP, the computers on the network using this printer must have the Client for Microsoft Networks component installed. In most cases, installing both components on all computers is easier. In this lab, you install and share a printer in a workgroup, and then use the shared printer on the network.

ESTIMATED COMPLETION TIME: 45 Minutes

 Activity

First you must physically attach the printer to one of the computers. Follow these steps.

1. With the computer off, connect the printer cable to the USB or parallel port on your computer, turn on the printer, and then boot the computer. What make and model of printer are you using and what kind of port does it use to connect?

_____

_____

2. If you are using a USB printer in Windows Vista, the printer drivers will most likely be automatically installed. In XP, if the Add Printer Wizard starts, click **Next** and then skip to Step 4.

3. If the drivers don't automatically install or the wizard doesn't start, click **Start, Control Panel, Hardware and Sound,** and **Printers**. Click the **Add a printer** button on the toolbar, and click **Add a local printer**. (In XP, click **Start, Printers and Faxes, Add a printer,** and **Next**. Select **Local printer attached to this computer** and click **Next**.)

4. Select the Port appropriate to your printer, and then click **Next**.

5. A list of manufacturers and printer models is displayed. Select the manufacturer and the model from the list, and then click **Next**. If your printer isn't listed and you have the correct printer driver on disk or CD, click **Have Disk**. Keep in mind that drivers designed for one Windows operating system might not work for a later version of Windows, so you need to make sure you have the correct drivers for your computer's version of Windows. (You can download printer driver files from the printer manufacturer's Web site.) If you select a manufacturer and model from the Windows list, a dialog box might open where you can specify the location of the Windows setup files. In that case, insert the Windows setup CD or select another location for the files.

6. The next window asks for a name for the printer. This name appears later in the list of available printers. Accept the default name Windows provides or enter your own, and then click **Next** to continue. What is the name of your printer?

   _____

7. In Windows XP, click **Share name** to indicate that this printer will be shared with others on a network, and then click **Next** to continue. If the Location and Comment window is displayed, you can describe the location of the printer, or leave it blank and click **Next**.

8. Click **Print a test page**. (In XP, click **Yes** to print the test page and then click **Next**.) Did your test page print correctly? What, if any, information did it contain?

   _____

   _____

9. Click **Finish** to complete the installation. Your printer should now be listed in the Printers (Printers and Faxes in XP) window. What other printers or devices are listed?

   _____

   _____

10. When you're finished, close any open windows.

Next, you need to verify that all computers that need to use the printer are in the same workgroup. Follow these steps:

1. Ask your instructor for the name of the workgroup you should use for this lab, and record the name here:

   _____

2. Click **Start**, right-click **Computer** (**My Computer** in XP), and click **Properties** in the shortcut menu. (In Windows XP, click the **Computer Name** tab and then click **Change**.) Click **Change Settings**. If a UAC box opens, click **Continue**. Then click **Change**. The Computer Name Changes dialog box opens.

22

3. To what workgroup does this computer belong?

_____

4. If necessary, change the workgroup assignment for both computers to match the one you wrote down in Step 1.

5. Close any open windows.

After the printer is installed, you need to make it possible for other computers in the network to access it. Follow these directions to share the printer with other computers in the workgroup:

1. On the computer with a locally installed printer, click **Start, Control Panel, Hardware and Sound**, and **Printers**. (In XP, click **Start, Printers and Faxes**.)

2. The Printers window (Printers and Faxes window in XP) opens, showing the printer you just installed, as shown in Figure 22-1. Right-click the printer and click **Sharing** in the shortcut menu.

Figure 22-1 The Printers window shows all available printers
Courtesy: Course Technology/Cengage Learning

3. The Properties dialog box for the printer opens with the Sharing tab selected. Click the **Change sharing options** button and click Continue if a UAC box opens. Select **Share this printer** and type a share name for the printer.

4. Click **Additional Drivers**, and select the operating systems that remote computers use. Windows can then provide remote computers with the necessary driver files when they first attempt to connect to the shared printer. Click **OK**, and then click **OK** to close the Properties dialog box.

The printer is now listed in the Network (My Network Places in XP) window on all other computers on the network. However, before a remote computer can use the printer, printer drivers must be installed on it.

There are two approaches to installing a shared network printer on a remote PC. You can perform the installation using the printer drivers installed on the host PC or using the drivers on CD (the Windows CD or printer manufacturer's CD). If you need to install the printer on several remote PCs, it's faster to use the drivers installed on the host PC. The disadvantage of this method is that you must share the C:\Windows folder on the host PC, which is considered a security risk. For this reason, as soon as the printer is installed on all remote PCs, you should unshare the C:\Windows folder on the host PC to protect that critical folder.

Follow these steps to install the shared printer on the other PCs:

1. On the computer with the printer connected locally, you need to share the C:\Windows folder so that the drivers in this folder are available to the other computers. To do this, right-click the **C:\Windows** folder in Windows Explorer, click **Properties** in the shortcut menu, click the **Sharing** tab, and click **Share** (**Share this folder** in XP) to share the folder. Click **Share** again. If a UAC box opens, click **Continue**, and then click **Done**. Don't require a password to access the folder unless you want to prevent some users from accessing the printer. Click **Close**. (Click **OK** in XP.)

2. On remote PCs, open Network (My Network Places in XP) and find the printer. Right-click the printer and click **Connect** on the shortcut menu.

3. Enter a name for the printer and print a test page to complete the installation.

4. After all remote computers have installed the printer, you should remove the shared option on the local computer's C:\Windows folder to protect this important folder.

5. When you're finished, try printing a page from the remote computer.

REVIEW QUESTIONS

1. What two Windows XP components must be installed before you can share a printer in a workgroup?

_____

_____

2. What would happen if the C:\Windows folder on the host PC wasn't shared when you tried to install the printer on remote PCs? How could you have installed the printer on a remote computer if you didn't have access to the C:\Windows folder on the host computer?

_____

_____

3. Name an advantage of setting up file sharing at the same time as printer sharing:

_____

_____

22

4. Can you still print from a remote computer when a host computer is shut down?

_____

5. Suppose you want to stop some people on the network from using a shared printer, but you still want the printer to be available to the local computer to which it's connected. Which Windows component would you remove?

_____

_____

LAB 22.2 INSTALL A NETWORK PRINTER

OBJECTIVES

The goal of this lab is to install a network printer and then print to it from a remote computer on the network. After completing this lab, you will be able to:

◢ Install a network printer

◢ Test the printer across the network

MATERIALS REQUIRED

This lab requires the following:

◢ Windows Vista/XP operating system

◢ Network printer, patch cable, printer driver files, and documentation

◢ A functioning network

◢ A workgroup of 2 to 4 students

LAB PREPARATION

Before the lab begins, the instructor or lab assistant needs to do the following:

◢ Verify that Windows starts with no errors.

ACTIVITY BACKGROUND

Sharing a local printer is one way to include a printer on your network, but it's not an ideal solution. The host computer must remain on and it can be slowed down while printing. A better solution is to install a network printer that connects directly to the network and doesn't require a host computer.

ESTIMATED COMPLETION TIME: 30 Minutes

 Activity

The following steps describe the default method for installing a network printer. However, printer manufacturers often provide specialized steps and/or software for installing their devices. In that case, you should follow the steps your printer manufacturer prescribes rather than the steps listed here.

Attach your printer to the network hub, switch, or router using a network patch cable. Then go to a computer on the network and follow these steps to install a network printer:

In Windows Vista:

1. Open the Printers window and launch the Add Printer wizard as you did in Lab 22.1.

2. Click **Add a network, wireless or Blutooth printer** and then click **Next** if necessary.

3. Notice that Windows will begin to search the network for available printers, as shown in Figure 22-2.

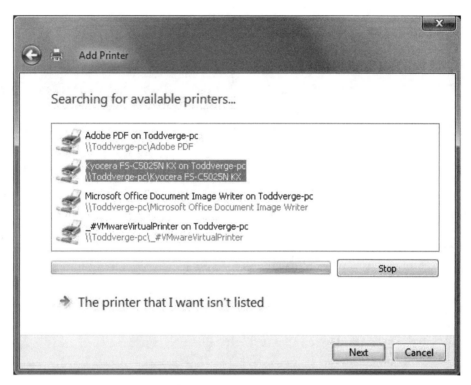

Figure 22-2   Windows automatically searches the network for available printers
Courtesy: Course Technology/Cengage Learning

4. If your printer is displayed, you can select it and then click **Next** and skip ahead to Step 8. Otherwise, click **The printer that I want isn't listed**.

5. If another computer, such as a server, were sharing the printer, you could select it by name. Because your printer is connected directly to the network, select **Add a printer using a TCP/IP address or hostname** and click **Next**.

6. Enter the IP address assigned to your printer. Most printers can print a status page telling you their IP addresses. Consult the printer's documentation or the Internet and figure out how to determine the IP address of your printer. How did you determine the IP address for your printer and what was it?

_____

_____

7. Enter the printer's IP address and click **Next**. Follow the instructions on-screen to complete the installation.

8. When the installation is complete, print a test page to test your printer.

22

In Windows XP:

1. Open the Printers and Faxes window and launch the Add Printer Wizard as you did previously. Click **Next** in the first wizard window.

2. Click **A network printer, or a printer attached to another computer**, and then click **Next** to continue.

3. Click **Browse for a printer** and click **Next** to locate the printer you'll install. The Browse for Printer window appears, which displays the network in a similar way to Windows Explorer.

4. Locate your printer by expanding the computer on which you installed and shared it. When you have found the correct printer, click to select it, and then click **Next**. If you can't find the printer when you browse, you can also try directly entering the printer's name or IP address in the printer text box.

5. In the Add Printer Wizard, verify that the path is correct, and then click **Next** to continue. If a warning dialog box opens, click **Yes** to continue.

6. If necessary, select the manufacturer and model or click **Have Disk**, depending on your printer and operating system.

7. Select whether to make this printer the default, and click **Next**. Complete the Add Printer Wizard.

8. Test your printer by printing a test page.

REVIEW QUESTIONS

1. A printer is connected locally on Computer1 but is shared on the network. Computer2 installs the shared printer and connects to it. Computer1 considers the printer to be a(n) _____ printer, and Computer2 considers the printer to be a(n) _____ printer.

2. Why should you use the manufacturer's prescribed method for installing its printer even if it differs from the default Windows method?

_____

3. Is it possible for a single printer to be both a local and a network printer? Why or why not?

_____

_____

_____

4. How can you determine the IP address of a network printer?

_____

_____

5. What would be the advantage of connecting a printer to a network server locally rather than having users connect to it directly through the network?

_____

_____

LAB 22.3 UPDATE PRINTER DRIVERS

OBJECTIVES

The goal of this lab is to give you experience in upgrading printer drivers. After completing this lab, you will be able to:

◢ Identify driver information

◢ Locate new drivers

◢ Install new drivers

◢ Test printer drivers for functionality

MATERIALS REQUIRED

This lab requires the following:

◢ Windows Vista/XP operating system

◢ Windows installation CD/DVD or installation files

◢ Administrator account and password, if applicable

◢ *Optional*: A file compression utility

◢ Internet access

◢ A local printer

LAB PREPARATION

Before the lab begins, the instructor or lab assistant needs to do the following:

◢ Verify that Windows starts with no errors.

◢ Provide each student with access to the Windows installation files, if needed.

◢ Verify that Internet access is available.

ACTIVITY BACKGROUND

Printer manufacturers often release new drivers for their existing printers to fix problems with earlier drivers, add new functions, support new applications, and accommodate new operating system features. A PC support technician needs to know how to update printer drivers as they become available. The process of updating printer drivers is similar to that for other devices. You must gather information about the device and the currently installed drivers, download the new drivers, and install them. Like other devices, after the drivers are installed, you should test the printer to be certain it's functioning correctly before turning it over to end users. Unlike many other devices, it's easy to verify that a printer is working correctly. You also learn that the process of updating printer drivers is similar across different Windows platforms and printer manufacturers. This lab gives you general instructions for updating printer drivers. Modify these instructions to fit your situation and printer.

22

Activity

The first step in updating printer drivers is to gather information about your current printer and drivers. Use Printers (Printers and Faxes in Windows XP) and any other resources at your disposal to research and answer the following questions:

1. How is your printer generally used (for example, text, photographs, or graphics)?

   _____

2. What operating system are you using?

   _____

3. Who is the printer manufacturer?

   _____

4. What is the model of the printer?

   _____

5. What is the printer interface (USB, parallel, network, other)?

   _____

6. Printers typically have many setup options that deal with print quality and paper handling. Open the Printers windows (Printers and Faxes in XP), right-click the printer, and click **Properties** in the shortcut menu. Note any important settings; you'll probably need to reapply them after the driver is updated:

   _____

   _____

   _____

Follow these instructions to identify the printer driver:

1. If necessary, open the Printers window (Printers and Faxes window in XP).

2. Right-click your printer icon, and click **Properties** in the shortcut menu. The printer's Properties dialog box opens.

3. Click the **Advanced** tab (see Figure 22-3). Note that tabs might differ from one printer to another.

4. What's the name of the driver listed in the Driver drop-down list?

   _____

5. When you're finished, close any open windows.

Follow these general directions to locate available driver updates:

1. Go to the printer manufacturer's Web site and locate the driver download section. Use Table 22-1 to help yourself find a Web site. What's the URL of the driver download page?

   _____

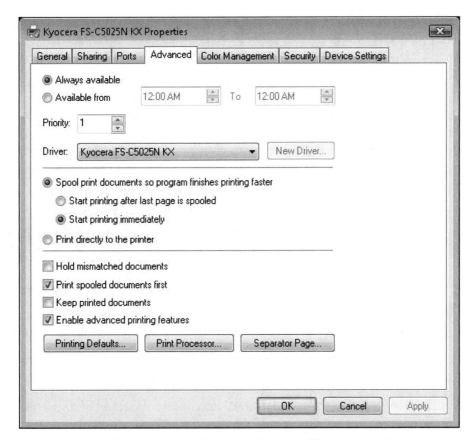

Figure 22-3   Use the printer's properties box to find information on your printer
Courtesy: Course Technology/Cengage Learning

Printer Manufacturer	Web Site
Brother	*www.brother.com*
Canon	*www.canon.com*
Hewlett-Packard	*www.hp.com*
IBM	*www.ibm.com*
Lexmark	*www.lexmark.com*
Okidata	*www.okidata.com*
SATO	*www.satoamerica.com*
Seiko Epson	*www.epson.com*
TallyGenicom	*www.tally.com*
Xerox	*www.xerox.com*

Table 22-1   Printer manufacturers

2. When you search for the correct driver on the Web site, you might find more than one driver that will work for your printer, operating system, or application. Generally, you should select the most recent version that matches your printer and operating system. There are exceptions, however. For instance, if a driver is listed as beta, it's still in development and has been released for evaluation. Usually, but not always, the

22

manufacturer has most of the kinks worked out. To be on the safe side, don't download a beta release driver. List all drivers, with brief descriptions, for your printer and operating system:

_____

_____

_____

3. What driver have you selected to download?

_____

4. Find and list any special installation instructions the manufacturer recommends:

_____

_____

5. Create a folder named **Downloads** on your C drive, if necessary. Then create a subfolder, such as C:\Downloads**Lexmark**, named for the manufacturer. What's your folder name?

_____

6. Download the driver you intend to install to that folder.

With any device, it's best to follow the manufacturer's recommended method of installation instead of the Windows approach. A good manufacturer tests the driver as well as the installation process. The exception is when you have several printers installed on a system and you think one set of drivers might overwrite files another printer needs. In this case, use the Windows method to update the drivers. Do the following to install the new driver using the manufacturer's installation process:

1. Print an example—a document or a digital picture—of the printer's main use. This printout verifies that your printer is working before you make any changes and is later used for comparison to verify that the new drivers are working.

2. In Windows Explorer, double-click the file you downloaded. If it's a compressed file, it self-extracts files or uses file compression software on your PC to extract the files. If an installation wizard starts, exit it.

3. Were any files extracted? List them here:

_____

_____

4. Locate any Readme.txt files for late-breaking information about the installation.

5. Double-click the setup or install program. Document the process you used to install the new drivers:

_____

_____

_____

Do the following to test the printer and new drivers:

1. Open the Printers window (Printers and Faxes window in Windows XP).

2. Right-click the printer icon and click **Properties** in the shortcut menu. Click the **Print Test Page** button and verify that the test page is legible.

3. Apply the correct printer settings you recorded in Step 6 at the beginning of this lab.

4. Reprint the typical document or photograph and compare it to the one printed before the driver update. List any differences you see:

_____

REVIEW QUESTIONS

1. List four reasons you might want to update a printer's drivers:

_____

_____

_____

_____

2. List four facts you should know about your printer before you start searching the Web for updated drivers:

_____

_____

_____

_____

3. What does the label "beta release" indicate about a driver?

_____

4. List the steps to print a test page in Windows:

_____

_____

LAB 22.4 MAINTAIN AND TROUBLESHOOT A PRINTER

OBJECTIVES

The goal of this lab is to give you experience supporting printers. After completing this lab, you will be able to:

◢ Use the Web to help with printer maintenance

◢ Correct common printer problems

MATERIALS REQUIRED

This lab requires the following:

◢ Internet access

◢ A printer

22

LAB PREPARATION

Before the lab begins, the instructor or lab assistant needs to do the following:

◢ Verify that Internet access is available.

ACTIVITY BACKGROUND

Printers require more maintenance than most other peripheral devices. Paper gets jammed, the ink cartridge or toner runs out, and image or document quality is degraded by dust and misalignment. Most manufacturers and many models have specific instructions for maintaining ink and toner cartridges and these instructions apply exclusively to the targeted printers; thus, you must rely on the printer manufacturer for instructions when maintaining a printer. In this lab, you investigate maintenance and troubleshooting instructions for several types of printers.

ESTIMATED COMPLETION TIME: 30 Minutes

Activity

Use the Internet to research how to solve the following problems. The printer is a high-end color laser printer, the LaserJet 9500, by Hewlett-Packard (*www.hp.com*). Answer these questions about routine maintenance for this printer:

1. Everything needed for routine maintenance of the LaserJet 9500 can be purchased in a printer maintenance kit. List the printer components included in this kit:

   _____

   _____

   _____

   _____

2. On the HP Web site, find the instructions for using the kit to perform routine maintenance. What should you wear while you do the maintenance?

   _____

3. How many pages can be printed before maintenance should be performed?

   _____

The next printer is an inkjet printer, the HP Deskjet 930c. Answer these questions:

1. Your computer displays a message to replace the ink cartridge. You replace the cartridge, but the message is still displayed. Also, you notice that the resume light on the printer is blinking. Search the HP Web site and locate the troubleshooting steps to solve the problem.

2. What is the first thing HP suggests you do when you see these errors?

   _____

3. One thing HP suggests is that you clean the cartridge contacts. List the steps:

   _____

   _____

   _____

   _____

4. If the problem isn't fixed, HP suggests you reclean the cartridge contacts, this time using a cotton swab dipped in what?

_____

Next, follow these steps to learn how to perform routine maintenance or troubleshoot problems on your local printer:

1. List the following information to identify your local printer:

   ◢ Printer manufacturer:

   _____

   ◢ Printer model:

   _____

   ◢ Printer interface (parallel, USB, other):

   _____

2. Search the manufacturer's Web site for troubleshooting and maintenance procedures and answer the following questions:

   ◢ What types of problems are addressed for your printer?

   _____

   _____

   _____

   ◢ Does the manufacturer offer a printer maintenance kit? If so, what components are included and how much does the kit cost?

   _____

   _____

   _____

   ◢ What maintenance tips for your printer can you find on the Web site?

   _____

   _____

REVIEW QUESTIONS

1. When a printer isn't working correctly, what are two ways the problem is communicated to users?

   _____

   _____

2. Why do printers require more maintenance than other peripherals?

   _____

22

3. How often should you perform printer maintenance using a maintenance kit purchased from the manufacturer?

4. After you replace an ink cartridge in an inkjet printer, an error message is displayed. What's the first thing you should do?

LAB 22.5 CRITICAL THINKING: SABOTAGE AND REPAIR A NETWORK PRINTER

OBJECTIVES

The goal of this lab is to learn how to troubleshoot problems with a network printer.

MATERIALS REQUIRED

This lab requires the following:

▲ Two or more computers connected to a network, one with a local printer attached and shared with the network

▲ Windows installation CD/DVD or installation files

▲ A workgroup of 2 to 4 students

LAB PREPARATION

Before the lab begins, the instructor or lab assistant needs to do the following:

▲ Verify that Windows starts with no errors.

▲ Provide each student with access to the Windows installation files, if needed.

ACTIVITY BACKGROUND

Problems with a network printer are common, and a PC support technician is often called on to solve them. This lab gives you practice solving these types of problems.

ESTIMATED COMPLETION TIME: 45 Minutes

 Activity

1. Using the knowledge that you've gained from previous labs, verify that each computer in a workgroup is able to print to a network printer that's locally installed on one of the computers in the workgroup.

2. Trade systems with another group, and sabotage the other group's system while that group sabotages your system. The following list has some suggestions for preventing a computer from using the network printer. Do something in this list, or think of another option.

   ▲ On the host computer, remove the sharing option for the printer.

   ▲ Uninstall the printer on a remote computer.

⊿ Pause printing on one or more computers.

⊿ Turn the printer off or turn it offline.

⊿ Disconnect the printer cable from the host computer.

⊿ Remove paper from the printer.

⊿ Introduce an error in the printer configuration on the host computer or a remote computer.

3. What did you do to sabotage the other team's system?

_____

_____

_____

4. Return to your system and troubleshoot it.

5. Describe the problem as a user would describe it to you if you were working at a help desk:

_____

_____

6. What is your first guess as to the source of the problem?

_____

7. List the steps you took in the troubleshooting process:

_____

_____

_____

_____

8. How did you solve the problem and return the printing system to working order?

_____

_____

9. What might cause this problem to happen again?

_____

_____

_____

REVIEW QUESTIONS

1. How did you initially test the printer to see that it was working?

2. What would you do differently the next time you encounter the same printing problem?

_____

22

3. Write down the steps you would use to make sure the printer itself is printing properly:

_____

_____

_____

_____

_____

4. Write down the steps you would follow to make sure the proper printer driver has been added on your computer:

_____

_____

_____

GLOSSARY

This glossary defines terms related to managing and maintaining a personal computer.

100BaseT An Ethernet standard that operates at 100 Mbps and uses twisted-pair cabling. *Also called* Fast Ethernet. Variations of 100BaseT are 100BaseTX and 100BaseFX.

80 conductor IDE cable An IDE cable that has 40 pins but uses 80 wires, 40 of which are ground wires designed to reduce crosstalk on the cable. The cable is used by ATA/66 and higher IDE drives.

802.11a/b/g *See* IEEE 802.11a/b/g.

A (ampere or amp) A unit of measurement for electrical current. One volt across a resistance of one ohm produces a flow of one amp.

A+ Certification A certification awarded by CompTIA (The Computer Industry Association) that measures a PC technician's knowledge and skills.

access point (AP) A device connected to a LAN that provides wireless communication so that computers, printers, and other wireless devices can communicate with devices on the LAN.

ACPI (Advanced Configuration and Power Interface) Specification developed by Intel, Compaq, Phoenix, Microsoft, and Toshiba to control power on notebooks and other devices.

active matrix A type of video display that amplifies the signal at every intersection in the grid of electrodes, which enhances the pixel quality over that of a dual-scan passive matrix display.

active partition The primary partition on the hard drive that boots the OS. Windows Vista/XP calls the active partition the "system partition."

adapter address *See* MAC (Media Access Control) address.

adapter card A small circuit board inserted in an expansion slot used to communicate between the system bus and a peripheral device. *Also called* interface card.

administrator account In Windows Vista/XP, an account that grants the administrator rights and permissions to all hardware and software resources, such as the right to add, delete, and change accounts and change hardware configurations.

Advanced Options menu A Windows Vista/XP menu that appears when you press F8 when Windows starts. The menu can be used to troubleshoot problems when loading Windows Vista/XP. In Vista, the menu is called the Advanced Boot Options Menu.

adware Software installed on a computer that produces pop-up ads using your browser; the ads are often based on your browsing habits.

Aero user interface The Vista user interface. *Also called* Aero glass.

AirPort The term Apple uses to describe the IEEE 802.11b standard.

alternating current (AC) Current that cycles back and forth rather than traveling in only one direction. In the United States, the AC voltage from a standard wall outlet is normally between 110 and 115 V. In Europe, the standard AC voltage from a wall outlet is 220 V.

ammeter A meter that measures electrical current in amps.

antistatic wrist strap *See* ground bracelet.

antivirus software Utility programs that prevent infection or scan a system to detect and remove viruses. McAfee Associates VirusScan and Norton AntiVirus are two popular antivirus packages.

APIPA (Automatic Private IP Address) An IP address in the address range 169.254.x.x, used by a computer when it can't successfully lease an IP address from a DHCP server.

ASCII (American Standard Code for Information Interchange) A popular standard for writing letters and other characters in binary code. Originally, ASCII characters were 7 bits, so there were 127 possible values. ASCII has been expanded to an 8-bit version, allowing 128 additional values.

ASR (Automated System Recovery) The Windows XP process that allows you to restore an entire hard drive volume or logical drive to its state at the time the backup of the volume was made.

AT A form factor, generally no longer produced, in which the motherboard requires a full-size case. Because of their dimensions and configuration, AT systems are difficult to install, service, and upgrade. *Also called* full AT.

ATAPI (Advanced Technology Attachment Packet Interface) An interface standard, part of the IDE/ATA standards, that allows tape drives, CD-ROM drives, and other drives to be treated like an IDE hard drive by the system.

ATX The most common form factor for current PCs, originally introduced by Intel in 1995. ATX motherboards and cases make better use of space and resources than did the AT form factor.

autodetection A feature on newer system BIOS and hard drives that automatically identifies and configures a new drive in CMOS setup.

autorange meter A multimeter that senses the quantity of input and sets the range accordingly.

Baby AT An improved and more flexible version of the AT form factor. Baby AT was the industry standard from approximately 1993 to 1997 and can fit into some ATX cases.

backup An extra copy of a file, used if the original becomes damaged or destroyed.

bandwidth In relation to analog communication, the range of frequencies a communications channel or cable can carry. In general use, the term refers to the volume of data that can travel on a bus or over a cable stated in bits per second (bps), kilobits per second (Kbps), or megabits per second (Mbps). *Also called* data throughput *or* line speed.

bank An area on the motherboard that contains slots for memory modules (typically labeled bank 0, 1, 2, and 3).

baseline The level of performance expected from a system, which can be compared to current measurements to determine what needs upgrading or tuning.

basic disk A way to partition a hard drive, used by DOS and all versions of Windows, that stores information about the drive in a partition table at the beginning of the drive. *Compare to* dynamic disk.

binary numbering system The numbering system used by computers; it has only two numbers, 0 and 1, called binary digits, or bits.

BIOS (basic input/output system) Firmware that can control much of a computer's I/O functions, such as communication with the hard drive and the monitor. *Also called* ROM BIOS.

BIOS setup The program in the system BIOS that can change the values in CMOS RAM. *Also called* CMOS setup.

bit (binary digit) A 0 or 1 used by the binary numbering system.

blue screen A Windows Vista/XP error displayed on a blue screen that causes the system to halt. *Also called* stop error.

Bluetooth A standard for wireless communication and data synchronization between devices, developed by a group of electronics manufacturers and overseen by the Bluetooth Special Interest Group. Bluetooth uses the same frequency range as IEEE 802.11b but doesn't have as wide a range.

Blu-ray Disc (BD) An optical disc technology that uses the UDF version 2.5 file system and a blue laser beam, which has a shorter wavelength than the beam used by DVD or CD discs. A Blu-ray disc can store more data than a DVD.

Boot.ini A Windows XP hidden text file that contains information needed to build the boot loader menu.

boot loader menu A startup menu that gives users the choice of which operating system to load, such as Windows Vista or Windows XP, which are both installed on the same system, creating a dual-boot system.

boot partition The hard drive partition where the Windows Vista/XP OS is stored. The system partition and boot partition can be different partitions.

boot record The first sector of a floppy disk or logical drive in a partition; it contains information about the disk or logical drive. On a hard drive, if the boot record is in the active partition, it's used to boot the OS. *Also called* boot sector.

boot sector *See* boot record.

boot sector virus An infected program that can replace the boot program with a modified, infected version of the boot command utilities, often causing boot and data retrieval problems.

bootstrap loader A small program at the end of the boot record that can be used to boot an OS from the disk or logical drive.

broadband A transmission technique that carries more than one type of transmission on the same medium, such as cable modem or DSL.

brownouts Temporary reductions in voltage, which can sometimes cause data loss. *Also called* sags.

BTX (Balanced Technology Extended) A form factor used by motherboards and computer cases that was expected to replace ATX. It has higher-quality fans, is designed for better air flow, and has improved structural support for the motherboard. The BTX form factor has not been widely adopted.

buffer A temporary memory area where data is kept before being written to a hard drive or sent to a printer, thus reducing the number of writes to devices.

bus The paths, or lines, on the motherboard on which data, instructions, and electrical power move from component to component.

bus speed The speed, or frequency, at which the data on the motherboard moves.

byte A collection of eight bits that's equivalent to a single character. When referring to system memory, an additional error-checking bit might be added, making the total nine bits.

cabinet file A file with a .cab extension that contains one or more compressed files and is often used to distribute software on disk. The Extract command is used to extract files from a cabinet file.

cable modem A technology that uses cable TV lines for data transmission, requiring a modem at each end. From the modem, a network cable connects to a NIC in the user's PC.

capacitor An electronic device that can maintain an electrical charge for a period of time and is used to smooth out the flow of electrical current. Capacitors are often found in computer power supplies.

CardBus The latest PCMCIA specification. It improves I/O speed, increases the bus width to 32 bits, and supports lower-voltage PC Cards, while maintaining backward compatibility with earlier standards.

cards Adapter boards or interface cards placed into expansion slots to expand the functions of a computer, allowing it to communicate with external devices, such as monitors or speakers.

CAT A rating for UTP cable. CAT-5 or higher cabling is required for Fast Ethernet.

CCITT (Comité Consultatif International Télégraphique et Téléphonique) An international organization that was responsible for developing standards for international communications. This organization has been incorporated into the ITU. *See also* ITU (International Telecommunications Union).

CD (compact disc) An optical disc technology that uses a red laser beam and can hold up to 700 MB of data.

CD (change directory) command A command given at the command prompt that changes the default directory, such as CD\Windows.

CDFS (Compact Disk File System) The 32-bit file system for CDs and some CD-Rs and CD-RWs that replaced the older 16-bit mscdex file system used by DOS. *See also* UDF (Universal Disk Format) file system.

CD-R (CD-recordable) A CD drive that can record or write data to a CD. The drive may or may not be multisession, but the data can't be erased after it's written.

CD-RW (CD-rewritable) A CD drive that can record or write data to a CD. The data can be erased and overwritten. The drive may or may not be multisession.

chain A group of clusters used to hold a single file.

child directory *See* subdirectory.

chip creep A condition in which chips loosen because of thermal changes.

chipset A group of chips on the motherboard that control the timing and flow of data and instructions to and from the CPU.

CHS (cylinder, head, sector) mode The traditional method by which BIOS reads from and writes to hard drives by addressing the correct cylinder, head, and sector. *Also called* normal mode.

circuit board A computer component, such as the main motherboard or an adapter board, that has electronic circuits and chips.

clean install An installation of an OS on a new hard drive or a hard drive that has a previous OS installed, but it's performed without carrying forward any settings kept by the old OS, including information about hardware, software, or user preferences. *Also called* fresh installation.

client/server A computer concept whereby one computer (the client) requests information from another computer (the server).

client/server application An application that has two components. The client software requests data from the server software on the same or another computer.

clock speed The speed, or frequency, expressed in MHz or GHz, that controls activity on the motherboard and is generated by a crystal or oscillator located on the motherboard.

clone A computer that's a no-name Intel- and Microsoft-compatible PC.

cluster One or more sectors that constitute the smallest unit of space on a disk for storing data. Files are written to a disk as groups of whole clusters. *Also called* file allocation unit.

CMOS (complementary metal-oxide semiconductor) The technology used to manufacture microchips. CMOS chips require less electricity, hold data longer after the electricity is turned off, are slower, and produce less heat than TTL chips. The configuration, or setup, chip is a CMOS chip.

CMOS configuration chip A chip on the motherboard that contains a very small amount of memory, or RAM, enough to hold configuration, or setup, information about the computer. The chip is powered by a battery when the PC is turned off. *Also called* CMOS setup chip *or* CMOS RAM chip.

CMOS setup The CMOS configuration chip, or the program in system BIOS that can change the values in the CMOS RAM.

CMOS setup chip *See* CMOS configuration chip.

cold boot *See* hard boot.

combo card An Ethernet card that contains more than one transceiver, each with a different port on the back of the card, to accommodate different cabling media.

command prompt window A Windows utility that is used to enter multiple commands to perform a variety of tasks.

compact case A type of case used in low-end desktop systems. Compact cases follow the NLX, LPX, or Mini LPX form factor. They are likely to have fewer drive bays, but they generally still provide for some expansion. *Also called* low-profile *or* slimline cases.

compressed drive A drive whose format has been reorganized to store more data. A compressed drive is really not a drive at all; it's actually a type of file, typically with a host drive called H.

computer name Character-based host name or NetBIOS name assigned to a computer.

console A centralized location from which to run commonly used tools.

continuity A continuous, unbroken path for the flow of electricity. A continuity test can determine whether internal wiring is still intact or whether a fuse is good or bad.

conventional memory Memory addresses between 0 and 640K. *Also called* base memory.

cooler A combination cooling fan and heat sink mounted on the top or side of a processor to keep it cool.

(CPU) central processing unit The heart and brain of the computer, which receives data input, processes information, and carries out instructions. *Also called* microprocessor or processor.

C-RIMM (Continuity RIMM) A placeholder RIMM module that provides continuity so that every RIMM slot is filled.

cross-linked clusters Errors caused when more than one file points to a cluster and the files appear to share the same disk space, according to the file allocation table.

crossover cable A cable used to connect two PCs into the simplest network possible. Also used to connect two hubs.

CVF (compressed volume file) The file on the host drive of a compressed drive that holds all compressed data.

data bus The lines on the system bus that the CPU uses to send and receive data.

data cartridge A type of tape medium typically used for backups. Full-sized data cartridges are 4 x 6 x ⅝ inches. A minicartridge is only 3¼ x 2½ x ⅗ inches.

data line protector A surge protector designed to work with the telephone line to a modem.

data path size The number of lines on a bus that can hold data, for example, 8, 16, 32, and 64 lines, which can accommodate 8, 16, 32, and 64 bits at a time.

data throughput *See* bandwidth.

DC (direct current) Current that travels in only one direction (the type of electricity provided by batteries). Computer power supplies transform AC to low DC.

DC controller A card inside a notebook that converts voltage to CPU voltage. Some notebook manufacturers consider the card to be a field replaceable unit (FRU).

DCE (data communications equipment) The hardware, usually a dial-up modem, that provides the connection between a data terminal and a communications line. *See also* DTE (data terminal equipment).

DDR (Double Data Rate) A type of memory technology used on DIMMs that runs at twice the speed of the system clock.

DDR2 A version of SDRAM that's faster than DDR and uses less power.

DDR3 A version of SDRAM that is faster than DDR2 memory and that can use triple channels.

default gateway The gateway a computer on a network uses to access another network unless it knows to specifically use another gateway for quicker access to that network.

default printer The printer Windows prints to unless another printer is selected.

defragment To "optimize" or rewrite a file to a disk in one contiguous chain of clusters, thus speeding up data retrieval.

desktop The initial screen displayed when an OS has a GUI interface loaded.

device driver A program stored on the hard drive that tells the computer how to communicate with an I/O device, such as a printer or modem.

DHCP (Dynamic Host Configuration Protocol) server A service that assigns dynamic IP addresses to computers on a network when they first access the network.

diagnostic cards Adapter cards designed to discover and report computer errors and conflicts at POST time (before the computer boots up), often by displaying a number on the card.

diagnostic software   Utility programs that help troubleshoot computer systems. Some Windows diagnostic utilities are Chkdsk and Scandisk. PC-Technician is an example of a third-party diagnostic program.

differential cable   A SCSI cable in which a signal is carried on two wires, each carrying voltage, and the signal is the difference between the two. Differential signaling provides for error checking and improved data integrity. *Compare to* SE (single-ended) cable.

digital certificate   A code used to authenticate the source of a file or document or to identify and authenticate a person or organization sending data over the Internet. The code is assigned by a certificate authority, such as VeriSign, and includes a public key for encryption. *Also called* digital ID or digital signature.

digital ID   *See* digital certificate.

digital signature   *See* digital certificate.

DIMM (dual inline memory module)   A miniature circuit board used in newer computers to hold memory. DIMMs can hold up to 2 GB RAM on a single module.

DIP (dual inline package) switch   A switch on a circuit board or other device that can be set on or off to hold configuration or setup information.

directory table   An OS table that contains file information such as the name, size, time, and date of last modification, and cluster number of the file's beginning location.

Direct Rambus DRAM   A memory technology by Rambus and Intel that uses a narrow, very fast network-type system bus. Memory is stored on a RIMM module. *Also called* RDRAM or Direct RDRAM.

Direct RDRAM   *See* Direct Rambus DRAM.

disk cache   A method whereby recently retrieved data and adjacent data are read into memory in advance, anticipating the next CPU request.

disk cloning   *See* drive imaging.

disk compression   Compressing data on a hard drive to allow more data to be written to the drive.

disk imaging   *See* drive imaging.

Disk Management   A Windows utility used to display, create, and format partitions on basic disks and volumes on dynamic disks.

disk quota   A limit placed on the amount of disk space that's available to users. Requires a Windows NTFS volume.

disk thrashing   A condition that results when the hard drive is excessively used for virtual memory because RAM is full. It dramatically slows down processing and can cause premature hard drive failure.

DMA (direct memory access) channel   A number identifying a channel whereby a device can pass data to memory without involving the CPU. Think of a DMA channel as a shortcut for data moving to and from the device and memory.

DMA transfer mode   A transfer mode used by devices, including the hard drive, to transfer data to memory without involving the CPU.

DNS server   A computer that can find an IP address for another computer when only the domain name is known.

docking station   A device that receives a notebook computer and provides additional secondary storage and easy connection to peripheral devices.

domain   In Windows, a logical group of networked computers, such as those on a college campus, that share a centralized directory database of user account information and security for the entire domain.

domain name   A unique text-based name that identifies a network.

DOS box   A command window.

dot pitch   The distance between the dots that the electronic beam hits on a monitor screen.

doze time   The time before an Energy Star® or "green" system reduces 80 percent of its activity.

DPMS (Display Power Management Signaling)   Energy Star® standard specifications that allow for the video card and monitor to go into sleep mode simultaneously. *See also* Energy Star®.

DRAM (dynamic RAM) The most common type of system memory, it requires refreshing every few milliseconds.

drive imaging Making an exact image of a hard drive, including partition information, boot sectors, operating system installation, and application software, to replicate the hard drive on another system or recover from a hard drive crash. *Also called* disk cloning and disk imaging.

drop height The height from which a manufacturer states that its drive can be dropped without making the drive unusable.

DSL (Digital Subscriber Line) A telephone line that carries digital data from end to end and can be leased from the telephone company for individual use. DSL lines are rated at 5 Mbps, about 50 times faster than regular telephone lines.

DTE (data terminal equipment) Both the computer and a remote terminal or other computer to which it's attached. *See also* DCE (data communications equipment).

dual boot The ability to boot using either of two different OSs, such as Windows Vista and Windows XP.

dual channel A motherboard feature that improves memory performance by providing two 64-bit channels between memory and the chipset. DDR, DDR2, and DDR3 DIMMS can use dual channels.

dual core A processor package that contains two core processors, thus supporting four instructions at once.

dual-scan passive matrix A type of video display that's less expensive than an active-matrix display and does not provide as high-quality an image. With dual-scan display, two columns of electrodes are activated at the same time.

dual-voltage CPU A CPU that requires two different voltages, one for internal processing and the other for I/O processing.

DVD (digital video disk or digital versatile disk) A faster, larger CD format that can read older CDs, store more than 8 GB of data, and hold full-length motion picture videos.

dynamic disk A way to partition one or more hard drives, introduced with Windows 2000, in which information about the drive is stored in a database at the end of the drive. *Compare to* basic disk.

dynamic IP address An assigned IP address used for the current session only. When the session is terminated, the IP address is returned to the list of available addresses.

dynamic volume A volume type used with dynamic disks for which you can change the size of the volume after you have created it.

ECC (error-correcting code) A chipset feature on a motherboard that checks the integrity of data stored on DIMMs or RIMMs and can correct single-bit errors in a byte. More advanced ECC schemas can detect, but not correct, double-bit errors in a byte.

ECHS (extended CHS) mode *See* large mode.

ECP (Extended Capabilities Port) A bidirectional parallel port mode that uses a DMA channel to speed up data flow.

EDO (extended data out) A type of RAM that can be 10 percent to 20 percent faster than conventional RAM because it eliminates the delay before it issues the next memory address.

EEPROM (electrically erasable programmable ROM) A type of chip in which higher voltage can be applied to one of the pins to erase its previous memory before a new instruction set is electronically written.

EFS (Encrypted File System) A way to use a key to encode a file or folder on an NTFS volume to protect sensitive data. Because it's an integrated system service, EFS is transparent to users and applications and difficult to attack.

EIDE (Enhanced IDE) A standard for managing the interface between secondary storage devices and a computer system. A system can support up to six serial ATA and parallel ATA EIDE devices or up to four parallel ATA IDE devices, such as hard drives, CD-ROM drives, and Zip drives.

emergency startup disk (ESD)   *See* rescue disk.

EMI (electromagnetic interference)   A magnetic field produced as a side effect from the flow of electricity. EMI can cause corrupted data in data lines that aren't properly shielded.

encryption   The process of putting readable data into an encoded form that can be decoded (or decrypted) only through use of a key.

Energy Star®   "Green" systems that satisfy the EPA requirements to decrease the overall consumption of electricity. *See also* Green Standards.

enhanced BIOS   A system BIOS that has been written to accommodate large-capacity drives (more than 504 MB, usually in the gigabyte range).

EPP (Enhanced Parallel Port)   A parallel port that allows data to flow in both directions (bidirectional port) and is faster than original parallel ports on PCs that allowed communication only in one direction.

EPROM (erasable programmable ROM)   A type of chip with a special window that allows the current memory contents to be erased with special ultraviolet light so that the chip can be reprogrammed. Many BIOS chips are EPROMs.

error correction   The capability of a modem to identify transmission errors and then automatically request another transmission.

escalate   When a technician passes a customer's problem to higher organizational levels because he or she cannot solve the problem.

ESD (electrostatic discharge)   Another name for static electricity, which can damage chips and destroy motherboards, even though it might not be felt or seen with the naked eye.

ESD (emergency startup disk)   *See* rescue disk.

Ethernet   The most popular LAN architecture that can run at 10 Mbps (ThinNet or ThickNet), 100 Mbps (Fast Ethernet), or 1 Gbps (Gigabit Ethernet).

Event Viewer (Eventvwr.msc)   A Windows tool useful for troubleshooting problems with Windows, applications, and hardware. It displays logs of significant events.

expansion bus   A bus that doesn't run in sync with the system clock.

expansion card   A circuit board inserted into a slot on the motherboard to enhance the computer's capability.

expansion slot   A narrow slot on the motherboard where an expansion card can be inserted. Expansion slots connect to a bus on the motherboard.

extended partition   The only partition on a hard drive that can contain more than one logical drive.

external SATA (eSATA)   A standard for external drives based on SATA that uses a special external shielded SATA cable up to two meters long.

faceplate   A metal plate that comes with the motherboard and fits over the ports to create a well-fitted enclosure around them.

Fast Ethernet   *See* 100BaseT.

FAT (file allocation table)   A table on a hard drive or floppy disk that tracks the clusters used to contain a file.

FAT12   The 12-bit-wide, one-column file allocation table for a floppy disk, containing information about how each cluster or file allocation unit on the disk is currently used.

fault tolerance   The degree to which a system can tolerate failures. Adding redundant components, such as disk mirroring or disk duplexing, is a way to build in fault tolerance.

file allocation unit   *See* cluster.

file extension   A three-character portion of the filename used to identify the file type. In command lines, the file extension follows the filename and is separated from it by a period, such as Msd.exe, with exe being the file extension.

filename   The first part of the name assigned to a file. In DOS, the filename can be no more than eight characters and is followed by the file extension. In Windows, a filename can be up to 255 characters.

file system   The overall structure that an OS uses to name, store, and organize files on a disk. Examples of file systems are FAT32 and NTFS.

file virus A virus that inserts virus code into an executable program file and can spread wherever that program runs.

firewall Hardware or software that protects a computer or network from unauthorized access.

FireWire *See* IEEE 1394.

firmware Software permanently stored in a chip. The BIOS on a motherboard is an example of firmware.

flash ROM ROM that can be reprogrammed or changed without replacing chips.

flat panel monitor A desktop monitor that uses an LCD panel.

FlexATX A version of the ATX form factor that allows for maximum flexibility in the size and shape of cases and motherboards. FlexATX is ideal for custom systems.

flow control When using modems, a method of controlling the flow of data to adjust for problems with data transmission. Xon/Xoff is an example of a flow control protocol.

folder *See* subdirectory.

forgotten password floppy disk A Windows XP disk created to be used in case the user forgets the user account password to the system.

form factor A set of specifications on the size, shape, and configuration of a computer hardware component, such as a case, power supply, or motherboard.

formatting Preparing a hard drive volume or floppy disk for use by placing tracks and sectors on its surface to store information (for example, the FORMAT A: command).

FPT (forced perfect terminator) A type of SCSI active terminator that includes a mechanism to force signal termination to the correct voltage, eliminating most signal echoes and interference.

FQDN (fully qualified domain name) A host name and a domain name, such as *jsmith. amazon. com*. Sometimes loosely referred to as a domain name.

fragmentation The distribution of data files on a hard drive or floppy disk so that they are stored in noncontiguous clusters.

fragmented file A file that has been written to different portions of the disk so that it's not in contiguous clusters.

FRU (field replaceable unit) A component in a computer or device that can be replaced with a new component without sending the computer or device back to the manufacturer. Examples: power supply, DIMM, motherboard, floppy disk drive.

FTP (File Transfer Protocol) The protocol used to transfer files over a TCP/IP network so that the file doesn't need to be converted to ASCII format before transferring it.

full AT *See* AT.

gateway A computer or other device that connects networks.

GDI (Graphics Device Interface) A Windows 9x component that controls screens, graphics, and printing.

GHz (gigahertz) 1000 MHz, or one billion cycles per second.

Gigabit Ethernet The newest version of Ethernet. Gigabit Ethernet supports rates of data transfer up to 1 gigabit per second but isn't widely used yet.

global user account Sometimes called a domain user account, the account is used at the domain level, created by an administrator, and stored in the SAM (Security Accounts Manager) database on a Windows 2000 or Windows 2003 domain controller.

GPF (General Protection Fault) A Windows error that occurs when a program attempts to access a memory address that isn't available or is no longer assigned to it.

graphics accelerator A type of video card with an on-board processor that can substantially increase speed and boost graphical and video performance.

graphics DDR (G-DDR), graphics DDR2, graphics DDR3 Types of DDR, DDR2, and DDR3 memory specifically designed to be used in graphics cards.

Green Standards A computer or device that conforms to these standards can go into sleep or doze mode when not in use, thus saving energy and helping the environment. Devices that carry the Green Star or Energy Star® comply with these standards.

ground bracelet An antistatic strap you wear around your wrist that's attached to the computer case, grounding mat, or another ground so that ESD is discharged from your body before you touch sensitive components inside a computer. *Also called* antistatic strap, ground strap, or ESD bracelet.

group profile A group of user profiles. All profiles in the group can be changed by changing the group profile.

guard tone A tone that an answering modem sends when it first answers the phone to tell the calling modem that a modem is on the other end of the line.

Guest user A user who has limited permissions on a system and can't make changes to it. Guest user accounts are intended for one-time or infrequent users of a workstation.

handshaking When two modems begin to communicate, the initial agreement made as to how to send and receive data.

hard boot Restart the computer by turning off the power or by pressing the Reset button. *Also called* cold boot.

hard copy Output from a printer to paper.

hard drive The main secondary storage device of a PC is a small case containing magnetic-coated platters that rotate at high speed.

hard drive standby time The amount of time before a hard drive shuts down to conserve energy.

hardware The physical components that constitute the computer system, such as the monitor, keyboard, motherboard, and printer.

hardware address *See* MAC (Media Access Control) address.

hardware cache A disk cache contained in RAM chips built right on the disk controller. *Also called* buffer.

hardware interrupt An event caused by a hardware device signaling the CPU that it requires service.

hardware profile A set of hardware configuration information that Windows keeps in the Registry. Windows can maintain more than one hardware profile for the same PC.

HCL (Hardware Compatibility List) The list of all computers and peripheral devices that have been tested and are officially supported by Windows 2000/XP (see *www.microsoft.com/whdc/hcl/default.mspx*).

head The top or bottom surface of one platter on a hard drive. Each platter has two heads.

heat sink A piece of metal, with cooling fans, that can be attached to or mounted on an integrated chip (such as the CPU) to dissipate heat.

hexadecimal (hex) notation A numbering system that uses 16 digits, the numerals 0 to 9, and the letters A to F. Hexadecimal notation is often used to display memory addresses.

hibernation A notebook OS feature that conserves power by using a small trickle of electricity. Before the notebook begins to hibernate, everything currently stored in memory is saved to the hard drive. When the notebook is brought out of hibernation, open applications and their data are returned to their state before hibernation.

hidden file A file that isn't displayed in a directory list. Whether to hide or display a file is one of the file's attributes the OS keeps.

high-level formatting Formatting performed by the Windows Format program, the Windows installation program, or the Disk Management utility. The process creates the boot record, file system, and root directory on the volume or logical drive and makes the drive bootable. *Also called* operating system formatting.

hive Physical segment of the Windows Vista/XP Registry that's stored in a file.

HMA (high memory area) The first 64K of extended memory.

host Any computer or other device on a network that has been assigned an IP address. *Also called* node.

host adapter The circuit board that controls a SCSI bus supporting as many as 7 or 15 separate devices. The host adapter controls communication between the SCSI bus and the PC.

host bus *See* system bus.

host name A name that identifies a computer, printer, or other device on a network.

hot-pluggable *See* hot-swappable.

hot-swappable A device that can be plugged into a computer while it's turned on and the computer senses the device and configures it without rebooting, or the device can be removed without an OS error. *Also called* hot-pluggable.

HTML (Hypertext Markup Language) A markup language used for hypertext documents on the World Wide Web. This language uses tags to format the document, create hyperlinks, and mark locations for graphics.

HTTP (Hypertext Transfer Protocol) The protocol used by the World Wide Web.

HTTPS (HTTP secure) A version of HTTP that includes data encryption for security.

hub A network device or box that provides a central location to connect cables.

hypertext Text that contains links to remote points in the document or to other files, documents, or graphics. Hypertext is created by using HTML and is commonly used on Web sites.

Hyper-Threading The Intel technology that allows each logical processor within the processor package to handle an individual thread in parallel with other threads being handled by other processors within the package.

Hz (hertz) Unit of measurement for frequency, calculated in terms of vibrations, or cycles per second. For example, for 16-bit stereo sound, a frequency of 44,000 Hz is used. *See also* MHz (megahertz).

i.Link *See* IEEE 1394.

I/O addresses Numbers used by devices and the CPU to manage communication between them. *Also called* ports or port addresses.

I/O controller card An older card that can contain serial, parallel, and game ports and floppy drive and IDE connectors.

ICF (Internet Connection Firewall) Windows software designed to protect a PC from unauthorized access from the Internet; updated to Windows XP Firewall in Service Pack 2.

ICS (Internet Connection Sharing) A Windows utility that uses Network Address Translation (NAT) and acts as a proxy server to manage two or more computers connected to the Internet.

IDE (Integrated Drive Electronics or Integrated Device Electronics) A hard drive with a disk controller integrated into the drive, eliminating the need for a controller cable and thus increasing speed and reducing price. *See also* EIDE (Enhanced IDE).

IEEE (Institute of Electrical and Electronics Engineers) A nonprofit organization that develops standards for the computer and electronics industries.

IEEE 802.11a/b/g/n IEEE specifications for wireless communication and data synchronization. *Also called* Wi-Fi. Apple Computer's versions of 802.11 standards are called AirPort and AirPort Extreme.

IEEE 1284 A standard for parallel ports and cables developed by the Institute for Electrical and Electronics Engineers and supported by many hardware manufacturers.

IEEE 1394 Standards for an expansion bus that can also be configured to work as a local bus. It's expected to replace the SCSI bus, providing an easy method to install and configure fast I/O devices. *Also called* FireWire and i.Link.

IEEE 1394.3   A standard, developed by the 1394 Trade Association, designed for peer-to-peer data transmission. It allows imaging devices to send images and photos directly to printers without involving a computer.

infestation   Any unwanted program that's transmitted to a computer without the user's knowledge and designed to do varying degrees of damage to data and software. There are a number of different types of infestations, including viruses, Trojan horses, worms, and logic bombs.

information (.inf) file   Text file with an .inf file extension, such as Msbatch.inf, that contains information about a hardware or software installation.

infrared transceiver   A wireless transceiver that uses infrared technology to support wireless devices, such as keyboards, mice, and printers. A motherboard might have an embedded infrared transceiver, or the transceiver might plug into a USB or serial port. The technology is defined by the Infrared Data Association (IrDA). *Also called* IrDA transceiver *or* infrared port.

initialization files   Configuration information files for Windows. System.ini is one of the most important Windows 9x initialization files.

ink-jet printer   A type of ink dispersion printer that uses cartridges of ink. The ink is heated to a boiling point and then ejected onto the paper through tiny nozzles.

intranet   A private network that uses TCP/IP protocols.

IP address   A 32-bit address consisting of four numbers separated by periods, used to uniquely identify a device on a network that uses TCP/IP protocols. The first numbers identify the network; the last numbers identify a host. An example of an IP address is 206.96.103s.114.

IrDA transceiver   *See* infrared transceiver.

IRQ (interrupt request) line   A line on a bus assigned to a device that's used to signal the CPU for servicing. These lines are assigned a reference number (for example, the normal IRQ for a printer is IRQ 7).

ISA (Industry Standard Architecture) slot   An older slot on the motherboard used for slower I/O devices, which can support an 8-bit or a 16-bit data path. ISA slots have mostly been replaced by PCI slots.

ISDN (Integrated Services Digital Network)   A digital telephone line that can carry data at about five times the speed of regular telephone lines. Two channels (telephone numbers) share a single pair of wires.

ISP (Internet service provider)   A commercial group that provides Internet access for a monthly fee. AOL, Earthlink, and CompuServe are large ISPs.

ITU (International Telecommunications Union)   The international organization responsible for developing international standards of communication. Formerly CCITT.

JPEG (Joint Photographic Experts Group)   A graphical compression scheme that allows users to control the amount of data that's averaged and sacrificed as file size is reduced. It's a common Internet file format. Most JPEG files have a .jpg extension.

jumper   Two wires that stick up side by side on the motherboard and are used to hold configuration information. The jumper is considered closed if a cover is over the wires and open if the cover is missing.

key   In encryption, a secret number or code used to encode and decode data. In Windows, a section name of the Windows Registry.

keyboard   A common input device through which data and instructions can be typed into computer memory.

LAN (local area network)   A computer network that covers only a small area, usually within one building.

laptop computer   *See* notebook.

large-capacity drive   A hard drive larger than 504 MB.

large mode   A mode of addressing information on hard drives that range from 504 MB to 8.4 GB by translating cylinder, head, and sector information to break the 528 MB hard drive barrier. *Also called* ECHS (extended CHS) mode.

Last Known Good Configuration   In Windows, Registry settings and device drivers that were in effect when the computer last booted successfully. These settings can be restored during the startup process to recover from errors during the previous boot.

LBA (logical block addressing) mode   A mode of addressing information on hard drives in which the BIOS and operating system view the drive as one long linear list of LBAs or addressable sectors, permitting drives to be larger than 8.4 GB. (LBA 0 is cylinder 0, head 0, and sector 1.)

LIF (low insertion force) socket   A socket that requires the installer to manually apply an even force over the microchip when inserting the chip into the socket.

Limited users   Windows user accounts; they have read-write access only on their own folders, read-only access to most system folders, and no access to other users' data.

line speed   *See* bandwidth or modem speed.

Lmhosts   A text file in the Windows folder that contains NetBIOS names and their associated IP addresses. This file is used for name resolution on a NetBEUI network.

local bus   A bus that operates at a speed synchronized with the CPU frequency. The system bus is a local bus.

local I/O bus   A local bus that provides I/O devices with fast access to the CPU.

local printer   A printer connected to a computer by way of a port on the computer. *Compare to* network printer.

local profile   A user profile stored on a local computer that can't be accessed from another computer on the network.

local user account   A user account that applies only to a local computer and can't be used to access resources from other computers on the network.

logical drive   A portion or all of a hard drive partition that the operating system treats as though it were a physical drive. Each logical drive is assigned a drive letter, such as C, and contains a file system. *Also called* volume.

logical geometry   The number of heads, tracks, and sectors that the BIOS on the hard drive controller presents to the system BIOS and the OS. The logical geometry doesn't consist of the same values as the physical geometry, although calculations of drive capacity yield the same results.

lost allocation units   *See* lost clusters.

lost clusters   File fragments that, according to the file allocation table, contain data that doesn't belong to any file. The CHKDSK/F command can free these fragments. *Also called* lost allocation units.

low-level formatting   A process (usually performed at the factory) that electronically creates the hard drive tracks and sectors and tests for bad spots on the disk surface.

low-profile case   *See* compact case.

LPX   A form factor in which expansion cards are mounted on a riser card that plugs into a motherboard. The expansion cards in LPX systems are mounted parallel to the motherboard instead of perpendicular to it, as in AT and ATX systems.

MAC (Media Access Control) address   A 6-byte hexadecimal hardware address unique to each NIC card and assigned by the manufacturer. The address is often printed on the adapter. An example is 00 00 0C 08 2F 35. *Also called* physical address, adapter address, or hardware address.

main board   *See* motherboard.

master file table (MFT)   The database used by the NTFS file system to track the contents of a logical drive.

MBR (Master Boot Record)   The first sector on a hard drive, which contains the partition table and a program BIOS used to boot an OS from the drive.

MDRAM (MultiBank DRAM)   A type of video memory that's faster than VRAM and WRAM but can be more economical because it can be installed on a video card in smaller increments.

memory Physical microchips that can hold data and programming, located on the mother-board or expansion cards.

memory address A number assigned to each byte in memory. The CPU can use memory addresses to track where information is stored in RAM. Memory addresses are usually displayed as hexadecimal numbers in segment/offset form.

memory bus *See* system bus.

memory dump The contents of memory saved to a file at the time an event halted the system. Support technicians can analyze the dump file to help understand the source of the problem.

memory extender For DOS and Windows 9x, a device driver named Himem.sys that manages RAM, giving access to memory addresses above 1 MB.

memory paging In Windows, swapping blocks of RAM to an area of the hard drive to serve as virtual memory when RAM is low.

memory-resident virus A virus that can stay lurking in memory even after its host program is terminated.

MHz (megahertz) One million Hz, or one million cycles per second. *See also* Hz (hertz).

microATX A recent version of the ATX form factor. MicroATX addresses some new technologies that have been developed since the original introduction of ATX.

MicroDIMM A type of memory module used on notebooks that has 144 pins and uses a 64-bit data path.

microprocessor *See* CPU (central processing unit).

Mini PCI The PCI industry standard for desk-top computer expansion cards, applied to a much smaller form factor for notebook expansion cards.

Mini-ATX A smaller ATX board that can be used with regular ATX cases and power supplies.

minicartridge A tape drive cartridge that is only 3 x 2 inches. It's small enough to allow two

drives to fit into a standard 5-inch drive bay of a PC case.

Mini-LPX A smaller version of the LPX motherboard.

MMC (Microsoft Management Console) A utility to build customized consoles. These consoles can be saved to a file with an .msc file extension.

MMX (Multimedia Extensions) Multimedia instructions built into Intel processors to add functionality such as better processing of multi-media, SIMD support, and increased cache.

modem From the words "modulate-demodulate," a device that modulates digital data from a computer to an analog format that can be sent over telephone lines, and then demodulates it back into digital form.

modem speed The speed at which a modem can transmit data along a phone line, measured in bits per second (bps). *Also called* bandwidth or line speed.

monitor The most commonly used output device for displaying text and graphics on a computer.

motherboard The main board in the computer. The CPU, ROM chips, SIMMs, DIMMs, RIMMs, and interface cards are plugged into the motherboard. *Also called* the main board or system board.

motherboard bus *See* system bus.

motherboard mouse *See* PS/2-compatible mouse.

mouse A pointing and input device that allows users to move a cursor around a screen and select programs with the click of a button.

MP3 A method to compress audio files that uses MPEG level 1. It can reduce sound files to as low as a 1:24 ratio without losing much sound quality.

MPEG (Moving Pictures Experts Group) A processing-intensive standard for data compression for motion pictures that tracks movement from one frame to the next and stores only the data that has changed.

MSDS (material safety data sheet) A document that explains how to handle substances such as chemical solvents; it includes information such as physical data, toxicity, health effects, first aid, storage, disposal, and spill procedures.

multicasting A process in which a message is sent by one host to multiple hosts, such as when a video conference is broadcast to several hosts on the Internet.

multimeter A device used to measure the components of an electrical circuit. The most common measurements are voltage, current, and resistance.

multiplier The factor by which the bus speed or frequency is multiplied to get the CPU clock speed.

multiscan monitor A monitor that can work within a range of frequencies and, therefore, can work with different standards and video cards. It offers a variety of refresh rates.

name resolution The process of associating a NetBIOS name or host name to an IP address.

NAT (Network Address Translation) A process that converts private IP addresses on a LAN to the proxy server's IP address before a data packet is sent over the Internet.

NetBEUI (NetBIOS Extended User Interface) A proprietary, and outdated Microsoft networking protocol used only by Windows-based systems, and limited to LANs because it doesn't support routing.

NetBIOS (Network Basic Input/Output System) An API protocol used by some applications to communicate over a NetBEUI network. NetBIOS has largely been replaced by Windows Sockets over a TCP/IP network.

network adapter *See* NIC (network interface card).

network drive map Mounting a drive, such as drive E, to a computer that's actually hard drive space on another host computer on the network.

network printer A printer that any user on the network can access, through its own network card and connection to the network, through a connection to a stand-alone print server, or

through a connection to a computer as a local printer, which is shared on the network. *Compare to* local printer.

NIC (network interface card) An expansion card that plugs into a computer's motherboard and provides a port on the back of the card to connect a PC to a network. *Also called* network adapter.

NLX A low-end form factor that's similar to LPX but provides more support for current and emerging processor technologies. NLX was designed for flexibility and efficiency of space.

node *See* host.

noise An extraneous, unwanted signal, often over an analog phone line, that can cause communication interference or transmission errors. Possible sources are fluorescent lighting, radios, TVs, lightning, or bad wiring.

nonvolatile Refers to a kind of RAM that's stable and can hold data as long as electricity is powering the memory.

normal mode *See* CHS (cylinder, head, sector) mode.

North Bridge That portion of the chipset hub that connects faster I/O busses to the system bus. *Compare to* South Bridge.

NOS (network operating system) An operating system that resides on the controlling computer in the network. The NOS controls what software, data, and devices users on the network can access. Examples of an NOS are Novell NetWare and Windows 2000 Server.

notebook A portable computer designed for travel and mobility. Notebooks use the same technology as desktop PCs, with modifications for conserving voltage, taking up less space, and operating while on the move. *Also called* laptop computer.

NTFS (NT File System) The file system for the Windows 2000/XP operating systems. NTFS can't be accessed by other operating systems, such as DOS. It provides increased reliability and security compared with other methods of organizing and accessing files. There are several versions of NTFS that might be compatible.

Ntldr (NT Loader) In Windows, the OS loader used on Intel systems.

NTVDM (NT virtual DOS machine) An emulated environment in which a 16-bit DOS application resides in Windows with its own memory space or WOW (Win16 on Win32).

null modem cable A cable that allows two data terminal equipment (DTE) devices to communicate; the transmit and receive wires are cross-connected, and no modems are necessary.

octet Term for each of the four 8-bit numbers that make up an IP address. For example, the IP address 206.96.103.114 has four octets.

ohm (Ω) The standard unit of measurement for electrical resistance. Resistors are rated in ohms.

on-board ports Ports that are directly on the motherboard, such as a built-in keyboard port or on-board serial port.

operating system formatting *See* high-level formatting.

OS (operating system) Software that controls a computer. An OS controls how system resources are used and provides a user interface, a way of managing hardware and software, and ways to work with files.

overclocking Running a processor at a higher frequency than is recommended by the manufacturer, which can result in an unstable system.

P1 connector Power connection on an ATX motherboard.

page fault An OS interrupt that occurs when the OS is forced to access the hard drive to satisfy the demands for virtual memory.

page file *See* swap file.

Pagefile.sys The Windows swap file.

page-in The process in which the memory manager goes to the hard drive to return the data from a swap file to RAM.

page-out The process in which, when RAM is full, the memory manager moves a page to the swap file.

pages 4 KB segments in which Windows 2000/XP allocates memory.

parallel port A female 25-pin port on a computer that can transmit data in parallel, 8 bits at a time, and is usually used with a printer. The names for parallel ports are LPT1 and LPT2.

parity An error-checking scheme in which a ninth, or "parity," bit is added. The value of the parity bit is set to 0 or 1 to provide an even number of 1s for even parity and an odd number of 1s for odd parity.

parity error An error that occurs when the number of 1s in the byte isn't in agreement with the expected number.

parity memory Nine-bit memory in which the ninth bit is used for error checking. A SIMM part number with 36 in it (4 x 9 bits) is parity. Older PCs almost always use parity chips.

partition A division of a hard drive that can be used to hold logical drives.

partition table A table at the beginning of the hard drive that contains information about each partition on the drive. The partition table is contained in the Master Boot Record.

passive terminator A type of terminator for single-ended SCSI cables. Simple resistors provide termination of a signal. Passive termination isn't reliable over long distances and should be used only with narrow SCSI.

PATA (parallel ATA) An older IDE cabling method that uses a 40-pin flat data cable or an 80-conductor cable and a 40-pin IDE connector. *See also* SATA (serial ATA).

patch An update to software that corrects an error, adds a feature, or addresses security issues. *Also called* update or service pack.

patch cable A network cable used to connect a PC to a hub.

path A drive and list of directories pointing to a file, such as C:\Windows\command.

PC Card A credit-card-size adapter card that can be slid into a slot in the side of many notebook computers and is used for connecting to modems, networks, and CD-ROM drives. *Also called* PCMCIA Card.

PC Card slot An expansion slot on a notebook computer into which a PC Card is inserted. *Also called* PCMCIA Card slot.

PCI (Peripheral Component Interconnect) bus A bus common on Pentium computers that runs at speeds up to 33 MHz or 66 MHz, with a 32-bit-wide or 64-bit-wide data path. PCI-X, released in September 1999, enables PCI to run at 133 MHz. For some chipsets, it serves as the middle layer between the memory bus and expansion buses.

PCI Express (PCIe) The latest evolution of PCI, which is not backward-compatible with earlier PCI slots and cards. PCIe slots come in several sizes, including PCIe x1, PCIe x4, PCIe x8, and PCIe x16.

PCMCIA (Personal Computer Memory Card International Association) Card *See* PC Card.

PCMCIA Card slot *See* PC Card slot.

PDA (personal digital assistant) A small handheld computer that has its own operating system and applications.

peer-to-peer network A network of computers that are all equals, or peers. Each computer has the same amount of authority, and each can act as a server to the other computers.

peripheral devices Devices that communicate with the CPU but aren't located directly on the motherboard, such as the monitor, floppy drive, printer, and mouse.

permissions Refer to the user accounts or user groups allowed to access data. Varying degrees of access can be assigned to a folder or file, including full control, write, delete, and read-only.

PGA (pin grid array) A feature of a CPU socket whereby the pins are aligned in uniform rows around the socket.

physical address *See* MAC (Media Access Control) address.

physical geometry The actual layout of heads, tracks, and sectors on a hard drive. *See also* logical geometry.

PIF (program information file) A file used by Windows to describe the environment for a DOS program to use.

Ping (Packet Internet Groper) A Windows and UNIX command used to troubleshoot network connections. It verifies that the host can communicate with another host on the network.

pinout A description of how each pin on a bus, connection, plug, slot, or socket is used.

PIO (Programmed I/O) transfer mode A transfer mode that uses the CPU to transfer data from the hard drive to memory. PIO mode is slower than DMA mode.

pixel A small spot on a fine horizontal scan line. Pixels are illuminated to create an image on the monitor.

polling A process by which the CPU checks the status of connected devices to determine whether they are ready to send or receive data.

port As applied to services running on a computer, a number assigned to a process on a computer so that the process can be found by TCP/IP. *Also called* a port address or port number. It is also another name for an I/O address. *See also* I/O address. A physical connector, usually at the back of a computer, that allows a cable from a peripheral device, such as a printer, mouse, or modem, to be attached.

port address *See* port or I/O addresses.

port number *See* port.

port replicator A device designed to connect to a notebook computer to make it easy to connect the notebook to peripheral devices.

port settings The configuration parameters of communication devices such as COM1, COM2, or COM3, including IRQ settings.

POST (power-on self test) A self-diagnostic program used to conduct a simple test of the CPU, RAM, and I/O devices. The POST is performed by startup BIOS when the computer is first turned on and is stored in ROM-BIOS.

power scheme A feature of Windows XP support for notebooks that allows users to create groups of power settings for specific sets of conditions.

power supply A box inside the computer case that supplies power to the motherboard and other installed devices. Power supplies provide 3.3, 5, and 12 volts DC.

power-on password A password that a computer uses to control access during the boot process.

PnP (Plug and Play) A standard designed to make installing new hardware devices easier by automatically configuring them to eliminate system resource conflicts (such as IRQ or I/O address conflicts). PnP is supported by Windows 9x, Windows 2000, and Windows XP.

primary partition A hard disk partition that can contain only one logical drive.

primary storage Temporary storage on the motherboard used by the CPU to process data and instructions. Memory is considered primary storage.

printer A peripheral output device that produces printed output to paper. Different types include dot matrix, ink-jet, and laser printers.

printer maintenance kit A kit purchased from a printer manufacturer that contains the parts, tools, and instructions needed to perform routine printer maintenance.

private IP address An IP address used on a private TCP/IP network that's isolated from the Internet.

process A running instance of a program together with the program resources. More than one process can be running for a program at the same time. One process for a program happens each time the program is loaded into memory or runs.

processor *See* CPU (central processing unit).

processor speed The speed, or frequency, at which the CPU operates. Usually expressed in GHz.

product activation The process that Microsoft uses to prevent software piracy. For example, after Windows XP is activated for a particular computer, it can't be installed on another computer.

program A set of step-by-step instructions to a computer. Some are burned directly into chips, whereas others are stored as program files. Programs are written in languages such as BASIC and C++.

program file A file containing instructions designed to be carried out by the CPU.

protected mode An operating mode that supports preemptive multitasking. The OS manages memory and other hardware devices, and programs can use a 32-bit data path. *Also called* 32-bit mode.

protocol A set of rules and standards that two entities use for communication.

Protocol.ini A Windows initialization file containing network configuration information.

proxy server A server that acts as an intermediary between another computer and the Internet. The proxy server substitutes its own IP address for the IP address of the network computer making a request so that all traffic over the Internet appears to be coming from only the proxy server's IP address.

PS/2-compatible mouse A mouse that plugs into a round mouse PS/2 port on the motherboard. *Also called* motherboard mouse.

public IP address An IP address available to the Internet.

RAID (redundant array of independent disks) Several methods of configuring multiple hard drives to store data to increase logical volume size and improve performance or to ensure that if one hard drive fails, the data is still available from another hard drive.

RAM (random access memory) Memory modules on the motherboard containing microchips used to temporarily hold data and programs while the CPU processes both. Information in RAM is lost when the PC is turned off.

RAM drive An area of memory treated as though it were a hard drive, but it works much faster than a hard drive. The Windows 9x startup disk uses a RAM drive. *Compare to* virtual memory.

RDRAM *See* Direct Rambus DRAM.

read/write head A sealed, magnetic coil device that moves across the surface of a disk reading data from or writing data to the disk.

ReadyBoost A Vista utility that uses a flash drive or secure digital (SD) memory card to boost hard drive performance.

real mode A single-tasking operating mode whereby a program has 1024K of memory addresses, has direct access to RAM, and uses a 16-bit data path. Using a memory extender (Himem.sys), a program in real mode can access memory above 1024K. *Also called* 16-bit mode.

Recovery Console A Windows 2000/XP command-line utility and OS that can be used to solve problems when Windows can't load from the hard drive.

Registry A database that Windows uses to store hardware and software configuration information, user preferences, and setup information.

re-marked chips Chips that have been used and returned to the factory, marked again, and resold. The surface of the chips might be dull or scratched.

Remote Desktop A Windows tool that gives a user access to his or her Windows desktop from anywhere on the Internet.

rescue disk A floppy disk that can be used to start a computer when the hard drive fails to boot. *Also called* ESD (emergency startup disk) or startup disk.

resistance The degree to which a device opposes or resists the flow of electricity. As the electrical resistance increases, the current decreases. *See* ohm and resistor.

resistor An electronic device that resists or opposes the flow of electricity. A resistor can be used to reduce the amount of electricity supplied to an electronic component.

resolution The number of pixels on a monitor screen that can be addressed by software (for example, 1024x768 pixels).

restore point A snapshot of the Windows Vista/XP system state, usually made before installing new hardware or applications.

RIMM A type of memory module developed by Rambus, Inc.

RJ-11 A phone line connection found on modems, telephones, and house phone outlets.

RJ-45 connector A connector used with twisted-pair cable that connects the cable to the NIC.

ROM (read-only memory) Chips that contain programming code and can't be erased.

ROM BIOS *See* BIOS (basic input/output system).

root directory The main directory created when a hard drive or disk is first formatted. In Linux, it's indicated by a forward slash (/). In Windows, it's indicated by a backward slash (\).

rootkit A type of malicious software that loads itself before the OS boot is complete and can hijack internal Windows components so that it masks information Windows provides to user-mode utilities such as Windows Explorer or Task Manager.

routable protocol A protocol that can be routed to interconnected networks on the basis of a network address. TCP/IP is a routable protocol, but NetBEUI is not.

sags *See* brownouts.

SATA (serial ATA) An ATAPI cabling method that uses a narrower and more reliable cable than the 80-conductor cable. *See also* PATA (parallel ATA).

SCSI (Small Computer System Interface) A fast interface between a host adapter and the CPU that can daisy-chain as many as 7 or 15 devices on a single bus.

SCSI ID A number from 0 to 15 assigned to each SCSI device attached to the daisy chain.

SDRAM (synchronous DRAM) A type of memory stored on DIMMs that runs in sync with the system clock, at the same speed as the motherboard.

SDRAM II *See* DDR SDRAM (Double Data Rate SDRAM).

secondary storage Storage that's remote to the CPU and permanently holds data, even when the PC is turned off, for example, a hard drive.

sector On a disk surface, it's one segment of a track, which almost always contains 512 bytes of data.

sequential access A method of data access used by tape drives, whereby data is written or read sequentially from the beginning to the end of the tape or until the data is found.

serial ATA cable An IDE cable that's narrower and has fewer pins than the parallel IDE 80-conductor cable.

serial mouse A mouse that uses a serial port and has a female 9-pin DB-9 connector.

serial port A male 9-pin or 25-pin port on a computer system used by slower I/O devices, such as a mouse or modem. Data travels serially, one bit at a time, through the port. Serial ports are sometimes configured as COM1, COM2, COM3, or COM4.

service pack *See* patch.

Service Set Identifier (SSID) The name of the access point for a wireless network.

SFC (System File Checker) A Windows tool that checks to make sure Windows is using the correct versions of system files.

shadow RAM or shadowing ROM ROM programming code copied into RAM to speed up the system operation because of the faster access speed of RAM.

shortcut An icon on the desktop that points to a program that can be run or to a file or folder.

SIMM (single inline memory module) A miniature circuit board used in older computers to hold RAM. SIMMs hold 8, 16, 32, or 64 MB on a single module.

simple volume A type of dynamic volume used on a single hard drive that corresponds to a primary partition on a basic disk.

single-voltage CPU A CPU that requires one voltage for both internal and I/O operations.

slack Wasted space on a hard drive caused by not using all available space at the end of clusters.

sleep mode A mode used in many "green" systems that allows them to be configured through CMOS to suspend the monitor or even the drive, if the keyboard and/or CPU have been inactive for a set number of minutes. *See also* Green Standards.

slimline case *See* compact case.

snap-ins Components added to a console by using the Microsoft Management Console.

SO-DIMM (small outline DIMM) A type of memory module used in notebook computers that uses DIMM technology and can have 72 pins or 144 pins.

soft boot To restart a PC without turning off the power, for example, in Windows XP, by clicking Start, Turn Off Computer, Restart. *Also called* warm boot.

soft power *See* soft switch.

soft switch A feature on an ATX system that allows an OS to power down the system and allows for activity, such as a keystroke or network activity, to power up the system. *Also called* soft power.

software Computer programs, or instructions to perform a specific task. Software can be BIOS, OSs, or application software, such as a word-processing or spreadsheet program.

software cache Cache controlled by software, whereby the cache is stored in RAM.

solid state device (SSD) A storage device that uses memory chips to store data instead of spinning disks.

SO-RIMM (small outline RIMM) A 160-pin memory module in notebooks that uses Rambus technology.

spacers *See* standoffs.

SPGA (staggered pin grid array) A feature of a CPU socket whereby the pins are staggered over the socket to squeeze more pins into a small space.

SPI (SCSI Parallel Interface) The part of the SCSI-3 standard that specifies how SCSI devices are connected.

spooling Placing print jobs in a print queue so that an application can be released from the printing process before printing is completed. "Spooling" is an acronym for "simultaneous peripheral operations online."

SRAM (static RAM)   RAM chips that retain information without the need for refreshing, as long as the computer's power is on. They are more expensive than traditional DRAM.

standby time   The time before a "green" system reduces 92 percent of its activity. *See also* Green Standards.

standoffs   Round plastic or metal pegs that separate the motherboard from the case so that components on the back of the motherboard don't touch the case. *Also called* spacers.

startup BIOS   The part of system BIOS responsible for controlling the PC when it's first turned on. Startup BIOS gives control over to the OS after it's loaded.

startup disk   *See* rescue disk.

startup password   *See* power-on password.

static electricity   *See* ESD (electrostatic discharge).

static IP address   An IP address permanently assigned to a workstation.

stop error   An error severe enough to cause the operating system to stop all processes. *See also* blue screen.

STP (shielded twisted-pair) cable   A cable made of one or more twisted pairs of wires and surrounded by a metal shield.

streaming audio   Downloading audio data from the Internet in a continuous stream of data without downloading an entire audio file first.

subdirectory   A directory or folder contained in another directory or folder. *Also called* child directory or folder.

subnet mask   A group of four numbers (dotted decimal numbers) that tell TCP/IP whether a remote computer is on the same or a different network.

surge suppressor or surge protector   A device or power strip designed to protect electronic equipment from power surges and spikes.

suspend time   The time before a "Green" system reduces 99 percent of its activity. After this time,

the system needs a warm-up time so that the CPU, monitor, and hard drive can reach full activity.

swap file   A file on the hard drive used by the OS for virtual memory. *Also called* page file.

synchronous SRAM   SRAM that's faster and more expensive than asynchronous SRAM. It requires a clock signal to validate its control signals, enabling the cache to run in step with the CPU.

Sysedit   The Windows System Configuration Editor, a text editor generally used to edit system files.

system BIOS   BIOS located on the motherboard.

system board   *See* motherboard.

system bus   The bus between the CPU and memory on the motherboard. The bus frequency in documentation is called the system speed, such as 400 MHz. *Also called* memory bus, motherboard bus, front-side bus, local bus, or host bus.

system clock   A line on a bus dedicated to timing the activities of components connected to it. The system clock provides a continuous pulse that other devices use to time themselves.

system disk   Windows terminology for a bootable disk.

system partition   The active partition of the hard drive containing the boot record and the specific files required to load Windows.

system resource   A channel, line, or address on the motherboard that can be used by the CPU or a device for communication. The four system resources are IRQ, I/O address, DMA channel, and memory address.

System Restore   A Windows utility, similar to the ScanReg tool in earlier versions of Windows, used to restore the system to a restore point. Unlike ScanReg, System Restore can't be run from a command prompt.

system state data   In Windows 2000/XP, files that are necessary for a successful load of the operating system.

System.ini   A text configuration file used by Windows 3.x and supported by Windows 9x for backward compatibility.

TAPI (Telephony Application Programming Interface)   A standard developed by Intel and Microsoft that can be used by 32-bit Windows communication programs for communicating over phone lines.

Task Manager (Taskmgr.exe)   A Windows utility that lets you view the applications and processes running on your computer as well as information about process and memory performance, network activity, and user activity.

TCP/IP (Transmission Control Protocol/Internet Protocol)   The suite of protocols that supports communication on the Internet. TCP is responsible for error checking, and IP is responsible for routing.

telephony   A term describing the technology of converting sound to signals that can travel over telephone lines.

terminating resistor   The resistor added at the end of a SCSI chain to dampen the voltage at the end of the chain.

termination   A process necessary to prevent an echo effect of power at the end of a SCSI chain, resulting in interference with the data transmission.

thermal compound   A creamlike substance that is placed between the bottom of the cooler heatsink and the top of the processor to eliminate air pockets and help to draw heat off the processor.

TIFF (Tagged Image File Format)   A bitmapped file format used to hold photographs, graphics, and screen captures. TIFF files can be rather large and have a .tif file extension.

top-level domain   The highest level of domain names, indicated by a suffix that tells something about the host. For example, .com is for commercial use and .edu is for educational institutions.

tower case   The largest type of personal computer case. Tower cases stand vertically and can be as tall as two feet. They have more drive bays and are a good choice for computer users who anticipate making major upgrades.

trace   A wire on a circuit board that connects two components or devices.

track   One of many concentric circles on the surface of a hard drive or floppy disk.

translation   A technique used by system BIOS and hard drive controller BIOS to break the 504 MB hard drive barrier, whereby a different set of drive parameters are communicated to the OS and other software than that used by the hard drive controller BIOS.

UART (universal asynchronous receiver-transmitter) chip   A chip that controls serial ports. It sets protocol and converts parallel data bits received from the system bus into serial bits.

UDF (Universal Disk Format) file system   A file system for optical media used by all DVDs and some CD-Rs and CD-RWs.

unattended installation   A Windows installation done by storing the answers to installation questions in a text file or script that Windows calls an answer file. With this installation type, answers don't have to be typed in during the installation.

upgrade install   The installation of an OS on a hard drive that already has an OS installed in such a way that settings kept by the old OS are carried forward into the upgrade, including information about hardware, software, and user preferences.

URL (Uniform Resource Locator)   An address for a resource on the Internet. A URL can contain the protocol used by the resource, the name of the computer and its network, and the path and name of a file on the computer.

USB (universal serial bus) port   A type of port designed to make installation and configuration of I/O devices easy, providing room for as many as 127 devices daisy-chained together.

USB host controller   Manages the USB bus. If the motherboard contains on-board USB ports, the USB host controller is part of the chipset. The USB uses only a single set of resources for all devices on the bus.

user account   The information, stored in the SAM database, that defines a Windows 2000/XP user, including user name, password, memberships, and rights.

user profile A personal profile about a user that enables the user's desktop settings and other operating parameters to be retained from one session to another.

USMT (User State Migration Tool) A Windows Vista/XP utility that helps you migrate user files and preferences from one computer to another to help users make a smooth transition from one computer to another.

UTP (unshielded twisted-pair) cable A cable made of one or more twisted pairs of wires that is not surrounded by a metal shield.

V (volt) A measure of potential difference in an electrical circuit. A computer ATX power supply usually provides five separate voltages: +12 V, -12 V, +5 V, -5 V, and +3.3 V.

value data In Windows, the name and value of a setting in the Registry.

VCACHE A built-in Windows 9x 32-bit software cache that doesn't take up conventional memory space or upper memory space, as SMARTDrive did.

video card An interface card installed in the computer to control visual output on a monitor. *Also called* display adapter.

virtual device driver (VxD or VDD) A Windows device driver that can have direct access to a device. It might depend on a Windows component to communicate with the device itself.

virtual memory A method whereby the OS uses the hard drive as though it were RAM. *Compare to* RAM drive.

virtual real mode An operating mode that works similarly to real mode provided by a 32-bit OS for a 16-bit program to work.

virus A program that often has an incubation period, can infect other computers, and is intended to cause damage. A virus program might destroy data and programs or damage a disk drive's boot sector.

virus signature A set of distinguishing characteristics of a virus used by antivirus software to identify the virus.

volatile Refers to a kind of RAM that's temporary, can't hold data very long, and must be refreshed frequently.

voltage Electrical differential that causes current to flow, measured in volts. *See also* V (volt).

voltmeter A device for measuring electrical AC or DC voltage.

volume *See* logical drive.

VRAM (video RAM) RAM on video cards that holds the data being passed from the computer to the monitor and can be accessed by two devices simultaneously. Higher resolutions often require more video memory.

VRM (voltage regulator module) A device embedded or installed on the motherboard that regulates voltage to the processor.

VxD *See* virtual device driver.

W (watt) The unit used to measure power. A typical computer can use a power supply that provides 400W.

wait state A clock tick in which nothing happens, used to ensure that the microprocessor isn't getting ahead of slower components. A 0-wait state is preferable to a 1-wait state. Too many wait states can slow down a system.

WAN (wide area network) A network or group of networks that span a large geographical area.

warm boot *See* soft boot.

wattage Electrical power measured in watts.

WFP (Windows File Protection) A Windows 2000/XP tool that protects system files from modification.

Wi-Fi *See* IEEE 802.11b.

wildcard A * or ? character used in a command line that represents a character or group of characters in a filename or extension.

Win.ini The Windows initialization file that contains program configuration information needed for running the Windows operating environment. Its functions were replaced by the Registry beginning with Windows 9x, which still supports it for backward compatibility with Windows 3.x.

Win386.swp The name of the Windows 9x swap file. Its default location is C:\Windows.

WLAN (wireless LAN)   A type of LAN that doesn't use wires or cables to create connections; instead, it transmits data over radio or infrared waves.

workgroup   In Windows, a logical group of computers and users in which administration, resources, and security are distributed throughout the network, without centralized management or security.

worm   An infestation designed to copy itself repeatedly to memory, on drive space or on a network, until little memory or disk space remain.

WRAM (window RAM)   Dual-ported video RAM that's faster and less expensive than VRAM. It has its own internal bus on the chip with a 256-bit-wide data path.

ZIF (zero insertion force) socket   A socket that uses a small lever to apply even force when you install the microchip into the socket.

zone bit recording   A method of storing data on a hard drive whereby the drive can have more sectors per track near the outside of the platter.

INDEX